PRO TOOLS® 7

OVERDRIVE!

EXPERT QUICK TIPS

Matt Donner

THOMSON

COURSE TECHNOLOGY™

Professional ■ Technical ■ Reference

PRO TOOLS® 7
OVERDRIVE!

Publisher and General Manager, Thomson Course Technology PTR: Stacy L. Hiquet

Associate Director of Marketing: Sarah O'Donnell

Manager of Editorial Services: Heather Talbot

Marketing Manager: Mark Hughes

Senior Acquisitions Editor: Todd Jensen

Marketing Coordinator: Jordan Casey

Project Editor and Copyeditor: Kim V. Benbow

Technical Reviewer: Leff Lefferts

PTR Editorial Services Coordinator: Elizabeth Furbish

Interior Layout Tech: Shawn Morningstar

Cover Designers: Mike Tanamachi and Nancy Goulet

Indexer: Larry Sweazy

Proofreader: Dan Foster

© 2006 by Thomson Course Technology PTR. All rights reserved. No part of this book may be reproduced or transmitted in any form or by any means, electronic or mechanical, including photo-copying, recording, or by any information storage or retrieval system without written permission from Thomson Course Technology PTR, except for the inclusion of brief quotations in a review.

The Thomson Course Technology PTR logo and related trade dress are trademarks of Thomson Course Technology and may not be used without written permission.

Beat Detective, Digi 001, Digi 002, Digidesign, HD, LE, Mbox, Pro Tools, and QuickPunch are either registered trademarks or trademarks of Avid Technology, Inc., in the United States. Apple, QuickTime, the QuickTime logo, Power Macintosh, and iMac are trademarks of Apple Computer, Inc., registered in the U.S. and other countries. Microsoft, Windows, and Internet Explorer are either registered trademarks or trademarks of Microsoft Corporation in the United States and/or other countries.

All other trademarks are the property of their respective owners.

Important: Thomson Course Technology PTR cannot provide software support. Please contact the appropriate software manufacturer's technical support line or Web site for assistance.

Thomson Course Technology PTR and the author have attempted throughout this book to distinguish proprietary trademarks from descriptive terms by following the capitalization style used by the manufacturer.

Information contained in this book has been obtained by Thomson Course Technology PTR from sources believed to be reliable. However, because of the possibility of human or mechanical error by our sources, Thomson Course Technology PTR, or others, the Publisher does not guarantee the accuracy, adequacy, or completeness of any information and is not responsible for any errors or omissions or the results obtained from use of such information. Readers should be particularly aware of the fact that the Internet is an ever-changing entity. Some facts may have changed since this book went to press.

Educational facilities, companies, and organizations interested in multiple copies or licensing of this book should contact the publisher for quantity discount information. Training manuals, CD-ROMs, and portions of this book are also available individually or can be tailored for specific needs.

ISBN: 1-59863-008-3

Library of Congress Catalog Card Number: 2005931877

Printed in the United States of America

06 07 08 09 10 PH 10 9 8 7 6 5 4 3 2 1

THOMSON

COURSE TECHNOLOGY
Professional ■ Technical ■ Reference

Thomson Course Technology PTR, a division of Thomson Course Technology
25 Thomson Place
Boston, MA 02210

http://www.courseptr.com

Acknowledgments

This is by no means an exhaustive book. It couldn't be. I'd have to be working on the team at Digidesign actually *writing* the code to be *that* on top of everything. *Those* guys are the deepest. This book is meant to approach each of the various types of jobs I've done over the years and the slick moves I've learned from doing them. I've bent the ears of the greatest Pro Tools gurus I know, guys who have helped me cover as much territory as I can for you, the reader. These are my mouse-armed heroes and they deserve listing here:

* The design and engineering team at Digidesign for creating, maintaining, and continually improving an AMAZING collection of technology!

* Sig Knapstad, my mentor, and all the gang at Cutting Edge Audio (www.ceag.com).

* Leff Lefferts, also of Cutting Edge for providing excellent technical editing (that is, fixing my goofs).

* Lev Perrey, Product Specialist at Digi, for being available to help throughout this edition—and for knowing Pro Tools cold.

* Ken Walden, former Digi Product Specialist and consultant to the stars (www.secretsofthepros.com).

* Dave Anderson, Sales Manager at Digidesign, for always supporting me and the never-ending hookups.

* Andy Cook, Digidesign Education Coordinator, for letting Pyramind be one of the first Digi schools ever.

* Andre Zweers from Skywalker Sound for his time and insights into the real world of film-score orchestration and surround sound.

* Gene Radzik and John Loose from Dolby Labs for being two extremely knowledgeable, accessible, and personable guys and for sharing their hard-won knowledge and tips.

* Hideki Yamashita for figuring out just about every technical Rubik's cube I've thrown at him.

* Steve Heithecker for all the graphics help.

* Dave Nelson for being the hardest-working man in independent film (no exaggeration).

* Scott Hirsch for joining the Pyramind team as another Pro Tools instructor and helping with Final Cut tips.

* Greg Gordon for believing in my vision for Pyramind and letting me grab the ball and run with it.

* Kim Benbow for all her copyediting and patience in getting this book finished.

* My wife Kimberly and our families for their tireless support and love.

* My son Marcus for providing 18 months of inspiration, sleep deprivation, and loads of smiles.

Let me take one last moment to thank the vets in Digi's tech pool who have bailed me out of one or two impending disasters over the past 12 years. Digi screens their techs hard, and they don't hire dummies. Those guys are sharp, experienced, and give great service, and it's not their fault if you broke your system; so when you call them next time for help, BE NICE! I bet they'll bail *you* out, too.

About the Author

Matt Donner has been using Pro Tools since before Digidesign owned it. Over the course of his career, Donner has seen Pro Tools develop into the amazing audio production tool it is today. He has used Pro Tools on Sundance feature films as well as hundreds of records. As one of the only Certified Pro Tools instructors in San Francisco, Donner teaches hundreds of students annually at the school he co-created, Pyramind (www.pyramind.com). His solo album, *Donner, Party of One,* was produced with Pro Tools version 5 and was released in 2002 (www.cdbaby.com/donner). It will be followed up with a second release in 2006 using version 7.

TABLE OF } Contents

} Introduction

Unless your studio is under a rock, you are well aware of the all-pervasive presence of Pro Tools. From a simple two-channel editor called Sound Designer to the 128-track 192k mother-ship HD, Pro Tools has grown into the leader and the standard in digital audio workstations. We'll let the conversation about whether it's the "best" stay between you and your friends over beer. I'll just say that it's everywhere, and if you want to work in this business, knowing Pro Tools cold is your career-building buddy.

I know this because my career was built on Pro Tools. My first step out of the coffee-making role of intern was due to my proficiency with Sound Designer, the Mac, and subsequently Pro Tools. I cut my first professional recordings to Pro Tools and continue that tradition today. I train about 50 Pro Tools engineers annually, and I still learn new tricks with every class—it's that deep.

It's so deep that Thomson Course has three books on the subject, each one catering to deeper levels of knowledge. This one is ALL about the tips and tricks of running Pro Tools in the studio with the client breathing heavily over your shoulder. I don't care how seasoned you are; there is always something new to catch from another Pro Tools user who has learned in the heat of battle. In interviewing some top-flight Pro Tools users in the San Francisco Bay Area, I learned about 10 new tricks myself, and I'm glad to share them with you.

I present this material with the hope that there are some sweet nuggets of trickery in here for you. Some of this is common knowledge among well-seasoned vets, and some of this is brand spanking new to those same vets. My experience is based on the Macintosh platform, and that's how I've organized this material. However, just about every production tip listed here is equally valid on PC platforms! Tips that pertain to the Mac OS have PC equivalents listed as well. Shortcuts on the Mac have equivalents, too: CMD(Mac) = CTRL(PC) and OPTION(Mac) = START(PC). I'll also leave the conversation about which platform is better to you and your friends over beer!

I have broken the book down into several different phases of the production process and tried to pull out some of my favorite moves for you. I have always tried to deliver the client my best work in the fastest way possible. I tend to work faster than others because I know some shortcuts (more than just key commands) and some techniques that have proven very valuable over time. I am sharing some of those with you here, including several from much heavier hitters than me.

Folks in the audio world often gravitate toward a single process in production, be it tracking, mixing, mastering, editing, sound design, post-production, or simple voice recording. For the single-process user, Pro Tools has two or three ways to do the same thing. Once you've got one job down one way, you tend to stay with that methodology because it works; and if it ain't broke DON'T BREAK IT! You may not have any clue that you're doing it the long and slow way, or you may already know this but don't have the time to learn a new trick (you old dog). That's why this book is for you.

Setup and Maintenance of the Mac

Before any good pilot hits the throttle and takes off, there is a long and detailed flight-check that occurs to ensure that all gauges are correct and all settings are optimal for a safe flight. Operating Pro Tools and the computer should be no exception. This chapter will dig into various "pre-flight" checks that should be performed regularly (if not every session) to ensure a trouble-free session for you, your talent, and your producer!

Keeping the Dock Out of the Way

The Dock defaults to the bottom of the screen, but it can interfere when you attempt to drag the screen around in Pro Tools. Every time you drag the horizontal locator in Pro Tools (the blue horizontal bar at the bottom of the Edit window) to the left or right, the Dock will present itself if you have set the Automatically Show and Hide option. You can deactivate this setting, but then the Dock will *always* be present, taking up potentially useful screen space. You can change the settings for the Dock quickly and get it out of the way using the Apple icon in the upper-left corner of your screen, as seen in Figure 1.1.

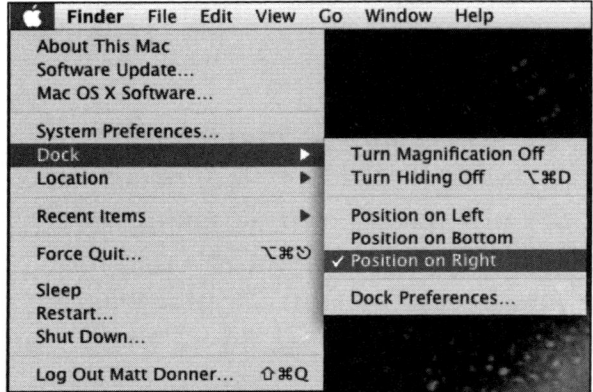

Figure 1.1

Finding the Dock preferences and locations from the Apple menu

The Dock's preferences allow you to adjust the Dock size to make the Dock bigger or smaller, as seen in Figure 1.2. You can also adjust the size of any icon when the mouse rolls up and down with the Magnification slider. Try to keep the Dock small enough to still recognize the application icon, and turn up the magnification so that scrolling through the list makes it easier to see which icon (application) you want. In addition, try to keep the Dock on the right side of the screen because you will be less likely to run into conflicts between Pro Tools and the Dock.

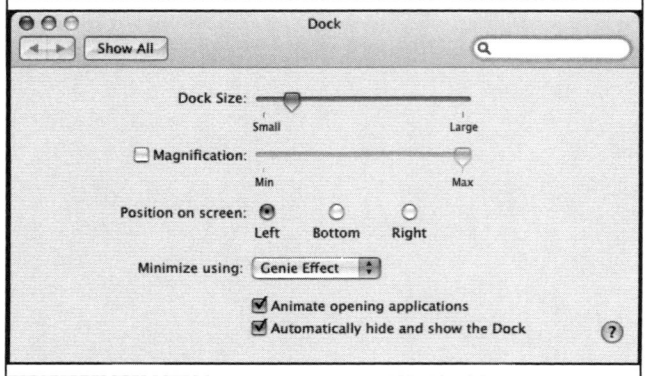

Figure 1.2

The Dock preferences within the System Preferences

If you have a second monitor, this works best. Some people disagree with the notion of keeping it on the right side, since you can scroll up and down the Edit window with the vertical locator on the right side of the screen. If this is you, you can certainly put the Dock on the left, or you can learn to scroll up and down the Edit window with the Page Up and Page Down keys instead!

If you still run into problems, resize the Pro Tools Mix and Edit windows so the Dock will never interfere with the Pro Tools screen. If you are using a single 17-inch monitor, you will quickly find that screen real estate is valuable and hiding the Dock for that extra half-inch is really important. See Figure 1.3 for a view of a single-monitor Dock solution.

You can achieve an effect similar to the auto-hiding Dock in Windows as well: Right-click the Taskbar, go to Properties, and check the Auto-Hide the Taskbar option, as shown in Figure 1.4.

Figure 1.3

Resizing the Edit window to fit the Dock on the right

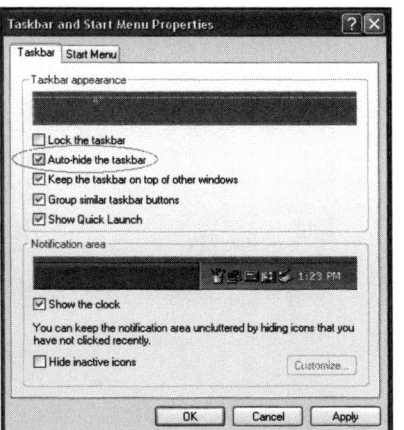

Figure 1.4

The Taskbar properties
in Windows

Customizing the Dock

You can drag any application you've installed to the Dock directly (as well as remove items from the Dock) by simply dragging them onto (or off of) the Dock. You might want to bring folders you use often here, such as your Pro Tools Sessions folder or your Applications folder, as seen in Figure 1.5. Notice that the My Pro Tools Sessions folder (at the bottom) is separated from the applications icons (at the top) by a divider. All folders and documents live below this divider.

I suggest you keep like applications together. For example, I often launch Reason (software) then ReCycle soon after, so I positioned them next to each other for quick access as you can also see in Figure 1.5. Similarly, I put Internet Explorer right next to Fetch when it's time to FTP work to a client. That way, the Dock is organized by application type.

Figure 1.5

Adding the PT Sessions folder to the Dock

In Windows, you can drag any icon onto or off of the Taskbar to make it a Quick Launch. Remember to check whether your Taskbar can have icons on it by right-clicking the Taskbar, selecting Toolbars, and making sure Quick Launch is checked. Also, make sure the Taskbar is not locked by right-clicking on it and ensuring the Lock the Taskbar option is not checked, as shown in Figure 1.6. If the Taskbar is locked, you won't be able to drag icons onto or off of the Taskbar. The difference between the Taskbar and a Toolbar is that a Toolbar is a subdivision of the Taskbar.

Figure 1.6

Quick Launch in the Taskbar

Setting Up Expose, the Dashboard, and Spotlight

One of the cooler gadgets that OS X provides is something called Expose. It is a hot-key switching function that allows you to jump between applications, which comes in handy when you are running Pro Tools with other applications, such as Reason or Live. It can also be confusing when you try to choose the Pencil tool and your windows go crazy because they default to sharing the same key-command (F11). To deactivate Expose (or to set any *other* key-commands to activate it) choose System Preferences > Dashboard and Expose and dese-lect the function keys in all positions. Figures 1.7 and 1.8 show the Expose Preferences and Expose in action, respectively. Note that the upper portion of the window is for hot-corner activation (drag the mouse to the corner and Expose/Dashboard becomes active) and the bottom half is for window-specific options.

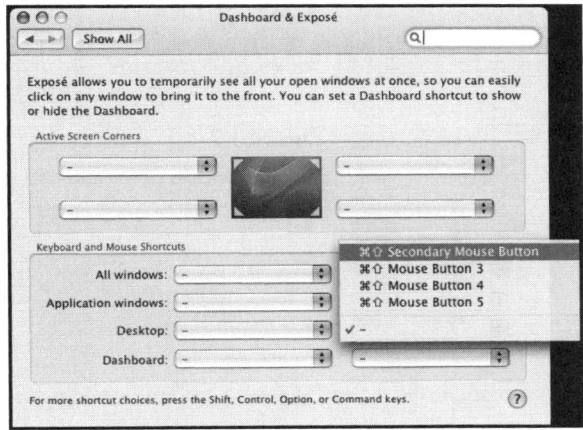

Figure 1.7

The Expose preferences with no hot keys enabled (-)

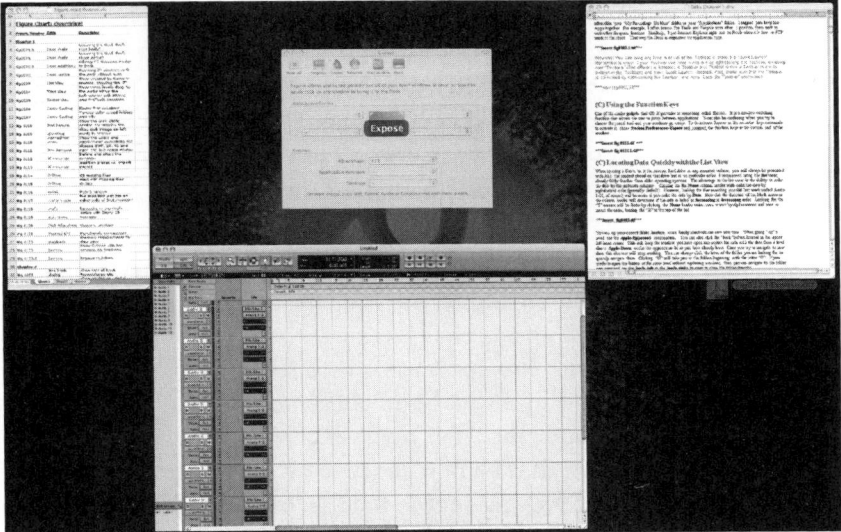

Figure 1.8

Expose in action, with all open documents visible

For those of you with mice that have more than one button, you can use the bottom-right options of the Preferences to select one of these buttons to activate/deactivate Expose or the Dashboard. Note that Figure 1.7 shows a custom button click including the modifiers SHIFT+CMD with the second mouse click. Simply hold SHIFT+CMD while setting the tab to the secondary mouse button and the new hot key is SHIFT+CMD+Second button! This is very handy for multi-purpose mice or for those of you on PCs with multi-button mice.

An alternative to using Expose to switch applications is the CMD+Tab shortcut, which will toggle through all your active applications. By holding down Command and hitting Tab repeatedly, you will cycle through the open applications. You can also use the left and right arrow keys (after hitting CMD+Tab) to navigate among them (as well as the mouse to click directly to any application without having to cycle through the list). OS X intelligently puts the last-used application next to the current one. To quickly switch back-and-forth between two applications among a list of active applications, hit CMD+Tab to switch to the first app, then hit CMD+Tab again to switch to the second app. Now, the CMD+Tab shortcut will default to going between only those two applications. Figure 1.9 shows the CMD+Tab list of active applications

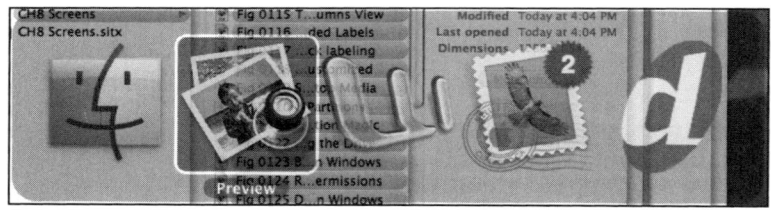

Figure 1.9

The list of active applications during the CMD+Tab shortcut

New to OS X 10.4 (a.k.a. Tiger) is a cool set of widgets called the Dashboard. This calls up a variety of user-definable subapplications ranging from poker screens to stock prices (available for free download from www.apple.com). Like Expose, it's very handy but defaults to the F12 key, which is sometimes reserved by Pro Tools as a Record hot-key. You can deactivate this by following the same directions as deactivating Expose. Choose System Preferences > Dashboard and Expose, and reset the hot key for the Dashboard to something not often used, like the F12+SHIFT keys. Since there are at least two other hot keys for quick recording (3 on the number pad and CMD+spacebar), it is a good bet that you won't have conflicts with the Dashboard, and you still get your hot keys for Record! Figure 1.10 shows some of my favorite widgets in action!

Although Expose and the Dashboard boast a high "cool" factor, a more important addition to Tiger is the Spotlight function. It's a new search engine for your Mac that organizes your search results into like-kinds. It's faster than other searches because it starts searching upon typing of the first letter! I'll talk more about how Pro Tools uses the Spotlight in the section "Spotlight Finds" in Chapter 3, but for now, let's just get Spotlight out of our way. Since one of the default shortcuts for Spotlight is CMD+spacebar, this poses a conflict. This is another shortcut for Record in Pro Tools, so it may come as a bit of a shock to hit the shortcut, expecting to record and instead be presented with the Spotlight search field (shown in Figure 1.11a).

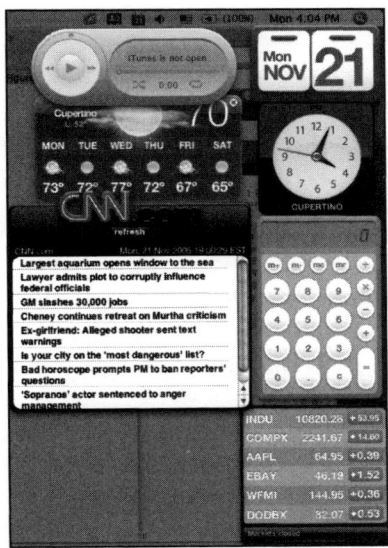

Figure 1.10
My Dashboard widgets in action!

The other Spotlight shortcut (CMD+OPT+spacebar) takes you to a more robust search window, as shown in Figure 1.11b.

Figure 1.11a
The Spotlight search field

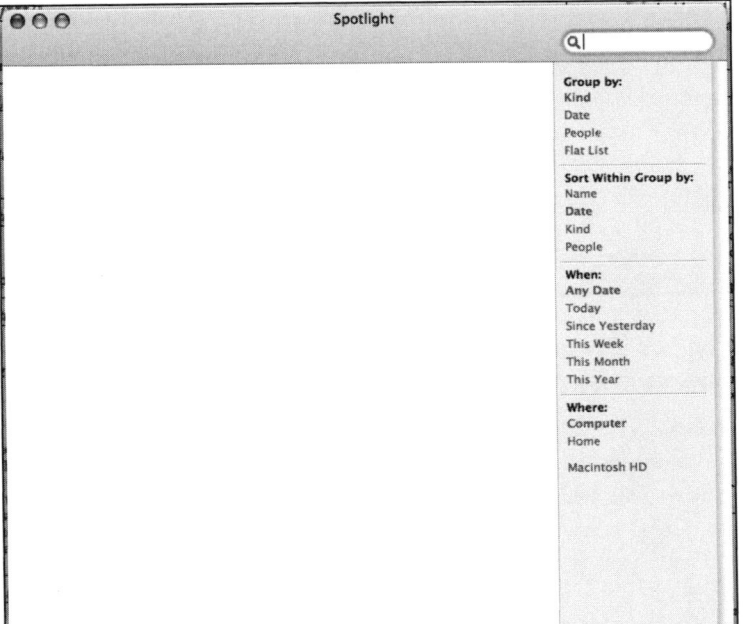

Figure 1.11b
The more detailed Spotlight search window

Locating Data Quickly Using the List View

When opening a drive, be it the internal hard drive or any mounted volume, you will be presented with *all* the content stored on that drive, but in no particular order. I recommend using the List view, with which you should already be familiar from older operating systems. The advantage to using the List view is that you have the ability to sort the data by the metadata columns. Clicking on the Name column header will order the data alphabetically (which is generally the default).

Note that the direction of the arrow in the column header will determine whether the data is listed in increasing or decreasing order. Looking for the Z session will be faster if you click the Name header twice—once to sort alphanumerically and once to invert the order, bringing the Z to the top of the list, as seen in Figure 1.12.

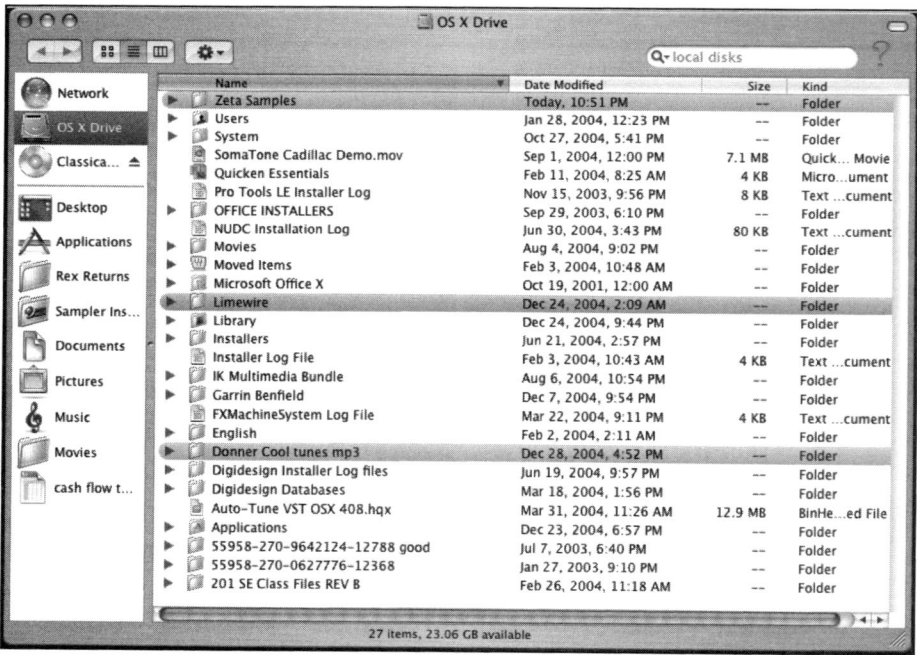

Figure 1.12

Macintosh file hierarchy, sorted by name in reverse

However, looking for that recording you did last week (called Audio 1-01, of course) will be easier if you order the data by date, as in Figure 1.13.

To change your current folder location, you can use some handy shortcuts to save time. To go up a level, use the CMD+up arrow combination. You can also click the Back button located in the upper-left corner of the window. This will keep the window open and replace the data with the data from the level above. CMD+down arrow works the opposite way and goes *only* as far as you have already been. Once you try to navigate to new data, this shortcut will stop working. In addition, you can always click the letter of the folder you are looking for to quickly navigate there. Clicking G will take you to the folders beginning with the letter G. If you prefer to open the folders at the same level without replacing windows, you can navigate to the folder you want and use CMD+left arrow or CMD+right arrow to open or close the folder directly.

When viewing files and folders in Windows Explorer (not to be confused with Internet Explorer), you can click View and select Details, as in Figure 1.14. Also, you can add metadata columns either by choosing View > Choose Details or by right-clicking a column and checking the metadata field you want as a column.

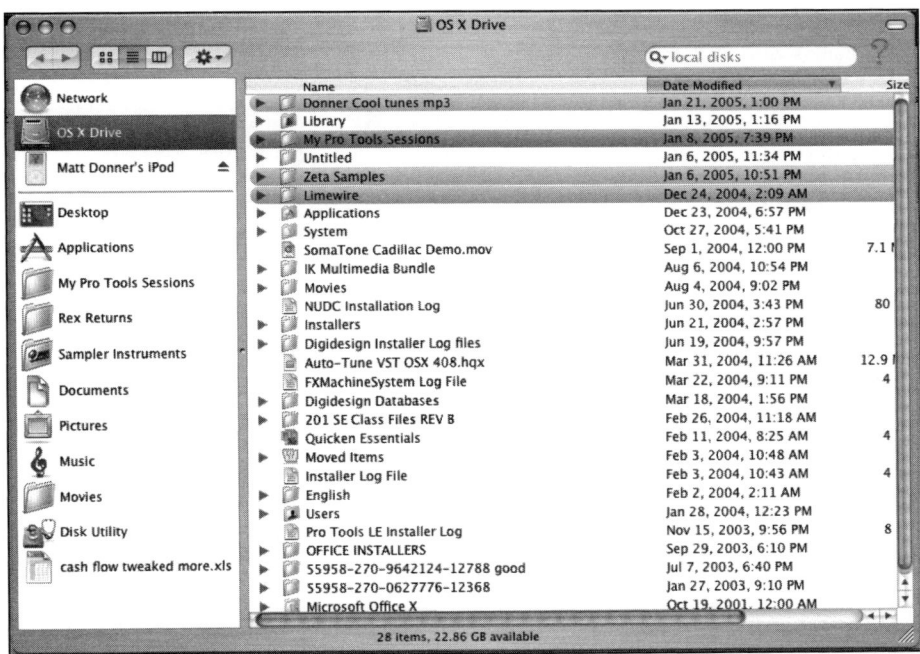

Figure 1.13

Macintosh file hierarchy, sorted by date

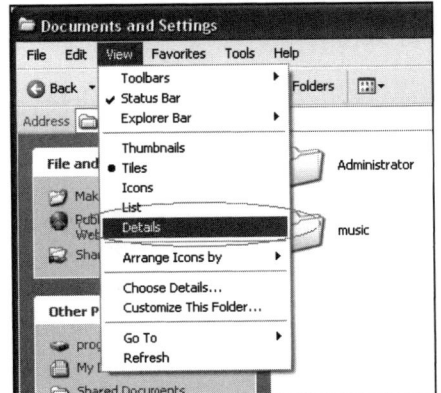

Figure 1.14

The Details view in Windows

Locating Data Quickly Using the Columns View

A disadvantage of the List view is that you are unable to see within a folder at any other level. This requires you to open the folder in another window (which clutters the screen) or open it on the same level (which eliminates your ability to letter-click and locate particular data). The biggest advantage of the Columns view is that it gives you the ability to see deeper (and shallower) levels of information at the same time, as shown in Figure 1.15. You can see at once whether the folder you are inspecting has the data you want directly within it or whether it is buried in subfolders.

NOTE

You can use either the Columns view or the List view when you are saving in Pro Tools by choosing a view preference in the upper-left corner of the Save dialog box.

Simply toggle left or right with the arrows, and you'll go forward or backward through the Columns view. It's much faster to navigate this way, but you have no hierarchy options, so searching by metadata other than the name is simply impossible.

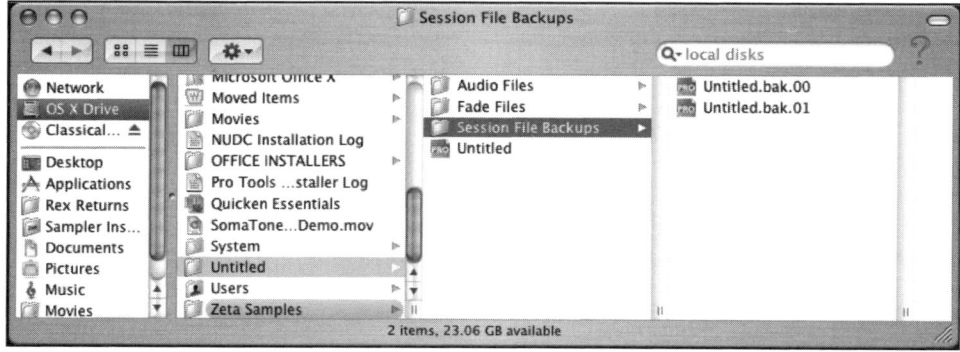

Figure 1.15

Macintosh file hierarchy—the Columns View

Locating Data Quickly Using Colors

When you are using either the List or Columns view, it is a good idea to organize your data by color. Coloring the folders makes them "pop" visually, and you can use the colors to mean different things related to how you run your studio.

You can name the colors to your liking (they default to simply color names) by going to the Finder level, clicking Finder > Preferences, then selecting the Labels tab. Here you'll see the colors that are available; you can rename them to whatever you want. In my studio, red means the session is live and not backed up, orange means it's an internal project not associated with any particular client, and green means it has been backed up and could be thrown out if space were needed. A customized color view is shown in Figure 1.16.

You can colorize the folders by highlighting them and clicking the Gear icon (also called the Action Menu) located next to the Columns/List view selector or by Control-clicking the folder (Figure 1.17) and choosing your color. The folder will then hold its color in both the List and Tiles views.

Figure 1.16

Color-coded labels

Figure 1.17

Control-click labeling

Organizing Drive Media Data on the Sidebar

It can cost you valuable time in a session to try to locate any data using the traditional List or Columns view if you are not sure what drive holds the data. You can quickly navigate between media by selecting the drive of choice in the top section of the left Sidebar when the drive information is visible. (Double-click any drive and a common Sidebar will appear in the window.) For studios working with a server that hosts a large sample library or backup station, the Network tab is a quick shortcut to navigate across the network to a remote location. You can also quickly eject any media device that is not permanently mounted to the system (like the boot drive) by clicking the Eject button next to the drive itself or by highlighting it and choosing CMD+E.

The top of the Sidebar is NOT user-definable but the bottom half is. The operating system supplies some of the standard shortcuts, such as Applications, Music, and Desktop, in the bottom of the Sidebar, but you can add or remove items at will, as shown in Figure 1.18.

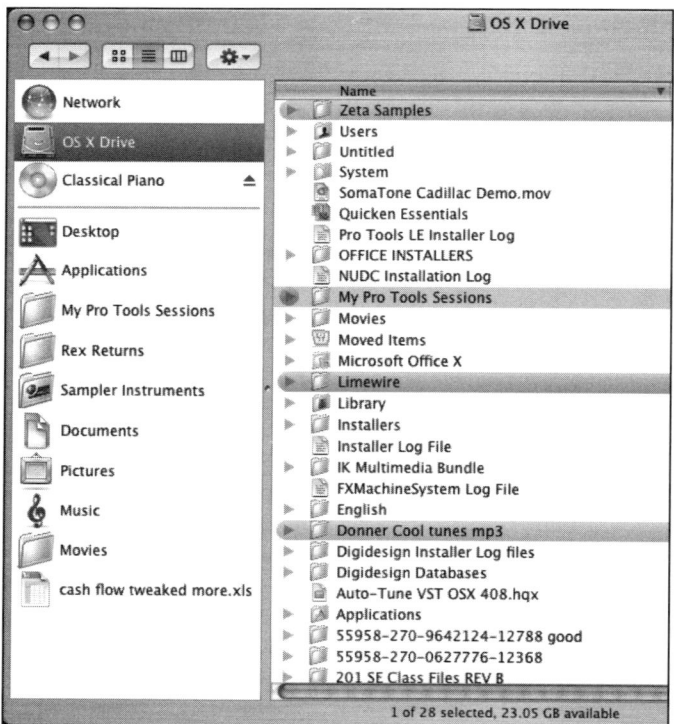

Figure 1.18
The Left Drive view customized

Be careful of the folder at the bottom called Music; it is *not* where you want to save your Pro Tools recordings. This folder is buried deep in your personal settings folder within the internal hard drive, and it will most likely not perform as well as another drive on the system. Even if you are running Pro Tools LE and you have no other drive, don't use this folder. If you are in this position, check out the section called "Maximizing Drive Performance with Single-Drive Systems" later in this chapter.

I suggest you remove folders you don't care about by simply dragging them off the window. Then you can drag the folders to which you *do* want to have quick access right onto this window. That way, you will have quick access to folders you always need without navigating through the folder hierarchy.

Drive Size Quick View

When you look at the Finder level, you can see how much space is being used on the drive and how much is left *before* you start your session. That way, you can deal with backups and making room before your vocalist gets warmed up and starts to deliver the perfect take, which you can't record because you have no room left on the drive.

At the Finder level, click View > Show View Options (CMD+J) and check the box labeled Show Item Info, as shown in Figure 1.19. (Note that the image says Hide View Options, as it has already been shown just to the right of the drop-down menu). Now, right on the desktop, you can determine whether you are really ready to start your session, as every media drive will tell you how much room is left. I recommend that you keep at least 2 GB free at all times. That's usually enough to handle a decent-sized last-minute session without worrying too much about having the room to perform for your clients. If you do run out of room during the session, they will be more understanding when you explain that you need to make room for the remainder of the session. If they look concerned, remind them that you didn't have time to back up other work because they are last-minute clients.

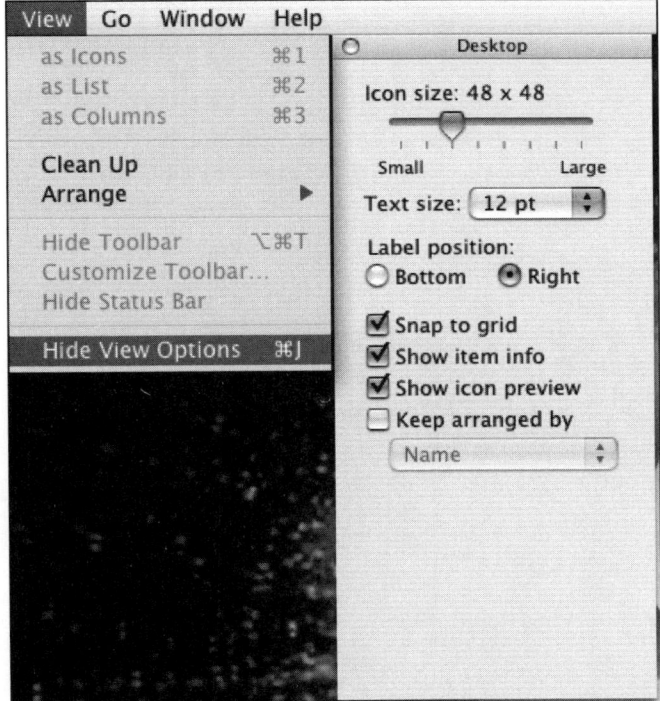

Figure 1.19

Showing item information on the desktop media

Maximizing Drive Performance with Single-Drive Systems

Laptop PT systems and many other PT LE systems often have the distinct disadvantage of operating with only a single hard drive—the internal system drive. This is particularly bad for laptops, which are usually packed with low-performance drives. Remember that in these single-drive systems, the drive now has to run the OS, as well as PT *and* the session data. In this case, you can speed things up somewhat by partitioning the drive into separate segments— one for the OS and applications and the other for PT sessions and audio data. Although it is still the same drive serving the data, by separating the two halves you can access the PT data quicker because there is less to search through to get at the audio.

First, back up your data drive to some other location (see the section "Creating System Backups" later in this chapter). While booting under an OS X 10.x version CD, choose Disk Utility > Partition. This will give you the option to resize the drive upon formatting (though all previous data will be lost). I suggest you break it into a 70/30 ratio, reserving the 70 percent for the PT sessions, as shown in Figure 1.20.

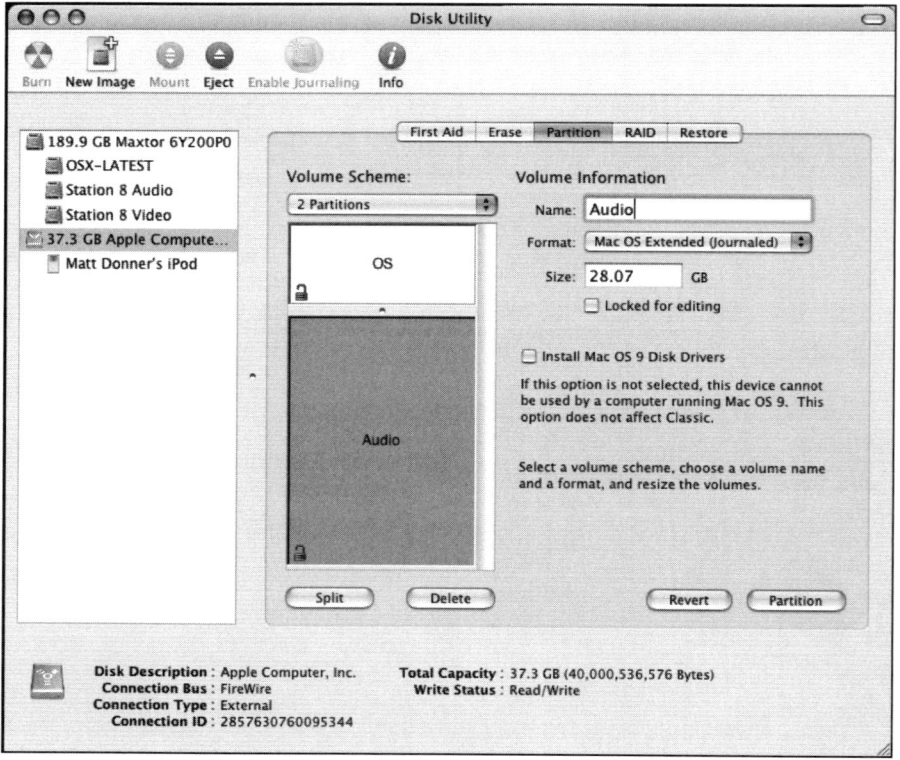

Figure 1.20

Two partitions

To partition a drive in Windows, you have to get your hands dirty with DOS. DOS comes with a utility called FDISK. To boot into DOS, you can boot from the Windows Installation CD or the boot disk, which you can create. Insert a 3.5-inch disk into the drive, open My Computer, right-click the A drive, and click Format. Check the box Create an MS-DOS Start-Up Disk in the Format window. Restart your new startup disk and type **FDISK** at the prompt. FDISK will now give you choices for what you want to do with the disk.

If you don't have a floppy, I strongly recommended that you use a third-party application, such as PartitionMagic (see Figure 1.21) or Partition Commander, because these and similar programs have a much more user-friendly interface, not to mention many additional cool features. If none of these help, consult your local Windows specialist to get you through this process.

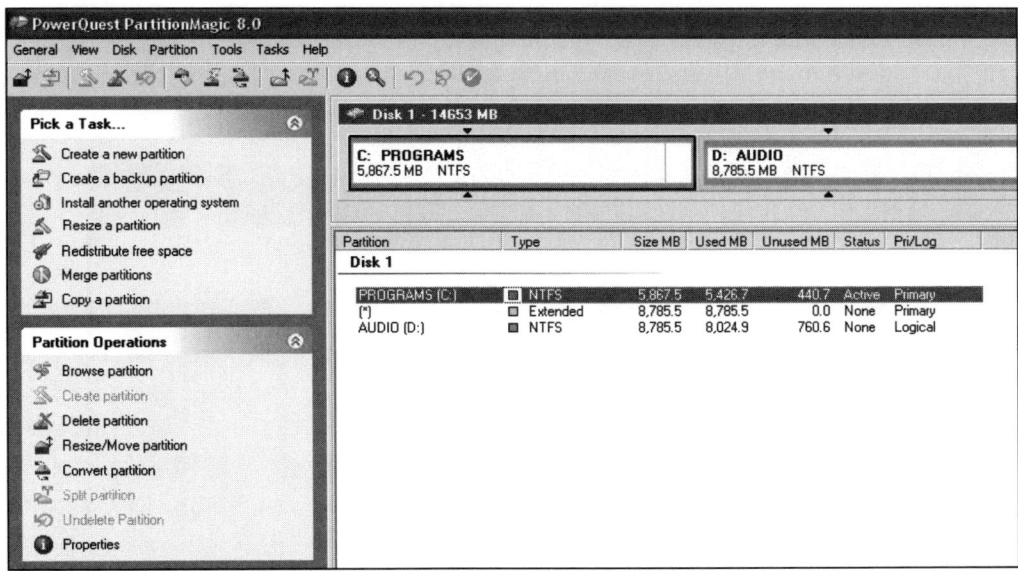

Figure 1.21

Partitioning in Windows with PartitionMagic

Creating System Backups

It will happen. It will happen when you don't want it to. It will happen at the worst possible opportunity. Murphy guarantees it. Your system drive will crash, and you'll be down. Many a studio has lost money and the confidence of a great client because of bad maintenance and worse contingency plans. Do us all a big favor and back up your system.

These days it's pretty easy to "ghost" a drive under OS X. You will need your friend Disk Utility, and you will need to boot off another drive (or OS X CD) to ghost your system drive. Ghosting will create a backup file (as large as your current system drive) and allow you to easily restore that ghost to any repaired drive. It will keep *everything*, so back up regularly because your system will *always* be changing.

Once you are booted under another OS, open Disk Utility and choose the drive from the left column, as shown in Figure 1.22. Then create a new image and put it where you have room. This image will be exactly as big your system, so be ready to store a 30 GB or larger file. Restoring is the opposite experience. Choose the image from the left column and click Restore.

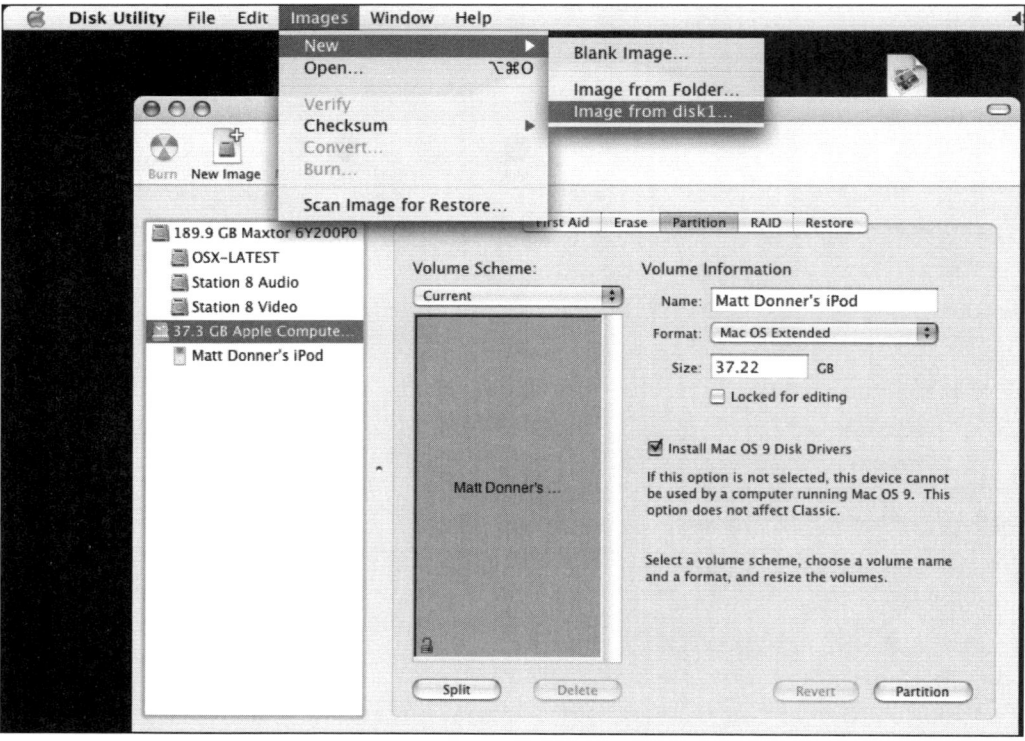

Figure 1.22

Ghosting the drive

Although this is theoretically good for the media drive too, it might be overkill if you have a separate FireWire drive. Drives are affordable enough now that you can have a drive per client and simply charge for the drive and store it on a shelf somewhere. If you want to make a backup (which is still a *very* good idea), you can simply copy the data to another drive or put it on multiple DVDs.

At Pyramind, we often perform redundant backups to DDS-4 DAT, which is slow and expensive but a lot less expensive than losing a favorite client. We also offer FireWire storage drives instead of DDS-4, since it is more popular and clients often take the backups, too. It's a good idea to sell the client a drive (instead of 2-inch tape) and let him or her take it with them. Offer the client a copy (backup) drive in house; this will not only make you more money, it will also save the client's butt when his or her assistant accidentally crashes the drive back at their office while playing online poker.

Backing up data in Windows is easy. Right-click the file, folder, or drive and select Properties. Under the Tools tab, click Backup Now, as shown in Figure 1.23. The Backup Utility wizard will guide you through saving your butt.

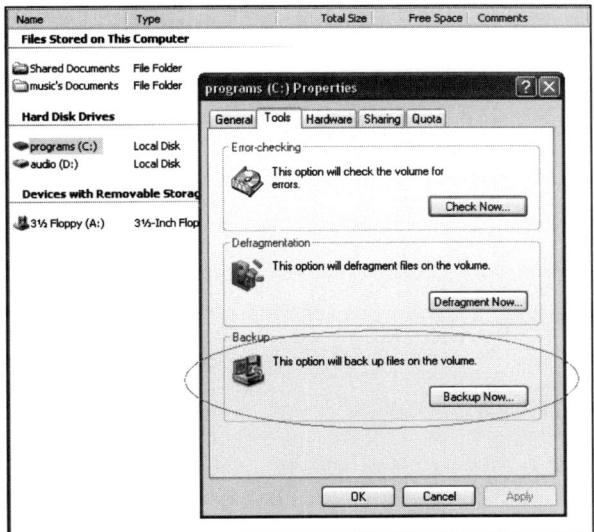

Figure 1.23

Backing up a volume in Windows

Saving a Crashing Drive Using Disk Permissions

Sometimes you get lucky, and you know your drive is about to crash. When this lucky day comes, try booting with the OS X CD and going back to Disk Utility. When you select the normal boot drive, you can both verify and repair the disk, as shown in Figure 1.24. This process will hunt through the OS and fix broken links and broken OS data. It's simple, useful, and good to do once a month. I also recommend you run this process on the media drive to keep things neat and organized.

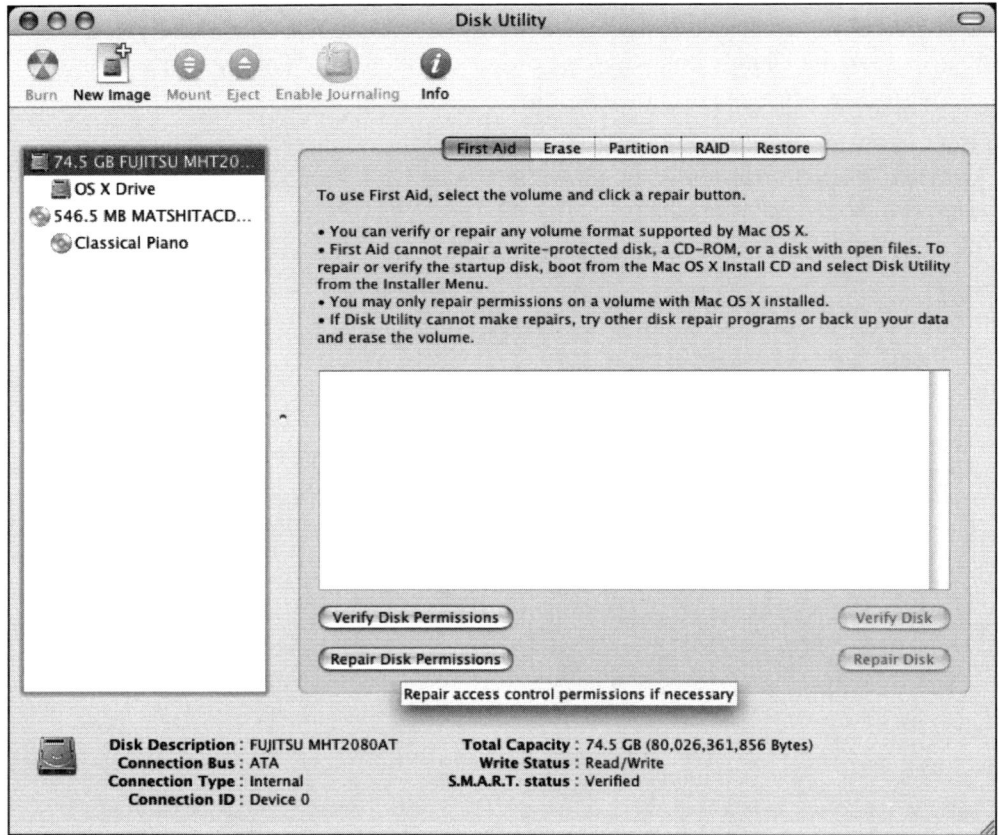

Figure 1.24

Repairing disk permissions

If your system drive isn't crashing, but exhibits slow and erratic behavior, you should consider backing up and reformatting the drive. Some people like to defragment their hard drive to "clean-up" the data, which requires separate software, like Disk Warrior."

Keeping your drive in good condition is a key to high performance and reliability. In Windows, right-click the target drive you want to optimize (see Figure 1.25), and then click the Tools tab. Here you'll find an option to error-check and defragment your hard drive. It's a good idea to defragment your drive once a month or so; remember to dedicate some time because it might take a while, depending on the size of the drive. It is possible to create an automated maintenance schedule by going into the Control Panel and opening Scheduled Tasks. Click All Scheduled Tasks, and the wizard will guide you through the process. It's a good idea to schedule maintenance tasks when the computer is idle, such as at the end of a long Saturday night session.

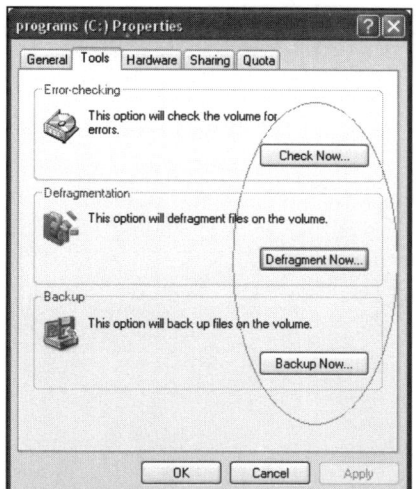

Figure 1.25

Defragmenting in Windows

Saving Your Drive by Booting as FireWire Target

I was recently the victim of a dead internal hard drive on my G4 laptop. The CD-ROM tray was also dead, so I was unable to restore the image or verify permissions. There was no way in. I was the Helen Keller of laptop owners.

OS X and the new Mac series of computers let you boot the computer itself as a FireWire drive, allowing another computer to serve as the boot drive and your computer to serve as the dummy drive. Turn off both computers and connect them to each other via FireWire. Fire up the healthy computer and wait for it to boot completely. Hold down the T key on the second Mac, and then fire it. After a few seconds, you'll see the blue screen with the dancing FireWire emblem, and your second computer will show up on the desktop of the first one, allowing you to image the drive, repair permissions, reformat, and start all over, if necessary.

Keeping Unwanted Visitors Out!

For that pesky intern/roommate/significant other who you don't want to have access to your system or your settings, OS X provides user definitions, permissions, and administrative powers to the owner of the computer. Separate user accounts allow you to maintain privacy and set restrictions for other users on the system. This is particularly useful at my school because it prevents the student populace from changing the desktop to display a favorite pet or copying or deleting applications. Different accounts can be created and managed in the System Preferences, as seen in Figure 1.26.

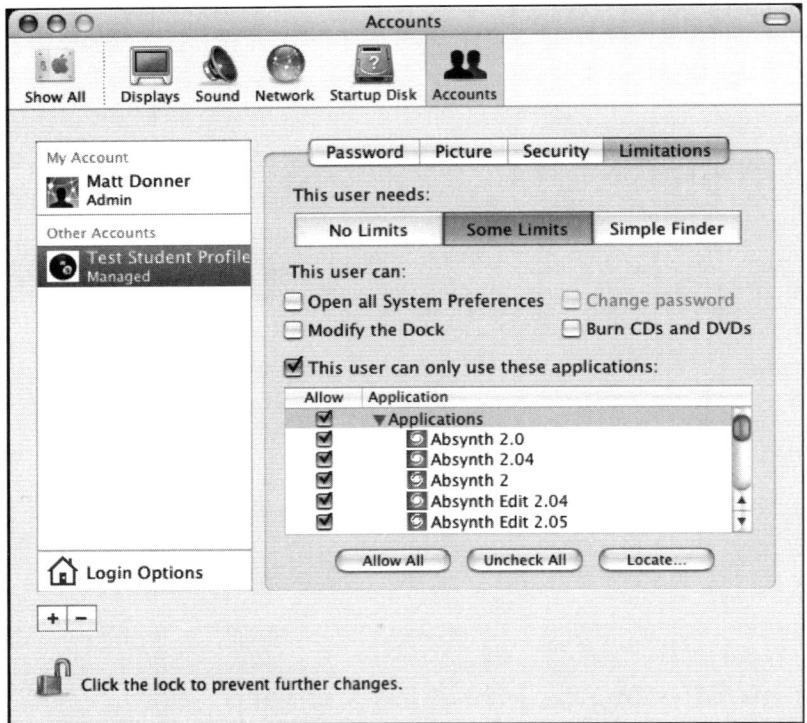

Figure 1.26

Creating various users

Creating different users and setting their permissions is generally reserved for the system administrator (the owner of the machine), but technically anyone with an Admin ID and password can make these changes. Each ID gets its own library (one per user), complete with applications, but may have limited ability to change the Control Panels, if desired. The system administrator has to administer the access granted to the secondary engineer and give everyone a password for their accounts.

To truly run PT under a non-admin user (first available with version 6.4), the system adminis-trator not only has to turn on the various applications associated with PT, but he or she also needs to do more work to get certain software peripherals to work. RTAS soft-synths, such as Native Instruments' Battery, for example, require that their permissions be turned on in both the System Preferences and the application itself. Highlight the Battery app (or whatever synth is troublesome—recognizable by a DAE-7400 error) and Get Info (CMD-I). Click Permissions and set it to all users and groups, as seen in Figure 1.27. This should give you full functionality in the non-admin world, allowing other computer users to operate PT while locking them out from changing the configuration of the machine itself.

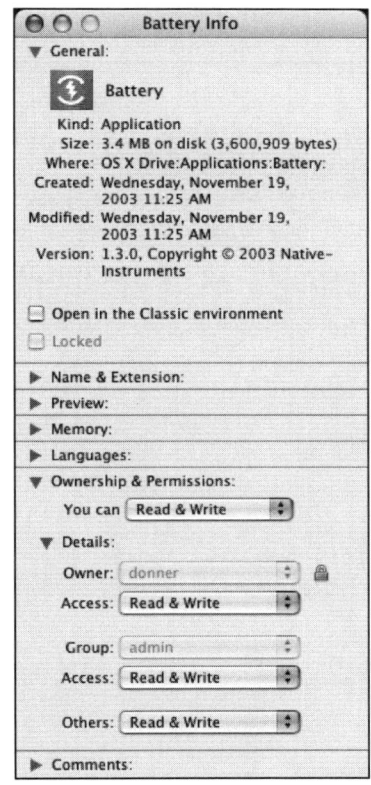

Figure 1.27

Permissions for soft synths

Deciding Which Format to Use

BWF? AIFF? SDII? 16 or 24? 44.1, 48, or higher? From your very first new PT session, you must choose different audio specifications, but which one is really right? You can make potentially brutal mistakes if you use the wrong specs, since Pro Tools won't allow you to change formats once you've created a session (see Figure 1.28). If you do make a mistake here, you may be able to deal with it later during the export process. (See "Exporting as Files" in Chapter 3 for more details.)

Caution

Once you choose a sample rate and a format type, you CANNOT change them within the current session, so choose wisely in the New Session dialog box.

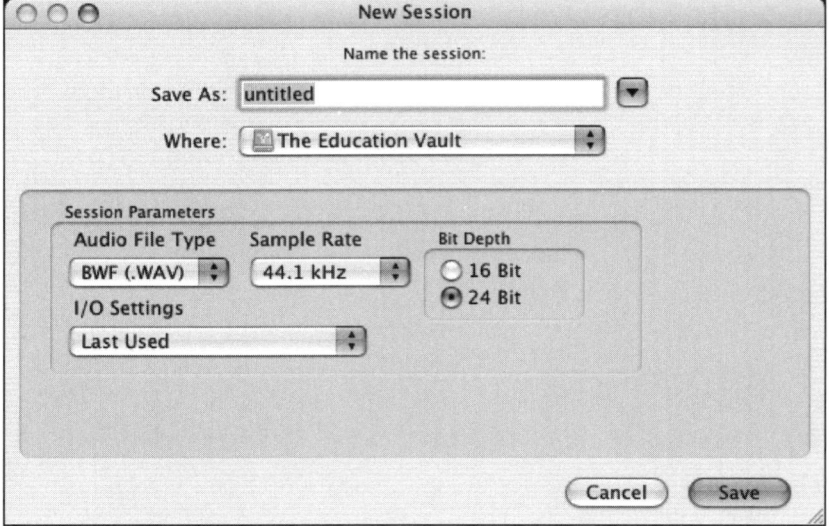

Figure 1.28

New Session dialog box

A good idea is to check out what the Grammy Association (NARAS) has to say about the matter. The P&E (Producers and Engineers) wing of NARAS has a document available at www.grammy.com/pe_wing/guidelines/index.aspx that recommends various settings to ensure both compatibility and quality. The formats you choose can depend on many factors, including what the client demands and what the receiving party expects. It is a good idea to ask the client before launching into your project. If the client doesn't know, he or she will depend on you for the answer. A background in digital audio may be necessary if you're not sure of the differences between formats.

Another intriguing question is which file format to choose: AIFF, SDII, or BWF. The most common file type is BWF; it is the de facto PC standard, and there are many more PCs than Macs out there. In fact, PT7 defaults to BWF format when creating new sessions for this reason! Note also that there is no more Enforce Mac/PC Compatibility button. All sessions default to cross-compatibility. Also keep in mind that PT7 no longer supports sessions of the +6 variety. All sessions have mixers that support fader gain of +12. This is important for two reasons—you have a greater dynamic range available on all faders, and you will run into problems going back to sessions/systems of version 6 or higher. For details about saving sessions to travel to older systems, see "Preparing Sessions for Delivery" in Chapter 3.

Deciding Which Sampling Rate to Use (Gene Radzik, Dolby Labs and Andre Zweers, Skywalker Sound)

Andre Zweers is the Pro Tools operator for the legendary Leslie Ann Jones, and if it's orchestral and recorded at Skywalker, Andre has recorded it. When I asked him about choosing sampling rates, the answer he gave was surprisingly familiar: Ask the producer and supervising sound editor. Although they sport a healthy Pro Tools 192 HD rig, Andre notes that often he'll record directly to 24, 44.1k as a matter of convenience for sessions ending as CDs. If a higher sampling rate is needed, he'll recommend 88.2 or 176.4, and *not* 192, because 88.2 and 176.4 divide into 44.1 more cleanly for CD. (While the computational power of a computer *shouldn't* affect the audio quality, it does—so choose wisely!) Whatever the sampling rate, he still bounces to disk to deliver roughs to the client on CD.

Gene Radzik has one of the greatest jobs there is. As senior Dolby Systems engineer, his function centers on setting up and calibrating music and post facilities everywhere for Dolby 5.1 compliance. He shows up, sets up, and then masters the final tapes for delivery. He concurs with Andre and lays out the various sampling rates from which to choose as such:

* Video sessions should be started at some variety of 48k because this is the de facto standard. Higher sampling rates should be multiples of it, yielding 96k and 192k. Since DVD Video supports audio of *only* 48k, choose these sampling rates for DVD-V as well.

* Music sessions should be started at some variety of 44.1k for obvious compatibility to CD. That yields 88.2k and 176.4k as primary high sampling-rate alternatives.

In either case, both Andre and Gene suggest you reference the down-sampled mix against the high-sample-rate mix to see whether your converter does a good job. In situations in which your sample rate converter is lacking, consider purchasing an external clock and converter that perform better.

Anatomy of a Pro Tools Session

When creating new Pro Tools sessions, organization is key. Being sloppy about your file management can mean the difference between keeping your clients happy (very good) and losing their lead vocals in between sessions (not so good). Pro Tools defaults to creating certain folders in a centralized location, and audio imported or recorded into the session *should* default to one of these locations.

When the session is created, the name you give it becomes both a session document (.ptf file) and a session folder. The folder holds all the subfolders within it, each of which holds the data that goes with the session. For example, the default folders are Audio Files, Fade Files, Session Backups (if the preference is selected; see "Don't Lose Your Work" later in this chapters), and Region Groups. ALWAYS keep these items together! While the default folders are handy for most things, you may find yourself creating more folders to keep organized. If you work with other applications often, and find yourself importing and exporting files a bunch, it's a good idea to create folders for these imports and exports. Figure 1.29 shows the defaults and some other folders I use often.

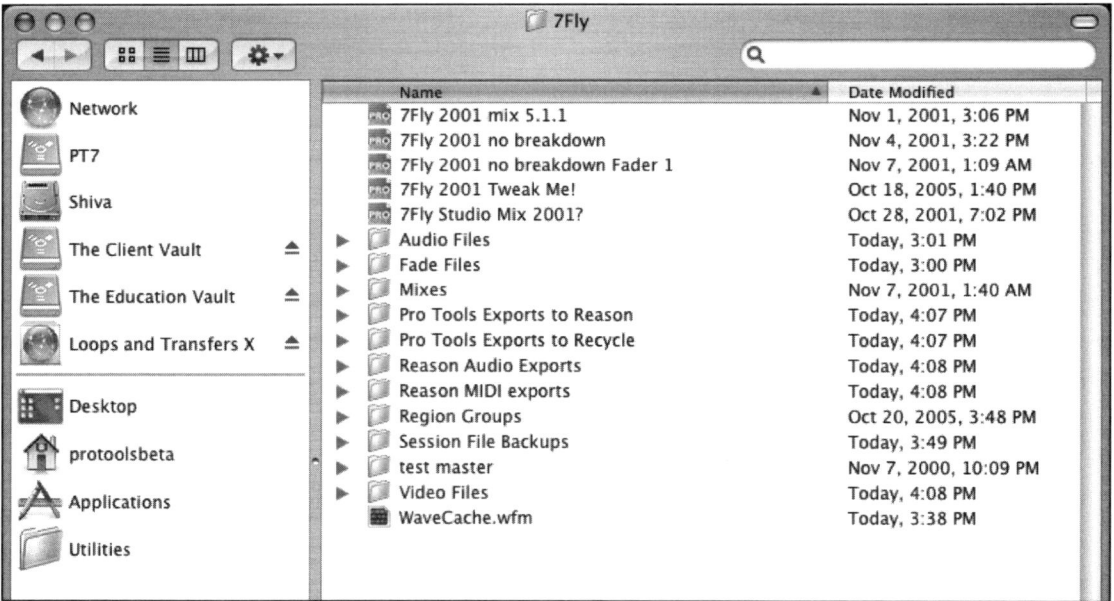

Figure 1.29

The anatomy of a Pro Tools Session with extra folders

Calibrating the I/O (TDM)—Gene Radzik, Dolby Labs

Gene recommends something that is often overlooked in HD and other TDM Pro Tools systems—calibration. The level you choose to calibrate to will determine how loud your studio plays and how well your mixes translate to other rooms. For specific applications, it may be wise to choose a different level to calibrate to. Most HD systems come pre-calibrated to −18dB FS. This example will cover full signal (0dB). For information regarding levels and other calibration techniques, you may need to do other research in audio engineering manuals or texts. Without much extra equipment, a few minutes can make a big difference in final audio quality. Here's how a calibration process might go.

The first step is to calibrate the outputs of the I/O. Once we know that the outputs are accurate, we can feed these outputs right back into the inputs of the I/O to calibrate them. Then, we know our I/O will accurately record and measure the signals present.

Pro Tools comes with a plug-in called Signal Generator, which is used to generate audio waves for calibration purposes. You'll need to decide whether to use a peak or RMS signal to calibrate with, which is somewhat dependent upon your work. For recording, use Peak mode, and for mixing or mastering, use RMS. Instant the plug-in on any Aux track and set Signal Generator's output volume to 0dB. When you instant Signal Generator, you can assign the channels' outputs to all eight outs of your interface by holding CTRL+Output assign and the single channel with Signal Generator will distribute the sound to each output equivalently. This is indicated by a + (plus sign) next to the output tab, as seen in Figure 1.30.

You'll need an external meter to measure the output signal. Connect Output 1 of your interface to the input of your pre-calibrated meter, and adjust the trim pots on the I/O until it reads the same as Signal Generator. Repeat this process until all eight (or more) of your outputs have been calibrated. Now, you can measure the Input section of the I/O.

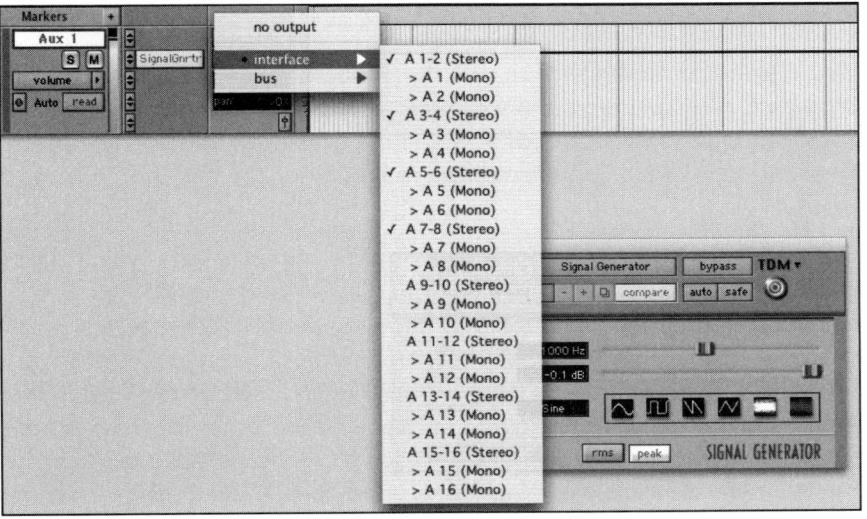

Figure 1.30

Signal Generator assigned to multiple outputs

Activate the Calibration mode by choosing Options > Calibration Mode, as seen in Figure 1.31. This puts Pro Tools into a mode in which you can measure incoming signals and determine whether the inputs are over- or under-calibrated. Using the recently calibrated outputs, route the signal from any output to the first input. Create a second Aux track and set it's input to Input 1. Adjust the trim pots on the I/O until the signal at the bottom of the Aux reads the same as the output from Signal Generator. Once Input 1 is calibrated, connect the output from Signal Generator to Input 2 and set the input of Aux 2 to Input 2 as well. Continue adjusting and moving the Signal Generator output throughout all the inputs until they are all calibrated. Now, you're ready for the session!

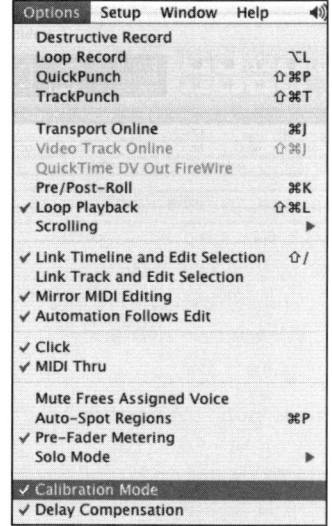

Figure 1.31

Calibration mode active

Labeling the I/O and Template Settings

When you are producing a band-recording session with Pro Tools, engineers often will become confused about which mic is plugged into which mic pre. There is usually a collection of tape strips to keep everything organized. But what about the preamps into the I/O—where should the engineer paste the tape in Pro Tools? And how would he or she find that tape in the second and third songs?

Because there is no way to mark the tracks in Pro Tools other than to use Comments (which takes up valuable screen real estate), the workaround is to label the I/O. Before the band lays down the first notes in your first song, customize the I/O setup by choosing Setup > I/O, shown in Figure 1.32, and start with the Input tab at the top. You will see stereo pairs of inputs, which you can "fold" open (so you can individually name the inputs) by clicking the gray arrows next to the pairs. Name all of the tracks the appropriate title (Input 1 > kick, Input 2 > snare top, and so on), and then click the Export Settings button. This will create a unique I/O setup, which you should call "Band X," and put in the folder Applications > Digidesign > Pro Tools > I/O Settings.

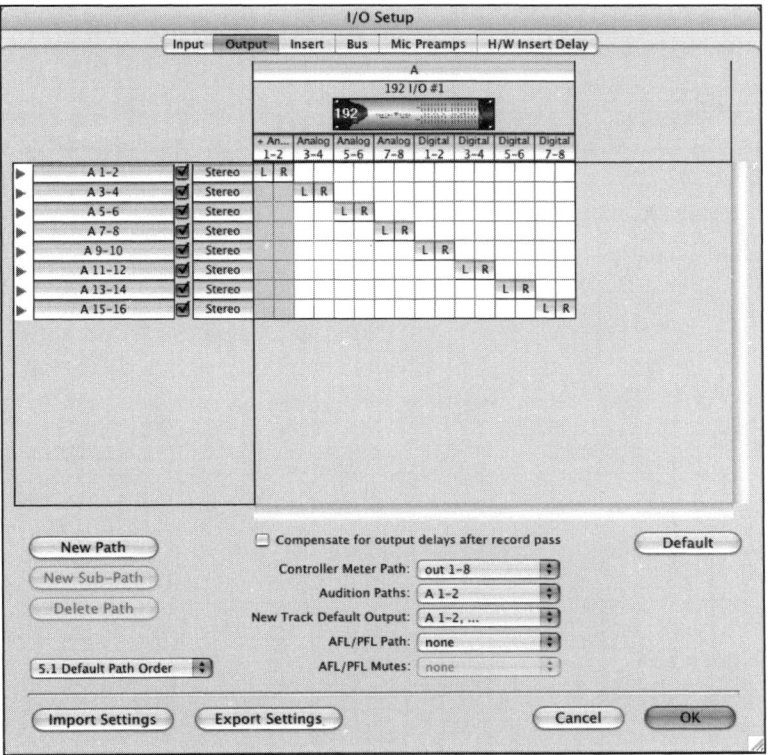

Figure 1.32

The I/O Setup dialog box

When you're done with the first song, save and close and get ready for the next one. Create the next song, but before you hit OK, look at the bottom-left corner and select the I/O Settings option. Choose the I/O settings from your last song, found in the hierarchy shown in Figure 1.33. Then, go right into the new song/session and you will be able to quickly create and name the necessary tracks, and all of your I/O settings from the first song will be available, shaving some time off your process. For more on switching songs and settings quickly, see the "Switching Songs" section in Chapter 2.

Another good idea is the use of the Stationery Pad. All Pro Tools documents have the ability to become Stationery Pads, which are a version of templates. If you have a setup that will be used repeatedly, you can turn a document into a Stationery Pad by choosing CMD+I (get info) on the document itself and checking the Stationery Pad box, as seen in Figure 1.34. Now, whenever you open the Stationery Pad Pro Tools document, Pro Tools will ask you to create a new session from it or edit the current document. If you're just messing around, then edit stationery. Otherwise, use this as the template and create a new session from this Stationery Pad. Just to be safe, verify the disk allocation after you've done this to ensure that the audio you will record will travel to the new location and won't end up with your Stationery Pad. See the section "Where Does It Record, Anyway?" later in this chapter for more on Disk Allocation.

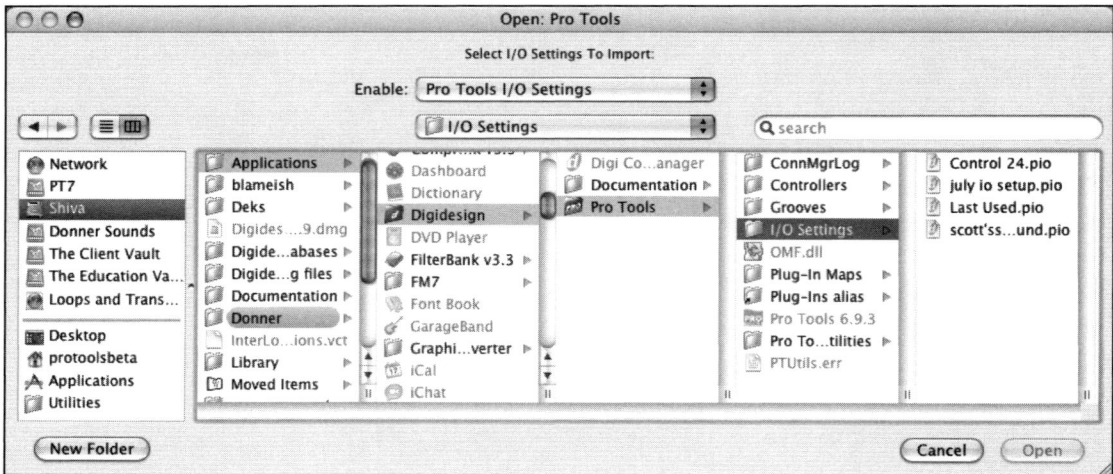

Figure 1.33

Importing the I/O settings

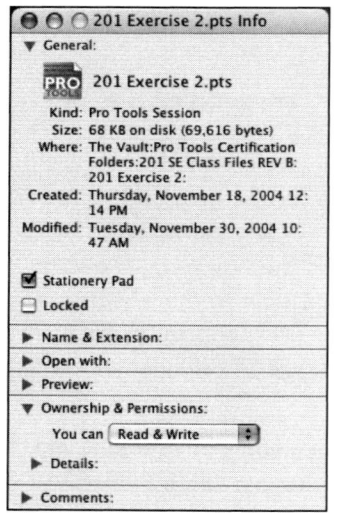

Figure 1.34

Stationery Pad

Keeping Organized with the Browsers

If you haven't been using the Workspace and its various browsers, you've definitely been doing things the hard way. The Workspace is a built-in database of everything on every drive in your system that Pro Tools can manage for you with ease—from locating files to direct imports, these databases can help you keep it together. The three browsers are as follows:

❋ **The Workspace.** This provides a representation of all the media and files mounted on your desktop. You can define what drives are set for Record (R), Transfer (T), and Playback (P) under the A and V columns (Audio and Video, respectively), as seen in Figure 1.35.

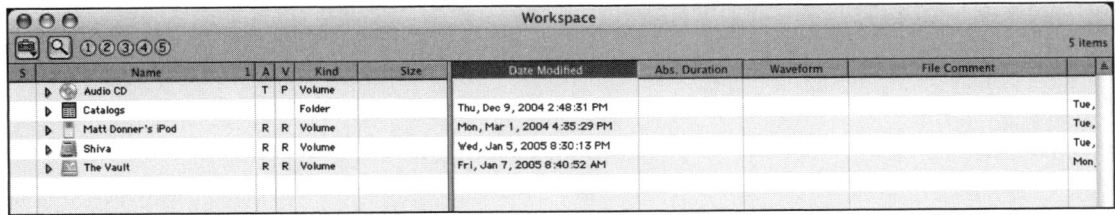

Figure 1.35

The Workspace

❋ **The Volume Browser.** This provides a detailed view of one of your drives (media) mounted on the desktop, shown in Figure 1.36.

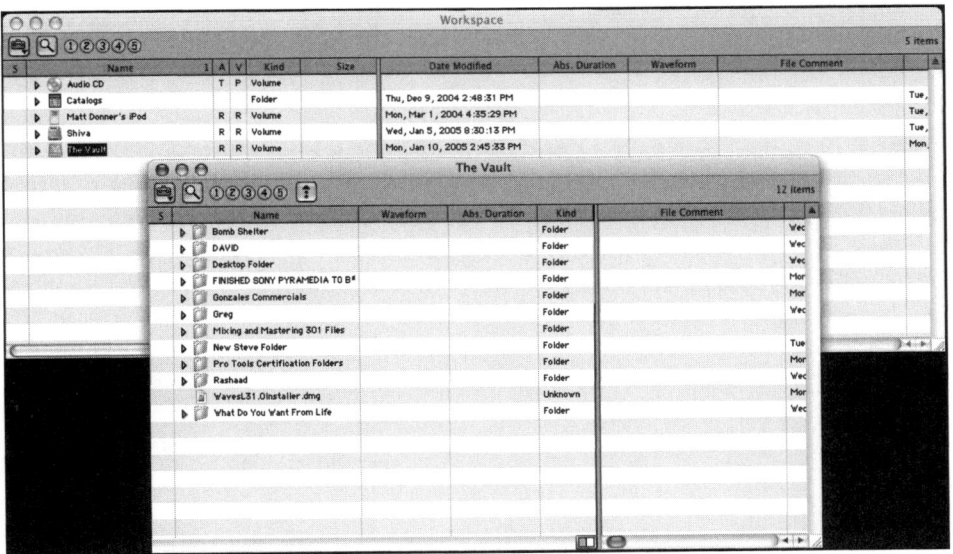

Figure 1.36

The Volume Browser

❄ **The Project Browser.** This provides a detailed view of your session and its audio/fade/other folders, as shown in Figure 1.37.

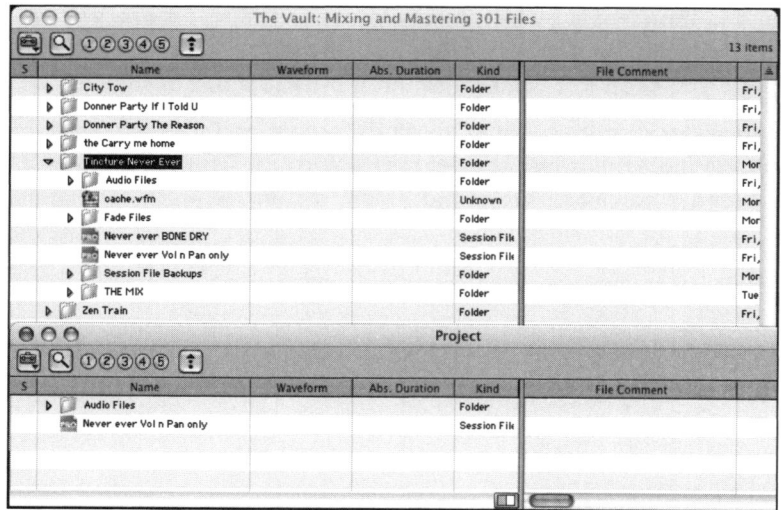

Figure 1.37

The Project Browser

When working in new studios, I like to set up the Workspace as the first thing. That way, all the information I will need is available at a glance, as shown in Figure 1.38. Press OPT+; (semicolon) (or Alt+O in Windows), and the Workspace will appear. It should be an exact copy of your desktop in chart form with some columns that display metadata columns such as Date Created, File Type, and so on. You should customize at least one view, but PT gives you five presets (similar to the zoom presets in the Edit window) for different views. I set up one view for generic searches, one just for searching for files and sounds, and a third for auditions and imports.

You can simply drag the columns back and forth between the panes to set up the columns as you want. To clean up the window, put unwanted information in the right pane and fold it closed using the Pane button on the bottom. After you've organized them how you want, store the preset by CMD+clicking (or Ctrl+clicking in Windows) the preset tab of choice. Now, as you work with PT, you can call up the browsers and quickly navigate to the collections of information you want.

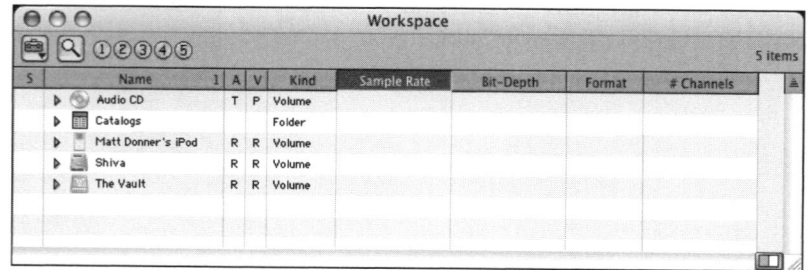

Figure 1.38

A customized Workspace

For example, when I need to import sounds, I call up the Browser, click the preset that shows the Name, Sample Rate, # Channels, Tempo (for .MID, REX and ACID files), File Type, Date Created, and Waveform columns. To verify files in the session (for example, which take was the right one?), I show the Waveform and Date Created columns only in the Project Browser. For searches, my preset looks like the Import preset, except that it also shows the Kind column (to search for video, audio, sessions, and so on).

A common error in PT that's associated with the Browsers is the following: "The disk <*disk name*> is in use and could not be ejected" (see Figure 1.39). The volume may in fact not be used at all, but the Digidesign Workspace may still be accessing it, forcing the OS to deliver the error. This can be confusing when the client wants to know why he or she has to wait for his or her iPod or CD back, and you tell them you have to quit Pro Tools in order to do it.

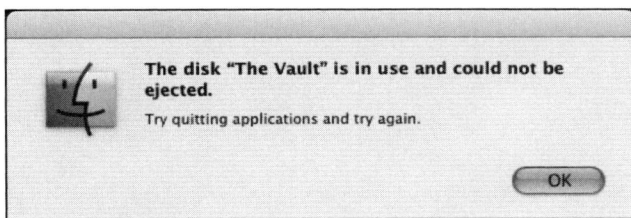

Figure 1.39

"Disk drive in use" error message

To avoid this, call up the Workspace, select the media you want to eject, and select Unmount from the Workspace menu, which looks like a construction worker's lunchbox (see Figure 1.40). This will give your client back his or her iPod in time to plug in (and ignore your awesome mix and listen to the Britney Spears rendition of the Lawrence Welk theme song instead!) and tune out. You could also quit Pro Tools, but that might not be appropriate if you are still working in the session and you can't afford the time to save, quit, and relaunch the program.

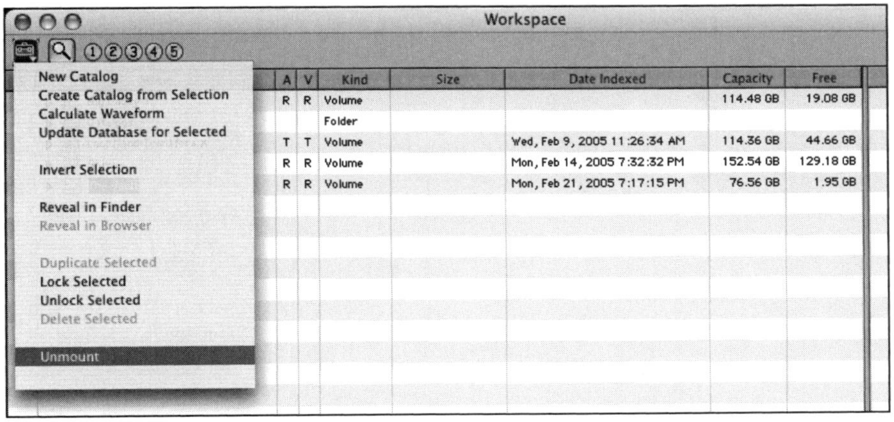

Figure 1.40

Unmounting media from the Pro Tools Workspace

What to Do about Those Missing Files

Either due to user error or drive amnesia, PT sometimes forgets where it puts the audio associated with a session—even though it's sitting right where it should be. When this happens, the
files are said to be *offline*, which means PT can't find them. It will maintain the regions with
light-blue boxes that approximate the edits until the audio is found. When the song opens,
PT will tell you about the missing files (see Figure 1.41) and ask what you want to do about
them—search manually (no fun), Skip All (makes for a quiet session), or search automatically
(there's an idea!). Most times, PT will find the files without a problem, but occasionally it won't.

Figure 1.41

The Missing Files dialog box

A moment of panic may ensue that you don't want to feel at the onset of the session. To fix
the problem, first visit the Tasks window shown in Figure 1.42, which eventually gets you to
the Relink window. (On the Mac, press Opt+' [apostrophe]; in Windows, press Alt+.[period].)
Relinking is the process of reconnecting the audio in the bin with the matching audio on the
drive. The Tasks window will most likely still be searching or will tell you that some files couldn't
be found. An alert will appear in the bottom of the window when PT is done searching, telling
you that certain files weren't found. Double-click on the alert, and the Relink window will
appear with the offline files at the bottom (see Figure 1.43). Select the offline files (one at a
time, unfortunately) and search using Find All Candidates, which will search for any possible
match for the file. When (if) your file comes up, select it and choose Commit Links.

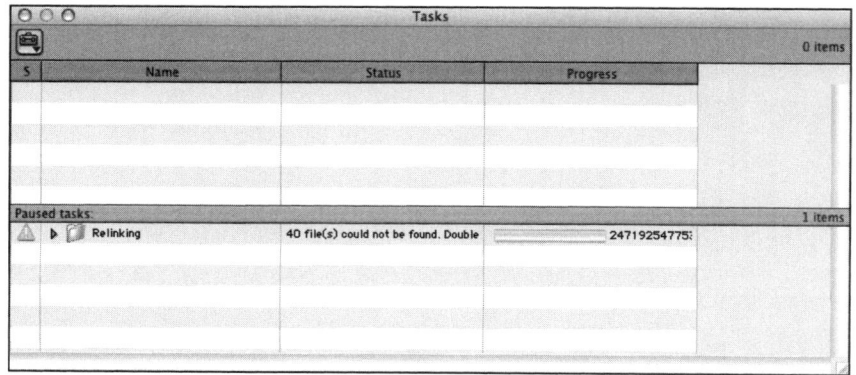

Figure 1.42

The Tasks window with
alert for missing files

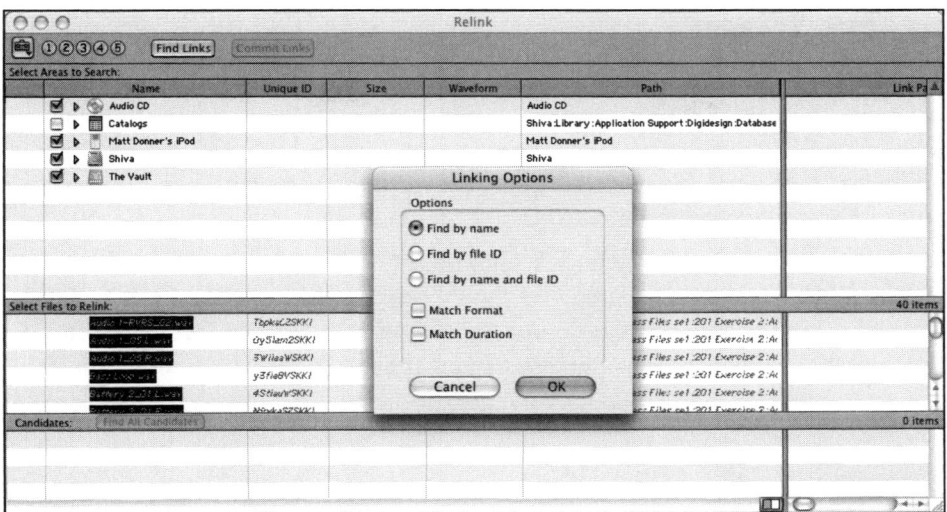

Figure 1.43

The Relink window manually finding links

If the system doesn't find your files this way, or if you can't spend the time to search one by one, you can perform other types of searches and relinks. Select all missing files and click Find Links. You will be presented with a search criteria box in which you can choose your parameters, like the one in Figure 1.43. (The widest search will be by name only, even though Pro Tools will tell you this is a bad idea.) This type of relink search bypasses the step of searching for candidates and goes directly to searching for established links. Once your links are found, choose Commit Links (see Figure 1.44), and your audio should come back online.

A third way to accomplish this task is to go directly to the Project Browser and choose Relink Offline from the menu. This will automatically select the offline regions and bring you to the Relink window with every one highlighted, saving you a step or two.

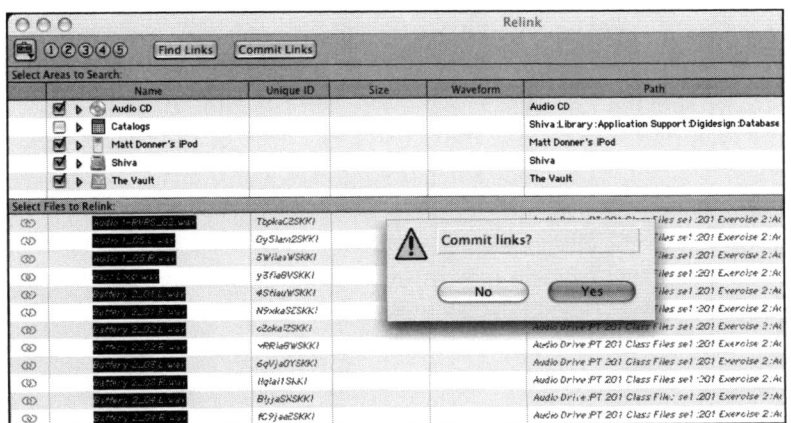

Figure 1.44

Committing links and relinking

Organizing Your Screen

For those of you transitioning from version 6x or lower to version 7, this section is very important because most of your familiar menus have moved. In an effort to be more GUI efficient, there are now new menus, such as Track, Event, Region, and View, where you will now find some of your old favorites. Most of this section is geared toward the View menu, so remember—most things are not where they used to be!

If you are new to Pro Tools or have simply forgot what a button does, Pro Tools now supports Tool tips, which display the function of a button by simply parking the mouse over it. You can disable (or re-enable) these tips by selecting Setups > Preferences > Display. Tool tips can display both the title and the function of every button as you choose. Figure 1.45 shows the Tool tips in action.

Figure 1.45

Tool tips at work

Although there are only the two main windows in PT, you can customize their look and feel somewhat to your work. For the best results with the least eyestrain, set up your windows before you get started. If you only have one monitor, this is even more important. First decide whether you're spending more time in the Edit window or the Mix window, and start there. For tracking sessions, edit sessions, and post-production, I work mostly in the Edit window, so that's where I start. For Mix sessions, you might work entirely in the Mix window, so set it up to taste. Let's look at the Edit window first.

Decide whether you need groups or access to the Track window (formerly the Show/Hide window). For simple tracking, you might not need either, so you should hide the bin with the chevrons in the bottom-left corner. Next, do the same for the Regions bin (formerly the Audio/MIDI bins). For edit sessions, you'll likely need these, but not for VO (voice-over)until the end. You should also decide about your column views in the Edit window (either View > Edit Window, as in Figure 1.46, or with the Edit Window View selector located directly under the modes, shown in Figure 1.47). If you wish to hide these columns again, simply deactivate them from the Edit Window View selector, or OPT-click the column title. For a mix session, choose View > Mix Window and activate the Inserts, Sends, I/O, and Comments if desired, or use the Edit Window View selector on the bottom left of the mixer. Figure 1.48 shows the new Mixer Window View selector on the mixer. You will now have access to all the information available in the Mixer window.

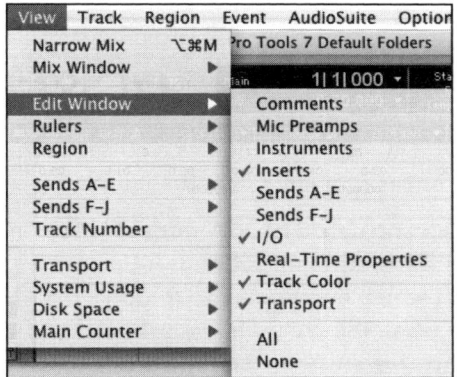

Figure 1.46

Customizing the views in the Edit and Mix windows

Figure 1.47

Customizing the view in the Edit window only

Figure 1.48

The Mix Window View selector

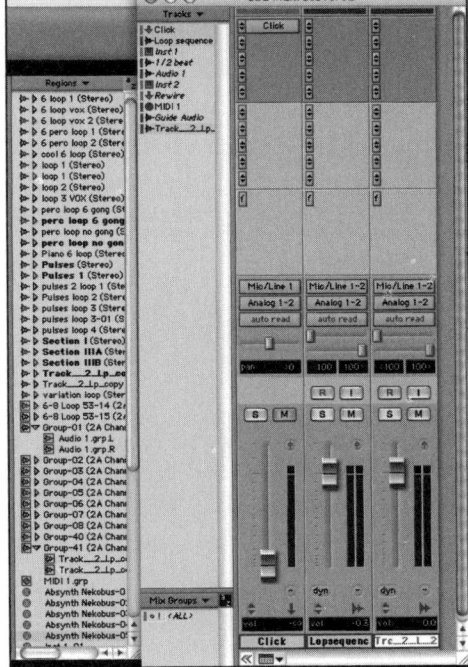

Figure 1.49

A two-screen setup

For two monitors, you can resize the Edit window so the Regions bin is just on the other side of the first monitor, giving you access to the bin but also giving you the rest of the first monitor for the Track view (see Figure 1.49). When you are deciding how to set up your screen, simply decide what you will need priority access to and show it. Anything you don't need often should be hidden because you will want the maximum amount of screen real estate available for the tracks themselves. This will minimize zoom time during the course of the session and speed up your work.

Resetting Pro Tools

Nothing will slow down your session like a crash. There's the obvious time lost due to having to restart and the time lost catching up on any lost work, but what do you do if you restart and PT *still* won't behave properly? Fortunately, your problem might not require tech support. The answer might be as simple as "Throw out your preferences and call me in the morning."

Pro Tools has four main components of its software that get corrupted (due to normal wear and tear) and need resetting. Each of them is responsible for a different set of user-defined preferences, so the nature of the crash will determine with which one you need to deal. The preferences files are rebuilt either when PT relaunches or when the computer is restarted. Within your system drive, you can reach them by choosing Users > Your User > Library > Preferences. The hierarchy is shown in Figure 1.50. In order, they are com.digidesign. ProToolsTDM.plist, DAE Preferences, DigiSetup OS X, and Pro Tools Preferences.

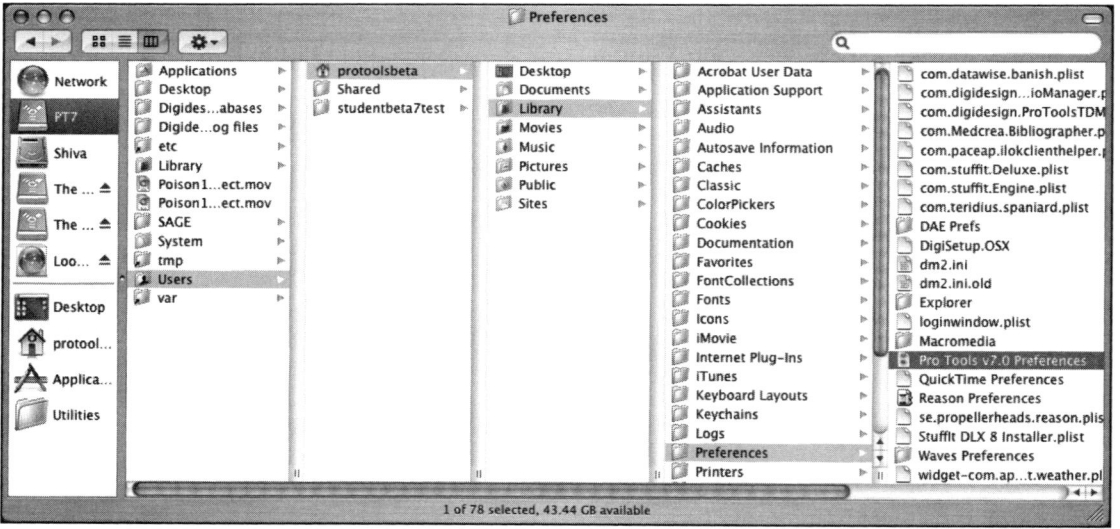

Figure 1.50

Hierarchy to the preferences

❋ **com.digidesign.ProToolsTDM.plist.** This preference is created by Pro Tools when a Navigation window (such as the New Session or Open Session window) is resized or otherwise modified. Otherwise, it doesn't exist, so throw it out at will . . . just in case.

✹ **DAE Preferences.** This folder contains all the settings for the preferences that relate to DAE. DAE is responsible for managing your I/O, plug-ins, memory, and other background Pro Tools applications. If your system can't remember how much RAM you have or if it consistently tells you more RAM is needed (when there is plenty), it is likely that your DAE preferences have gotten funny. Throw out the whole folder and relaunch PT. You might be asked to reset certain preferences related to the Playback Engine and disk allocation.

✹ **DigiSetup OS X.** This one controls your hardware settings and your hardware's ability to manage A-D/D-A conversion. If your audio is screwed up or won't play, this preference is corrupt. This can happen if there is an accidental power outage, your intern accidentally powers off your interface, or your clock source is interrupted. This will require a computer restart if you throw it out.

✹ **Pro Tools Preferences.** Snafu is the best way to describe the feeling you get when the PT preferences are corrupt. No matter how many times you tell the system to turn off the Timeline Insertion Follows Playback preference, it keeps turning back on. That's a pretty good sign that your Pro Tools preferences are corrupted.

Don't Lose Your Work

If the restaurant business is built on the phrase "location, location, location," then the Pro Tools production business should be built on the mantra "save, save, save." However, remembering to save while you're in the middle of working is not always easy. Choose Setup > Preferences > Operation and select the Enable Session File Auto Backup function shown in Figure 1.51. I suggest you keep the last 10 to 15 versions and save every minute or two. When you crash and want to go back to where you were, locate your session, locate the Session Backups folder, and sort by date to find the most recent file. You can go back as far as you like (depending on the AutoSave settings) to retrace your steps. Launching a backup file will force you to rename the session before you work.

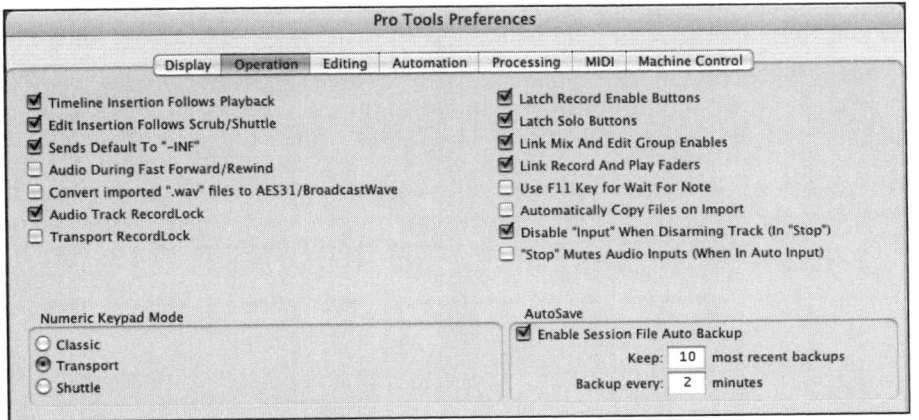

Figure 1.51

AutoSave

Where Does It Record, Anyway?

Normally, Pro Tools will set the recording location option to the Audio Files folder within your session. However, you might want to set the Disk Allocation preference (the default location each track will record its audio to) to a unique place for quick organization. To manually set the Disk Allocation option, choose Setup > Disk Allocation. For example, if you are working with an existing session and you want to record the dialogue in a new language, you can create a new dialogue track (per actor) and assign its disk allocation to a folder called Actor 1, as shown in Figure 1.52. The advantage to this is that when the session is over, all the takes are in a single location, ready for transfer to the client drive, iPod, CD, DVD, or FTP site.

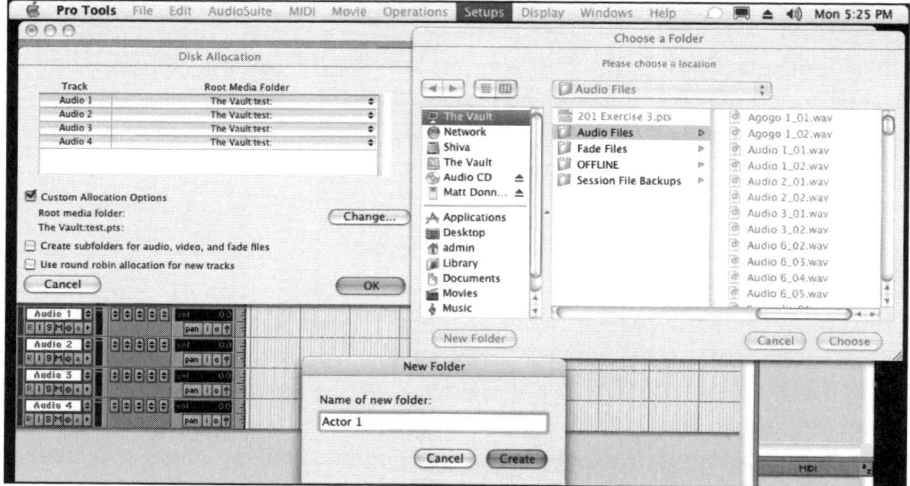

Figure 1.52

Disk allocation

You also can choose something called Round Robin if you have two record drives. Round Robin will alternately set the disk allocation from one drive to the next as you create new tracks. The advantage to this is that you split the amount of data that each drive is responsible for, and you can sometimes get better performance from weaker drives. The disadvantage is that you need to be aware of the *second folder* with the session name on the *second* drive when you attempt to give the client the work to go to another studio. In addition, there will be a moment of panic when the client opens the session in the next studio and it tells him that 85 files are missing because they are in the *other* Audio Files folder.

NOTE

Round Robin will ONLY spread the session across drives that are defined as RECORD drives in the Workspace. See "Keeping Organized with the Browsers" earlier in this chapter.

Adding a Second Interface (Mix and Mix Plus Users— Version 6x or Earlier)

Note

This section is ONLY for Mix and Mix Plus (and beyond) TDM hardware owners running version 6x or earlier. Digidesign officially stops support for non-HD TDM systems with version 7.

A common mistake when setting up a second interface on a Mix or Mix Plus TDM system is found in telling Pro Tools *where* you've installed and connected the interface. A proper setup is shown in Figure 1.53. To properly configure a second interface, three things need to happen: You need to properly connect it to a voice card, you need to properly connect the clock cables (we'll assume you figured out the audio cable portion), and you need to tell Pro Tools where you've connected the interface to the voice card. Generally, you will connect the second interface to the second card (if you have one), but you might choose to connect it to the first card as well via the proprietary Digidesign Y cable. Often, when the former is used, the Pro Tools setup matches the latter. This won't work.

NOTE

HD systems are self-recognizing, and you shouldn't need to go through this process to identify your interfaces.

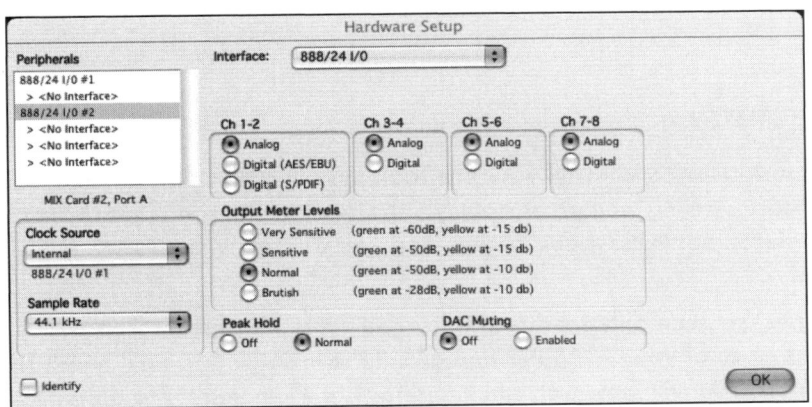

Figure 1.53

Multi-I/O setups in the playback engine

When I connect a new I/O, I often toss the DigiSetup OS X preference (see "Resetting Pro Tools" earlier in this chapter), and then shut down the computer to attach the interface. After the interface is connected and powered up, you should start the computer, and then start Pro Tools. You can also set up the I/O by launching the Digidesign CoreAudio Driver, (launched in Figure 1.54) located in your Digidesign folder within your Applications folder. After you click the HW Setup button, you will be presented with a dialog box looking for peripherals. In the upper-left corner, you will see a list of peripheral connections (one for each card and port, two per card).

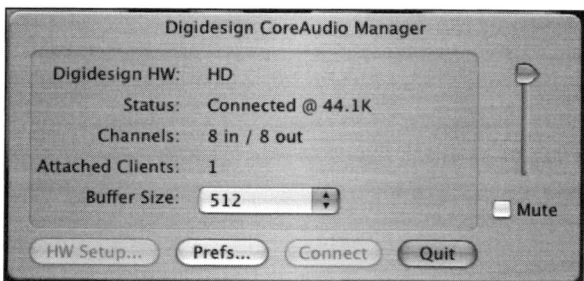

Figure 1.54

Digidesign CoreAudio Driver

If you have connected the interface to the second card and not the Y cable, you need to skip the second available peripheral on this dialog box. This is the stumbling block. Each interface can ONLY be connected to one card if there is no Y cable. Where there is no Y cable, Interface 1 should connect to Card 1 and Interface 2 connects to Card 2. In the CoreAudio Driver, the second interface will actually show up on the *third* port shown, which is the A port on the second card.

Note

The Digidesign CoreAudio Driver (version 6.4 and later) is now multi-client, which means that multiple programs can access the Digidesign hardware at once. The DCAD will tell you how many programs are logged in (connected clients). Previous versions forced the user to manually add programs via the Supported Applications button.

Managing Your Memory

Memory can play a large part in how successful your Pro Tools system is when the session starts getting large or you start working with other applications, such as Reason. To set your memory requirements, choose Setups > Playback Engine, and you will see where to set your memory requirements.

For single-processor machines, you can only set the CPU usage limit to 85 percent. This will prevent you from asking too much of your computer and give it the breathing room it needs to run both the OS and Pro Tools. You will, however, run into difficulty when you try to do too much with Pro Tools and another application, such as Reason. Dual-processor systems can set at least one of them to 90%, as shown in Figure 1.55. Version 7 now supports multi-processors, meaning that several processors can be set to dedicate to Pro Tools, making LE systems extremely powerful. You can also choose how many processors can be dedicated to RTAS processing. A balance will need to be struck between dedicating the processors to Pro Tools the application versus RTAS. While processing many tracks with deep automation, shift the balance to the CPU side; while using many plug-ins, you will need the CPU load shifted to RTAS.

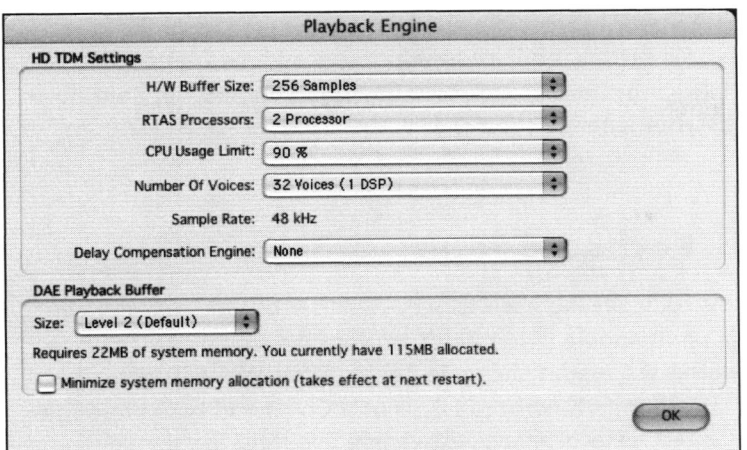

Figure 1.55

Memory requirements

More challenging than the CPU usage is the playback buffer size. Having a higher buffer will allow Pro Tools to keep playing if the system starts to get "heavy" with processing. Pro Tools will buffer playback by the amount of memory selected here. Although this is necessary for PT to keep playing, it can adversely affect other functions. A high buffer setting will make recordings potentially late and will certainly affect MIDI functions, as well as ReWire functions. You might need to jockey this setting back and forth until you find a happy medium between enough memory for playback and accurate timing on other functions. If none of this works, either put more RAM in your machine or print some of your parts. (See "Using Program Changes to Save Voices" in Chapter 5.)

What Do I Do about Shortcuts on My Laptop?

The best part about using my laptop is being able to produce in Pro Tools while waiting for my plane at Tokyo International Airport. The worst part is that I have to retrain my brain to work quickly without my favorite shortcuts. Be sure to activate the Command Focus (see "Command Focus," next in this chapter) to get some very handy quick key shortcuts for your laptop or tower.

❈ **Opening Windows.** Since there is no number pad on your laptop, there is no option to open the Transport with CMD+1. The secret, as with all shortcuts on a laptop, is the Fn key. For example, opening the Transport can be accomplished with Fn+CMD+J, where J=1 (see Numeric shortcuts below).

❈ **Switching modes/tools.** You can still switch with the function keys, but you might run into conflict with the OS system presets for some features, such as brightness, volume, and expose. (See "Setting Up Expose, the Dashboard, and Spotlight" earlier in this chapter.) If you can't get them to work or you or are bothered by the interference with the other functions, you can switch modes using the Esc key and tools using the ~ (tilde) key (as well as CMD+1-6 for tools and OPT+1-4 for modes).

❄ **Numeric shortcuts.** For whatever reason, the numbers across the top of the keyboard *never* work as numeric shortcuts, both on laptop and standard keyboards. To quickly call up windows (such as the Transport window) on your laptop, hold down the Fn (function) key and hit your letter of choice: 1=J, 2=K, 3=L, 4=U, 5=I, 6=O, 7=7, 8=8, 9=9, 0=M

Command Focus (a.k.a. Keyboard Focus)

Speed and accuracy with Pro Tools radically increase with the number of shortcuts you can master. Some shortcuts are simply unattainable if you don't activate the Command Focus key, located in the upper-left corner, below the modes shown in Figure 1.56. While its name has changed to Keyboard Focus, I'll interchange Keyboard Focus and Command Focus throughout the book. After this key is activated, several shortcuts become available via the keyboard. Some of most useful ones are

❄ **E.** When regions are selected, hitting the letter E will zoom the selection to fill the screen (large zoom).

❄ **R/T.** These are two other shortcut keys for zooming horizontally, with R zooming out and T zooming in.

❄ **N.** This shortcut toggles the Timeline Insertion Follows Playback option, a useful preference to set how the cursor behaves during playback. With this feature activated, the cursor will follow playback and position itself at the point of play stoppage. Be careful of the letter N, as it is closely positioned near the spacebar. With Command Focus activated, people accidentally hit the N key and deactivate (or reactivate) this option, which can be very frustrating.

❄ **D, F, G.** These are for fades, where D creates a fade-in from the beginning of a region to the current cursor location and G creates a fade-out from the cursor location to the end of the region. F is the default crossfade, which you can set in the preferences (see "Faster Fades" in Chapter 4).

❄ **6, 7, 8, 9.** These handy functions allow for one-key play options during editing. 6 will play to the current cursor location from a position earlier by the pre-roll amount, 7 plays from the edit start, 8 plays to the edit end, and 9 plays from the edit end. For more information, see "Auditioning Edits" in Chapter 4.

❄ **P/L/:/>.** These keys shift the selection or cursor up, left, right, and down, respectively.

Figure 1.56

The Command Focus (a.k.a. Keyboard Focus) button

2 } Recording

This chapter will cover some best practices and shortcuts for the recording process. The simple part may be getting the signal into Pro Tools, but here you'll find ways to record your sound while *also* sending your sound *out* to the artist in new ways. There are also several shortcuts for making your work with *multiple* artists faster and more effective!

New Track Shortcuts

Using the keyboard while creating new tracks can speed up the process of choosing and creating the tracks you need to record for your session. After hitting the SHIFT+CMD+N shortcut (see Figure 2.1), try using the CMD+arrow combination to choose more quickly the types of tracks you want. The left and right arrows (remember to hold CMD) will toggle between the stereo and mono functions (including formats into surround sound; see Chapter 8, "Working with Picture and Surround"), whereas the up and down arrows will toggle between the Audio/Aux/MIDI/Master and the New Instrument types of tracks. The shortcuts now include SHIFT+CMD+arrows (up or down) to create and remove new tracks. Figure 2.2 shows multiple tracks being created in different timescales at once.

Also new in this window is the ability to select how each track will behave with respect to the timescale. This means that track by track you can choose which will follow an absolute timescale and which will follow a relative timescale. Hit the Tab key to select the track of choice, and then hit CMD+OPT+CTRL+up/down arrows to toggle this track between ticks and samples (relative versus absolute) timescales. For more on this, see "Keeping the Music/SFX Still When the Picture Changes" in Chapter 8.

Figure 2.1

The New Tracks dialog box

Figure 2.2

Multiple track types and timescales in version 7

Naming Track Shortcuts

Many people waste time naming tracks one at a time by double-clicking on the track name (channel select), hitting OK, and then moving on to the next track. The next time you name a track, notice the Next and Previous buttons (shown in Figure 2.3), which allow you to switch to the next track and name it.

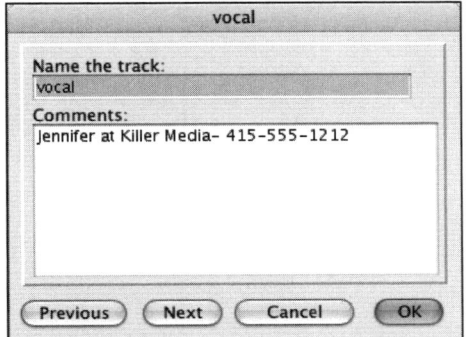

Figure 2.3

The Track Name dialog box

For several tracks that share a name (Vocal Take 1, Vocal Take 2, and so on), try copying the name without the number and pasting it into the next track, and then adding the number. You can also switch tracks by hitting the CMD+arrow combination. (The up/down or left/right combinations perform the same functions.) See the "New Track Shortcuts" section earlier in this chapter.)

Signal Checks

Following is a good checklist to run through before you record to a track. It will save you headaches and save everyone in the room earaches from feedback.

❄ **Run through the default/custom I/O setup** to make sure your inputs are named appropriately. Much confusion can ensue if your labels match the room the session was initiated in instead of *your* room, as shown in Figure 2.4.

❄ **Check your hardware setup** to ensure that all of your inputs are appropriately set to the incoming signal. For incoming digital signals, be sure you have set your clock source correctly. This will be particularly critical when you are using the ADAT light-pipe connection because these signals require very strong clocks to avoid jitter (see Figure 2.5).

❄ **Start your signal with no plug-ins on the chain**. If you are using a plug-in and it happens to have run out of its demo time, it will kill the signal on the track, and you'll never know why you can't hear it.

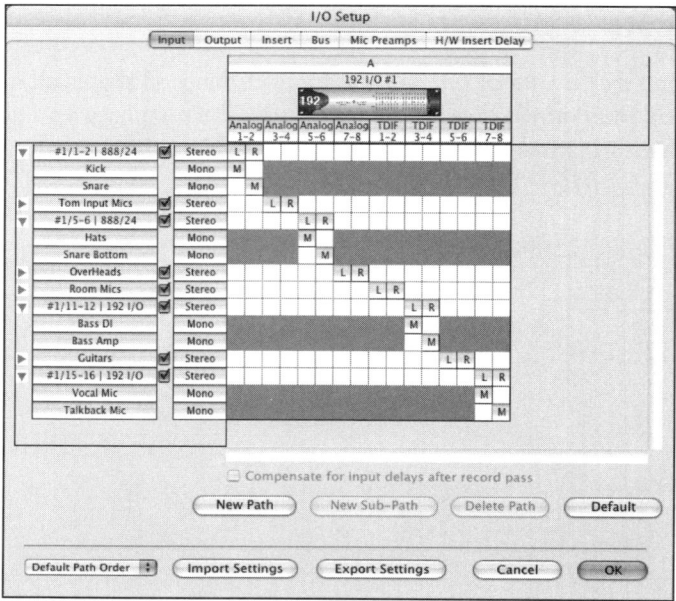

Figure 2.4

Custom I/O setup inputs

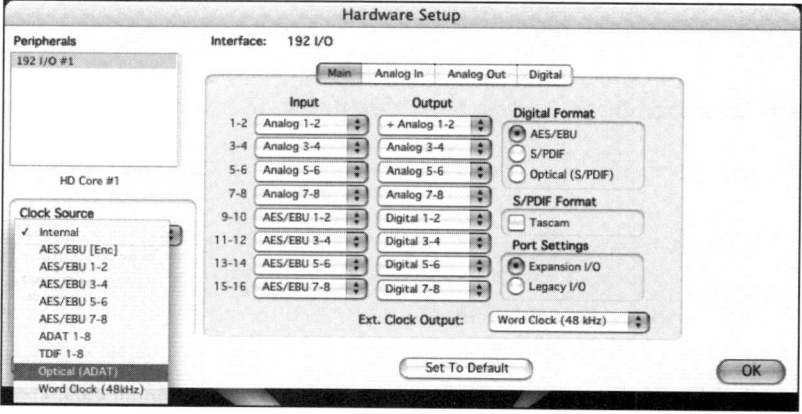

Figure 2.5

The hardware setup with a digital clock from an ADAT

* **Always mute the channel first!** Many a session has gotten off on the wrong foot due to screeching feedback on the record channel (see Figure 2.6). Perhaps your intern miked up the playback speaker instead of the guitar cabinet, or perhaps your artist was warming up his best "Good Morning, Vietnam!" impression when you record-enabled the channel. In either case, you can be assured of an earful of fun if you don't mute the channel first.

* **Verify the disk allocation** for the record track, as seen in Figure 2.7. (For more on this, see "Where Does It Record, Anyway?" in Chapter 1.) This will prevent you from having to search for the "missing" file later.

Figure 2.6

The muted record-ready channel with feedback

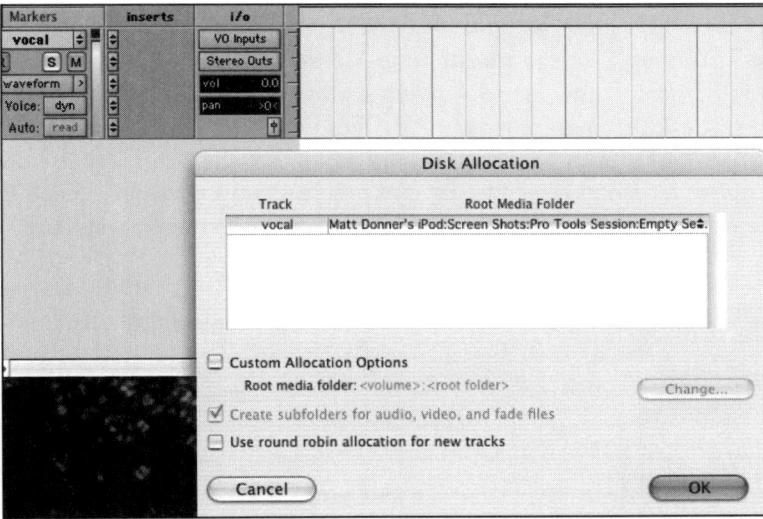

Figure 2.7

The Disk Allocation dialog box

* **Keep the monitor volume low** until you have success. Even if the signal path is set up well, you can scare your producer by randomly opening the channel with the speakers on full blast.

* **Test the talkback system before you open the channel**. This will not only verify that the talent can hear you, it will serve as a good wakeup call to the talent to stop his or her screeching so you can safely open the channel and begin work. Assure the talent that it is appropriate not to hear himself or herself because he or she is muted while waiting for the final signal check.

* **Name the track before you record**. This will ensure that your Region List isn't full of files all named Audio 01-xx. In answer to your next question: No, you can't name the track in the middle of recording and expect PT to "catch" the name...it won't.

Talkback Options

Obviously, communication through the glass can be critical to the flow of recording. For the artists, it's easy; they have the mic in front of them. The challenge is usually in getting sound *to* the artist. Most consoles come equipped with a talkback button, but it may or may not allow you to send a combination of Pro Tools output pairs with the talkback signal. (See the "Creating Discrete Headphone Mixes" sections later in this chapter.) Control surfaces, such as the Icon, Control 24, and the Pro Control, make it easy but others don't.

A good workaround assumes you have *no* console at all. In this case, Pro Tools will be fed to the artist (again, see "Creating Discrete Headphone Mixes"), and you need to get the talkback mic to Pro Tools. Create a new mono Aux input channel and set its input to the I/O connected to your talkback mic, as seen in Figure 2.8. That way, you speak into Pro Tools (without using a track voice), and both you *and* the mix make it to the artist. Try to keep the channel muted when you're not speaking so there isn't any feedback or weird phase issues. When you *do* open the channel, be careful what you say because the artist will hear everything!

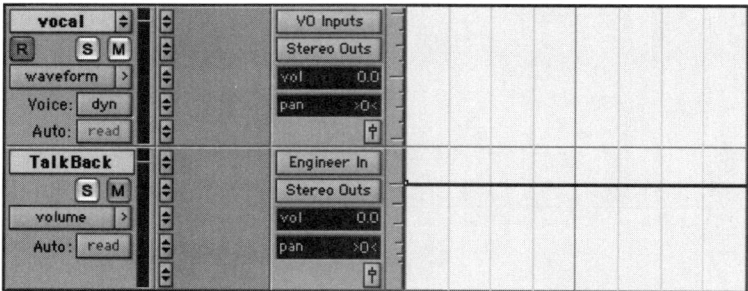

Figure 2.8

Aux channel for the engineer's talkback

A good idea to keep the two-way communication smooth in band situations is to set a mic in the middle of the live room and simply leave it open the entire time. If you've ever recorded a drummer and watched him lean over to yell into the snare mic to talk to you, you know this is a good idea. I suggest either a decent mic set to OMNI (which listens everywhere around it equally) or a PZM (*pressure zone microphone*). Route the channel to an Aux input within Pro Tools for monitoring between takes, as seen in Figure 2.9. This will allow you to hear everything that the band says at all times, allowing you to act quickly and keep the vibe flowing.

You can choose to route the talkback mic to an audio channel if you want to print the tone anyway, as a poor man's room mic. Sometimes it provides a certain dimension to drums with a healthy amount of pleasing bleed from the bass and guitar, helping you tie the discrete sounds together later. Other times, it provides terrible phase shift that will destroy your stereo image of the overhead mics and sound bad when referencing in mono.

Figure 2.9

Aux channel
for room
talkback mic

Monitoring with the Mbox and Mbox 2

The Mbox has made Pro Tools available to almost everyone by being both USB-powered and so affordable. As you might have guessed, though, something had to give—you can't get *everything* for such an attractive price.

The biggest shortcoming is the Mbox's ability to handle zero-latency monitoring—it can't. It comes close, though, with the Input/Playback knob, which allows you to blend between the track and the input signal. In the Mbox's defense, I should point out that no USB-powered audio interface allows for full-duplex monitoring without a certain amount of latency (the delay in time between the input of the signal and its return through the outputs of the interface). With the Mbox, as you turn the knob toward Playback, you get a stronger level of playback and a weaker level of the input signal (no latency). Finding the right blend, however, may be impossible. As you turn the knob toward Input, you get a stronger input signal (no latency) but a weaker playback signal. In either case, if you are also listening to the record track, you hear both the input (no latency) and the playback of the same signal (latency). Although this is a fun delay effect, it will destroy your concentration and the artist's. A simple solution is to mute the recording track, removing the latent signal from the "live" signal. However, this may lead to awkward headphone mix issues with the artist.

To properly monitor the playback and the input signal without latency, you will need more hardware. Refer to Figure 2.10 for a potential zero-latency monitoring solution. I like the Mackie 1202-VLZ Pro for this function because the signal is clean and quiet, and it provides four decent mic preamps; but any mixer could do. Route Pro Tools to any of the four stereo input pairs at the end of the mixer, 5 through 12, and route the mic to any of the mic channels (1 through 4). You will need to send the headphone mix to the artist from the Mackie itself. Mute the record channel in Pro Tools. You will have much more control over the blend of the input and output of Pro Tools without the delay of the latency throwing you both off. Unmute the Pro Tools record channel when you are ready to monitor the performance *after* the recording.

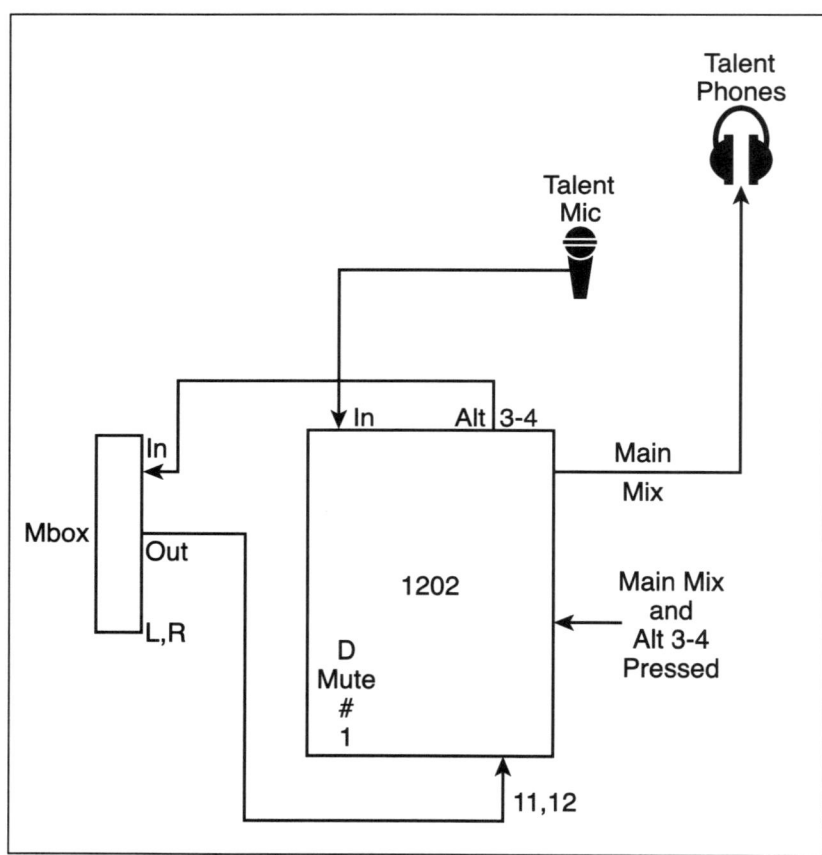

Figure 2.10

Diagram of Mbox monitoring system

Creating Discrete Headphone Mixes (Single Artist)

Invariably, your artist will want to hear the mix differently than you do. You will want to hear it as it will sound when it is done, but the artist will want to hear the "more me" mix. If you share the same mix, one of you has to suffer (and we all know who that'll be, don't we?). This technique works for all systems *except* LE Mbox systems. (See "Monitoring with the Mbox and Mbox2" earlier in this chapter.)

Create a send on all your channels to a pair of outputs on your hardware I/O. I use 7–8 (as shown in Figure 2.11) as the default because they are out of the way of other potential output pairs (as in 5.1 surround). For M-Powered Pro Tools with other hardware, like the Ozonic, you'll need to use any output pair other than outs 1–2 (the Ozonic has 2 stereo outs, so use 3–4). You can then build the mix to the artist's specifications track by track if required. You should build his or her mix by plugging a pair of your own cans into the headphone amp connected to the output pairs going to the artist (assuming the amp supports more than one pair at a time). You can then listen with the artist, hear what he or she hears, and build it that way. More sophisticated setups allow you to connect the 7–8 output to *both* the talent and your monitors so you can quickly switch back and forth to adjust them to taste.

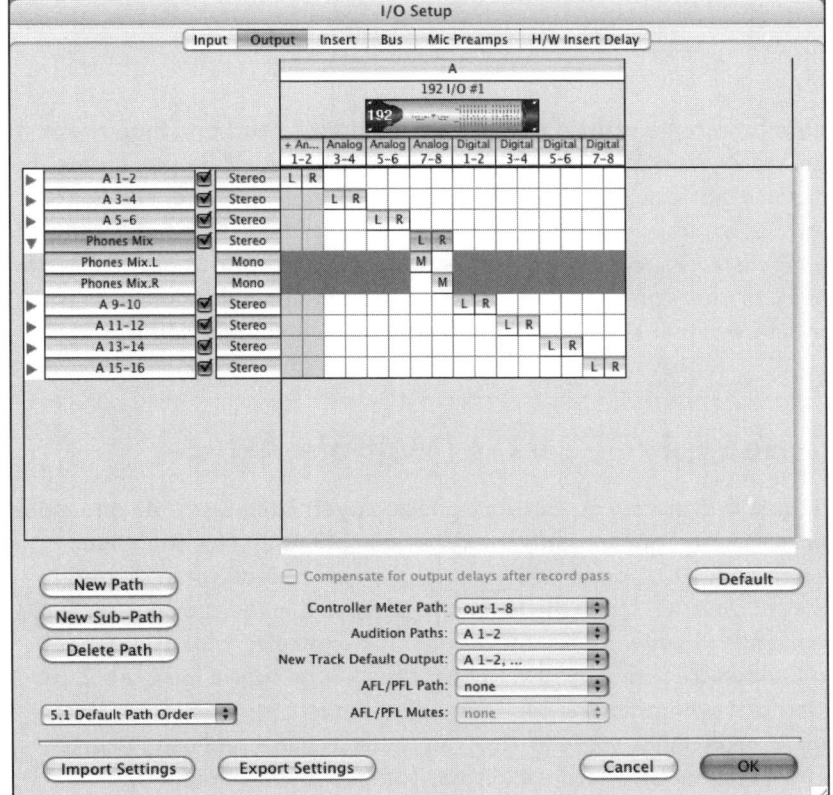

Figure 2.11

Interface 7–8 as headphone out mix

Keep in mind that version 7 offers up to 10 sends per track. Even though you may not be using all 10, it's still a good idea to create your headphone mix sends on send J, just in case your mix becomes more complex than you originally expected. That way, when you fire up the mix and your artist tells you she wants just one more pass at the main vocal, you can create your headphone mix send with little worry that you'll have to restructure the mix to accommodate her!

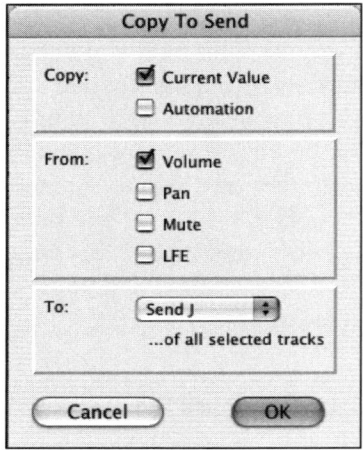

Figure 2.12

Use Copy to Send to build a headphone mix from the faders

A quick way to share your mix with the artist is to copy the mix to the send and then tweak it to taste. First, create a send to 7-8 on all channels (hold the Option key while you create the send). Again, prudence dictates that you choose send J to avoid conflict with other sends. Then, select all your tracks (hold Option while you channel select) and choose Edit > Automation > Copy to Send, as seen in Figure 2.12. You will have the option to copy various parameters to the mix. Ask your talent if he or she wants to hear that crazy pan in the middle or other automation clues to determine whether she needs automation or only volume and pan.

Creating Discrete Headphone Mixes (Multiple Artists)

Your drummer wants more bass and more kick, but your guitar player wants less bass and more kick. Your bassist wants more kick and guitar, and your singer complains that he can't hear himself. Provided you have enough I/O, you should be able to create at least three discrete mixes for the band and one for yourself. Using the technique discussed in the previous section, send at least three different sends to three different I/O pairs. For example, route Aux send A to Outputs 3-4, send B to Outputs 5-6, and send C to Outputs 7-8, as shown in Figure 2.13. Individually copy the mix to each send pair. You can then adjust the mix for each artist. When you are adjusting the mixes, it might make sense to view the sends as individual assignments (choose View > Sends F-J > Assignments), which will display faders instead of outputs.

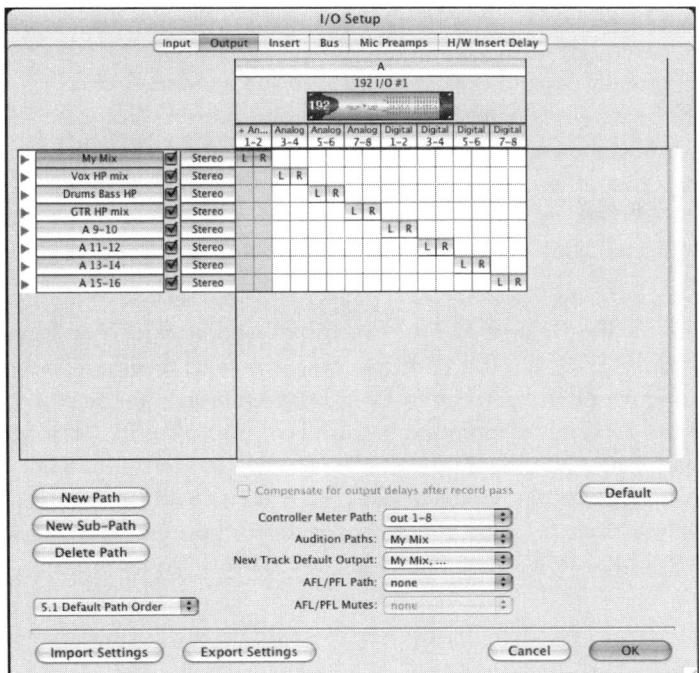

Figure 2.13

Multiple headphone mixes
from multiple output pairs

In both this example and the previous one, I should point out that these discrete sends are still susceptible to interference from you, the engineer. By adjusting any of the volume faders, you have an impact on the send levels, thus messing with the mix to the artists. When you are using sends to create headphone mixes, you should *always* set them to Pre-fader by clicking on the P on the send itself, as shown in Figure 2.14. This will isolate the send volume from the volume fader, allowing you to create your own mix while leaving theirs alone—even while recording!

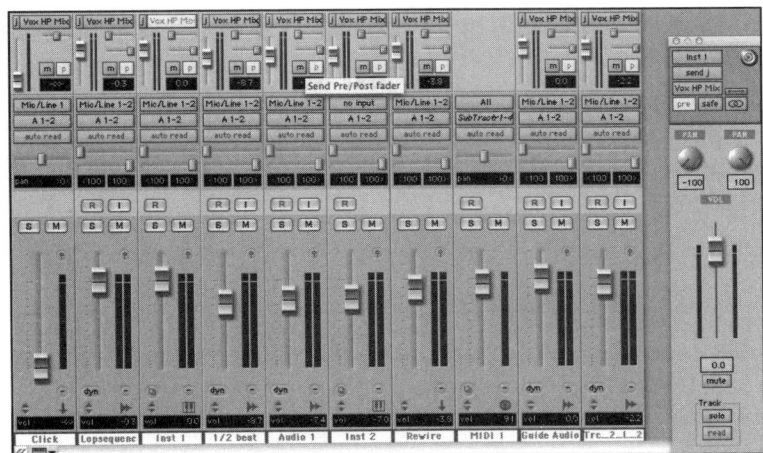

Figure 2.14

Sends set to Pre-fader

Creating Mix-Minus Sessions

A mix-minus session is one in which incoming signal is *not* fed back to the sender. A classic case of this is a radio show in which the caller doesn't get his or her signal back. Doing so would cause an analog delay at best and feedback at worst. However, the caller needs to hear the DJ, and the DJ needs to hear the caller. I recommend setting up the system and testing with a cell phone in the control room before you go to air. There are several boxes on the market to interface the phone to Pro Tools. Look for ones that have crosstalk control and a pass through for a local phone unit.

You will need at least two tracks—one for the DJ and one for the caller—and each should have its own discrete input source, as in Figure 2.15. On the DJ track, create a send to an unused interface port (mono is preferred), and turn the signal up to 0dB. I use Output 5 because it's nowhere near 1-2 or 7-8 (which I use to send to someone in the vocal booth), and it's not likely to be accidentally used. Call in to the system with a cell phone and "answer" the call. Speak into the cell phone to test for a signal at the caller track. (The track should be record-ready and muted.) Have the DJ talk into the mic to test the signal to the cell phone. (The track should be record-ready and unmuted.) After you've set the levels for comfort, you can hang up the call and begin your session.

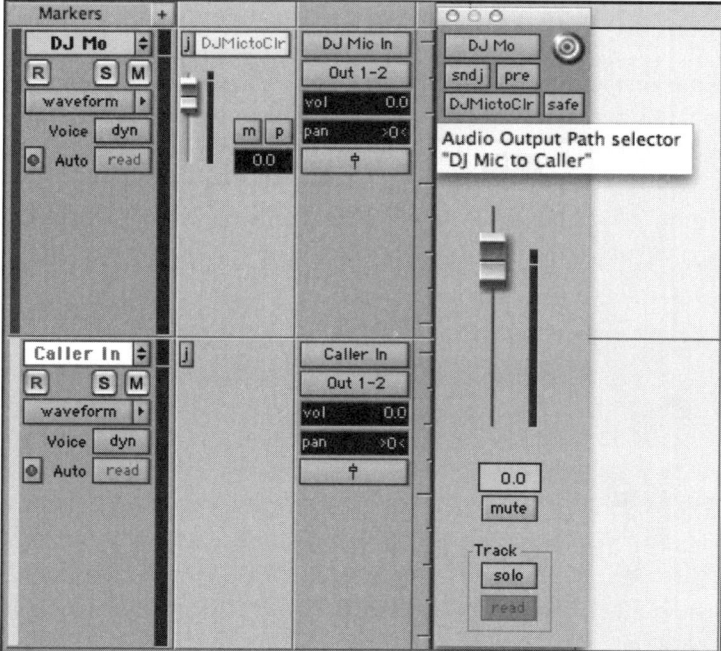

Figure 2.15

Two-way mix-minus setup with send J to caller

Another situation in which this might come in handy is when a distant producer wants a phone-patch session with a local talent. Suppose the client is in Texas, but her favorite voice actor is in San Francisco. She wants to hear the voice talent on the phone clearly (without you holding the phone to the speaker and screaming, "Isn't that great?"). This is only slightly more complex than the aforementioned situation because your talent is in the voiceover booth speaking to the producer, but *you* might be nowhere in the conversation.

If your console and patch bay don't support the built-in talkback going to the caller, then get your own mic and plug it into a discrete input on Pro Tools (Input 3 at this point—1 for VO, 2 for caller, and 3 for you). Send your mic to an Aux track (if they don't want slates, an audio track if they do) because the Aux track obviously won't record. Create a send on your track (labeled "Engineer") to the caller send, as in Figure 2.16. (I use I/O number 5 because it has nothing to do with any other outputs. Remember that 7–8 are being used to send the mix to the talent.) Now, when the client wants to talk to *you*, you can talk back.

As before, remember to mute this track so the client doesn't hear you comment to your intern about how bad the talent sounds that day.

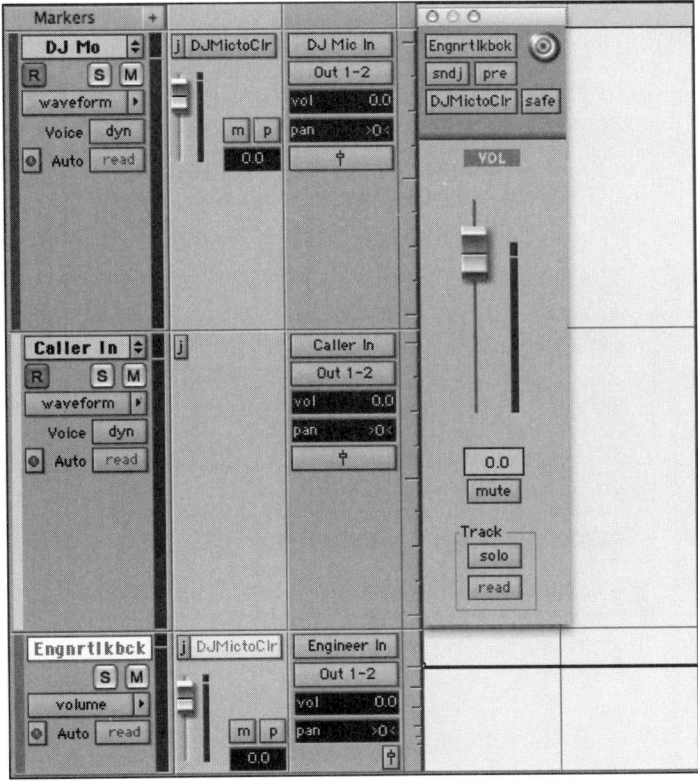

Figure 2.16

Three-way mix-minus setup
with send J to caller

Switching Songs

Nothing will slow down the recording process more than having to set up a new PT session for every song *without* saving the settings. If you create a perfect headphone mix and recording levels to disk on the first song, the odds are you won't be able to recreate it from memory for each song. Even if you could, it would take too long and the band would lose energy, missing that perfect take. Following are three different ways to get around this.

❋ **Simply keep recording.** Don't bother to switch songs, just keep recording. You will be left with one master session containing all the songs back to back, as in Figure 2.17. The problem is that the sound files do not have differentiated names (like Kick Song 1versus Kick Song 2). The other problem is that trying to separate them afterward (and trying to create unique mixes later) is challenging and requires extra work. You'd have to open the master session, save it as Song 1, and then select and delete the other sound files. Then you'd have to reopen the original master session and repeat the process for each other song. This would provide you with individual sessions (albeit with shared audio folders) with only one song per session. Oh boy...fun, fun, fun!

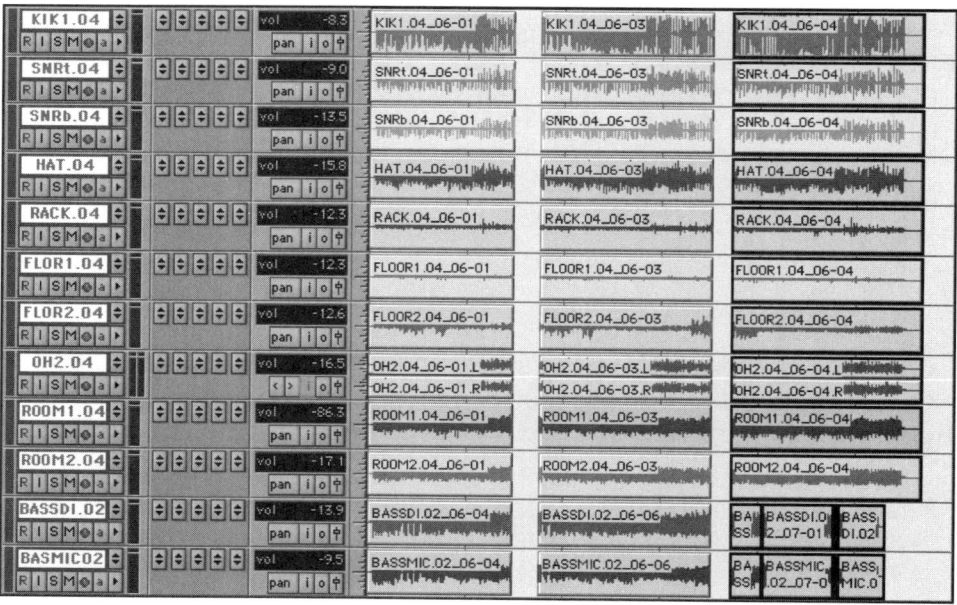

Figure 2.17

Back-to-back songs in one session

✱ **Create the first song and set all the levels** the way you like them and in a way that works well for the band. Save the song before you record the first note. On the desktop, click once on the session document (which selects the document but does not open it) and go to Get Info (CMD+I). Check the box next to Stationery Pad (see Figure 2.18) and return to Pro Tools. Now, for every new song, open the song's Stationery Pad first. Pro Tools will prompt you to create a new session (or edit the original, which I don't recommend) that you should call Song 2. You will quickly have everything set as desired, and you will already have a unique session per song. The problem here is that you still run the risk of sharing all your audio in the same Audio Files folder, so be sure to change your disk allocation (see "Where Does It Record, Anyway?" In Chapter 1).

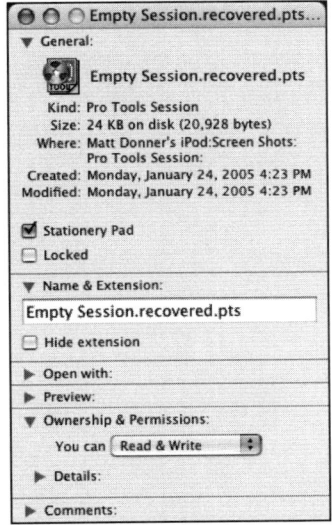

Figure 2.18

Stationery Pad document

✱ **Create the perfect setup for song one and print the tune**. Save the song as Song 1. Close the session and create a new session in a new location called Song 2. When you create this song, don't forget to choose the I/O setup you exported from Song 1. (See "Labeling the I/O and Template Settings" in Chapter 1.) Immediately choose File > Import Session Data and inspect the dialog box, as shown in Figure 2.19. You have several options here, but for now simply OPTION+click the first track in the list and select Import as New Track. Directly below this list (verify that *all* the tracks are set to Import as New Tracks), you will find a drop-down menu asking what information you want to import with the tracks. From the list, deselect Regions and Media as well as anything related to automation. (There shouldn't be any automation, so it's okay if you forget this step.) Then, click Import. You will see all of your tracks as they were, complete with sends for headphone mixes and inserts for compressors/EQs/verbs, with all inputs preset. This is the smartest way to switch songs during the recording process because it takes the same amount of time (or less) than the other options, and it leaves you with clean versions of each song with its own Audio Files folder.

Keep in mind that any tracks that were hidden in the original session will import into the new session but will still be hidden after import!

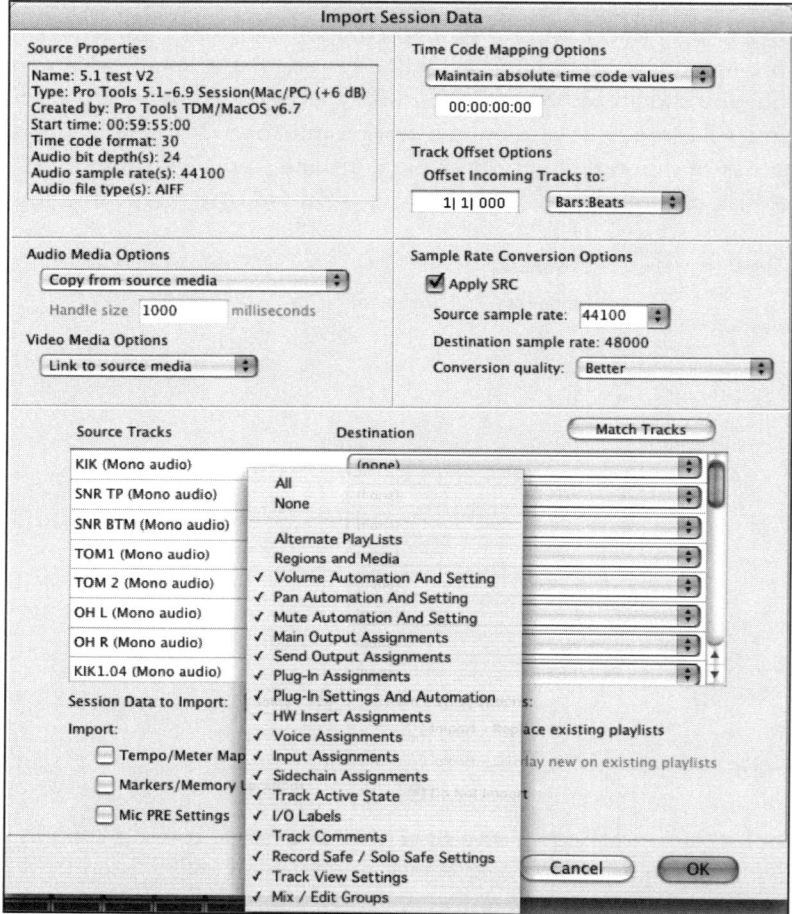

Figure 2.19

Importing the session data without the media

Switching Takes (Andre Zweers, Skywalker Sound)

It's no surprise that Andre would have a killer tip in this section because he records all day long. This one is priceless!

Because Andre records large orchestras and is responsible for the quick operation of the system (sometimes 256 people paid by the hour wait for him to press buttons), he has found a great way to quickly set up for fast punches *and* multiple takes.

The first half of this process is to identify the groups (sections) that would conceivably need punching, fixing, or overdubbing. After this is done (with the producer calling the shots, of course), Andre groups the section tracks together by choosing Track > Group (CMD+G) as seen in Figure 2.20. This includes the All group (created by default in every Pro Tools session).

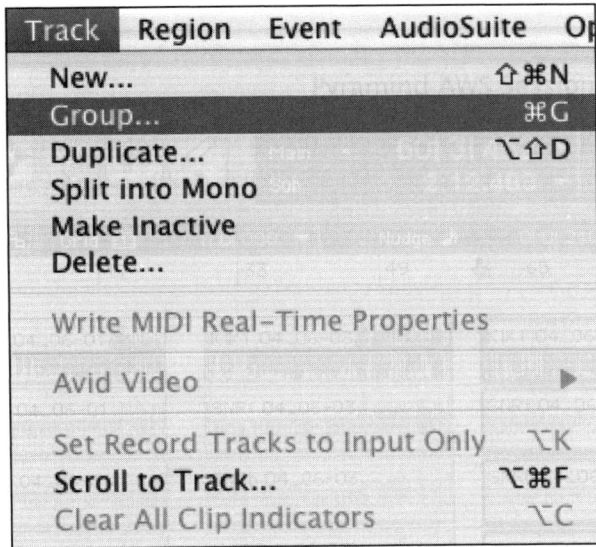

Figure 2.20

Grouping the drum tracks with Track > Group

Because the default playlist is actually called Playlist-00, Andre first activates the All group and switches to a new playlist first, as shown in Figure 2.21. That way, the first recording is actually performed on Playlist-01, synchronizing with the takes performed (take 1-playlist1, and so on). Any section that needs to be replaced first gets the group activated (*without* the All group), and then has its playlist switched for quick replacement. Note that if a single track has already been named, it is faster to duplicate the playlist as opposed to creating a new one because the duplicate automatically keeps the name and simply adds the playlist number (that is, Playlist Vocal becomes Vocal-01). With multiple tracks, either a new or duplicate playlist will automatically create new playlists and simply add the playlist number.

Figure 2.21

New Playlists menu

The MO-ME Mix (Turn Me Up!)

There is a headphone box out there called the MO-ME, which is an appropriate name for almost every singer out there. We always need to hear more of ourselves than anyone else. It is a function of the instrument that we need strong monitor mixes to determine our relative pitch and dynamic (and strength of ego!).

It may come to pass that the vocal track's fader is already at +12 and it's not enough gain for the artist. In this case, a quick move to give the artist more when no more exists is to simply lower everybody else and turn up the overall volume. The quick way to do this without destroying your mix is to select every channel except the vocal and group them as a Mix group called Instruments by choosing Track > Group (or CMD+G) as seen in Figures 2.22 and 2.23. (For more on grouping, see "Faster Working with Groups" in Chapter 4.)

Figure 2.22

The Track > Group menu option

Figure 2.23

The New Group dialog box

Clicking any track fader will allow you to trim the faders of the rest of the mix (relative to every other fader) and keep the vocal fader high. Then, tell the artist to turn it up at her box.

If you have complex routing to processors in your session, it might adversely affect your mix, at which point you have three choices:

❋ You could print the music to a stereo mix as is and import it into another session to record the vocals against (see "Shaving DSP in TDM Systems" in Chapter 6). This way, you simply turn down the music track and tell her to turn her headphones up.

❋ You could add processing to the vocal track to make it louder. A limiter or compressor can achieve this effect easily.

❋ Route every track other than the vocals to a single Aux input and turn it down, trimming the volume of the music only.

If automation occurs on the other tracks, the previous tips won't really work unless you do one of the following things:

❋ OPTION-click any track's automation button to temporarily set the automation mode to Auto-Off for *all* tracks. You can always reactivate the automation after the recording and get your mix back.

❋ See "Automating the Whole Mix" in Chapter 7.

Recording the Audio with Effects

As a guitar player, I tend to play to the sound of the guitar. If the tone is bluesy, I'll play bluesy. If the tone is '70s rock, I'll play with more Zeppelin flavor (sloppy and beautiful). With Pro Tools, one of the great options available is the amplifier simulator. With dozens of classic amps to choose from and good tone among them all (insert your favorite here), it's easy to whip up a decent tone quickly. You can even change your mind later if you no longer like it.

However, because I play to the tone, switching the tone later can make the performance suffer because I didn't play to *that* tone, and it might not fit. I often print my guitar tracks with the simulator tone permanently, committing both the tone and the performance with inspiration. If it doesn't work later, I can always replay it. (I *hate* when that happens!) Besides, this is how guitars have been recorded for decades, even back when we didn't have simulators.

To do this in Pro Tools, you will need two tracks—one for the plug-in and one for the recording. The first should be a Mono Aux input, and it should have its output routed on a mono bus to the input of the Audio track (for guitar tracks, because the guitar is generally mono… but the bus can be stereo if the sound is stereo). Set the input of the Audio track to the *same* bus as the output of the Aux track, as shown in Figure 2.24. On the Aux track, insert your favorite amp simulator (or EQ, or whatever you want to print with), and you will be recording to the Audio track *with* the plug-in active, creating a track with the effect printed permanently. It is a good idea to mark the amp and settings in the comments or to save a preset of the tone in the Session Plug-In Settings folder. (See "Storing Presets" in Chapter 6.) Remember that this take is permanent, so play well!

Figure 2.24

Aux track with effect routed to the Audio track

Keep in mind that this is different than simply adding the effect to the record track and recording directly to that track (without an Aux track). This is easiest to accomplish, but should your session travel to another studio where the chosen plug-in is not available, you'll only have the unprocessed track to deal with. If you only have RTAS plug-ins at your disposal, you might need to use the two-track setup, since RTAS plug-ins switch to bypass when the Audio track they're on is record-enabled! This is not true anymore with version 7, but there is a side-effect.

Let's say you're using an RTAS guitar amp simulator directly on an Audio track. Once you record-enable the track, the plug-in will remain active (version 7), but the plug-in will steal two voices—one for the input and one for the output. This will matter if this guitar track is a last-minute idea and is also the 32nd voice in your 32-voice system. Since there are no more voices to steal, you won't hear the effect on the track.

Recording with Hardware Inserts

If you own hardware processing and you want to employ it with Pro Tools during recording, here are a few ways to integrate your hardware during recording.

❋ Insert an analog I/O on your record channel, as shown in Figure 2.25. Connect the output of that I/O to the input of your processor and the output of your processor back to the input of the *same* I/O port. Keep in mind that your insert I/O needs to be a discrete connection that is not otherwise being used in your session, such as the main output pair 1–2. You might experience a delay in the signal because of this procedure (although users of HD TDM with PT version 6.7 should not experience this), due to the time necessary for the signal to leave Pro Tools (digital-analog conversion) and re-enter after processing (analog-digital conversion). If this is the case, you might need to monitor the signal before printing to Pro Tools, effectively ruining the purpose of performing the I/O insert in the first place. In which case, try the next tactic.

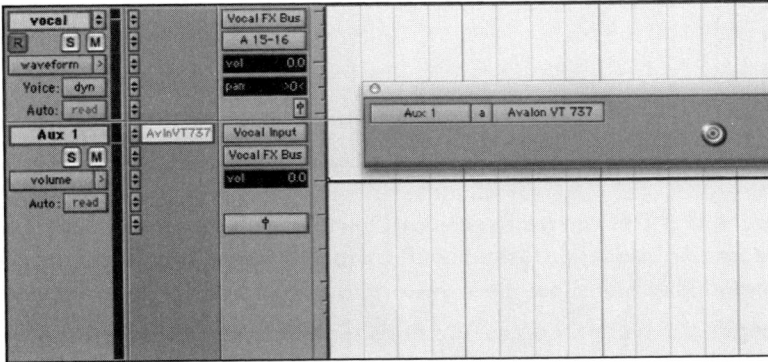

Figure 2.25

A hardware I/O plug-in on Aux input for recording

❋ Connect the hardware before you connect Pro Tools. This will process the signal permanently. You will not have the option to tweak the settings later; it will happen in real time, but it will not adversely affect your monitoring of the signal.

❋ For Mbox users, connect the processor to the back of the unit at the connection labeled Insert using a standard TRS send-return cable. You might need to create a cable to suit your needs because these standard cables don't always have the appropriate connectors for your processor. Monitoring won't be affected (other than the standard monitoring latency in the Mbox). See "Monitoring with the Mbox and Mbox2" earlier in this chapter.)

Selection Recording (Punching In)

After the initial take is printed, there might be imperfect moments in the performance, but perhaps the rest of the performance is great. Using the Selector tool, highlight the region that needs rerecording, and Pro Tools will record over *only* that section. This is standard procedure for production. Following are some good practices to use when recording selections like this.

1. Zoom in closely on both the beginning (in) and end (out) of the selection to ensure that you have highlighted the audio at a zero-crossing point, as shown in Figure 2.26. This will prevent you from generating any unnecessary pops and clicks in the recording. (See "Zero-Crossing Edits" in Chapter 4.)

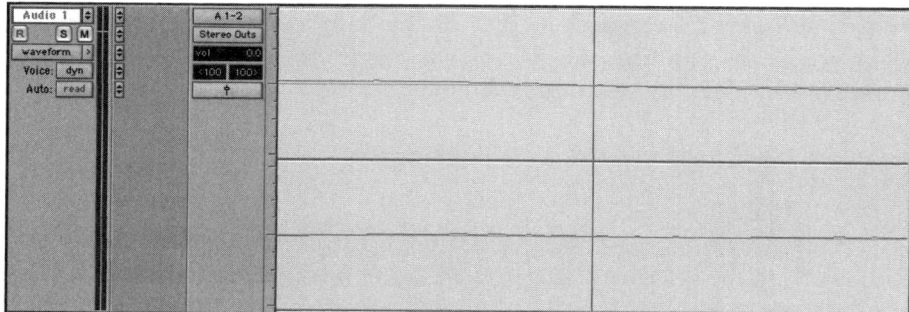

Figure 2.26

Zero-crossing point at the In of the punch selection

2. Be sure to deselect either Destructive Record or QuickPunch because they can be detrimental to your recording process. Destructive Record will *permanently* erase whatever it records over and neither will show the waveform during recording.

3. Try to select a length of time that begins and ends slightly earlier and later than what you need (maybe a word or two for vocals and a note/phrase or two for music). This will give you the option to trim and crossfade the selection to perfection later. Without recording extra time, you might not be able to crossfade at all after the recording, as shown in Figure 2.27. (See "Faster Fades" and "Batch Fading" in Chapter 4.)

4. Drag the arrows (red) earlier and later to adjust the selection. The arrows refer to the In and Out markers for the recording.

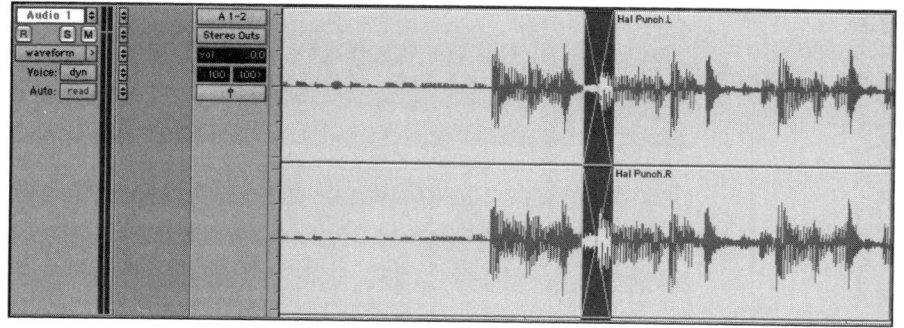

Figure 2.27

A crossfade over the In of the punch

QuickPunch

QuickPunch , when active, allows the user to hit record at anytime during playback and achieve seamless punch-ins. QuickPunch requires having a voice in reserve in order to function. In fact, with QuickPunch active, Pro Tools is *always* recording—it just doesn't draw a waveform throughout the take!

Take the following situation:

Your singer is listening to the song for the first time and is belting out various ideas, lots of which are worth remembering. In normal situations, you'd have to go back and say something like, "That was cool. Do that moaning thing again … you know, the 'nnnnngggggaaaaahhhhh' thing you did!" You should be met with a blank stare or furrowed brows as the artist starts to wonder whether you took your medication that morning!

To activate QuickPunch , choose Options > QuickPunch. With QuickPunch , simply start playback. You'll recognize QuickPunch as active when the Record button on the Transport has a P in it, as shown in Figure 2.28. When the moaning thing starts, hit the Record button (either F12, CMD+spacebar or 3 on the numeric keypad [FN+L for laptops]). Pro Tools will begin drawing waveforms at the time of punch-in until you punch-out, but remember that it is *always* recording! If you missed something cool, simply trim the region earlier with the trim tool, and voilá! Pro Tools caught the *whole performance!* Now you can simply play back the moaning thing without the dirty looks!

Figure 2.28

QuickPunch menu from the Transport window

Recording with Pre- and Post-Roll

Activate pre-roll and post-roll to get a head start and to hear how well the punch-in dovetails into the next section. (Use CMD+K or activate pre- and post-roll in the Transport window.) You can adjust the amount of pre- and post-roll by moving the green flags before (pre-roll) and after (post-roll) the selection. Try to begin the pre-roll at the beginning of the previous phrase or two so it doesn't start awkwardly, as seen in Figure 2.29.

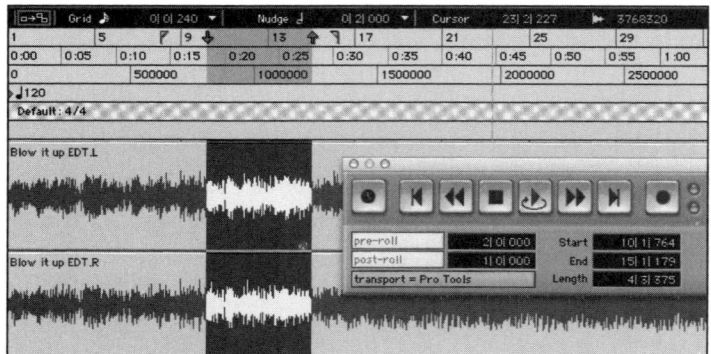

Figure 2.29

Pre-roll on the Transport window and the Ruler

After you've punched-in, you can audition the In and Out separately without losing the selection! Hold CMD+OPTION+right arrow to listen to the punch-out with pre-roll and post-roll. This will allow you to play up to the end of the punch and into then next section to determine whether the take was correct. Similarly, press CMD+OPTION+left arrow to audition the punch-in the same way. If the end is good but the beginning is not (or vice versa), you can select a smaller section to fix and leave the good punch alone. Repeat this procedure until the entire section meets your expectations. Remember from Chapter 1 that there are other shortcuts here when Command Focus is active. Notably the numbers 6, 7, 8, and 9 on the keyboard (NOT the number pad) will provide alternate audition capabilities.

Using Markers During Recording

Memory Location Points, or *markers*, are wonderful things that are often underused. You can use markers during the recording process to either point out mistakes as they happen (see Figure 2.30) or to set song pointers like the Verse, Chorus, and so on, if you've never heard the song before (for example, on the first take of the first song of a new client's band).

While recording (or playing, for that matter), hit the Enter key. The Memory Location dialog box will open. Name the section (Intro, Verse 1, and so on) and hit Enter again to create the marker. You should also show the markers along the Ruler (Track > Ruler Shows > Markers).

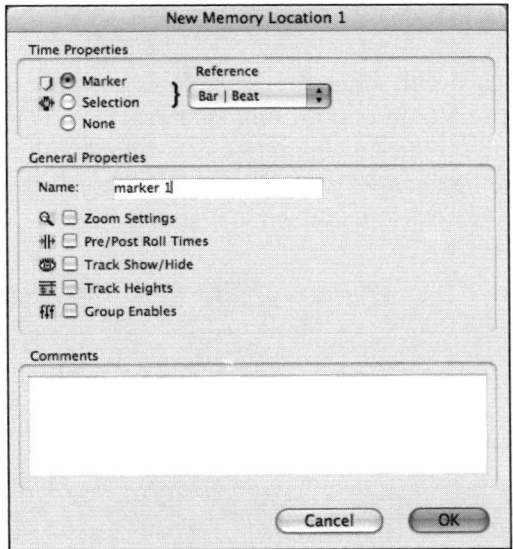

Figure 2.30

The Memory
Location dialog
box

Then you can use the markers to select sections that require punching in by SHIFT-clicking the two markers that define the region to be replaced. If the selection is imperfect, click and drag the markers to the exact locations desired, and then reselect the region.

If you find that there is not enough time to name the marker during the recording process, you can choose to auto-name the markers in the Memory Locations drop-down menu, as shown in Figure 2.31. You can name the markers after the recording by double-clicking the marker along the Ruler.

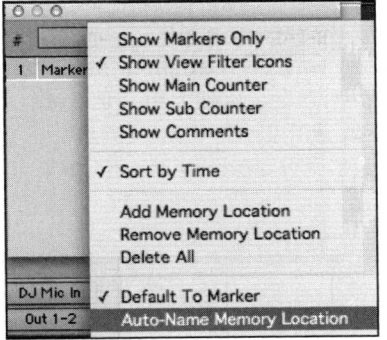

Figure 2.31

Auto-Name selected on the Memory Location drop-down menu

Setting a Temporary Effect for the Artist

Almost every artist (it's usually the singer) likes to record with some effects—mainly reverb. To do this without committing to the effect, create an Aux send *and* an Aux input track. Insert the artist's effect of choice *on the Aux input* and set the Aux input to any available bus. (Use pairs for stereo effects.) Create an Aux send on the channel to which you are recording, and set its output to the same bus as the input of the Aux track, as shown in Figure 2.32.

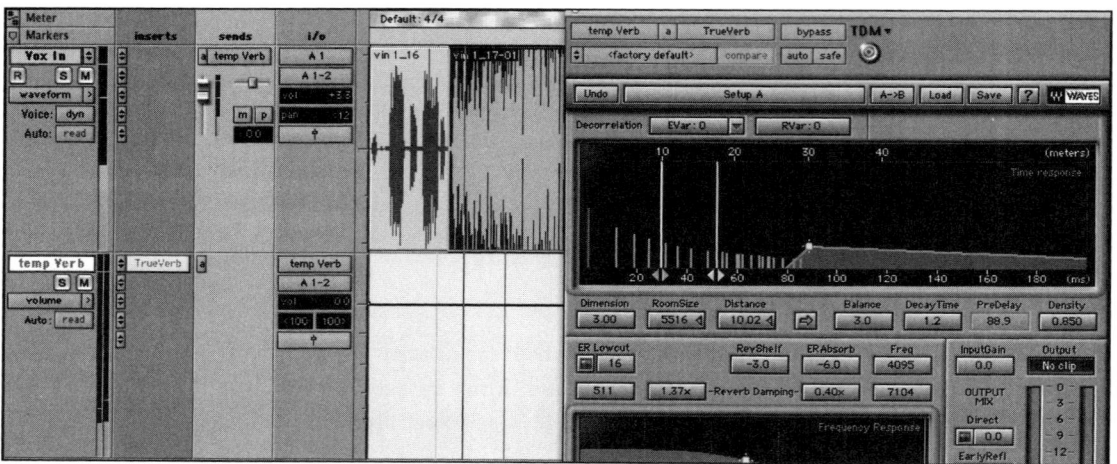

Figure 2.32

A temporary effect

Be sure that you are sending the effect signal to the headphone mix as well, and turn up the Send level (to the phones) to your taste. (See "Creating Discrete Headphone Mixes" earlier in this chapter.) If you are recording through an Aux input to print with effects, make sure you create the temporary effect send on the record track and not the Aux input with the printable effect. (See "Recording the Audio with Effects" earlier in this chapter.) If you don't set the effect send on the record track, then when you play back the take, it will play without the temporary effect.

Stereo or Dual Mono?

Few things get confused more than the concept of stereo versus dual mono. I want to take a moment to define the two.

❈ **Stereo.** This refers to a recording of one source by two microphones in some stereo technique. The two mics can and should be panned left and right to recreate the stereo image of the performance. An example would be recording a piano with two mics over the soundboard, with one facing the low strings (left) and one facing the high strings (right). An acoustic guitar, percussion, sections of instruments, and drums are other good examples.

❈ **Dual mono.** This refers to two recordings of a source performed at different times, generally overdubbed. One mic is often used to record the artist doubling the part, and then panning take 1 left and take 2 right. Vocals are usually done this way, as are rock guitars.

You can switch between the two types by creating both a stereo track *and* two mono tracks. When you record guitars, you might record take 1 to Track 1 (mono) and take 2 to Track 2. When you are satisfied with the performances, select them both (use CMD+A to ensure you've highlighted them all) and drag the two onto the stereo track. You have "stereo-ized" the two, but you have *not* created a true stereo part. This is still dual mono; it's simply housed on a stereo track. Look at Figure 2.33 to see both the mono tracks and the "stereo-ized" track with both of them.

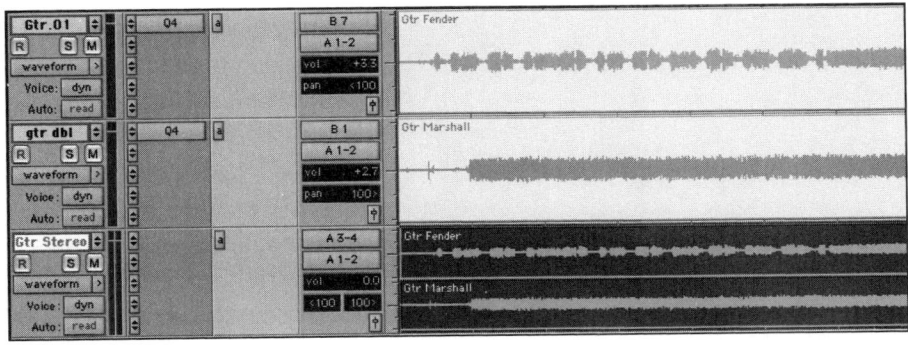

Figure 2.33

Two files brought together on a stereo track

Loop Recording

Inevitably, there will be parts that an artist will want to record over and over again until he or she has performed them to perfection. Loop recording will do this easily, but what happens to the takes *after* the loop record is complete and the artist says, "I think there's a good one in there"?

After loop recording, highlight the looped section and switch to the Selector tool. Then, CMD+click on the highlighted section, and you will be shown the Takes list, as shown in Figure 2.34. But this might *also* show much more than you expected.

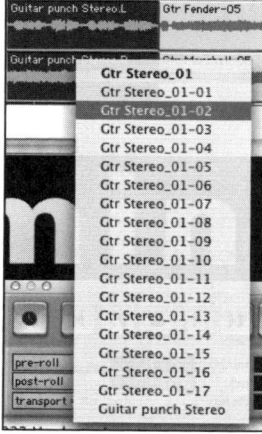

Figure 2.34

The Takes list

If you first look under Setup > Preferences > Editing, you notice that the Matching Start Time Takes List section gives you the indication that the section you've looped will also show you regions that match the start time (see Figure 2.35). This might give you too many choices, so I suggest you also check the Take Region Name(s) That Match Track Names and Take Region Lengths That Match boxes (at least choose the matching name). That way, the takes list will *only* present the takes that fit your loop recordings. Note that all the takes will be numbered sequentially.

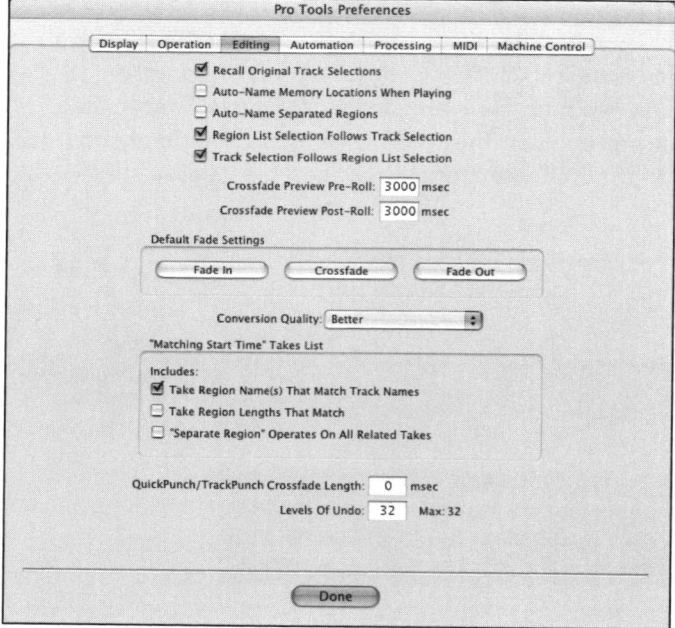

Figure 2.35

The Matching Start Time preferences section

You should only hit Stop after the artist tells you she is done and the loop goes back to the beginning for yet another loop. That way, if the last take had any good stuff in it, it will show up under the Takes list. If you cut the loop short, the length won't match and it won't even show in your Takes list (if you've activated the Take Region Lengths That Match option under the preferences). It will still be in the bin, however, and you can still drag it onto the track for auditioning if necessary.

Using Destructive Record to Avoid Editing

When performing large VO (voice-over) recordings, the client will usually want to walk away with a single audio file matching a script. Other times, the client will want to walk with many files. Obviously editing is a part of this process, but the editing can often take longer than the recording, making a longer session for you and a higher bill for your client. Even after editing, there is still the process of merging all the edited clips into single files for delivery, presenting you with the time-consuming task of either bouncing (which takes a *really* long time) or consolidating (which doubles your hard-drive requirements) after editing.

When presented with this scenario, try using Destructive Record and pre-roll to create a single clip without having to edit later.

1. Record the talent's read until there is a mistake. A professional should be able to go fairly far before goofing and should be able to be interrupted and resume the take without a problem.

2. Stop the talent and drop the cursor at the farthest zero-crossing point *before* the mistake. This is usually the end of the last word before the mistake. That way, if the talent comes in earlier than before, you will catch the first word in its entirety, as shown in Figure 2.36.

3. Activate pre-roll and set it to a point that makes sense for the talent, usually a sentence before the goof.

4. Activate Destructive Record and record from the insertion point (you will notice a D in the Record button on the Transport indicating Destructive Record). This will allow the talent to hear the pace and energy of the previous read and pick up at the mistake point while making it seem like a seamless read. You will be presented with a continuance of the same file that you were recording, leaving no need to edit afterwards.

Figure 2.36
The VO recording with Destructive Record

3} Importing, Exporting, and Managing

Recording isn't the only way to get audio into Pro Tools. In fact, you'll probably spend enough time importing and exporting audio, MIDI, and sessions that these topics deserve their own chapters! From the simplest Import Audio command to more complex preparations of sessions for traveling clients, this chapter covers some known and unknown ways to make the job easy...or at least less painful!

The Many Ways to Import Audio

Audio will exist in many places on your drive, and you need to be able to bring that audio into your session at any time. The following sections provide various options for importing audio from their various sources.

Drag-and-Drop Support

While the traditional methods of importing audio and MIDI still exist, Pro Tools 7 supports drag-and-drop importing from two sources—the desktop and the Workspace. Now, simply CMD+Tab to the desktop (or use Expose), find your file, and drag it onto any track to import the file to that track. If you drag the file to an empty space in the Edit window, the file will create a new track for itself intelligently. This means that stereo files create stereo tracks and mono files create mono tracks. In addition, the imported file will automatically copy to the Audio folder, making it harder for the file to become offline afterwards. For more on this, see "Collecting, Finding, and Adding Sounds" later in this chapter.

Direct Importing to the Bin

Choose File > Import > Audio to Region List (CMD+SHIFT+I), as shown in Figure 3.1. You will be presented with an Import Audio dialog box, shown in Figure 3.2, giving you the option to audition the file (with independent volume control), and then either add, copy, or convert it, depending on its sample rate and bit depth. After the file is in the Regions Currently Chosen section in the lower-right portion of the dialog box, you can click Done to bring the file into your session.

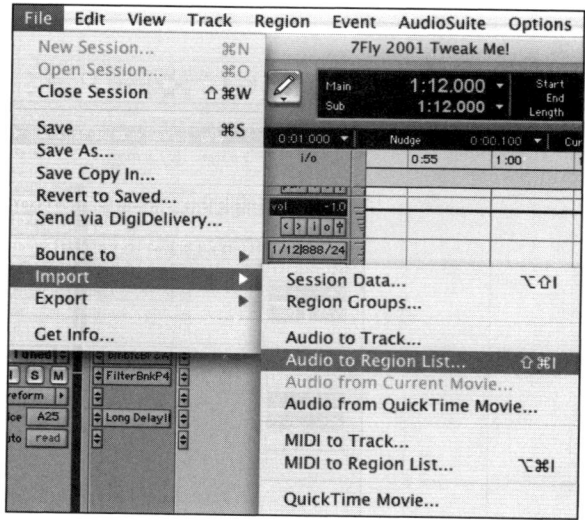

Figure 3.1

Importing to the Regions
List menu option

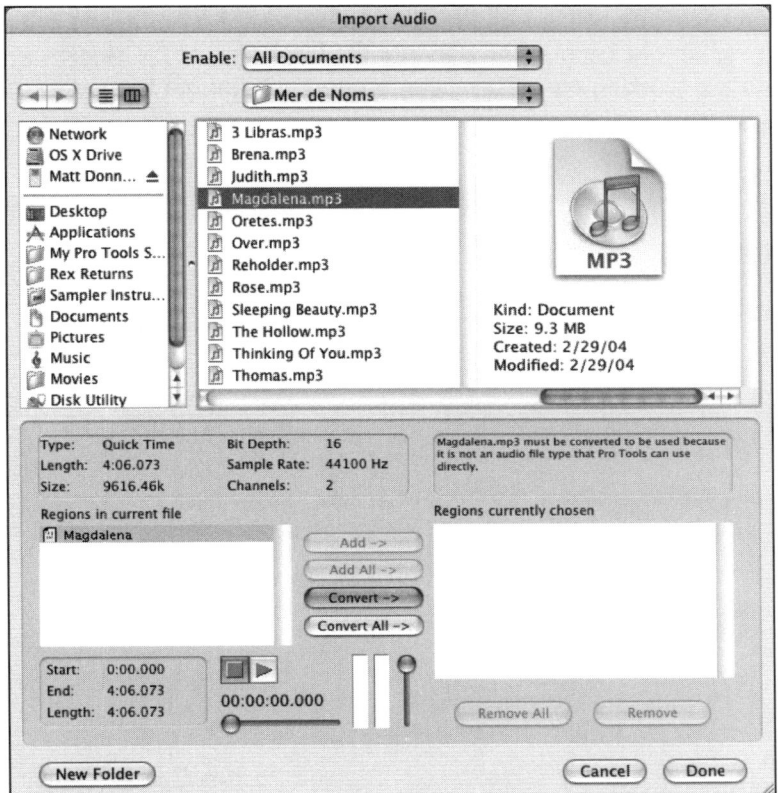

Figure 3.2

The Import Audio dialog box

I am a firm believer in always copying or converting the file! If you choose to simply add the file, Pro Tools will leave the file in its original location and *not* bring it or a copy into your current session's Audio Files folder. This means if you delete the folder with the *original* Audio Files folder, you will no longer have that audio in your current session. The media will be considered offline, and you will not be able to hear it again. Ever.

If you copy the file, Pro Tools will make a copy and put it in your *current* Audio Files folder, ensuring that the clip will never go offline. If the file has a different bit depth or is of a different file type, the only option available is to convert the audio on import, which is just as good as copying. Although copying doubles the hard drive requirements (because audio is now in two places instead of one), it is a small price to pay when you consider the alternative of potentially losing audio.

Importing to Track

As the name implies, this option (choose File > Import > Audio to Track, as seen in Figure 3.3) will not only import the audio, but it will create an appropriate track for it, name it, and bring it into the session on that new track. All the rules from the previous section still apply. This is useful in situations in which you know you will use all the files and you want a track for each one. The drawback is that this option always puts the audio at the beginning of the session, which can be a drag when you are working on a 90-minute feature and you are trying to grab the file to play at 01:15:32.26.

Figure 3.3

Import Audio to Track

Importing Session Data

Suppose the producer wants to try something weird and borrow the main vocal from one song and use it as a background for the current song. However, the other song's main vocal was compiled from seven takes and consists of 23 regions, making importing the raw audio impossible. You could close this song and open the other, soloing the vocal and its respective effect channels, and bounce out a complete vocal (which takes time), but you'd get stuck with the effects and inserts on the channel at the time, as well as any editing mistakes. You could bypass the effects and bounce the file dry (which takes more time), but then you'd have to de-bypass the effects and be sure not to save your song to avoid changing its performance. You'd then have to open the current song again and import the vocal, at which point the producer might realize she wants to revisit some of the other takes instead. Oh boy.

As you saw in the "Switching Songs" section in Chapter 2, it is easy to import the data from other sessions and not bring in the audio. In this scenario, you should do the opposite to save time and hassle. Choose File > Import > Session Data, and select the session from the other song in question. In the Import Session Data dialog box, shown in Figure 3.4, you can choose to remap the timing to your current song timing (avoiding the part showing up an hour past the end of the song) as well as select only the main vocal for importing. From the Session Data to Import drop-down menu, deselect everything you don't want (including the insert effects, if desired), but be sure to check Regions and Media to import the track and its audio as is.

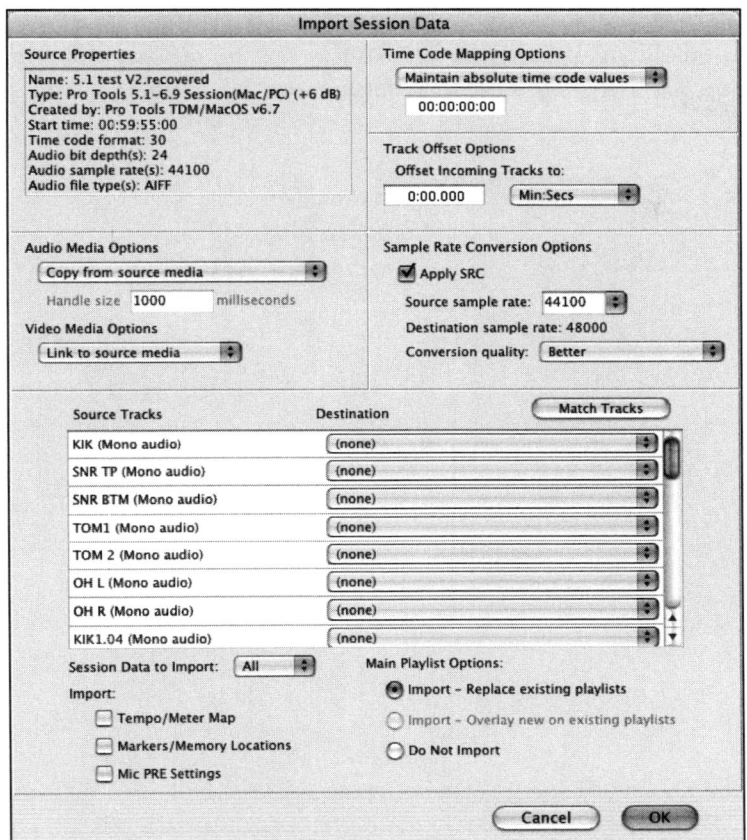

Figure 3.4

The Import Session Data dialog box

In the upper-left corner of the Import Session Data dialog box, choose Copy From Source Media to ensure that any imported tracks and audio get moved into the current session's Audio Files folder. Depending on which Playlist option you choose, the imported track might show up as a new track or it might overwrite another playlist. It is *always* safer to import as a new track to avoid losing something important.

Importing from CD (Option 1)
As of version 6.0, Pro Tools now imports red book audio directly from CD without you needing QuickTime to bridge the gap. When a CD is in the CD-ROM tray and mounted on the desktop, choose a method of importing audio (either Import Audio or Import Audio to Track). Navigate to the CD in question, and select the track of choice. In this case, because the audio lives on a different drive than your session, you will be forced to either copy or convert the audio upon import.

When you are choosing the track from the CD, you can skip to later sections in the song by dragging the horizontal time bar below the Stop and Play buttons in the Import Audio dialog box. When you are sure that this is the track, you can select it for import by bringing it into the right side of the dialog box (Convert or Copy Audio), as seen in Figure 3.5.

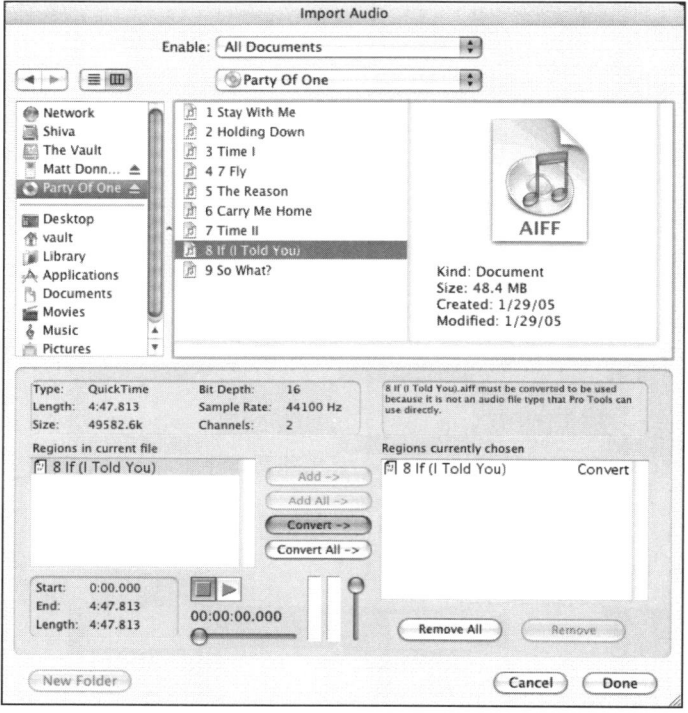

Figure 3.5

The Import Audio dialog box for importing CDs

Importing from CD (Option 2)

When you want to import audio from a CD, you can save time by importing directly through the Workspace. Open your Workspace by selecting Window > Workspace (OPTION+;). From there, double-click the CD mounted on your Workspace, opening the Volume Browser. You should see the tracks listed in the order of the CD tracks. If you do not see the waveform next to the file, be sure you are seeing the waveform column in the view. (See "Keeping Organized with the Browsers" in Chapter 1.) Select the files by clicking CMD+A, and go to the Browser menu and select Calculate Overviews. You can now listen to the file by clicking and holding the speaker icon next to the waveform. The file will audition (in summed mono) as long as you hold the mouse button. To skip ahead, click and hold later on the waveform.

After you have verified your file, simply drag it onto a blank section of the session (or onto a newly created track to house it). Again, because the track is on a separate drive from your current session (as well as being stereo interleaved, which Pro Tools will de-interleave anyway), Pro Tools will copy the file to your Audio Files folder, ensuring that it will stay online throughout your session. The waveform will be a light blue box until the import function is complete. The region is said to be offline at this point. Don't worry, it will come online in a second. If you open the session later and there's still a blue box where the audio should be, see the section on "What to Do about Those Missing Files?" in Chapter 1.

Batch Importing

When you are designing sound for post-production, you generally need many sounds to create the scene. For example, you might need four different types of gunshots to match four actors carrying four guns. You might not know which sound will match which gun until you import the audio. In this case, it makes more sense to directly import instead of using the Import Audio to Track function because you might not even use half of what you import.

In this case, a batch import will be most useful. There is no menu option called Batch Import—simply perform the standard import audio function and fill the Regions Currently Chosen area with any sound that might even be close to what you need, as shown in Figure 3.6. Audition and fill the bin until you've exhausted all the possibilities, and then hit the Done key. This fills the bin with the gunshots, allowing you to build the gun tracks sound by sound and actor by actor, matching the gun sound to the screen gun perfectly and quickly.

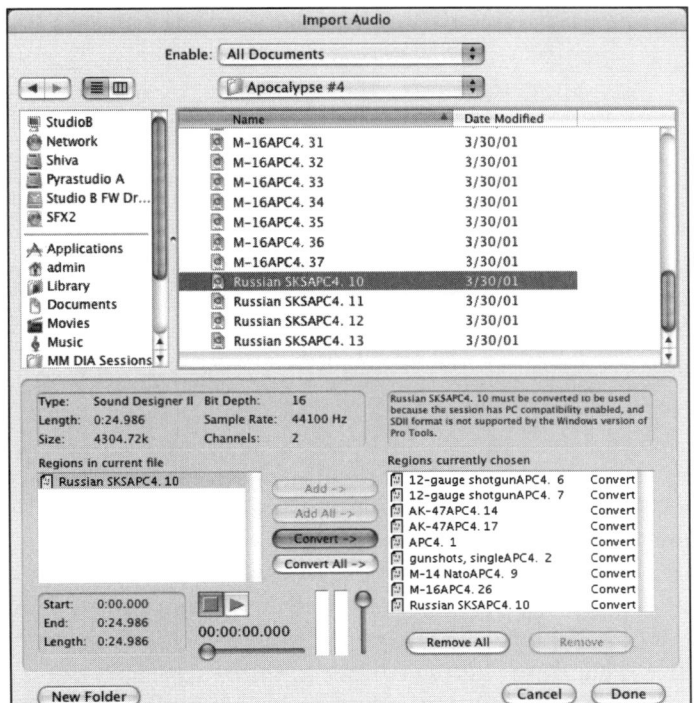

Figure 3.6

Multiple audio files
prepared for batch importing

Importing MIDI Files

Now that Pro Tools supports drag-and-drop MIDI as well as audio, the easiest way to import MIDI is to simply find it (either on the desktop or through the Workspace) and drag it onto a blank section of the Edit window. This will create a new MIDI track to house the region. From there, assign the output to your synth of choice, and it should play.

When you find the MIDI file on the desktop, you can now simply double-click it and it will bring up the Workspace (if Pro Tools is launched) and immediately audition it to see if this is the correct file. The big questions is what sound will Pro Tools use to audition the MIDI file? The answer is in the preferences. Choose Setup > Preferences > MIDI, and look at the Default Thru selection. Whatever is chosen there will be the default player for all MIDI auditions. For more on this, see "Setting Default Thru" in Chapter 5.

If you want to bring the MIDI file directly into a track, choose File > Import > MIDI to Track (seen in Figure 3.7). A new dialog box will appear, asking what you'd like to do with the MIDI, as seen in Figure 3.8. This dialog box will want to know if you'd like to remove existing tracks as well as whether or not to bring in the tempo associated with the MIDI file or conform the file to the session tempo.

Figure 3.7

The Import > MIDI to Track menu option

Once you are past this dialog box, a track will be created for the MIDI, and the part will arrive at the beginning of the session. As with direct MIDI imports, the part will play at the tempo of the song because MIDI is played on a *relative* timescale based on the tempo. Lastly, you can import MIDI directly to the Region List by choosing File > Import > MIDI to Region List. As with audio, this will create a region in the Region List but will not play the MIDI until you drag the region to a track and set an output. This is handy for Instrument tracks, since drag-importing MIDI to the Edit window naturally creates a MIDI track, not an Instrument track.

MIDI imports automatically create MIDI tracks that are set to the Ticks options and will naturally conform to the tempo of the session. You can now set MIDI tracks to be sample-based, meaning that no matter what the tempo, the MIDI will play at the tempo it now plays. For more on this, see " Keeping the Music/SFX Still When the Picture Changes " in Chapter 8.

Figure 3.8

The Import MIDI Settings dialog box

Importing Standard MIDI Files

The standard MIDI file is one way to transfer song data between different applications. If, for example, your client works in a different sequencer program, you can still import the file track by track as *MIDI* if you have the client save the song as an SMF. The process is usually simple; the option to do so is usually found in the File menu of the host application.

In Pro Tools, choose either method to import the SMF. If this is a new song imported into a new session, I suggest you use the Import > MIDI to Track method (shown in Figure 3.9), which will bring in the song track by track at the session tempo. Now, you can re-voice each MIDI track to the synth of your choosing contained in your studio.

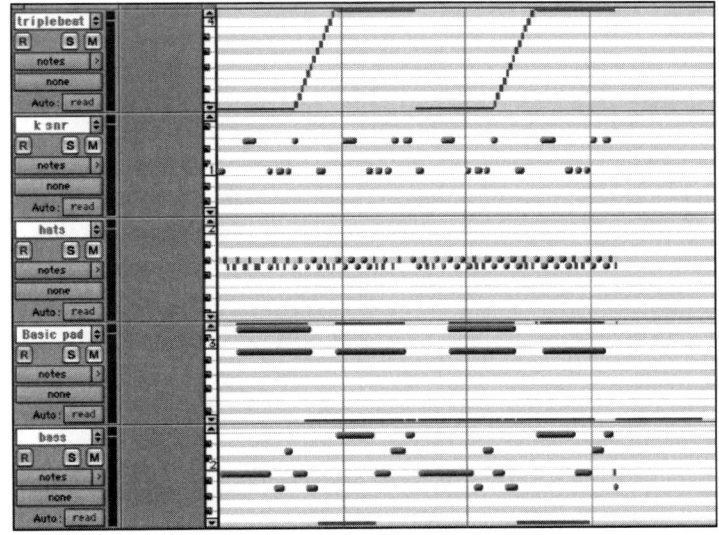

Figure 3.9

A standard MIDI file imported to track and re-voiced

Creating Standard MIDI Files

When the MIDI song has been started in Pro Tools and needs to go to another studio for more tracks or finishing, and the other studio is running another sequencer, you must export the SMF for delivery. You should keep in mind that the SMF will only transfer the MIDI data, so any audio must either be sent alongside it (see "Exporting as Files" later in this chapter) or bounced out separately and delivered alongside the SMF (see "Bouncing the Mix" in Chapter 7). The third option is to export an OMF.

Select all the tracks (OPTION-click the channel select of one track) and choose File > Export > MIDI. You will be presented with the Export MIDI Settings dialog box, shown in Figure 3.10. When you are exporting SMFs, be sure the client exports as a type 1 SMF. This type will retain all the MIDI data as separate tracks, allowing you to easily import the SMF and re-voice the MIDI. If you choose a type 0 SMF, all MIDI tracks will be merged into one track. When creating SMFs, choose the format expected by your client and hit Export. If you've also selected Audio tracks, it doesn't matter; Pro Tools will *only* export the MIDI parts for your SMF. Note that there is an option called Apply Real-Time Properties. This will hard-quantize any real-time MIDI properties to the SMF—either region-based or track-based.

Figure 3.10

Exporting MIDI as an SMF

Verifying Path Names

No matter how diligent you are about importing audio and copying the files to your Audio Files folder, it is a good idea to verify the path names of your session every once in a while to ensure that *all* your files are in the local Audio Files folder.

The Region List should default to showing you all the regions in your session. If you've done any finding through the Region List (CMD+SHIFT+F), then the list will be limited to what was most recently shown. To get back to showing all regions, choose Clear Find (CMD+SHIFT+D) from the Region List menu to show all regions again. Stretch your Region List to its largest available size by dragging the vertical divider to the left. From the Region List drop-down menu, choose Show > Full Path (as seen in Figure 3.11). Scroll slowly down the list and verify that the files all live in the Audio Files folder of this session. When you are satisfied, deselect the Full Path option, and resize the bin to a more appropriate view size.

Figure 3.11

Show > Full Path with the bin stretched

Fixing Bad Path Names

Following are three different ways to fix audio that has been improperly imported into the session.

❊ In the case of a file that accidentally was added to your session and *not* copied, as in Figure 3.12, there is still hope of bringing the file to your Audio Files folder. Obviously, you can re-import the file (if you remember where it was) and choose Copy this time. If you've forgotten where it lives, show full path names, mark where it lives, and then re-import it. If the file is a region of a larger file, be prepared to re-edit the file to match your session if it has already been edited.

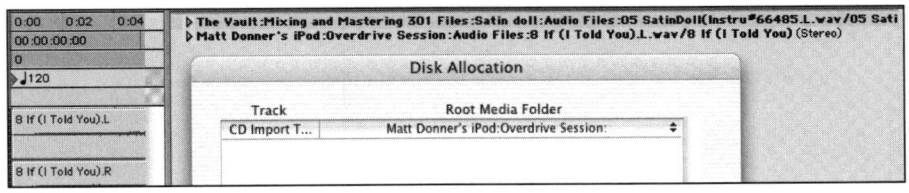

Figure 3.12

Full path name of incorrectly imported file

❊ Another solution is to create a new file from the bad one in the correct location. Choose Setup > Disk Allocation to verify that all tracks are pointing to the Audio Files folder of this session. Then choose Setup > Preferences > Editing, and make sure that the Edit Selection Follows Region List Selection and the Region List Selection Follows Edit Selection options are both checked, as shown in Figure 3.13. When these two preferences are selected, highlighting on the track will highlight the same region in the bin and vice versa. It's a good idea to leave these preferences on because they "link" the tracks and the bin.

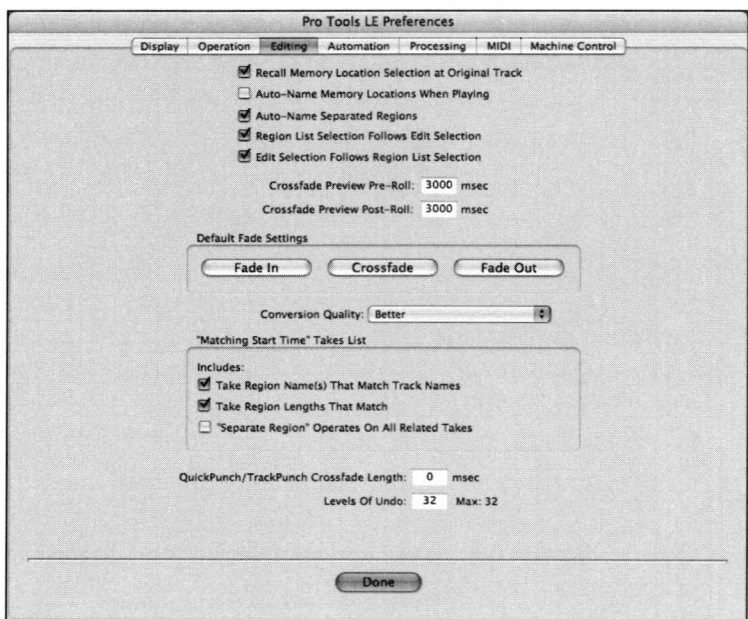

Figure 3.13

Edit Selection preferences

Then, highlight the region/file with the bad path name in the bin, also selecting the region on the track. Choose Edit > Consolidate Selection (or SHIFT+OPTION+3; see Figure 3.14) to create a new file from the old region, which will live in the Audio Files folder. You also can select AudioSuite > Duplicate to perform a similar function.

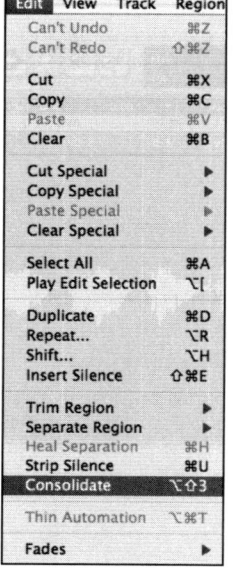

Figure 3.14

Consolidate Selection

By doing this, you create new files from the original regions, which are then stored in the current session's Audio Files folder. These new files have no "handles" anymore, so the option of using the Trimmer to extend them to their original size no longer exists. If you think you might need some handles before consolidating, you should trim the region out to its original form (or at least as large as you might need it) before consolidating.

✻ Find the region that had a bad path name. Locate its parent file (it will be in bold in the Region List because it is the parent file), and choose Export Selected as Files from the Region List drop-down menu. (See "Exporting as Files" later in this chapter.) Choose the Audio Files folder for this session, and then choose the appropriate file type and bit depth (which should match your current session). Then, re-import the file and, if necessary, re-edit it to taste and location. You then can clear the incorrect file from the bin. (See also "Cleaning the Region List" later in this chapter.)

Note

For sessions with more than one file with bad path names, see "Preparing Sessions for Delivery" (later in this chapter) as an alternative to fixing bad path names.

Collecting, Finding, and Adding Sounds

There are several functions in Pro Tools that make the process of collecting and adding sounds easy and smart. Since this is a process that people spend a *lot* of time on, there's bound to be a workflow that works best for you. Following are a few ways to gather, find, and add your sounds.

Spotlight Finds

The "old school" way of performing this type of search-import function is through the desktop. Either CMD+Tab until you're in the Finder, use Expose, or set a handy shortcut for Spotlight. As you saw in "Setting Up Expose/Spotlight" in Chapter 1, it's just as easy to search and drag from the Finder, but you don't get any of the metadata columns or the audition functions. Switch to spotlight, type in your search criteria, and the results will start piling up as soon as the first letter is typed. Once you find what you are looking for, simply drag it into the Edit window or double-click it to bring it up in the Workspace.

Searching from the Browser

When looking for specific audio to bring into your session, many engineers CMD+Tab to the desktop and perform searches from there. However, the Workspace has a very sophisticated search engine with the distinct advantage of built-in metadata and audition capabilities. Next time you're searching for audio, click the magnifying glass in the upper-left corner of the Workspace, and type in your search criteria, as seen in Figure 3.15.

Figure 3.15

The Search button within the Workspace

Be sure to check the boxes next to all the drives you wish to search through. Once you type in the search criteria and hit Enter, all audio files that match the search name will appear in the bottom of the Workspace. From there, click and hold the speaker icon to audition the file. Pro Tools now supports auditioning in stereo through the Workspace.

When searching for ACID, REX, Region groups, or MIDI files, be sure to look on the right side of the column at the tempo, if this is a part of the search criteria. To find out how to audition MIDI files, see "Setting Default Thru" in Chapter 5. Once you find the right one, drag it onto a blank space of the Edit window, and you're done!

Region Find History

Assuming all of your audio is already in the session, but you need to find it in the Region List, you can search within the Region List through the Find function. You can get to the Find function through the Region List drop-down menu, shown in Figure 3.16, or through the shortcut CMD+SHIFT+F.

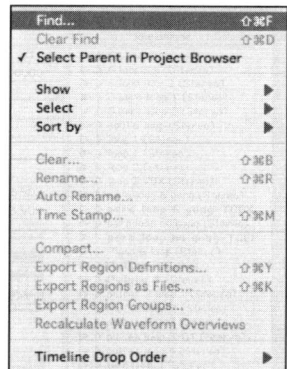

Figure 3.16

The Find function seen from the Region List drop-down menu

The advantage to this function is that only the regions matching the search criteria will appear in the Region List. Repeating the Find function with different search criteria will change the list shown in the Region List to only what fits the latest search. Best of all is the new Find History, which can be accessed through the arrow on the right of the Find dialog box, shown in Figure 3.17. From here, you can repeat finds to show only the results you want over and over again!

To show all the files in the Region List again, select Clear Find from the Region List drop-down menu, shown in Figure 3.18.

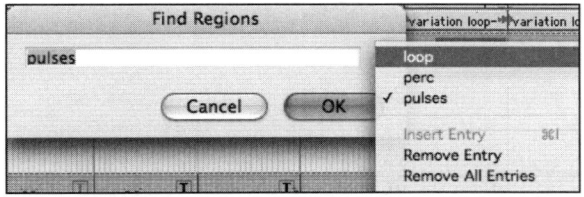

Figure 3.17

The Find History option

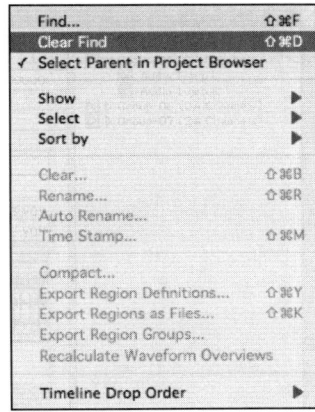

Figure 3.18

Clearing the Find menu to show all the regions

Drop Order

Finding single files and dragging them into the session is simple, but there is an added level of complexity when dealing with multiple files. If you've selected multiple files to import through drag-and-drop, Pro Tools will want to know how you'd like them imported—either all on one track or all at the same time with each on a new track. This is known as the Timeline Drop Order, as seen in Figure 3.19.

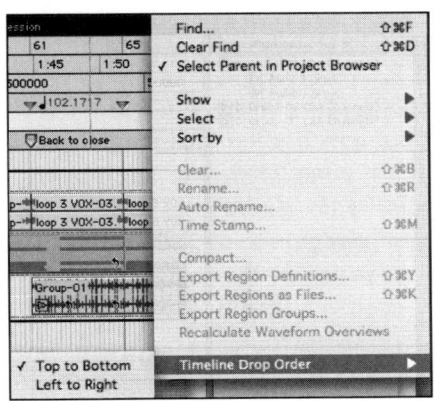

Figure 3.19

The Timeline Drop Order

Exporting Definitions and Importing Regions

As you've seen in the Import Audio dialog box, Pro Tools will import any audio file on the system. Unfortunately, it won't find the edits from another session, so how do you import only the region edited in that other session? To do so, follow these steps.

1. Close the current session and open the session that contains the region in question. When you've located it, select it and choose Export Regions as Files, shown in Figure 3.20. (See the next section, "Exporting as Files.") Then, you can reopen the new session and import the file. Because the region has become a new file, any portions of the original file outside the edit boundaries no longer exist. Therefore, it is imperative that the region selected in the original file is enough to satisfy your needs. Also, keep in mind that if you need several regions from the original session, you should export them all at once to avoid wasting time going back and forth.

Figure 3.20

The Export Regions as Files menu option

2. As mentioned earlier, close the current session and open the original session containing the sought-after region. Find it and select it, but this time choose Export Region Definitions. Region definitions are what Pro Tools remembers when audio is edited, so by exporting the region definitions, Pro Tools is effectively exporting the edit points, which can be reapplied to the original file, recreating all the regions as well.

After you export the definitions, Pro Tools will show you a dialog box telling you that it normally saves the region definitions to the session document, but now it will attach the definitions to the audio itself, like the one in Figure 3.21. When this is completed, you can reopen the current session and choose Import Audio. When you point to the Audio Files folder of the original session, find the parent file that created the sought-after region. Now, when you search the files in the Audio Files folder, each file will also show you *all* the regions defined by editing in the original session (and exported by you), as seen in Figure 3.22.

Figure 3.21

The Export Region Definitions menu option

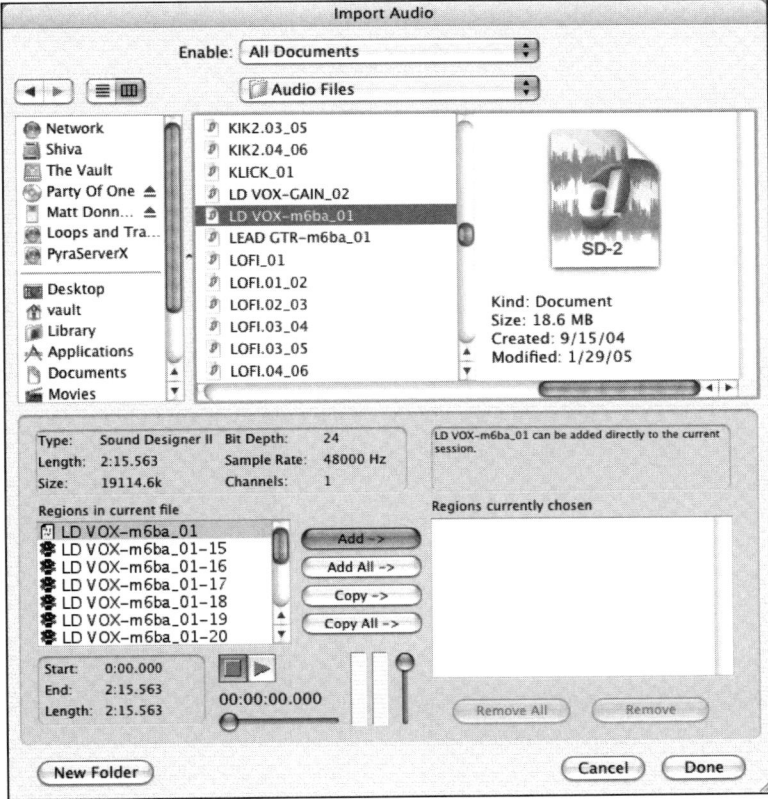

Figure 3.22

The Import Audio dialog box with regions

If this is something you will do often, get in the habit of exporting the region definitions for *all* the audio in the session. That way, you will know that you have access to *every* region of every audio file from that session.

Exporting as Files

As mentioned earlier, it is very common to export regions from one session into others. The most common method is to use the Export Regions as Files feature, found in the Region List drop-down menu. When the region in question is selected, choosing Export Regions as Files will allow you to create an entirely new parent file from the region. However, the new file will have no handles and no ability to trim back to its original size.

In voiceover sessions, it is very common to record and edit 300 individual files or more for delivery. In situations like this, exporting as files is the perfect solution. After the files are recorded and edited to taste, select them all and export them for delivery. When you are presented with the Export Selected dialog box (seen in Figure 3.23), choose the file type and bit depth required in the top section. In the middle section, click the Choose button. This will tell Pro Tools where to export the files. I suggest you create a new folder at the same level as the session and the Audio Files folder, and call it Exports. Then, you can simply deliver to the client the Exports folder and all the edited files contained therein.

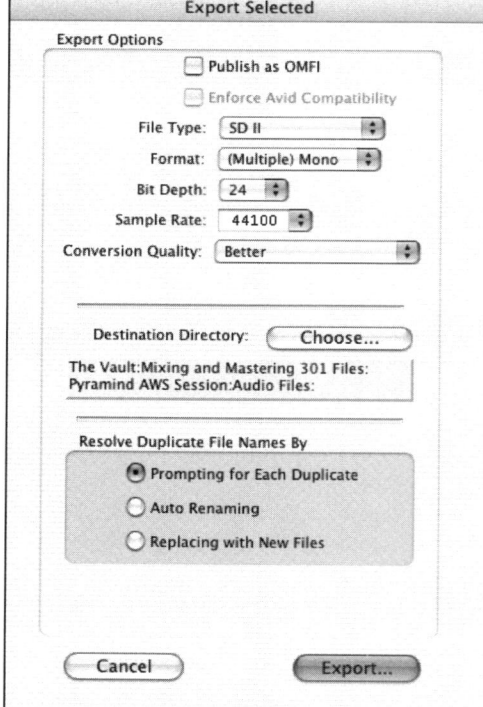

Figure 3.23

The Export Selected dialog box

Batch Naming and Exporting

In the situation previously described, in which the voiceover session and client require files be exported for delivery, we assume that the files are perfect and ready for exporting. However, because these sessions usually happen extremely fast, stopping to name each file after editing (or even during editing) can be a waste of time. In the scenario in which the files take sequential names (such as Clip 01, Clip 02, and so on), Pro Tools can save a lot of time for you and the client.

This is, however, a multi-stepped process utilizing a function of Pro Tools called the *Timestamp*. This bit of information is a timing reference that is stamped onto all files and regions. There is the Original Timestamp (which refers to the timeline position of the file as it was created/recorded) and the User Timestamp (which refers to a timeline position of the user's preference).

After your takes are edited, you will usually (but optionally) line them next to each other according to time and naming conventions. For example, VO take 24, which is the third final region, will eventually be called VO_3, so its timestamp will want to be the third latest. When files are moved, however, their timestamps do not change, so simply moving the files into order and expecting them to get stamped at their new positions and be ordered chronologically doesn't work, as seen in Figure 3.24. (Notice that the files are named sequentially on the track, but they do NOT follow the same convention in the bin!)

By duplicating the region (AudioSuite > Other > Duplicate), you create a new region with a timestamp that matches the current position, allowing you to line them up in the bin for renaming. You could also use Edit > Consolidate (SHIFT+OPTION+3) to do the same thing. Be sure to select the Create Individual Files option if you use Duplicate so your individual clips are retained; otherwise, Pro Tools will merge them all into a single audio file.

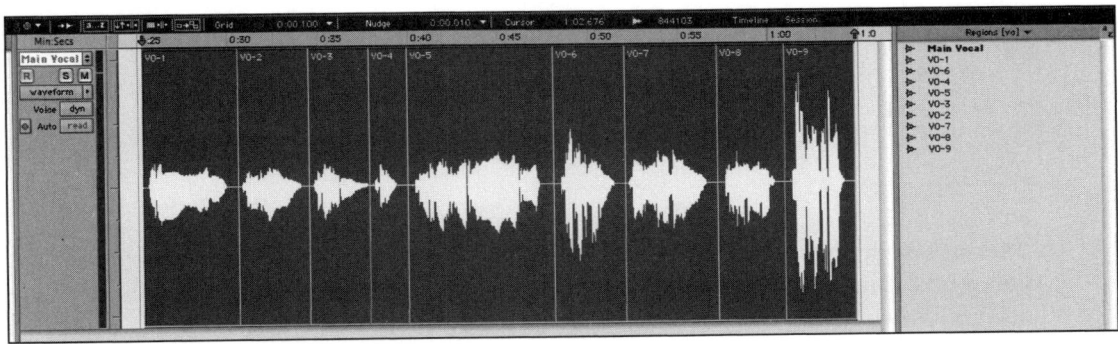

Figure 3.24
Files named in order, sorted by an out-of-order timestamp

Perform the following sequence of moves to prepare and rename your files in numeric order.

1. Select all the files on the track after editing.

2. Choose AudioSuite > Other > Duplicate to duplicate the files in position, recreating the Timestamp at the current location, as seen in Figure 3.25.

Figure 3.25

Duplicating files

3. With the files selected, sort by timestamp by choosing Sort By > Original Time Stamp option from the Audio drop-down menu (see Figure 3.26). This will order the files in the bin by their timestamps and align them in the same order as they are on the track.

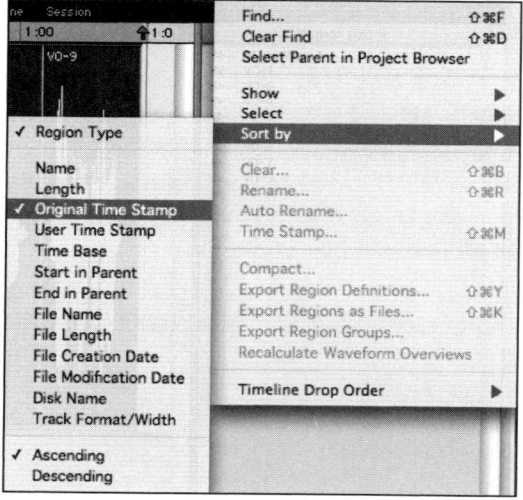

Figure 3.26

Sort By > Original Time Stamp

4. Choose Auto Re-Name Selected from the drop-down menu. You'll be presented with a dialog box (see Figure 3.27) that will allow you to give the file name (VO Clip, in this case) and the naming protocol (01, 1, 001, and so on), as well as dictate any extension to the file (such as .wav). If you are creating .wav files, you don't have to name the extension here; you can choose to add the extension when exporting the files. Another good idea is to start with Number 1 (the default is 0) because your clips will all be offset by one number, driving your producer crazy (along with her Web programmer), which means no repeat business for you!

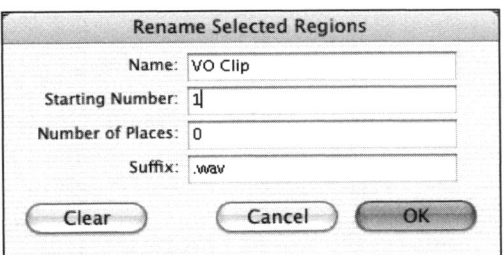

Figure 3.27

The Rename Selected Regions dialog box

When you have renamed the files to your liking, you should use the Export Regions as Files option and direct them to a new folder you create for your client, called VO Clips. If your client wants the files tagged with the extension, you can choose this option in the Rename Selected Regions dialog box, but Pro Tools will generally do this on export, which will make your .wav files VO Clip 01.wav.wav... which I think is from the Department of Redundancy Department.

With Pro Tools version 7, there is a handy new sort function called Sort by Time Base, which absolves the user from having to go through the duplication process to order the Region List by ruler position. In this case, you can skip the sections that ask you to either duplicate or consolidate, since you no longer need to re-timestamp the regions for them to line up correctly in the Region List. Simply choose Sort By > Time Base from the Region List drop-down menu (shown in Figure 3.28), and all the files will be in the correct order for renaming!

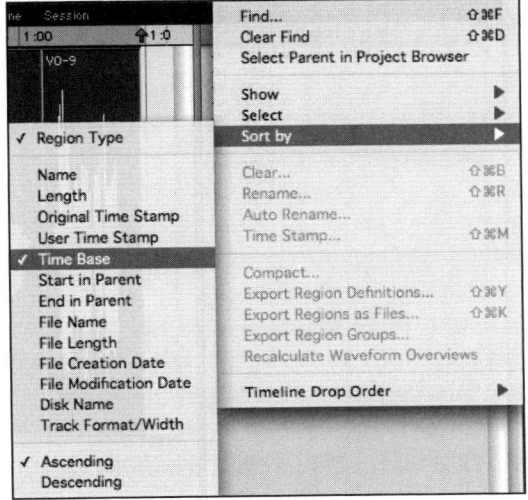

Figure 3.28

Sort By > Time Base from the
Region List drop-down menu

Preparing Sessions for Delivery

It is common for artists to want to work with several producers and engineers on a project, and sometimes on a single song. Usually, the artist will travel with a portable drive containing the session so all the work is intact, but occasionally the session will start at a studio without the traveling drive and will need to be prepared to travel on another medium, such as CD or DVD. The following tips present a few ways to prepare the session for traveling and ensure that it arrives without a problem.

Cleaning the Region List

By the sheer nature of working and recording in Pro Tools, you will have *many* unused audio files and regions. When the song has reached a level of acceptability at which the artist or producer says it's finished, it becomes a good idea to clean out the Region List to make the session as efficient as possible for traveling.

1. Choose Select > Unused from the Region List drop-down menu, highlighting any files (or regions) that are not used on any playlist. You could also choose Select > Unused Audio Except Whole Files, which will do the same thing, minus the parent files, as shown in Figure 3.29.

Figure 3.29

Selecting unused files

2. Choose Clear Selected from the Regions List drop-down menu. You will be presented with the Clear Audio dialog box (see Figure 3.30). If the regions selected are whole files and not just regions, you will be presented with two possibilities: Remove or Delete.

   - **Remove.** This option will take the files and regions out of the Region List, but will retain the parent files in the Audio Files folder. If you make a mistake, you'll be happy you did this because you can re-import the parent files and recreate the edits if necessary.

   - **Delete.** This option will remove the files from the session *and* the hard drive. This is preferable if you are preparing for travel on a smaller medium, such as CD, because it could shrink your session size in half.

Although clearing the Region List is a good idea, be sure you've told the producer that you will *permanently* be removing files and that he or she should be sure this is okay. After she says, "Okay," ask again and explain that this will *permanently* remove files—and also ask if she wants to hear it one last time to be sure. She might get annoyed, but at least you will be covered when she panics and realizes that means you tossed the alternate vocal that she also wanted (but never bothered to actually tell you)!

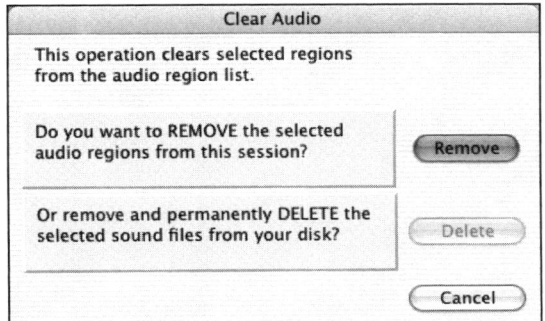

Figure 3.30

Clearing the selected regions

Duplicating the Session

When you clean the Region List to prepare for delivery, you run the risk of deleting files that were important, even if the producer said it was okay. A safer way to prepare the session is to make a copy of it as is.

1. Choose File > Save Copy In (see Figure 3.31). You will be presented with the Save Copy In dialog box (Figure 3.32).

Figure 3.31

The Save Copy In menu option

2. Point to the file to save to a unique place on either your drive or the artist's drive. This will avoid the possibility of confusing the original session with the copy.

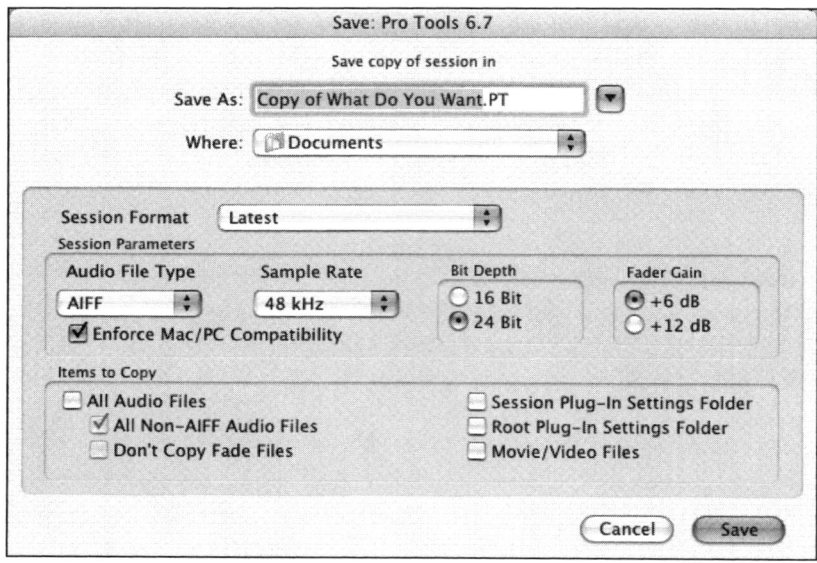

Figure 3.32

The Save Copy In
dialog box

3. At the bottom of the dialog box, check the Items to Copy box and select all options. If you don't do this, you will copy the session *only*, leaving all the audio on the original drive. This is a big problem, especially if the artist is traveling far, to someplace like Europe.

4. You can also select *not* to copy over fade files. If you are troubled by many corrupt fade files that always show up as missing when you open your session, this is a handy workaround because the new session will try to recreate the fades when you open it after the copy.

5. Choose BWF for the file type and check the Enforce Mac/PC Compatibility box. I recommend this to all clients—it is the most common form of Pro Tools session because you never know when this will end up at a PC studio. If you *don't* do this, you could put your client in a very bad position if the next stop is a PC studio.

Compacting the Session

If the producer says the piece is finished and he is absolutely sure it is, the most efficient way to pack the session for delivery is to compact it. Compacting removes all the unused edits from the parent files, deletes the parent files, and creates new parent files from the regions left on the playlists, which is more efficient than selecting and deleting unused regions.

1. Select all audio in the Region List by choosing Select All from the Region List drop-down menu. The shortcut is SHIFT+Apple+A.

2. Select Compact Selected from the drop-down menu. You will be presented with the Compact Selected dialog box (see Figure 3.33). This dialog box describes the process of compacting in greater detail and gives you only one option—handle size.

3. Choose the handle size you like, and hit Compact. *Handle size* is the amount of space left at the beginning and end of the new parent files in case some last-minute trimming is in order. I suggest a handle size of at least 1000 ms (1 second) because any editing should be much closer than that by now, right? If not, then increase this to 5000 ms.

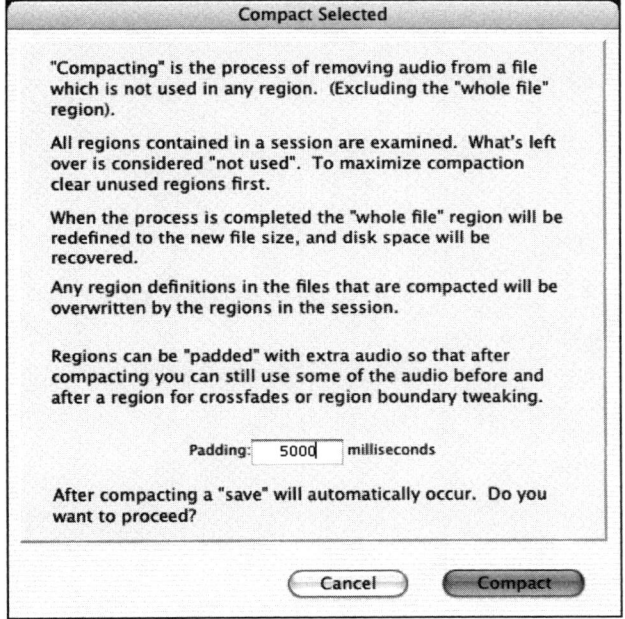

Figure 3.33

The Compact Selected dialog box

Importing OMFs

The Open Media Format allows multiple programs and platforms, such as Avid and Final Cut Pro, to send files to each other while maintaining the integrity of all the audio *and* the edits. OMFs come in two flavors—one with the audio embedded into the document (which is preferred) and another with an OMF document and a folder full of the audio files to which it refers.

To import the OMF, you must also have DigiTranslator, a separately sold software component that is built into Pro Tools. (It is unlocked ONLY when a valid authorization is recognized on your iLok.) Owning this software unlocks Pro Tools' ability to both import and create OMFs for working with other platforms.

To import the OMF and into a new Pro Tools session, first create a blank document. Open the Workspace, and navigate to the OMF file. Simply drag the OMF into the blank Edit window, and you will be presented with the Import Session Data dialog box (see Figure 3.34).

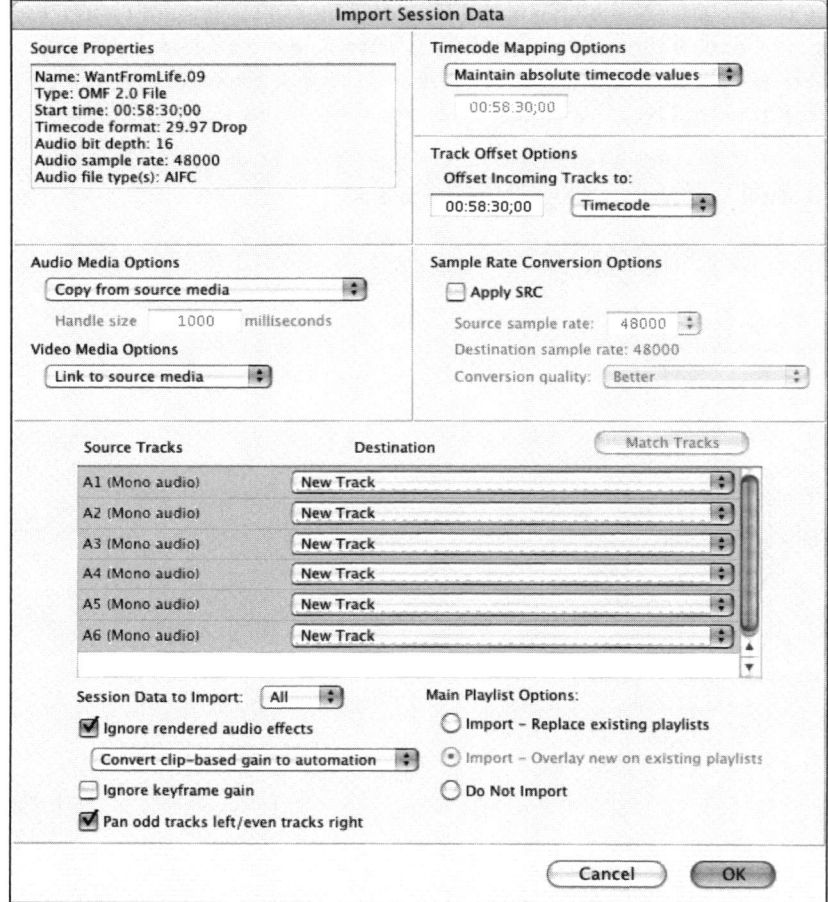

Figure 3.34

The Import Session Data dialog box for an OMF document

Depending on your circumstances, there are several decisions to make during this OMF import. Following, you'll find all the options and what they mean.

❖ **Audio Media Options.** Here you tell Pro Tools whether to simply refer to the audio with the OMF, copy the audio to the new session's Audio Files folder (preferred), or consolidate from the original OMF. Consolidating is similar to copying, except that it won't necessarily keep your handles (the extra audio underneath the trimmed region boundary). This means that copying the audio is more a flexible option.

❖ **Video Media Options.** These are the same as the Audio Media options, except for video files.

❋ **Timecode Mapping Options.** Generally reserved for OMFs from video-editing platforms, such as Avid systems or Final Cut Pro, this option will allow you to shift the start time of the incoming sequence to any Timecode location by choosing the Map Incoming Timecode option. You can choose Maintain Absolute Timecode Values to keep the incoming audio at the Timecode position originally held in the video-editing system, or you can choose Maintain Relative Values to keep everything in position but shift it to the beginning of the session. You can change this later if you want. (See "What Happens When You Change the Start Time?" in Chapter 8.)

This is particularly important in video OMFs. Generally, the OMF will come with a predetermined start time (determined by the video editor), and you should not mess with it. You can throw the entire mix out of time with the video, or do even worse with other processes you are not involved with. A quick confirmation call can avoid serious issues, but generally, if there is *already* Timecode information in this window, chose the Maintain Absolute Timecode option, and your session will open at the beginning of the Pro Tools document in perfect time.

❋ **Operation/Destination Track.** This gives you the option to either ignore the track (Do Not Import) or import the track. This is similar to importing session data. (See "Switching Songs" in Chapter 2.) The fast move here (assuming you are importing the OMF as a fresh session) is to OPTION-click any track and set the Import as New Playlist option, which will set all the tracks to import to new playlists.

❋ **Session Data to Import.** Again, this is similar to importing session data.

❋ **Main Playlist Options.** These options only kick in when you are importing OMFs into existing sessions in which the incoming tracks are sent to destinations already in play by other tracks. For example, you can choose to import a kick track from the OMF to the kick of the existing session, and then decide what happens to the audio on the existing kick track.

❋ **Ignore Rendered Audio Effects.** In video systems, this means that each audio file (clip) can have independent volume controls (automation) permanently mapped to the file. This is a destructive process, rendering certain sounds useless. I *always* suggest you activate the Ignore button and choose Convert Clip-Based Gain to Automation, which will bring the mix over exactly as the editor left it, giving you a sense of what he or she heard and liked as a starting point.

❋ **Pan Odd/Even Tracks Left/Right.** The name says it all. This should tell you that stereo tracks don't come over as stereo tracks, but as mono left/right tracks panned accordingly. You should "stereo-ize" these tracks by dragging them onto new stereo tracks. (See "Stereo or Dual Mono?" in Chapter 2.)

Creating OMF Documents

If you have a Pro Tools session that needs to travel to another studio that doesn't run Pro Tools, you can pack the session as an OMF for delivery. The OMF format will retain almost all of your session (it won't port over markers) that can be unpacked by other software like AVID, Final Cut Pro, Logic Pro and others. If you own DigiTranslator, you can access the OMF creation menu option by choosing File > Export OMF/AAF.

The OMF will pack any selected tracks, so be sure to OPTION-click (selects all the tracks) before you pack the OMF to ensure that you are packing everything! Also remember that you will need to export a separate SMF (standard MIDI file) if your session has MIDI in it as the OMF won't carry that information.

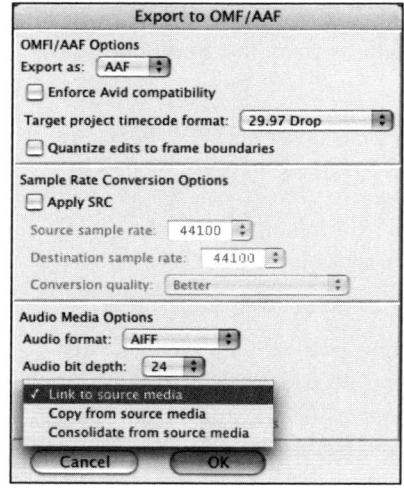

Figure 3.35

The Export to OMF/AAF dialog box

You will be presented with the Export to OMF/AAF dialog box, seen in Figure 3.35, which presents several options to you during the OMF packing process. In most cases, you will leave things alone, but occasionally you'll need to adjust things. First, choose between OMF and AAF. Ask the receiving studio which they prefer, and make your decision accordingly. The same goes for enforcing AVID compatibility. The frame rate will come up as it is in your session (probably 30, but maybe 29.97 for video jobs), and if you don't know, then ask. I would stay away from quantizing edits to frame boundaries unless you know the receiving studio can't handle audio at the sample level. Older video systems may suffer from this, so again, ask. If you're not sure, ask. If they don't know, have them ask someone there. If they don't know whom to ask, then leave it unchecked for safety. If they complain later, your butt is well covered.

Generally, I suggest you create an OMF with consolidated audio (choose Consolidate from Source Media in the Media drop-down menu), as there will be less confusion later. This will create a large OMF document and all the audio will be embedded within it. You can only get to the audio through OMF unpacking, so for some clients, this presents a problem. For those clients, create the OMF document and a separate folder (Copy from Source Media) to house the audio. That way, in a pinch, you could at least access the files and re-create some of your edits by hand if necessary. It's not pretty, and it defeats the purpose of the OMF, but at least there is some recourse this way.

Remember that most of the work with OMFs is at the unpacking stage (see "Importing OMFs" earlier in this chapter). For those of you working with Final Cut Pro, be sure to read the section "Helpful Hints for Final Cut Pro Users" in Chapter 8.

4 Editing, Arranging, and Navigation

Most Pro Tools users already know how to edit audio and are generally pretty good about getting around, too. However, no matter how fast you are and how clean you edit, there's always a faster way to get it done. For anyone working with music and audio for clients (and are charging by the hour), this chapter will shave hours off your session times, saving your clients money and keeping them coming back to you!

Simple editing tips can be lifesavers when the client asks you to backtrack and you can't, creating quick loops that hold up over time will prevent having to do it over and over again, chopping words together for the perfect vocal performance can help sell the product for the client, as well as following the vocal part with the lyrics attached to the waveform will help speed the punch-in process and keep the session flowing smoothly. These and many more power tips are covered in this chapter, so buckle up and get ready to go very, very fast!

Zero-Crossing Edits

When editing audio with Pro Tools or any other DAW, the most important decision you can make is where to make the cut. *All cuts should be made at zero-crossing points. Period.* Audio is effectively an AC electrical signal that has both positive and negative energy. The wave will cross the zero-voltage line several million times throughout the session, as seen in Figures 4.1 (zoomed way in) and 4.2 (zoomed slightly in), giving you plenty of opportunity to find places to make the cut. If audio is cut at a point on the wave where the energy is either positive or negative, there will be an audible click when it is played, known as a Fourier click (pronounced *four-yay*). So repeat after me: "I promise to always cut at the zero-crossing point!"

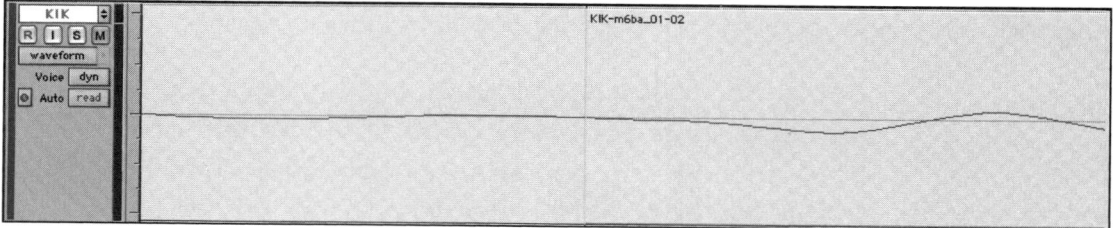

Figure 4.1

Zero-crossing point for editing, zoom 1

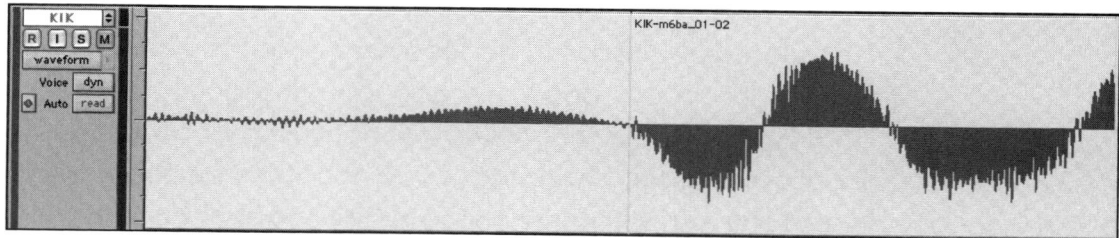

Figure 4.2

Zero-crossing point for editing, zoom 2

Editing Safely

Nothing is worse than performing hours of editing (including some destructive edits), only to have the producer say, "I changed my mind. Put it back to how it was at the beginning, and let's start over." Not only did you waste your time, it is often very difficult to recreate the track.

Before you begin an editing session, start by copying the entire track (or tracks) to a new playlist. Hit CMD+A or choose Edit > Select All. When the track(s) are highlighted, copy the audio (CMD+C or Edit > Copy). Click the arrow to the right of the track name (the Playlist tab) and select Create New Playlist, as shown in Figure 4.3. Name the track Safety Edit 1, and then paste the audio (CMD+V or Edit > Paste).

Figure 4.3

The Playlist menu

You can skip some of this process by simply highlighting the audio, and then selecting Duplicate from the Playlist drop-down menu. However, you don't get the option of naming the playlist during this process; you must name it afterward.

Locating Positions

If you are constantly trying to find your way through the session and you are always clicking in random locations, you are used to positioning the cursor slightly off the desired location. A more accurate way of locating the cursor to any position is by clicking directly in the Main Time Indicator and typing the location, as shown in Figure 4.4. You must hit the Enter key to jump to the typed-in location. The shortcut is to hit the * (asterisk) key on the number pad. For laptops without number pads, press Function+P (Fn+P).

Figure 4.4

Main Time Indicator highlighted

Auditioning Edits

Once you've made the cuts you like (where did you make them again?), you'll probably be re-assembling the cut pieces together in some new and improved fashion. Once re-assembled, you'll most likely spend time moving the cursor around to audition the re-assembly, but you'll get annoyed putting the cursor at the beginning, then the end, repeatedly, to audition both sides of the cut. If so, here are a few handy audition techniques to make life a little easier for you—just remember to activate the Command Focus button (see "Command Focus" in Chapter 1).

- ✸ 6 plays to the beginning of the selection by the pre-roll amount (OPT+left arrow)
- ✸ 7 plays from the beginning of the selection by the amount of post-roll (CMD+left arrow)
- ✸ 8 plays to the end of the selection by the pre-roll amount (OPT+right Arrow)
- ✸ 9 plays from the end of the selection by the post-roll amount (CMD+right Arrow)
- ✸ CMD+OPT+left arrow will play to the beginning of the selection by pre-roll AND will play through the region boundary by the post-roll amount.
- ✸ CMD+OPT+right arrow will play to the end of the region by the pre-roll amount AND will play through the region boundary by the post-roll amount.

The last two are very handy for auditioning composite edits (comps) as they not only tell you how well they merge together vis-à-vis timing, but they also tell you whether they merge together vis-à-vis zero-crossing Fourier clicks.

Zoom Options

Let's face it—most time spent in Pro Tools involves zooming in and zooming out. Here are some ways to help you zoom in/out faster and smarter.

- ✸ **Zoom toggle.** Sometimes known as the "E" zoom, this back-and-forth tool is a great way to jump between two different zoom settings. Zoom toggle is activated by hitting the letter E (with Command Focus active) or by clicking the Zoom toggle button under the Zoom tool, as seen in Figure 4.5.

Figure 4.5

The Zoom toggle button

Zoom toggle starts at the medium level and when clicked again, will zoom to large with the selection filling the screen. However, the Zoom toggle is intelligent in that you can set the size toggled between. Once you activate Zoom toggle, change the view to the height you like, and Pro Tools will remember this. Hit the Zoom toggle again, and set the next view size. Pro Tools will then switch back and forth between the two zoom views!

❊ **Marquee Zoom**. New to Pro Tools 7 is the Marquee Zoom, which is a real-time zoom function available in conjunction with the Zoom tool. Hold the Control key while click-dragging on any region, audio, or MIDI. Dragging up and down will zoom in vertically (much like the up/down Zoom buttons) while dragging left and right will zoom in horizontally.

❊ **MIDI view options**. Pro Tools now defaults to showing all MIDI tracks "all full" in that all notes will be displayed as large as possible in the Regions view, as seen in Figure 4.6. In Notes view, the notes will shrink to a small size, and the view height ruler will show the octave value as well, as shown in Figure 4.7. This note-size view will maintain throughout the MIDI track playlist options, like Velocity.

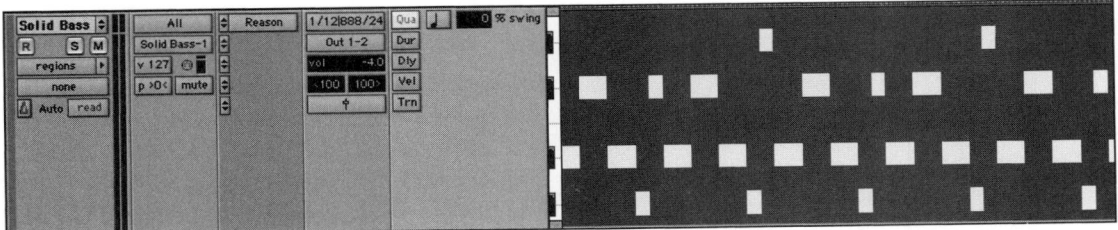

Figure 4.6

The MIDI Regions view with all notes large

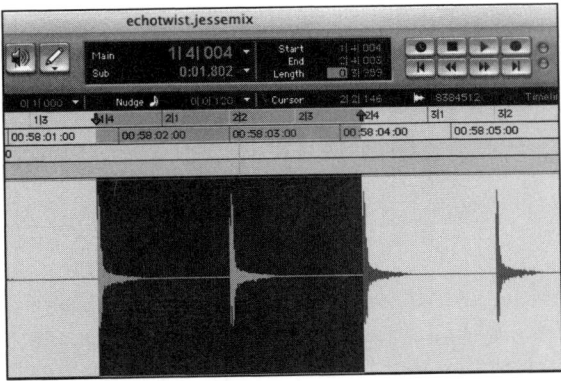

Figure 4.7

The MIDI Notes view with the octave displayed in the track height ruler

Finding Tracks Easily

"Where did that background track go? It used to be at the top, but I guess I moved it. . . . Hmmm, maybe if I search track by track. . . ."

Does this sound like you? If so, here are some handy ways to keep from getting lost.

✳ **Color codes**. Tracks have the ability to be color-coded, which makes them instantly visible—if you actually use a color-system! A good organizational idea that will help you find tracks easily is to devise a color system. For example, in a music session, think about color-coding the drum tracks blue, the bass orange, and so on. Consider keeping the groups that match the tracks the same color. Colors can be added to tracks by choosing Window > Color Palette, as shown in Figure 4.8. New to v7 is the Hold button, shown on the Color Palette window in Figure 4.9. This keeps the last color chosen as the default color so it is readily available for the next track you select.

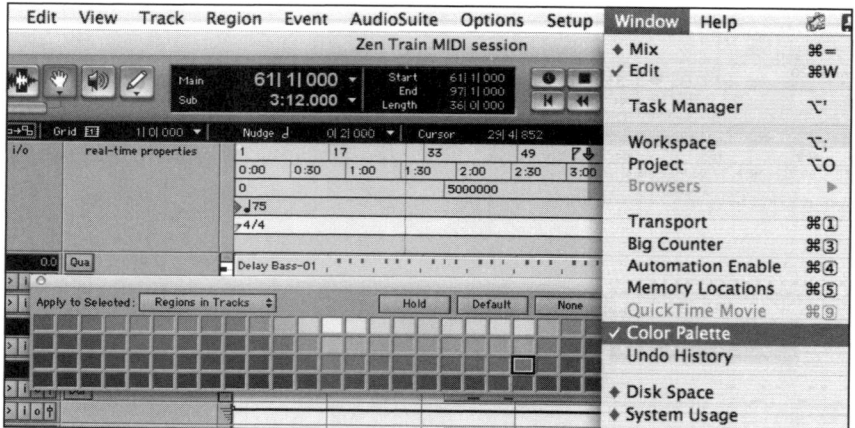

Figure 4.8

The Color Palette drop-down menu

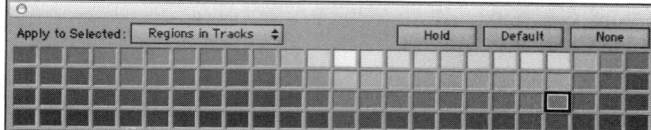

Figure 4.9

The Color Palette window

✳ **Link Track and Edit Selection**. This new feature allows the user to select a region in the Edit window and have the track selected as well. This is handy if you can't remember the name of the track, but you know the region that belongs to the track. You can activate this under the Trim tool, as shown in Figure 4.10.

Figure 4.10

Link Track and Edit Selection

❋ **Scroll to Track**. Just as its name indicates, choosing Track > Scroll to Track (shown in Figure 4.11) will present you with a dialog box asking what track position you'd like to find. Tracks are numbered in vertical fashion, with the top-most track being position 1. Simply type in the track number position desired, and Pro Tools will find it and select it.

Figure 4.11

The Scroll to Track menu option

Region Looping

New to version 7 is the region looping function, found by choosing Region > Loop or with the shortcut CMD+OPT+L (see Figure 4.12). The region looping function takes any selection and loops it based on the settings you choose. When you choose Region > Loop, you are presented with a dialog box, like the one in Figure 4.13.

Once here, you can tell Pro Tools to loop a certain number of times, loop for a specific length, or loop until the end of the session—or until the next region on the track, whichever comes first. This would be cool enough on it's own, but the slick factor goes one step beyond—loops can be resized at any time and *all loop iterations will instantly readjust to match!*

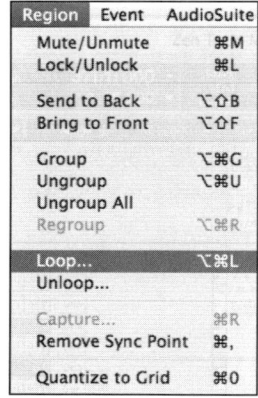

Figure 4.12

The Region > Loop menu option

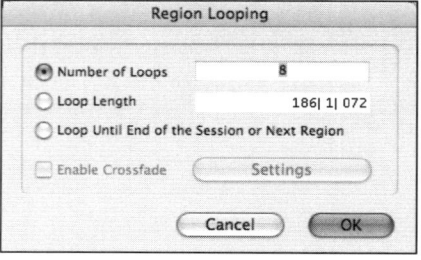

Figure 4.13

The Region Looping dialog box

Let's be clear—this is huge. This means that the 2-bar loop that you've pasted for 150 bars that your producer now wants to be a 1-bar loop can be so—instantly! Before this, you would have needed to select all but the first loop, delete them, cut the first loop to 1 bar, then reloop (by hand, no less) back to 150 bars. Now, simply choose the Trim tool and position it on the loop icon in the bottom right of the region, shown in Figure 4.14. Trim the region in half, and watch all loop iterations change instantly!

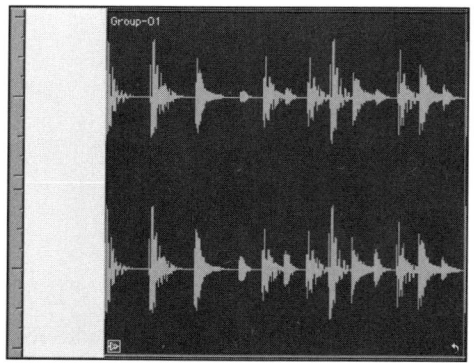

Figure 4.14

The region looping icon

Be careful of one thing when editing looped regions—once the loop has been cut, there will be two loop iterations, one before the cut and one after. Loops changed in the first iteration will no longer affect changes in the second. For more ways to use this to your advantage, see "The Great Shrinking Region Trick" later in this chapter.

Faster Editing

For those of you trying to edit out the kick drums from that favorite drum loop so you can copy them to another track and EQ them, your hours of editing have just shortened—to 10 seconds!

New in Pro Tools v7 are two new quick editing options: Separate Region > On Grid and Separate Region > At Transients, both seen in Figure 4.15. By separating the region at transients, you allow Pro Tools to find all the hits and separate the region at those transients, leaving you with lots of little regions.

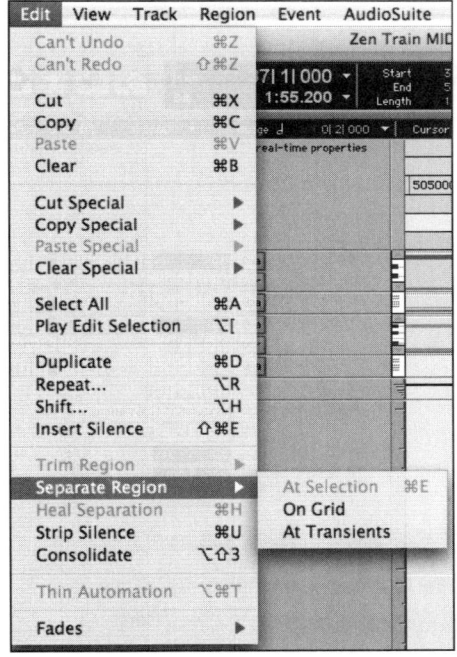

Figure 4.15

Separate Region > On Grid and
Separate Region > At Transients options

By contrast, separating on the grid will leave you regions parceled into perfect grid-ready sections. Keep in mind that the grid resolution will need to be set first in the Ruler Grid Size menu option, as shown in Figure 4.16.

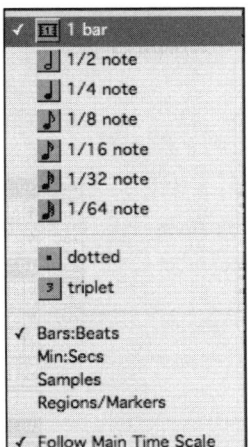

Figure 4.16

The grid resolution drop-down menu

Boxing the Slices

In the section "The Many Ways to Import Audio" in Chapter 3, you learned that Pro Tools v7 now supports drag-and-drop importing of both REX and ACID files. When the file is imported, Pro Tools will "wrap" it in something called a Region Group. New to v7, the Region Group is effectively a "boxing" of individually sliced regions into a single, movable region group as if it were a single region—because it is.

A Region Group can be "unwrapped" into its individual slices at anytime by choosing Region > Ungroup, shown in Figure 4.17. Region Groups can be nested, meaning that several Region Groups can be grouped into a larger Region Group. To get back to the individual slices from a nested Region Group, choose Region > Ungroup All. Figures 4.18 and 4.19 show a REX file imported as a Region Group and ungrouped as individual slices, respectively.

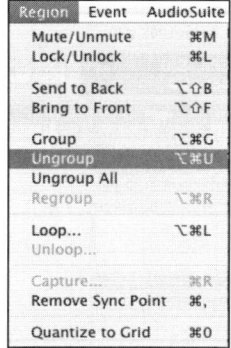

Figure 4.17

The Region > Ungroup menu option

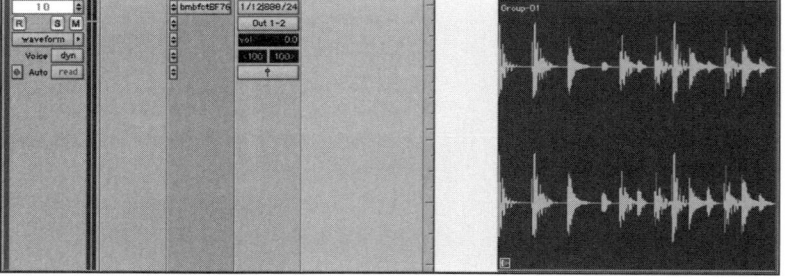

Figure 4.18

An imported REX file
as a Region Group

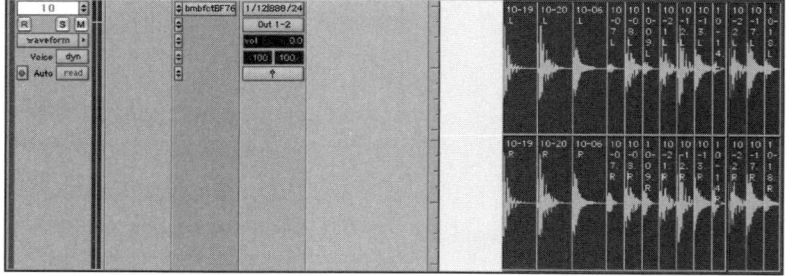

Figure 4.19

The REX file as
individual slices

(Almost) Elastic Audio

If you import an ACID file and it shows up as a Region Group, will it conform to the session tempo? Will it conform to a new tempo if you decide to speed up the song? Just like ACID? Just like a REX player in Reason?

YES!! YES!! YES!! PRO TOOLS SUPPORTS ELASTIC AUDIO . . . almost.

Yes, if you import an ACID file or a REX file, it will conform to the session tempo if its been imported to a fresh track. Pro Tools will create a new track for the file and set the track to tick-based. Because the track is a tick-based track, any regions on the track are linked to the Bar|Beat location. This means that the imported REX file, secretly wrapped in a Region Group, will reconform the individual slices to whatever tempo the session holds. In fact, the Region Group will conform to multiple tempos within a single session, meaning that any tempo changes throughout the song require no extra work to reconform the audio to the new tempo! Figure 4.20 shows a single Region Group conforming to multiple tempos within a single session.

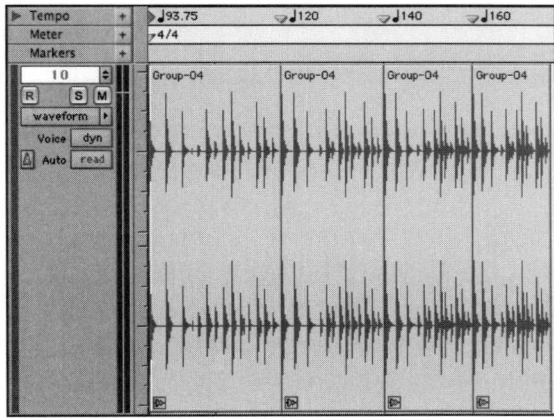

Figure 4.20

A single Region Group conforming to multiple tempos in a single session

Group and Loop

If attempting to turn a loop into a Region Group and have it behave like an ACID file when the original file is *not* an ACID file, the trick is not as easy. You'll need to import the file, select it, and choose Edit > Separate Region > At Transients to slice it into its individual hits. Figure 4.21 shows the region on one track as the original and the other track as the slices after separating at the transients. From there, conform the session tempo to the length of the loop through the Identify Beat function (see "Using Loops to Create a Tempo Map" in Chapter 5). Once the tempo matches the loop, you're as good as an ACID file!

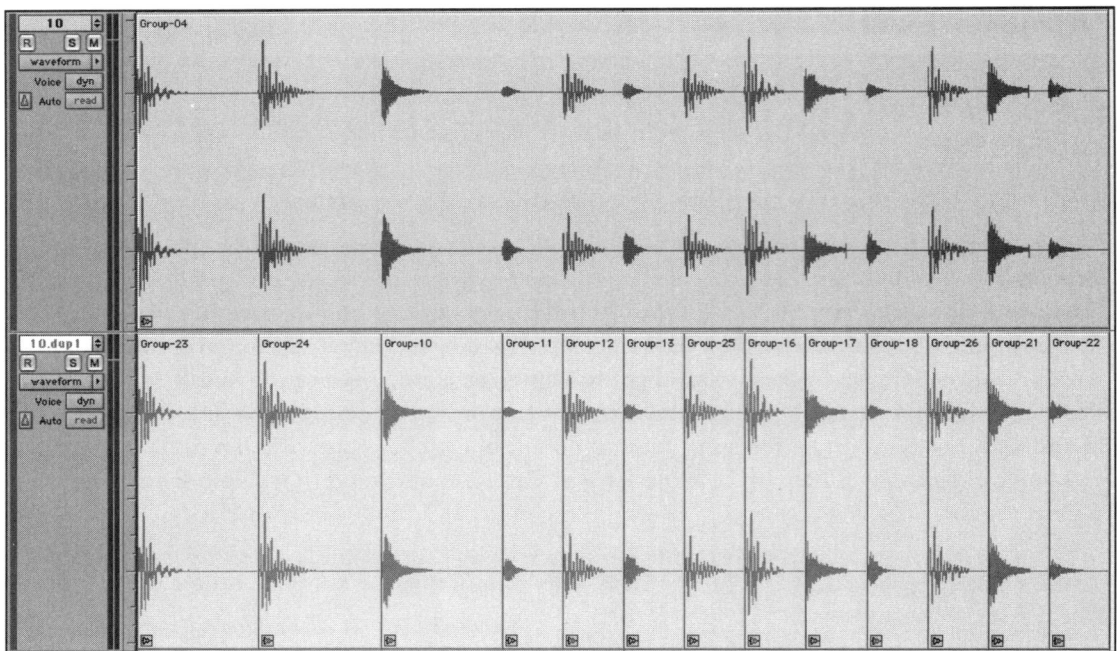

Figure 4.21

A loop before and after separating at the transients

Now, you can perform what I call the Group and Loop function. First, select all the slices and create a Region Group by choosing Region > Group. This will "box the slices" into a Region Group. Then, if desired, you can loop the new Region Group by choosing Region > Loop. The cool shortcuts for the Group and Loop function are CMD+OPT+G (group) and CMD+OPT+L (loop). Figure 4.22 shows the boxed slices as a Region Group looped afterwards.

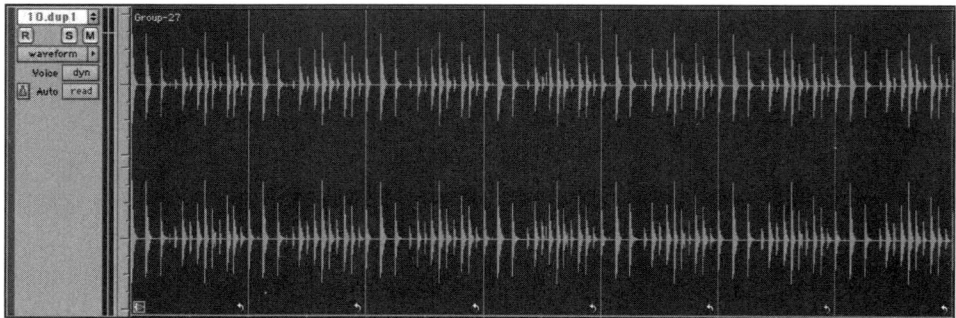

Figure 4.22

The boxed slices looped and grouped afterwards

The Great Shrinking Region Trick

I've been listening to a lot of electronic music these days, and I hear a trick in quite a few tracks. I call it the Great Shrinking Region trick, and it involves repeating a loop from 1 bar in length to a half bar to a quarter, then 1/8th, and finally 1/16th notes. It might sound like "doom-di-ba-di, doom-di doom-di, doom-doom-doom-doom, do-do, d-d-d-d-" You can do it by hand-editing or by utilizing the Separate by Grid function.

Option 1: Editing by Hand

Select the 1-bar loop in question and repeat it a few times. Determine where you want the trick to occur and start by looking at the last two loops. On the second-to-last region, separate it in half and delete the second half (be sure to use Grid mode to ensure quality cuts). Then, repeat the first half. This will give you two half-bar sections, as shown in Figure 4.23. Then duplicate one of the half sections twice more, except here, you'll separate into quarters. Delete the last three sections and repeat the first quarter section three times, as shown in Figure 4.24. Delete the last quarter, and separate the third quarter in half, making 8th notes. Repeat the first 8th note three times, as shown in Figure 4.25. Finally, delete the last 8th note and separate the first 8th note into two 16th notes. Select the first 16th note and repeat it three more times, as shown in Figure 4.26.

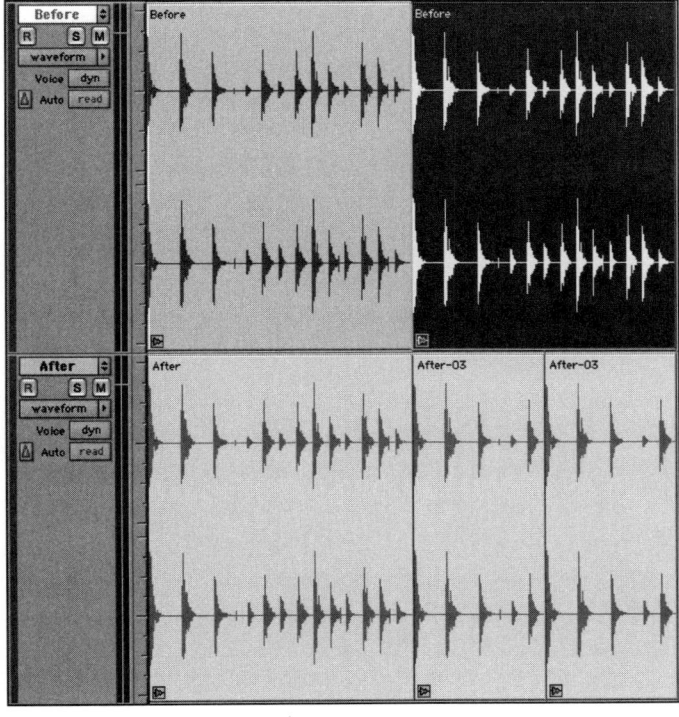

Figure 4.23

A 1-bar loop before and after editing it into half-note loops

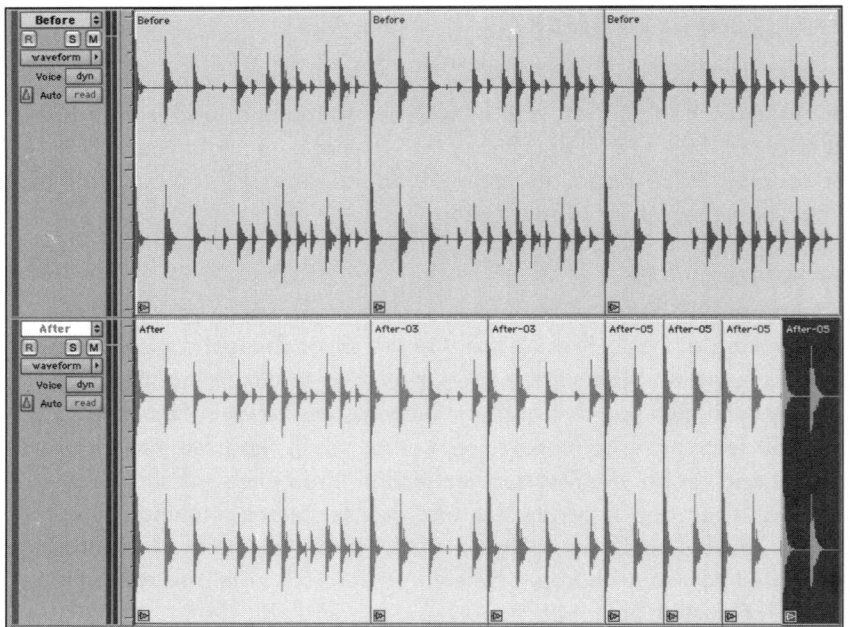

Figure 4.24

The half-bar loop separated into quarter notes and repeated

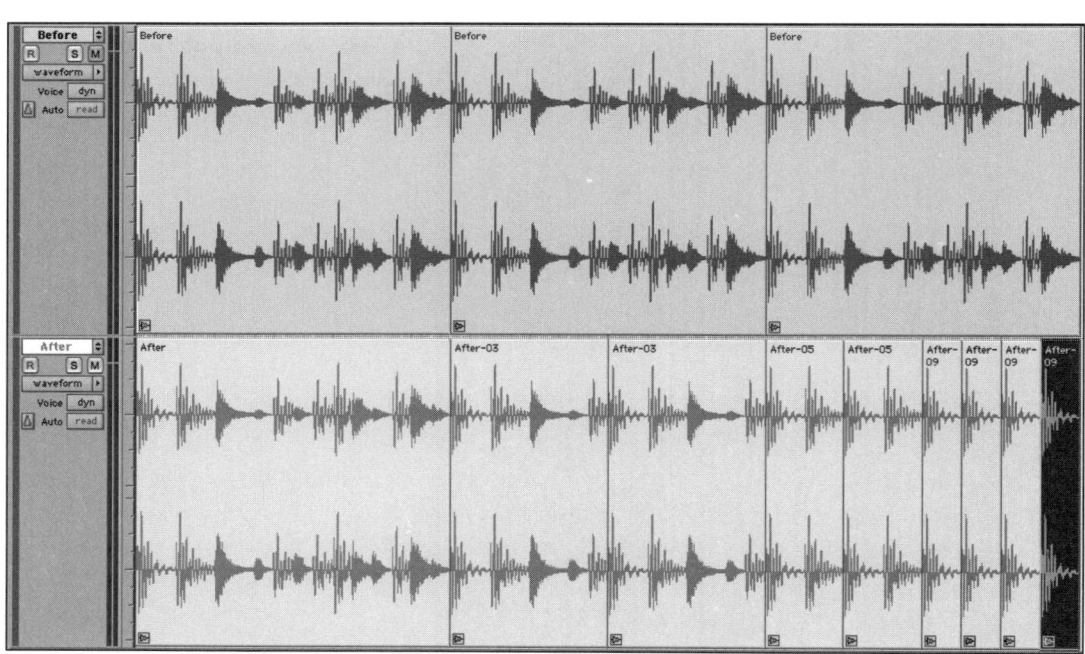

Figure 4.25

The quarter notes separated and repeated as 8th notes

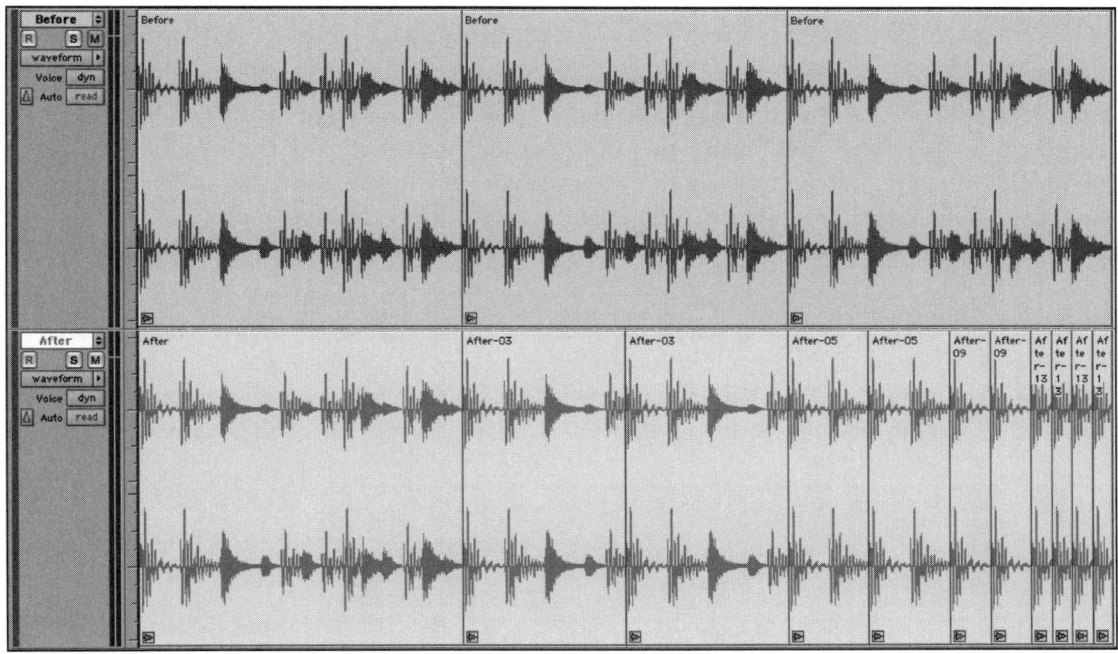

Figure 4.26

The final 8th note separated and repeated as 16th notes

Option 2: Separate on the Grid

Repeat the loop once and select the second loop. Set the grid resolution to 16th notes and
select Edit > Separate on Grid. Select the first half of the sections and create a Region Group
(CMD+OPT+G). Repeat three times, making three half-bar sections, as shown in Figure 4.24.
Select the third half bar and separate again on the grid. Select the first half again (quarter
note) and Region Group, then repeat three times. Select that last quarter note, separate on
the grid, select the first half of the regions, Region Group, and then repeat three times.
Sensing a theme here? Continue the process until the last regions are four 16th regions so
it looks just like Figure 4.26.

Locating and Selecting Loops

When the producer asks you to loop from measure 33 through 48, most operators will use the mouse and get as close as they can, creating awkward loops that require adjustments, frustrating the producer, and making things harder for themselves. You can avoid this by being in Grid mode, but this still requires some finesse and sometimes some squinting to see the screen well enough. It is fastest and most accurate to type the loop into the Start/End/Length Indicator.

Hit the / key (the division key on the number pad, or Fn+0 [zero] on laptops) to highlight the Start field in the Start/End/Length Indicator, located to the right of the Main Time Indicator, like the one in Figure 4.27. If you continue to hit the / key, you will cycle through the Start/End/Length dialog box. When the Start field is highlighted in the dialog box, use the arrows to move the selection to the right, making more accurate selection positions.

Figure 4.27

Start/End/Length
Indicator highlighted

Creating Loops on the Fly

When you want to create a loop to play or create a region, using the Start/End/Length Indicator will create a region based on the grid, but there is no guarantee that the loop will actually match the audio. To create the loop while listening, use the arrow keys during playback. Position the cursor somewhere a few seconds before the desired loop or activate pre-roll. During playback, hit the down arrow to mark the beginning of the loop (the In) and the up arrow to mark the end of the loop (the Out). You will notice that the arrows represent the loop across the Ruler as well, shown in Figure 4.28. You can adjust the In and Out to taste by dragging the blue arrows earlier or later.

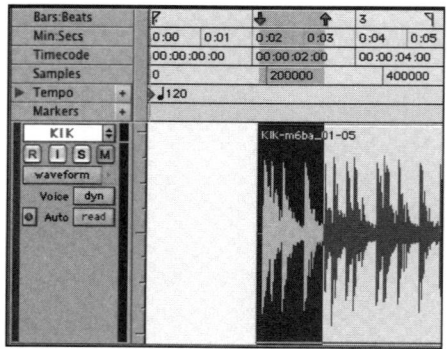

Figure 4.28

Up and down arrows indicating
the In and Out of the new selection

N o t e

Adjusting loop size will *only* update the playback if you adjust the blue arrows *during* play!

Looping Throughout the Song

When you are working with loops, it is easy to make mistakes when you are copying the loop throughout the song. A familiar comment might be something like, "The loop sounds great for the first eight bars, and then it starts to drift from the click track."

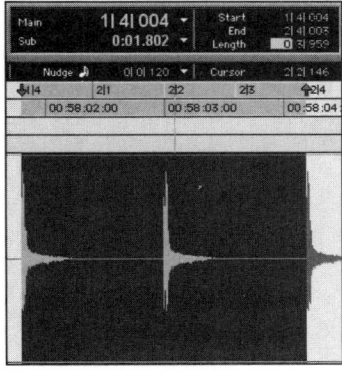

Figure 4.29

A good-sounding loop slightly off the grid

In this situation, pay attention to the Start/End/Length section across the top of the Edit window. What usually happens is that the loop is selected, sounds great, and works well with the click track while you are looping playback. However, without paying attention to the Start/End/Length section, you won't notice that the loop selected is either slightly shorter or longer than the bars needed for a clean loop, like the one in Figure 4.29.

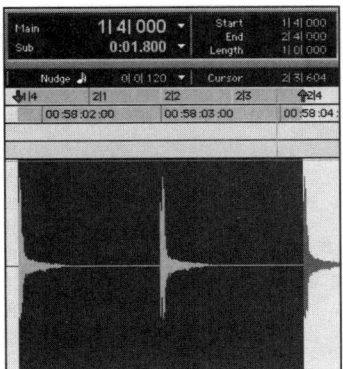

Figure 4.30

The same loop over-selected to match the grid

Before you create the loop or region, adjust the selection slightly (use Slip mode for fine adjustments) until the Length Indicator shows you an exact bar length that matches, like the one in Figure 4.30. (If you want a 2-bar loop, adjust until you read 2|0|0, and so on.) Now you can copy and paste the loop as many times as necessary, and it will fit your click track perfectly. You can use Duplicate or Repeat from the Edit menu for multiple repeats and for saving time. For situations in which the loop has no click or where the click needs to conform to the loop, see "Using Loops to Create a Tempo Map" in Chapter 5.

Loops Off the One

Creating loops that start and end on beat 1 (on the "one") is easy, but how do you deal with loops that start *before* beat 1? In Latin music, for example, the beat is usually started before beat 1 on pickup notes. For loops like this, the same rules as discussed in the previous section apply. You still need to select a loop that has a length of 2|0|0 (a 2-bar loop).

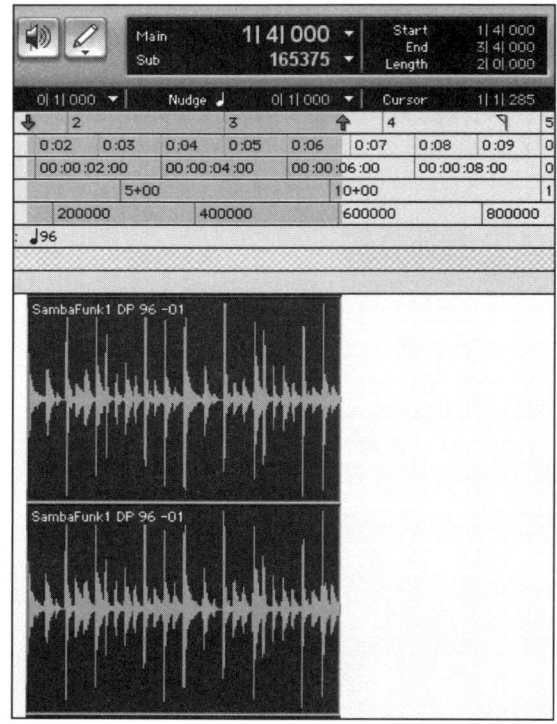

Figure 4.31

A 2-bar loop off the one

However, in this case, the loop won't start on 1|1|0; it will start at something like 1|4|000 (a quarter note early). Adjust your selection (again, using Slip mode) until both the start and end have the same 4|000 and the length is a 2|0|0 loop, like the one in Figure 4.31. You can then successfully copy (repeat) the loop, and it will fit your click. You should notice that all the copied loops will start and end with |480. For situations in which the loop has no click, see "Using Loops to Create a Tempo Map" in Chapter 5.

Relative Grid and Loops Off the One

Another way to deal with loops that don't start or end on the one is to use Relative Grid mode, shown in Figure 4.32. Select the loop (verify this in the Start/End/Length Indicator box when the length is on the bar), and then switch to Relative Grid mode. Pro Tools will then operate as if the grid is on, but it will retain the integrity of the beginning time of your loop *relative* to the grid.

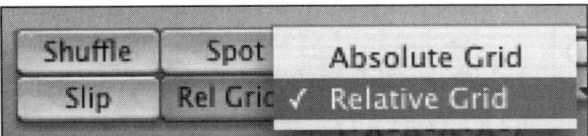

Figure 4.32

Relative Grid mode

In other words, if your loop is exactly two bars and it matches your click but starts on 4|4|234, Relative Grid mode will allow you to OPTION-drag (making a copy) the region to 5|4|234, retaining the loop relative to the grid, as shown in Figure 4.33.

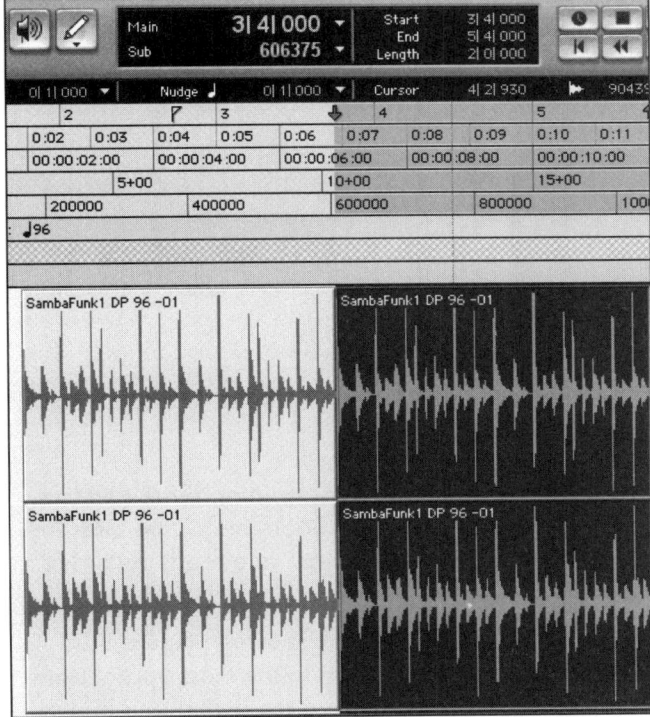

Figure 4.33

A loop drag-copied to the next location with Relative Grid mode

Sync Points and Loops Off the One

In situations in which the loop starts and ends before the one, another handy shortcut similar to Relative Grid mode is the use of Sync Points. A Sync Point is a marker placed within a region, marking a point of interest (importance) within the region. In this case, it would be the one, which occurs *after* the start of the region itself.

Position the cursor at the one and choose Edit > Create Sync Point (CMD+,). After the Sync Point is marked, you can snap the Sync Point to the "one" of the grid using the standard Grid mode (shown in Figure 4.34) and still maintain the integrity of the preceding upbeat.

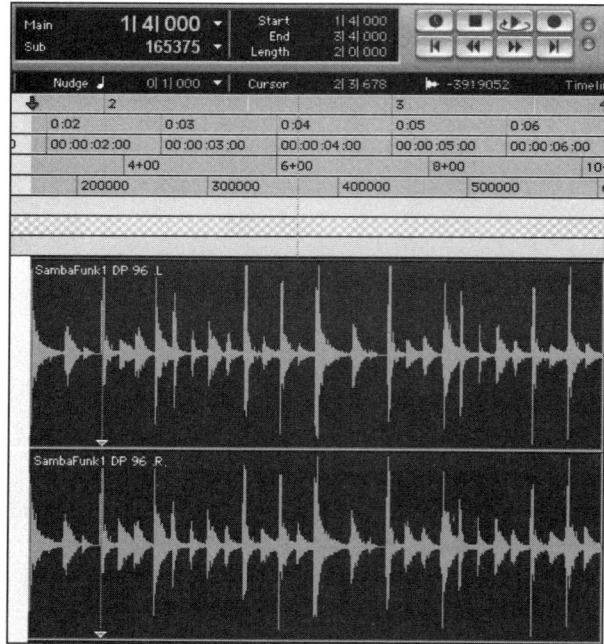

Figure 4.34

Using Sync Points to mark the one within a region

Loops and the TCE Trim Tool

Sometimes the right loop just doesn't fit. Whether you start it earlier or later, there's just no fitting it to the click and the rest of the song. You could adjust the click to match the loop (see "Using Loops to Create a Tempo Map" in Chapter 5), but what if you've already recorded parts and you can't adjust the click to the loop?

Select the loop, switch to Grid mode, and choose the TCE Trim tool, shown in Figure 4.35. Align the loop's start to the nearest bar line, and click-drag the end to the most appropriate bar line. This means that if the loop is supposed to be two bars, drag the end region boundary to the grid that represents two bars later than the start. The region will time compress (or time expand) to fit the grid, as seen in Figure 4.36. Verify that the loop is now the proper length by both listening and looking at the Start/End/Length Indicator. This method works for quick, non-critical time adjustments, but you might hear unacceptable audio artifacts. In these situations, either select a different loop or see the "Exact Beat Slicing Using the Beat Detective" section in this chapter. For other tools that perform similar functions, see Digidesign's Web site for a list of Development Partners and their respective tools.

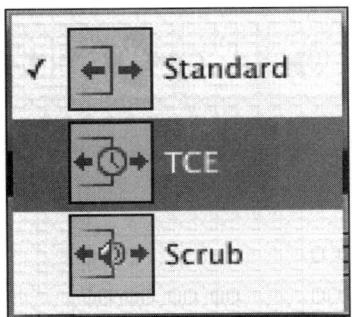

Figure 4.35

The TCE Trim tool

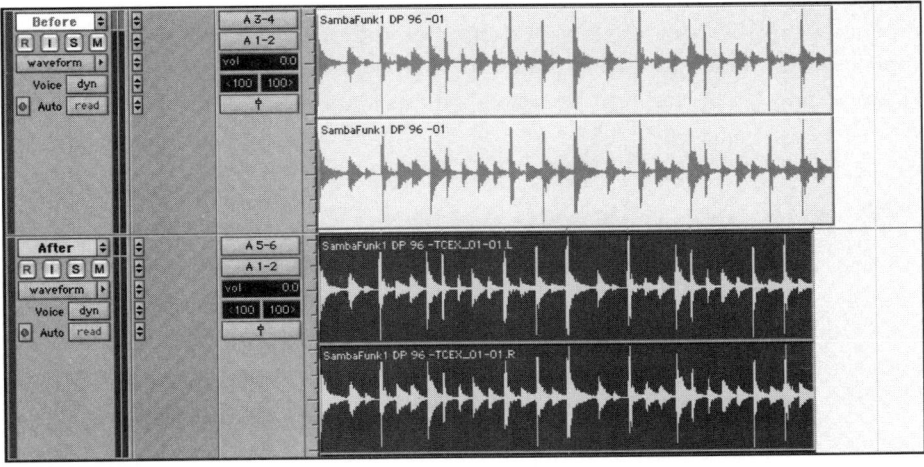

Figure 4.36

The loop before and after applying the TCE Trim tool

You can accomplish the same function by using the AudioSuite TCE tool. In this case, choose AudioSuite > Time Compression Expansion, type in the desired length, and check the Constant Pitch box. Pro Tools will stretch (or shrink) the region to fit the grid.

If the performance is great but a single hit is simply too early (or late), try the TCE tool on only the bad note. This works well for monophonic sounds, such as bass or kick drums. If the hit is early, move to Slip mode and position the cursor at the zero-crossing just before the early note. Cut there and also at the end of the note. Switch to the TCE Trim tool in Grid mode and TCE the hit to the grid. You can do the same for the last note before the early one to stretch it to fill the gap left by shrinking the early hit, shown before and after in Figure 4.37.

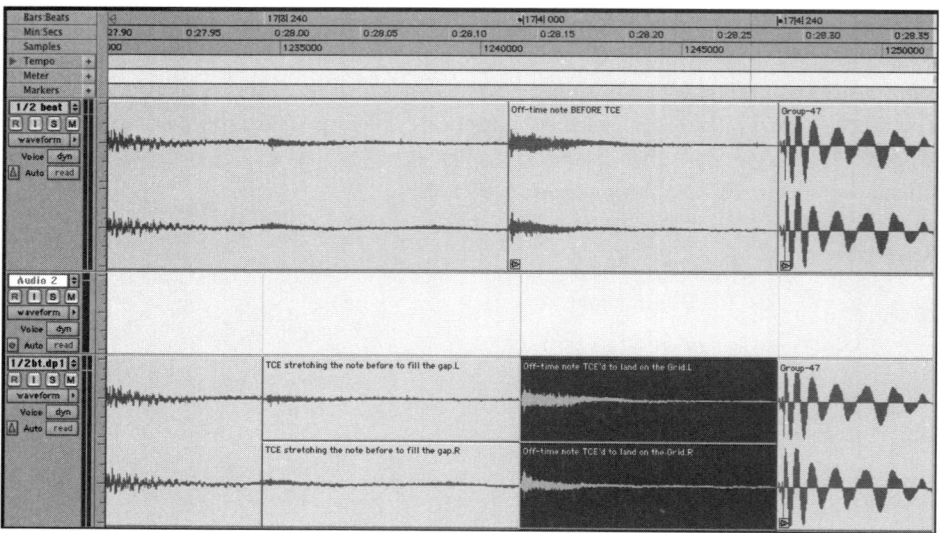

Figure 4.37

TCE tool
fixing a single
off-time note
(before
and after)

Note that this last technique only works when the sound is close to the grid, but not exactly on it. In addition, none of the TCE tool maneuvers guarantee that the stretched sound will fit the feel of the song—just that the length will fit the click. To make a loop fit the feel and the click, see "Exact Beat Slicing Using the Beat Detective" in this chapter.)

Creating Loops with the Tab-to-Transient Function

When you create loops, using the arrow keys or the Start/End/Length Indicator, or simply selecting by ear and eye, sometimes takes too long to get it exactly. When time is of the essence, activate the Tab-to-Transient function (see Figure 4.38). Tab-to-Transient seeks strong attacks (sharp volume increases, such as in drums or other percussive sounds) and positions the cursor at the nearest zero-crossing point for quick editing.

Figure 4.38

The Tab-to-Transient button

First, position the cursor slightly before the downbeat of the loop and tab the cursor to the beginning of the hit. Separate the audio by hitting CMD+E, B (assuming the Command Focus is on) or by choosing Edit > Separate Region. Then, tab continually until the cursor lands after the end of the desired loop, and separate the audio again. You have separated the region quickly based on the performance (attacks), creating a very usable loop very quickly.

Stripping Vocals

One annoying by-product of vocal recordings, either spoken or sung, is the sound of breaths between words and phrases. Most producers request the removal of these noises, and in VO sessions, it is a mandatory process. You could edit by hand, but this could take a few hours just for two hours of dialog, resulting in a high bill for the client and a mind-numbing editorial experience for you. When you are presented with a vocal requiring de-breathing, there are two ways to shave time effectively: Tab-to-Transient or Strip Silence.

The advantage to using Tab-to-Transient is the accuracy of Pro Tools' ability to find the zero-crossing points. The biggest disadvantage is Pro Tools' inability to find the breaths themselves. The system doesn't know whether the next attack is a word or a breath. In recordings in which compression was overused, this is worse. You will spend extra time auditioning envelopes to determine whether the sound is intentional or an unwanted breath.

With Strip Silence, Pro Tools allows you to set the volume parameters at which breaths and silence are determined. The four parameters let you determine what is silence and unwanted sound based on volume and time. Anything below the threshold (minimum of 48 dB) and of fitting length is removed, leaving only the regions desired. Strip Silence will show you where it interprets the noise and audio to be before actually stripping. You can sometimes visually tell whether the settings you have will work.

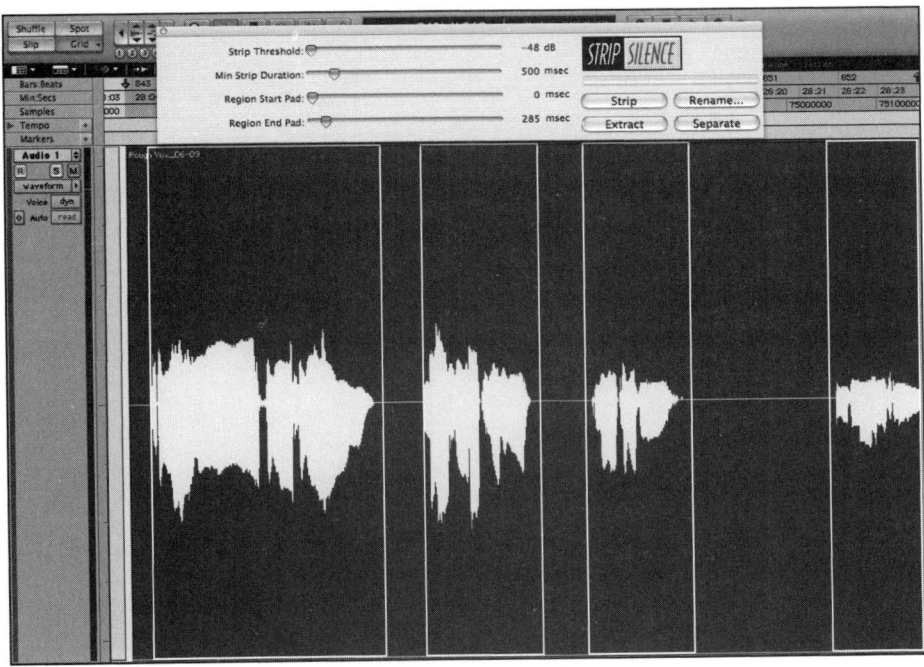

Figure 4.39

Strip Silence with preview over track

Following is some good advice when you are recording vocals for these situations:

❋ Use little compression when recording. This will help ensure that the vocal is louder than the breaths and silence, making Strip Silence more effective.

❋ If compression is requested, set the threshold and the ratio high. This will add compression to the loudest sounds without affecting the breaths of lower volume.

❋ For VO, make sure the talent is presenting the information in the most even delivery possible. This will prevent volume fluctuations that can be confused for unwanted breaths.

Assuming the vocal was recorded well, open Strip Silence by selecting Edit > Strip Silence. You'll be presented with the Strip Silence window. In order, slide the threshold upward until you start to see the potential cuts show up over the wave, as seen in Figure 4.39. I suggest you separate one breath first so you can see how appropriate the settings are on the breaths. When the volume looks appropriate, set the length until the tiny slivers of silence between the words are no longer set to separated. Then, adjust the Start and End pads until Strip Silence adjusts the beginning and end cut points to accommodate for extra audio at the ends of the region.

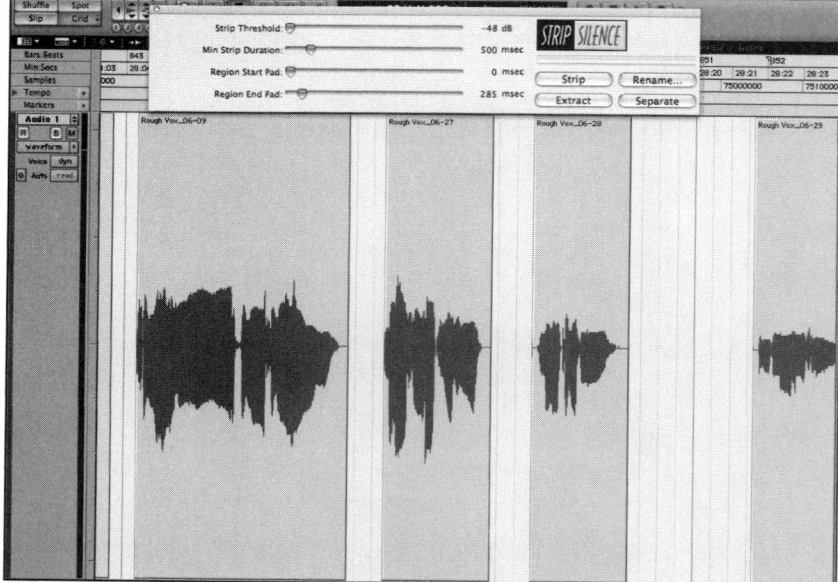

Figure 4.40

After Strip Silence

The biggest disadvantage to Strip Silence is that the settings for one breath might not work for all the breaths. Although 80 to 90 percent of the breaths will work well (saving you time you would have spent tabbing through the breaths), you will need to perform a QC test and listen to each edit to ensure the quality of the strip, then repeat the process until all the breaths are gone, as in Figure 4.40. If the edit is abrupt, use the Standard Trim tool to extend or retract the region to better quality.

Crisper Words

Suppose a VO recording was perfectly recorded, stripped, and all edits were cleaned. Then, the producer noticed that some words were missing the final, punctuating syllable needed for proper intelligibility. Situations like this are usually discovered about two minutes after the talent has left for that flight to New Zealand.

In these situations, it is possible and even encouraged to perform some micro-edits to help the situation. If the last syllable is a T, for example, yet it sounds like a D, you can edit a T from a crisper performance and paste it onto the end of the softer syllable. Find the best T, P, S, and K, and keep them as stored regions in the Region List. Be sure to capture the regions and *not* separate them. When the syllable is required, simply drag it onto the appropriate word to fix the performance, as shown in Figure 4.41. You might need to find short versions for words in the middle of the read and long versions for the close of the word.

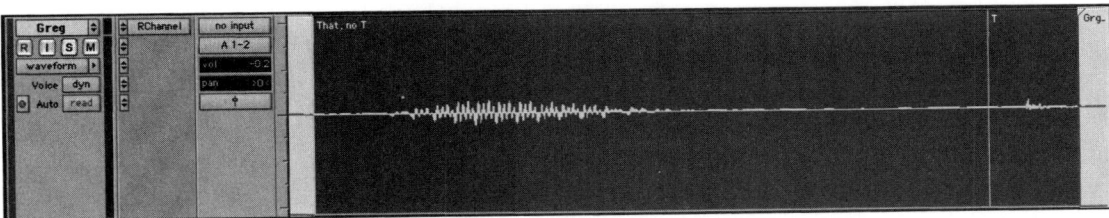

Figure 4.41
Micro-editing the punctuation of the word at the end

Adding and Fixing Syllables (Words) That Don't Fit

In VO situations in which the words aren't recorded or pronounced properly, you can sometimes edit ending syllables or even complete words (such as "and," "but," "or," and so on) from other words and fix the performances. However, in some situations, the syllable can only be found on words that were pronounced with different intensities and speeds.

For this pronunciation plastic surgery, following are three tools that can help smooth over the graft-edit.

✳ **Pitch Shift.** Often the replacement syllable will come from a word said with much greater (or less) intensity than the desired one. Most times, a simple pitch shift will allow the editor to adjust the pitch and format of the replacement syllable to fit it into place. Use the AudioSuite Pitch Shift (in Figure 4.42) because it gives you the ability to audition the tone to see whether your settings will make the sound work.

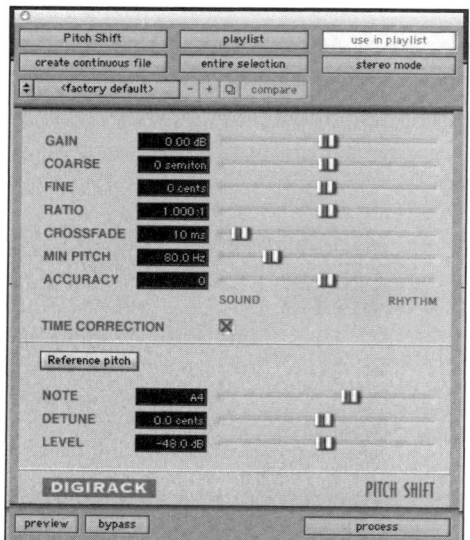

Figure 4.42

AudioSuite Pitch Shift window

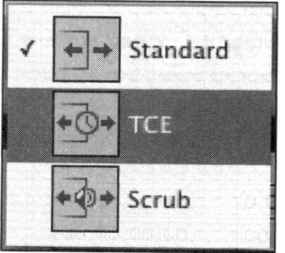

Figure 4.43

The TCE Trim tool

❋ **Time stretch.** In other situations, the intensity fits but the pace does not. For these situations, try time stretching (or compressing) the syllable so it fits the pacing of the overall delivery. Although the TCE Trim tool (see Figure 4.43) in Pro Tools can produce unwanted artifacts, it might be perfectly acceptable for small syllables or words.

❋ **Crossfade.** You already know the crossfade can smooth over awkward edits and can be particularly useful in this micro-grafting of language. For syllables that are grafted onto the ends of words, try using a very short crossfade at the head of the edit with a very sharp slope, as seen in Figure 4.44. This will trick the ear into thinking that the two were pronounced more naturally together than a long crossfade with a shallow slope will.

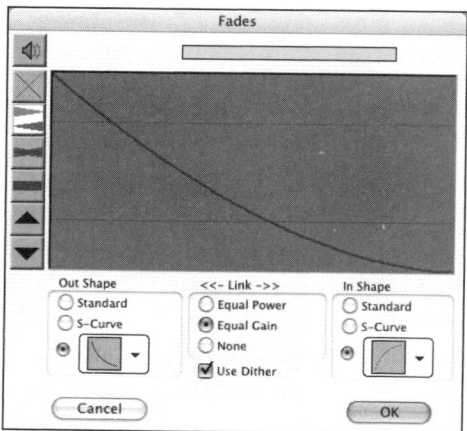

Figure 4.44

Crossfade window with custom slopes

Room Tone Fixes

Although most VO is recorded in quiet rooms, location recordings almost never have good, dry vocal sound. When you are editing these parts later, there might be awkward gaps when the talking stops and the room sound dies, as seen in Figure 4.45, leaving the track unnaturally dry. Generally, the recordist will capture 30 seconds of room tone, which is the ambience of the room without anyone making noise.

When you attempt to edit dialogue recorded in the field, keep the room tone handy on a nearby track. When you perform an edit that needs filling with room tone, measure the length of the "hole" and cut that length of time from the room tone. (Refer to the Start/End/Length Indicator to tell you whether you have enough.) Paste it to fit the hole, and trim out the ends to taste. A crossfade usually smoothes this edit to a natural delivery, as shown in Figure 4.46. Be sure to capture room tone from the middle of the file because you will need some handles from which to trim!

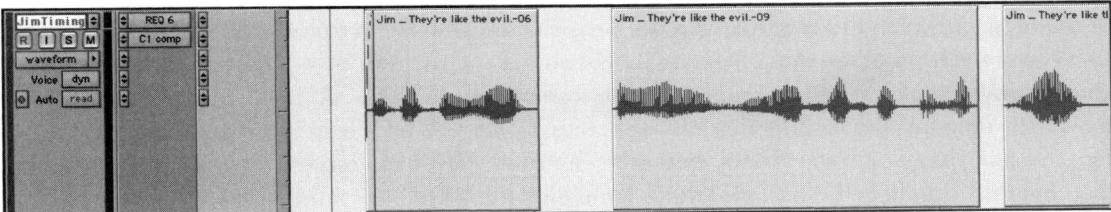

Figure 4.45

VO edited with gap in room tone

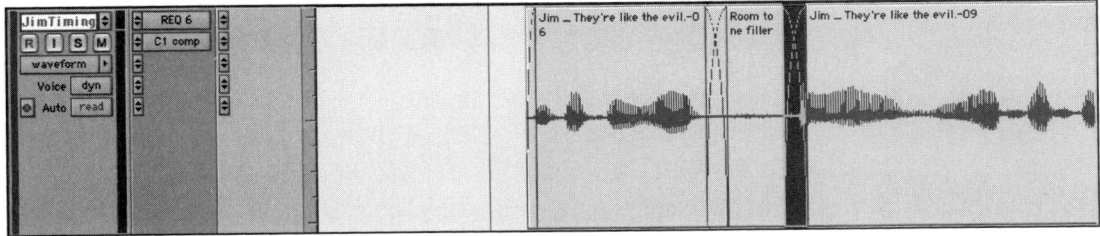

Figure 4.46

Grafted and crossfaded room tone

Another way is to loop the room tone throughout the track, ignoring the holes, as shown in Figure 4.47. Although this works technically, keep in mind that you now have twice the energy of the room tone throughout the track—once on the room tone track and once throughout the VO while speaking. This can make your overall mix noisy, but sometimes if time is really short, you can get away with it.

Also be careful of the loop points of the room tone. Even though room tone has no distinctive sounds within it, the loop points might be very noticeable if left exposed. Verify that the tone loops well before you commit to this technique.

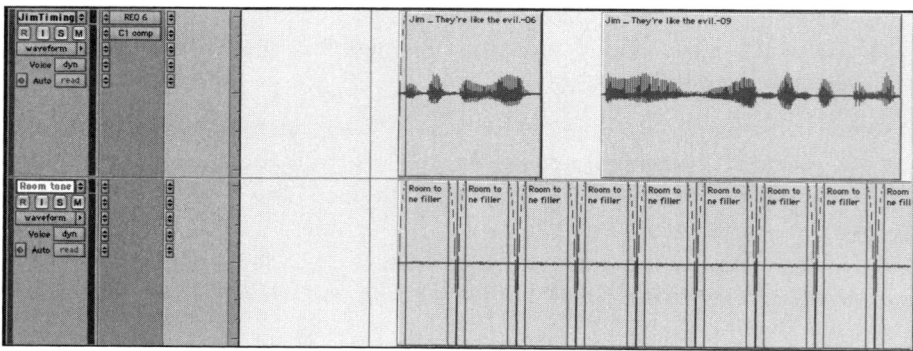

Figure 4.47

Room tone track with looped tone region

In situations in which the recorder did not provide you with room tome, you might need to edit small sections from other short silences (between the words) and paste them to fit. These, of course, never really fit. What used to be the standard and is now simply a cool trick is taking the short region of the room tone and repeating it until you fill the space. You might notice that the edits are audible, cyclical, and unacceptable. Move the regions over each other until they overlap significantly, and crossfade them until the edits blur. If they are still noticeable, try reversing some of the room tones, and crossfade those together until they are gone, shown in Figure 4.48.

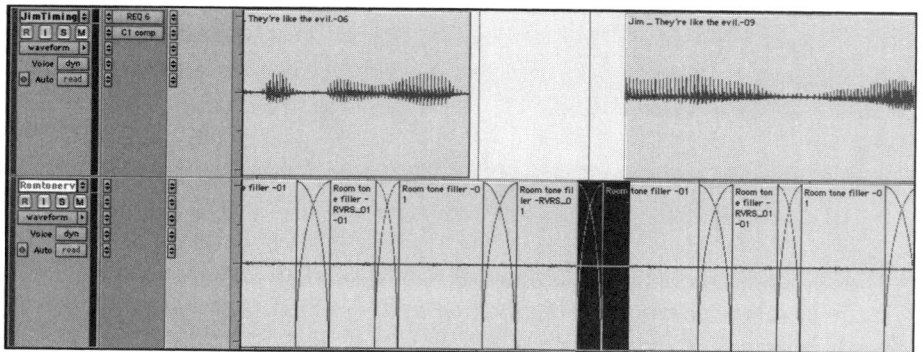

Figure 4.48

Tiny room regions reversed and crossfaded

Of course, the easiest way to do it (now you tell me!) is to copy the track, select the dialog on the copy, and remove the room tone from the dialog through Strip Silence. Since Strip Silence now can extract the noise and remove the dialog, simply set the faders as you like and click the Extract button. For more on how to set the faders in Strip Silence, see "Stripping Vocals" earlier in this chapter.

Lyrics in the Regions (Ken Walden)

Ken Walden was the product specialist for Digidesign for seven years. He had a bird's-eye view of Pro Tools during its greatest era of expansion, and he now runs a company called Secrets of the Pros, producing DVDs that showcase some of the best tips he's culled over the years. He shared with me one of his favorite little-known nuggets of wisdom for music sessions in Pro Tools—lyrics tracks.

Unfortunately, there is no method of adding lyrics to a Pro Tools session to keep track of where each vocal line exists. However, here are some cool techniques for creating your own lyric sheets within the song.

Version 1

1. Section the main Vocal track into regions matching certain lines or phrases.

2. Name each region with the lyric of the section or a phrase that tells you what is being sung, as shown in Figure 4.49.

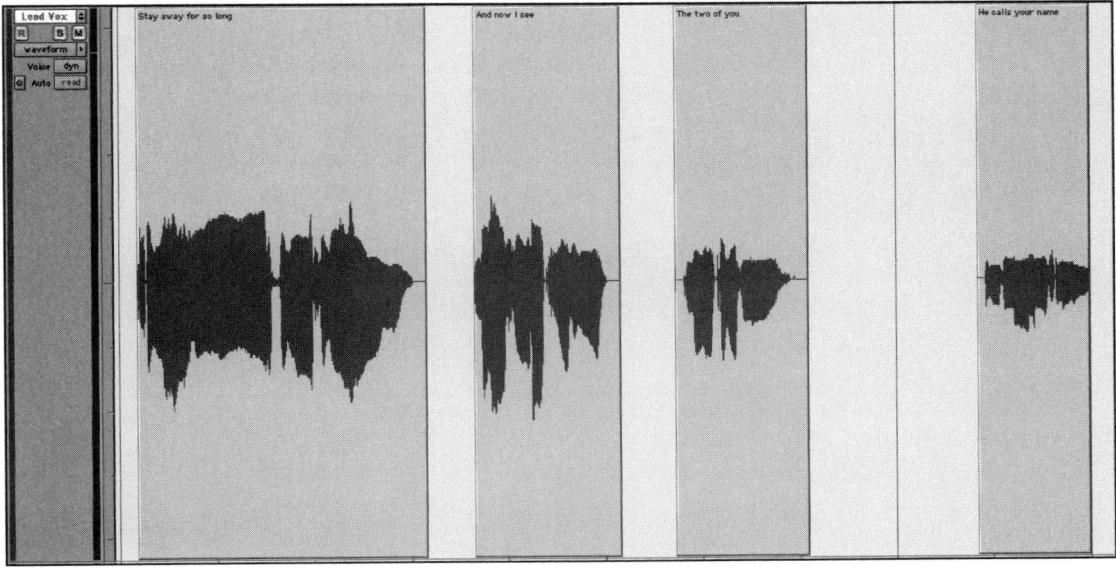

Figure 4.49

Lyrics named onto the regions of the lead vocal

Version 2

1. Create an Audio track either above or below the main Vocal track.

2. Listen to the vocals and create regions on the Lead Vocal track in a fashion that works for the song, either line by line or section by section.

3. Select the region corresponding to the first phrase, and move the selection down (or up) to the new Audio track.

4. Hold SHIFT+OPTION+3 (consolidate selection) to create regions of empty space that match the regions created on the Lead Vocal track.

5. Name the empty region with the lyrics of the section, as shown in Figure 4.50.

6. Repeat throughout the song.

7. Choose Edit > Heal Separation while highlighting the original Lead Vocal track to reconnect the regions if desired.

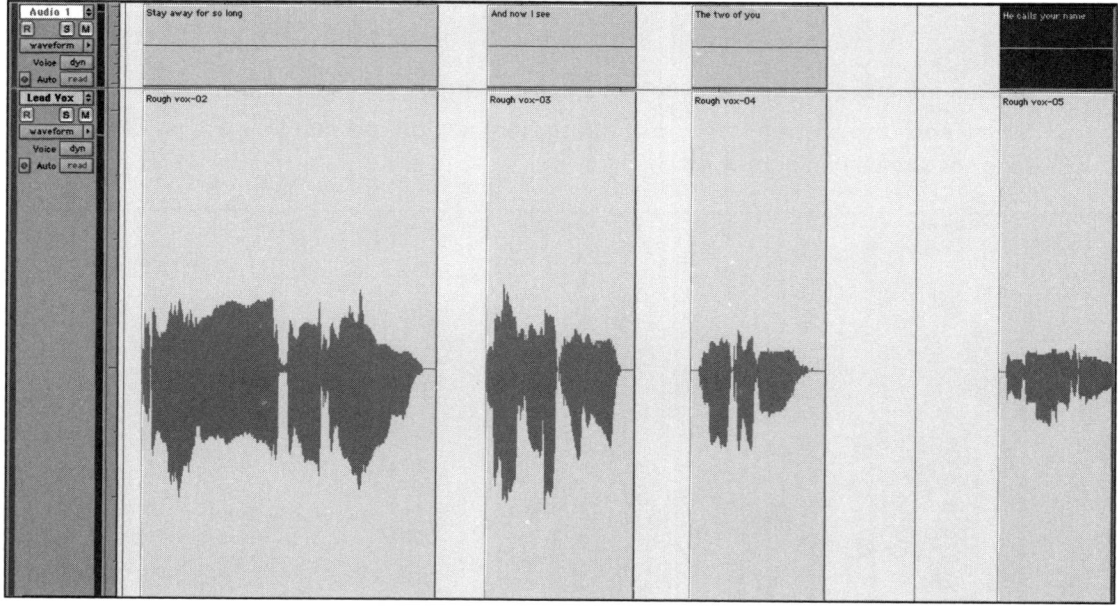

Figure 4.50

Lyrics named on empty spaces above the Lead Vocal track

Version 3

1. Create a new MIDI track either above or below the main Vocal track.

2. Listen to the vocals and create regions in a fashion that works for the song, either line by line or section by section.

3. Select the region corresponding to the first phrase, and move the selection down (or up) to the new Audio track.

4. View the track as notes and pencil-draw a single note for the length of this selection.

5. Switch the track to Regions view. You should see regions that match the lyric regions from your main Vocal track.

6. Name the empty region with the lyrics of the selection, as shown in Figure 4.51.

7. Repeat throughout the song.

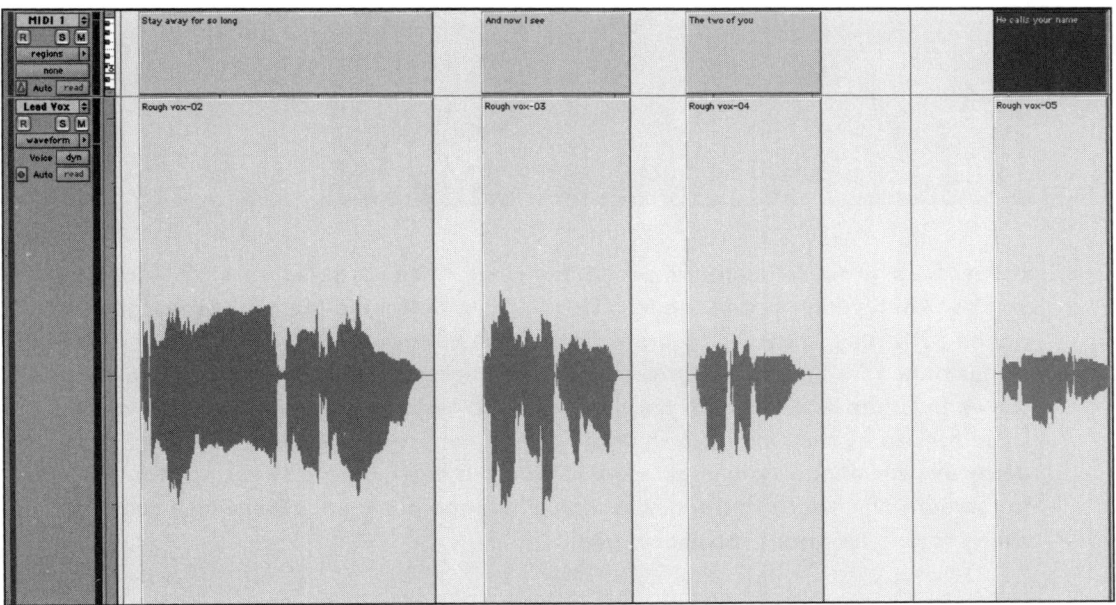

Figure 4.51

MIDI track with lyrics in the regions

Switching between Multiple Takes

The take is done and it's perfect, but *now* your artist wants to redo it in three new ways. This is standard operating procedure for most vocalists. Following are a few ways to handle the request without going crazy.

1. Create three or more new Audio tracks, and mute the ones that you are *not* working with. You should name them Intense Vocal or Softer Vocal to match the style of delivery, as seen in Figure 4.52. This will use three other voices as well, which might be a problem if you are close to or at your voice limitation. You can immediately switch between takes by muting and unmuting the tracks you want to switch from and to, respectively. You also will need to recreate any inserts and sends to match the tone between takes, which might be overly taxing for your processor.

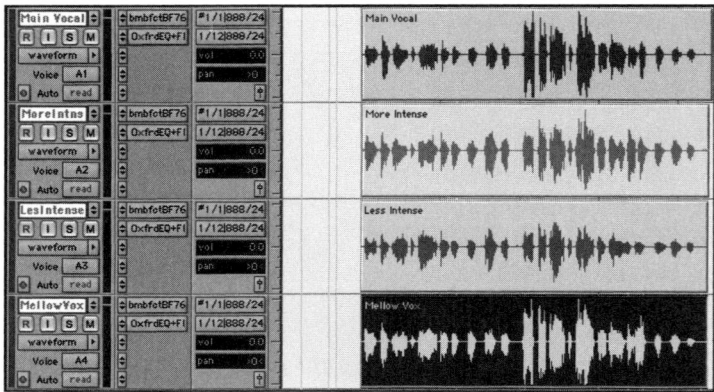

Figure 4.52

Four tracks with four setups and voices

2. Follow Step 1, but set all four tracks to the same voice, as in Figure 4.53. That way, you can keep your voice usage to a single voice. Select the Mute Frees Assigned Voice option (HD only; shown in Figure 4.54) to switch between the four tracks quickly. (If this option isn't available, you will need to choose the Track > Make Inactive option, shown in Figure 4.55, to hear the next track.) When you mute one track, its voice is freed for use by the next track in priority (the one directly below it). There might be a delay in switching, so you might want to stop playback before switching. You will need to recreate any inserts and sends to match the tone between takes, which might be overly taxing for your processor as well.

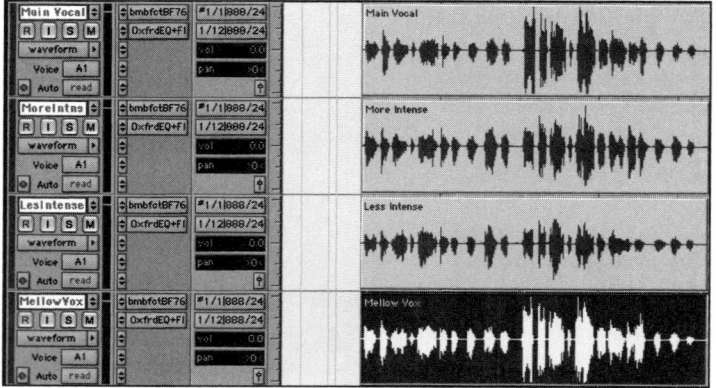

Figure 4.53

Four tracks with the same voices

3. Create a separate playlist for each take by clicking on the Playlist tab, just to the right of the Channel Select. Name each playlist Vocal Soft or Vocal Intense so that when PT shortens the name, it still starts with VOC. You can switch between tracks by switching playlists, as shown in Figure 4.56, but you might also experience a slight delay in switching. You should stop playback before switching to avoid this. However, all playlists will retain the insert chain and send chain so they sound the same without using up extra processing.

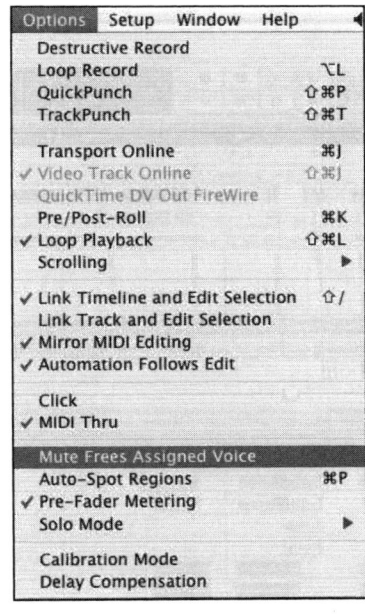

Figure 4.54

The Options > Mute Frees Assigned Voice option

Figure 4.55

The Track > Make Inactive option

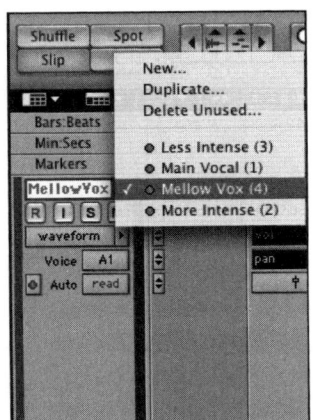

Figure 4.56

List of vocal playlists

Composite Edits with Multiple Takes (Comping Tracks)

When recording and punching-in, or when performing multiple takes, you will eventually be presented with the task of compiling (compositing) the various good sections into one master take. Depending on the technique of your takes, you will want to proceed differently for each method. In this section, you'll take a look at the different methods and some good techniques for each.

Multiple Tracks and Voices

1. When you have multiple tracks, you should start with the best overall track and delete any regions that aren't good. When you are finished, you will be left with holes that require recorded parts from other takes, as shown in Figure 4.57.

2. Move this track to the top of the multiple takes and mute the others.

3. Put the cursor at the beginning of the first hole and SHIFT+Tab to the end, selecting the entire hole.

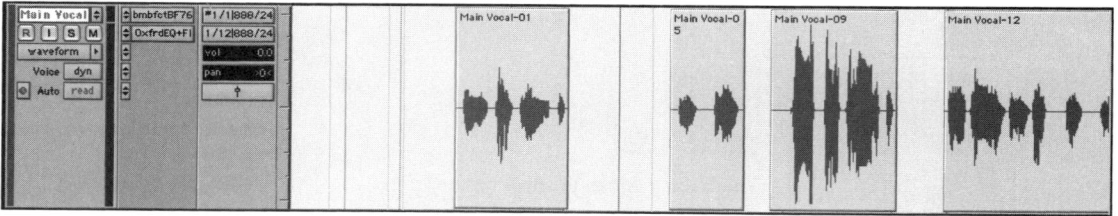

Figure 4.57

A great take with sections missing

4. Move the selection to the next track, highlighting the same length of time on the second take. If the waveform looks like the start and end are not lining up properly (perhaps the talent came in early or went too long on that take), then move on to the next available track.

5. After you find a selection that looks like it fits, I recommend you use the Separation Grabber to pull this region onto the first track, filling the space. (You can hold the OPTION key to leave the take intact and drag a copy to the hole.) You can also perform a reverse edit. Remove the audio that matches the "keeper" audio from the first track, leaving the possible sections to fill the holes on Track 2, as shown in Figure 4.58, *then* drag them into position on the "keeper" track.

6. Activate both pre- and post-roll (one or two bars), and then audition the comp. If it works, then move to the next bad section and repeat these steps. When you are finished, you should have composited all the good sections into one master take.

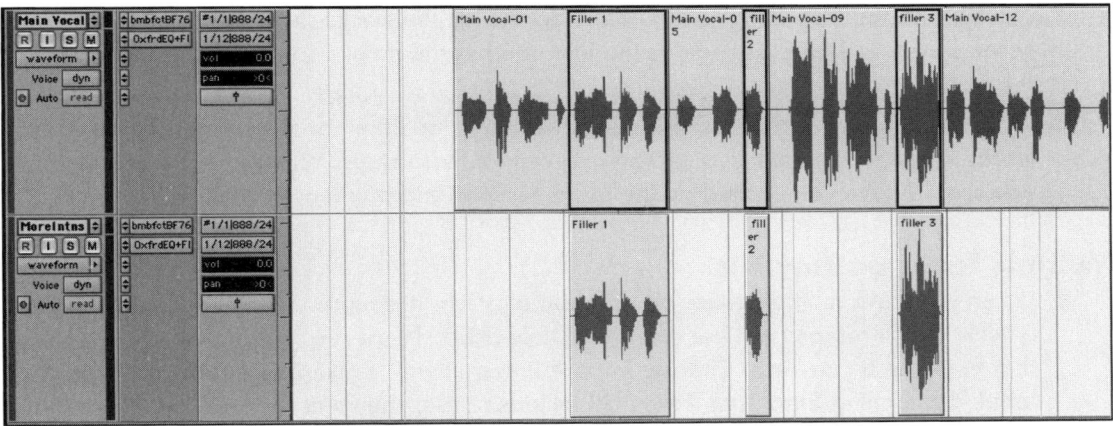

Figure 4.58

Sections taken from second take

Multiple Tracks with the Same Voice

1. Put the track with the best overall take at the top of the multiple takes and cut holes for the bad sections, as seen in Figure 4.59.

2. Because the first hole is the first section that requires replacing, the beginnings of all other takes are unnecessary. I suggest cropping them all (SHIFT-click on the Standard Trim tool) so they all start at the beginning of the first hole. With Command Focus active, you can hit A to trim them to the cursor location, which should be the beginning of the first hole. Do this by putting the cursor at the beginning of the first hole and moving down each track. Press OPTION+SHIFT+Tab to select to the beginning of that take, and then delete it.

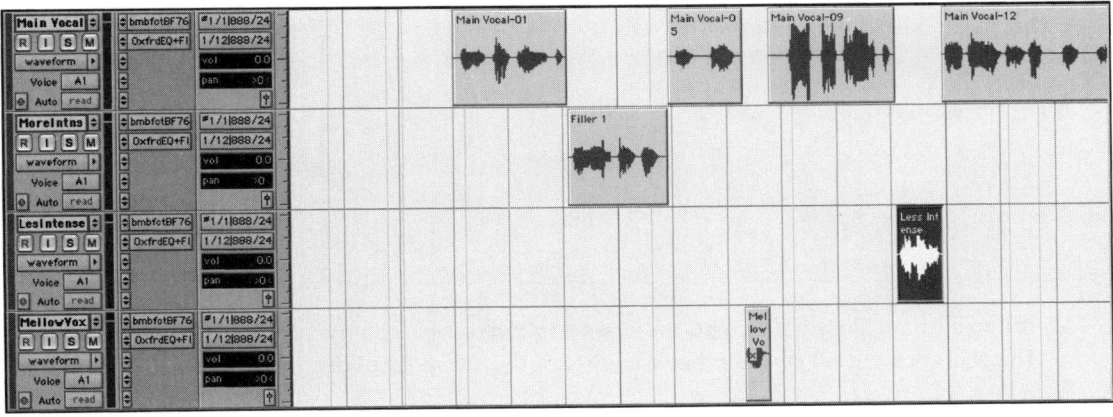

Figure 4.59

Multiple takes with good sections trimmed out on the same voice

3. Tab back to the beginning of the hole. Because all the tracks share the same voice, the second track will play as soon as the first one hits the hole, allowing you to audition the comp.

4. Activate both pre- and post-roll (one or two bars), and then audition the comp. If it works, move to the next bad section and repeat these steps. When you are finished, you should have composited all the good sections into one master take.

Multiple Takes on Playlists

1. When you have multiple takes on different playlists, it is more difficult to determine quickly which regions will become good hole-fillers. There is a handy preference setting that might help you here. Choose Setup > Preferences > Editing, and look at the section labeled Matching Start Time Takes List Includes area, shown in Figure 4.60. There, you can activate the Separate Region Operates On All Related Tracks check box.

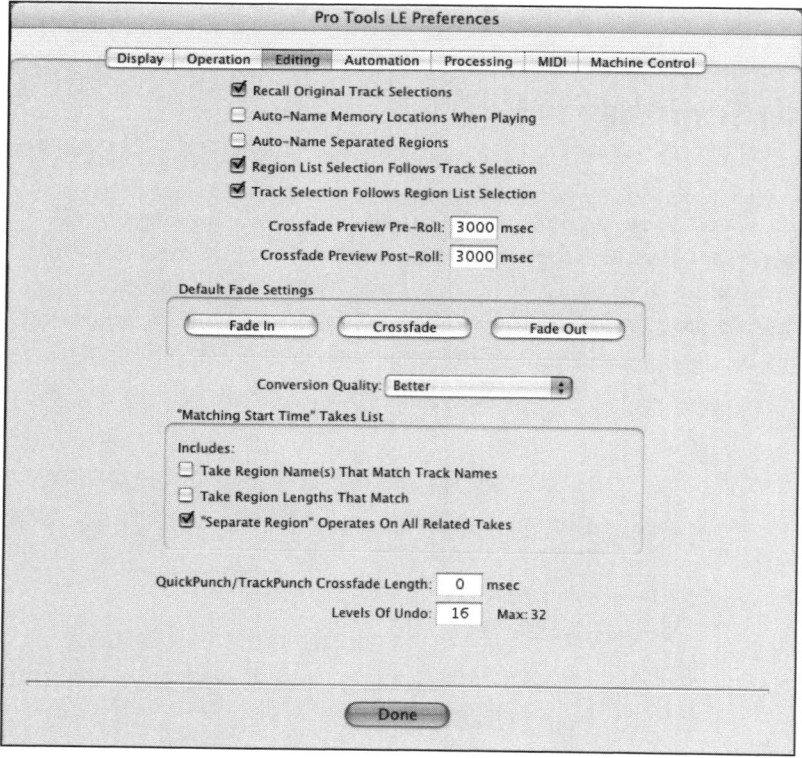

Figure 4.60

The Separate Region Operates On All Related Tracks check box

2. Instead of creating holes, you only need to make separations at the points of the holes. This will also cut all of the other playlists at the same location.

3. Delete the first bad section, creating your first hole.

4. SHIFT+Tab from the beginning of the hole to the end, selecting the hole itself, as shown in Figure 4.61.

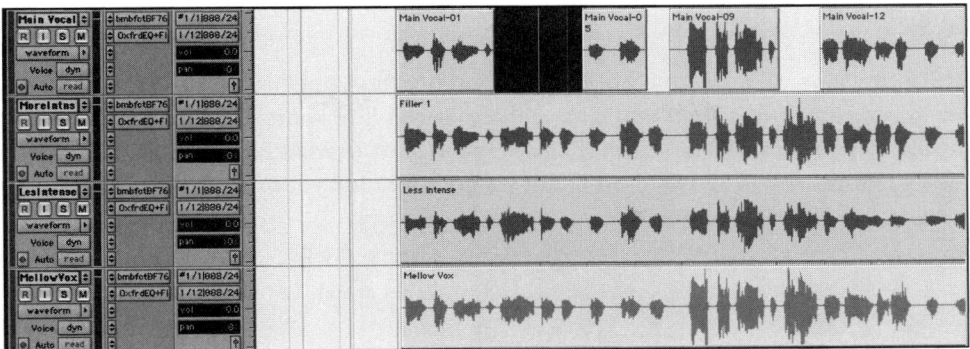

Figure 4.61

Removed section highlighted

5. Switch to the first playlist, and copy the audio in the same selection time as the hole, as seen in Figure 4.62. If the waveform looks like the start and end are not lining up properly (perhaps the talent came in early or went too long on that take), then move on to the next available track and copy and past it into place.

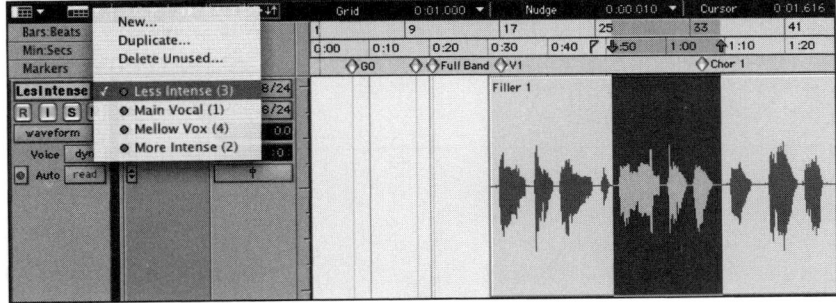

Figure 4.62

Same highlighted section on second playlist

6. Activate both pre- and post-roll (one or two bars), and then audition the comp. If it works, then move to the next bad section and repeat these steps. When you are finished, you should have composited all the good sections into one master take, as shown in Figure 4.63.

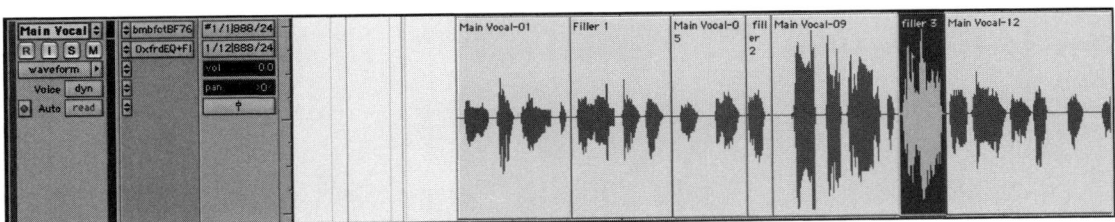

Figure 4.63

Comped track from multiple playlists

Zoom Presets: Edit Window

Because you probably spend more time zooming in and out than anything else, the ability to jump right to a zoom setting can save you a lot of time. In the Edit window, five zoom presets are user-definable to your favorite horizontal zoom settings, as seen in Figure 4.64. Although there are already five presets, you will most likely set up a few for your favorite settings.

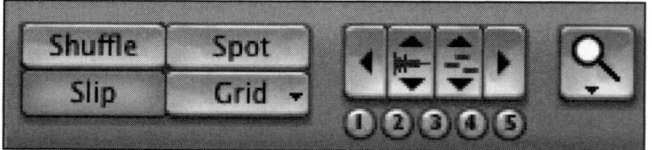

Figure 4.64

Zoom presets

For example, you might want to set up Preset 1 to be the length of the full song, whereas Preset 5 might be set to the sample level for detailed zero-crossing edits. I recommend you start with a small, medium, and large approach (shown in Figure 4.65), with the small being the sample level (Preset 5), the large being the full song (Preset 1), and the medium somewhere in between (Preset 3). To set the presets, zoom in to the level desired, and then CMD-click the zoom preset number. After the zoom is set, you can save time by simply hitting the zoom preset of choice or using the key command, such as CTRL+1, CTRL+2, and so on to CTRL+5.

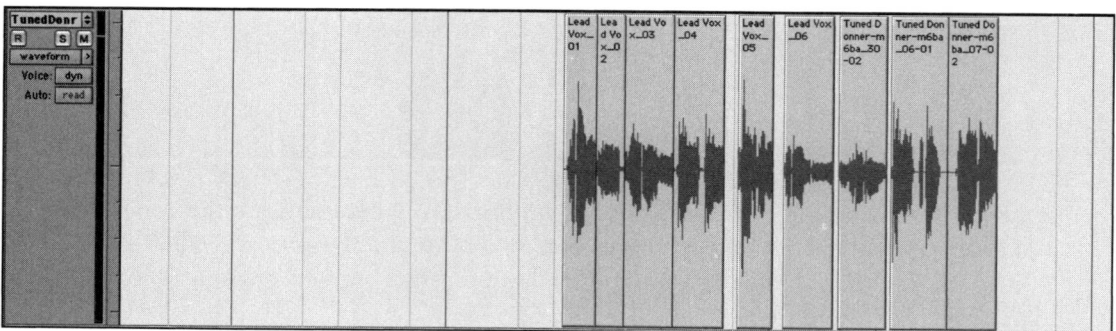

Figure 4.65

Three shots of three preset zooms

Zoom Presets: Memory Locations

Because Pro Tools gives you 999 (200 in v6x and earlier) memory locations, you might as well use them. A lot of Pro Tools engineers use the first 10 or so memory locations for the first 10 or so sections of a piece, but nothing beyond that. Because memory locations can store zoom presets and track heights, try using them as zoom presets.

After you've marked the first 10 or so memory locations, you can continue to create dummy ones until your next memory location is number 21 (or the nearest number that's easy to remember). Remember to set them to None (*not* Markers) to ensure that the Markers Ruler doesn't get crowded with dummies, as shown in Figure 4.66. Set the cursor to the location of the first memory location (probably the song start). *Before* you create memory location 21, set the track heights to mini and the zoom setting to fill the screen with all the tracks, then position the cursor at the beginning of the song. Call this All Full, as shown in Figure 4.67. Now create memory location 21 and use the following settings: None (not Marker), Track Heights, and Zoom Settings. Now whenever you recall memory location 21, you will return to All Full.

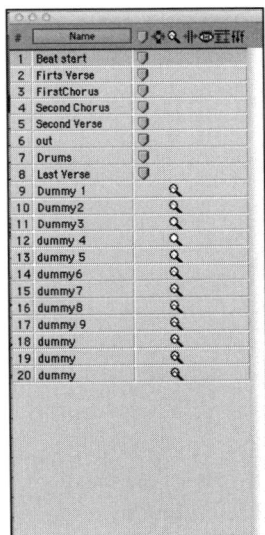

Figure 4.66

Dummy markers up to number 21

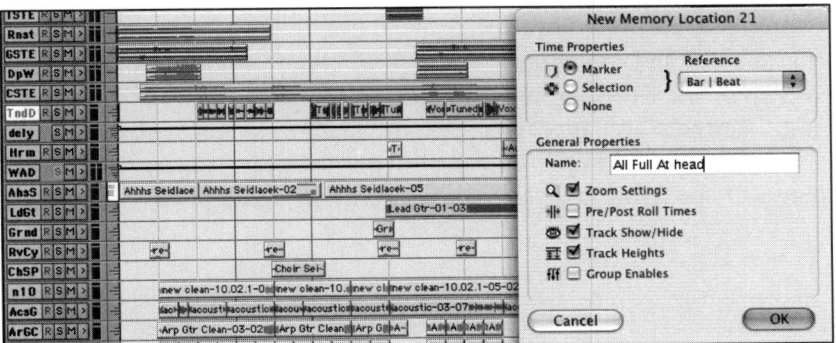

Figure 4.67

Twenty memory locations, with number 21 called All Full

Repeat this process with various tracks set to track heights at different settings. For example, you could make number 22 All Full with the Lead Vocal track set to large (see Figure 4.68), and number 23 with the drums all set to medium, and so on. Once you've filled the 20s, you can do similar functions with the 30s. For example, you could make the 20s All Full at the different song locations (21 at Marker 1, 22 at Marker 2, and so on), and then use the 30s to do the same with the Lead Vocal track set to large (31 at Marker 1 with lead vox large, 32 at Marker 2 with lead vox large, and so on).

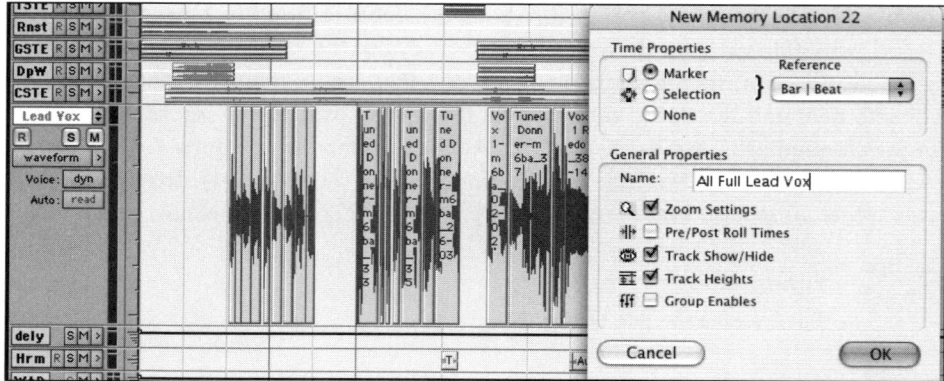

Figure 4.68
Memory location 22 All Full at Marker 1 with Lead Vocal set to large

Lift-Cuts with the Separation Grabber (TDM Only)

A very common move is to select a word from one performance (or phrase, note, and so on) and copy it to another location to fix the second occurrence. Normally, you would simply select the part, copy it, move it to the new location, and paste it in (four moves). Perhaps you'd select the region, use the Capture Region or Separate Region function, name it, and then move to the new location and drag the region to the location from the Region List, adjusting it into place (six moves).

The fastest way to do this is to select the region, and then OPTION-drag the region to its new location (two moves). The Separation Grabber, seen in Figure 4.69, allows you to lift-cut any selection without having to go through the Separate Region or Capture Region commands. The OPTION key tells Pro Tools to copy the region, leaving the part intact in its current location. An OPTION-dragged region with the Separation Grabber is shown in Figure 4.70. This method is very fast.

Figure 4.69

The Separation Grabber

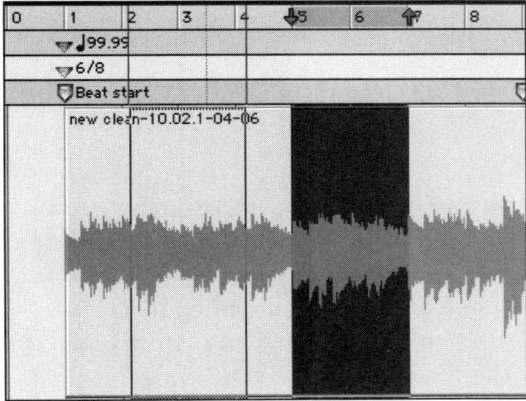

Figure 4.70

Separation Grabber lift-cut (and copy) to a new location

Finding Your Way through the Universe (TDM)

In extremely long sections, the process of finding sections without knowing the time location is a big waste of time. It would be easy to find the love scene if you knew it happened at 01:27:24.05, but without that information, you'd just have to guess or scroll until something looked familiar. Both processes can waste serious time.

One method around this is by using the Universe window (TDM only; see Figure 4.71). The Universe window provides a graphical representation of the entire session, laid out horizontally with all tracks shown. If you are looking for a section of a movie that is obvious (such as the love scene), it might be noticeable by the section with only one track active—the music. You can simply click on that position in the Universe window, and Pro Tools will locate the section. You should, of course, have markers set for these scenes, but that's another matter.

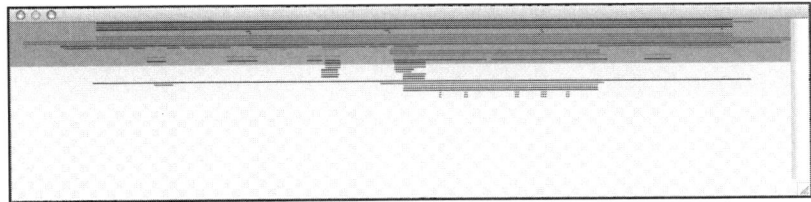

Figure 4.71

The Universe window

Moving Around Quickly

Most of us find ourselves grabbing the blue locator along the bottom and right (vertical) side of Pro Tools to drag the screen up and down and left to right, searching for various sections and regions. The faster way to scroll around the screen is to use handy key commands. To navigate up and down (bank selecting vertically), press the Page Up and Page Down keys on the keyboard. OPTION+Page Up (and Page Down) will navigate the screen left and right, making track searches and time searches much faster.

Where Did My Cursor Go?

Some people like to work with screen scrolling active during playback, others prefer it to be active after playback (options shown in Figure 4.72), and some simply turn it off. I can't stand either active scroll, but my partner can't seem to work without one of the two active. It drives me crazy. If I start to work on the system after he's been on it, I hit Play and listen to the piece, and then hit Stop when I hear the first problem. The screen then jumps to the stopped location, and I lose the cursor on the screen. AAARRRRGGHHH!

Figure 4.72

Scrolling After Playback active

In this situation, the Main Time Indicator tells you that the cursor is at the beginning of playback (not necessarily the beginning of the song or session), but it isn't in the screen view. If you have a selection, then pressing Return or typing a location in the Main Time Indicator will cause you to lose that selection. Dragging the blue bar around is annoying, and OPTION+Page Up/Down might not be exact enough for you.

You will notice in these situations (and in any situation in which the cursor is outside of the visual field) that there is a small blue arrow in the top-right (or top-left) corner of the Ruler, indicating where the cursor is, as seen in Figure 4.73. This will at least tell you in which direction to scroll to find it, but that is not enough. When the cursor is off the field and you want to bring it to the beginning of the screen *without* losing any selections, hit the left arrow on the keyboard. This will bring the cursor into view and maintain the selection...even if someone left scrolling on before you got there!

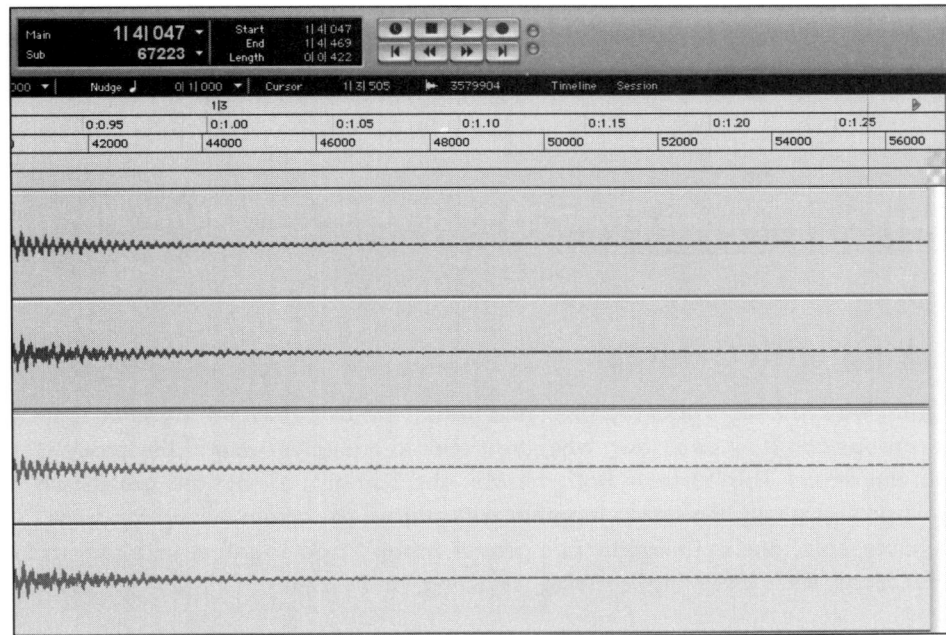

Figure 4.73

Small blue cursor location indicator

Listening Away from the Selection

It's a rare situation, but occasionally it is handy to select one thing but listen to another. Consider the following situation....

While selecting a loop for possible copying and pasting, the producer has been meticulous about the starting and ending points. After 10 minutes, he feels satisfied but wants to hear the first verse version before committing to this second verse selection (that you just spent 10 minutes highlighting). Do you create a region to "hold" your locations, and then move to the first verse to listen? What if the producer changes his mind about the region you've just created? Do you move back to the original location, reselect the loop, and tell yourself it won't take 10 minutes this time?

The answer is no. If you've spent time selecting something but you are not ready to commit to it, try deselecting the Link Timeline and Edit Selection button, shown in Figure 4.74. This will cause the Ruler to no longer follow the selection on any track. In the fussy producer scenario, this tactic is *very* handy because you can keep your selection, deselect the Link Timeline and Edit Selection button, and then click anywhere on the Ruler to play that location. Pro Tools will keep the selection, allowing you to click on any location and play from there. Reselecting the button will tell the Ruler to resync to the selection, putting you right back where you started. Nice!

Figure 4.74

The Link Timeline and Edit Selection button

Faster Working with Groups

Grouping is a great way to keep tracks together and treat them as if they were on the same track. However, groups can slow you down when you seek to maneuver one of the group members without the others. This is true in both the Mix and Edit groups (options are shown in Figure 4.75). Mix groups group the tracks together with regard to certain mixing functions, such as volume, mute, solo, and automation. Edit groups group tracks together with regard to certain editing functions, such as cutting, copying, selecting, and pasting.

Figure 4.75

The New Group dialog box

I *only* use Mix and Edit groups because I never know what I want to do to the group before-hand. If I need to perform a cut on a group member but not the whole group, I can easily suspend groups temporarily by choosing Suspend All Groups from the Group menu bar, shown in Figure 4.76. Then, I can make my cut and reactivate the groups using the same command (SHIFT+CMD+G). I also could simply click on the group name in the Edit Groups List to suspend *only* that group.

However, there may be times when you only wish to make an individual group type. For example, you can choose to create Edit Groups when you want to have individual volume control but grouped editing, as with several drum tracks. Conversely, you may wish to create Mix Groups when you are pre-mixing sessions that will end up on Icon systems, as they translate much better.

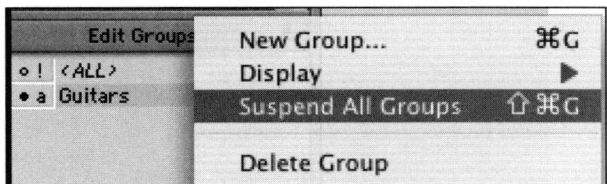

Figure 4.76

The Suspend All Groups menu option

An even better move is to hold down the Control key when you are adjusting certain mix functions, such as volume, to suspend the group only for the length of time the Control key is held down. This is a very handy way of working without having to remember (or check constantly) for active groups during the session.

Section Arrangements

So the song is perfect and ready to print, until the vocalist walks in and wants you to change the ending. She never liked the hard end (see Figure 4.77), and she wants you to duplicate the chorus and fade the song. After dropping this bomb, she capriciously walks out of the room, laughing too loudly on her new cell phone. I love this business!

Never fear—it's only a key click away, really. To copy, paste, or simply delete entire sections, All Group is your best friend. Activate the All Group option, as shown in Figure 4.78, and select the section to copy (or delete). In this case, you'll select a full round of the outro chorus (before the big end) with the All Group option active, and then copy the section. Switch to Shuffle mode and paste repeatedly. When you confirm that the sections flow smoothly (you may need to polish automation curves to help accomplish this), create your fade on the Master Fader, as seen in Figure 4.79 and call that pesky singer back in to approve it!

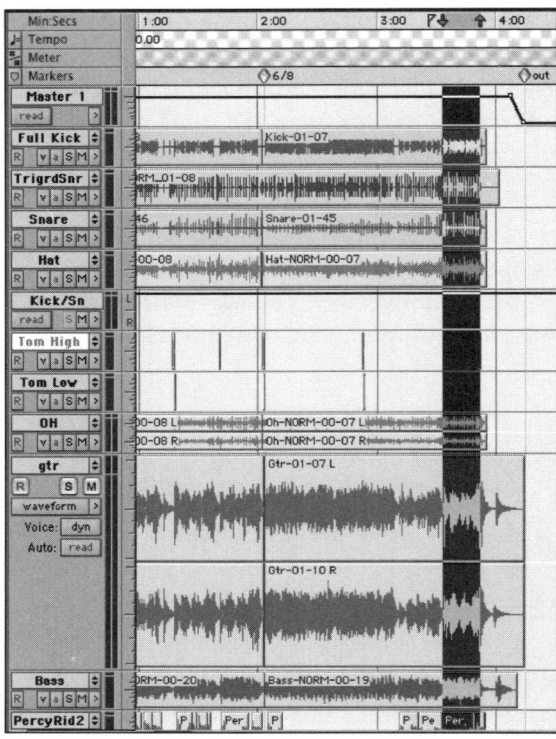

Figure 4.77

Song with hard end

Figure 4.78

The All Group
option active

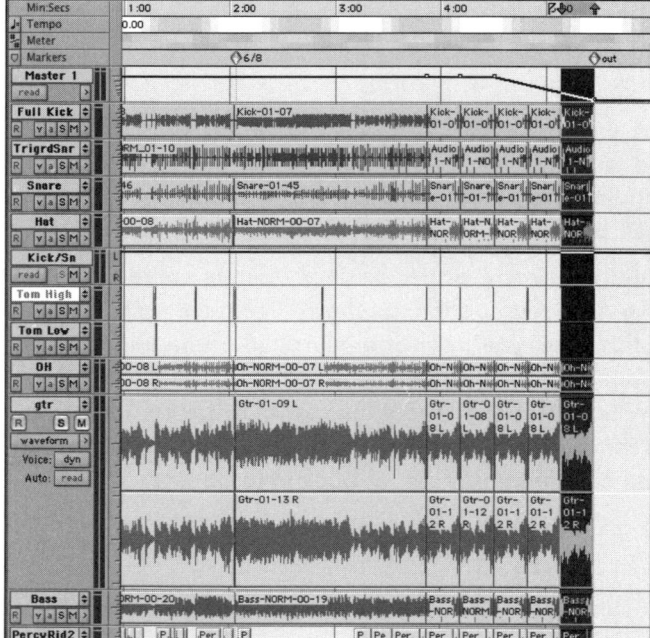

Figure 4.79

Song with copied, faded outro chorus

Another way to perform this
maneuver would be to use the
Region Group function. Simply
select the outro of the song, and
create a Region Group. Then,
simply copy/paste or loop until
satisfied (see "Group and Loop"
earlier in this chapter).

Erasing with the Pencil Tool

Are nasty pops and clicks randomly destroying your session? Couldn't get the drummer to stop hitting the mic? Did your vocal talent forget the pop filter again? These are common recording no-nos, but they happen anyway. Sometimes you can remove pops and clicks from vinyl recordings (or even add them) by using certain plug-ins (which is nice for heavy, pop-laden material), but for the once-in-a-while pop it's overkill. When you are zoomed in to the sample level at the moment of the pop, the Pencil tool becomes active with several drawing options available from its drop-down menu. Select the freehand Pencil tool and try drawing a smooth curve where there is currently a spike, as shown in Figure 4.80. This can radically reduce the sound of the pop (and further experimentation can remove it completely) without cutting the file, potentially shifting things out of whack (Shuffle mode) or leaving a funny silent hole (Slip mode). If this doesn't work, you might need to cut the spike out and fill the space with another performance. (See the sections "Adding and Fixing Syllables (Words) That Don't Fit" and "Room Tone Fixes" earlier in this chapter.)

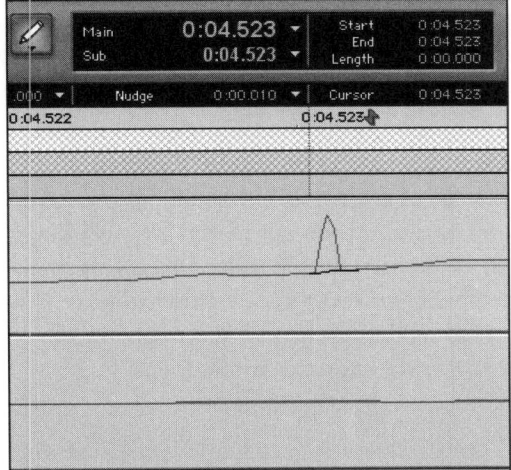

Figure 4.80

The Pencil tool rewriting a spiked wave

Batch Fading

I hate the sound of toms ringing sympathetically to the rest of the drum set. Every time the snare is hit, the toms make a tonal ringing that just takes up frequency space and makes the overall set sound muddy. Gating can fix this, but some hits are soft and don't make it past the gate. Others are long and get cut off by the gate. Editing by hand is sometimes the only way to fly. However, each end edit can require serious attention due to bleed from the hi-hat and the snare. A fade out would be nice, but you might need to create many of them. Because you just edited by hand, it would be *really* nice not to have to fade by hand, too.

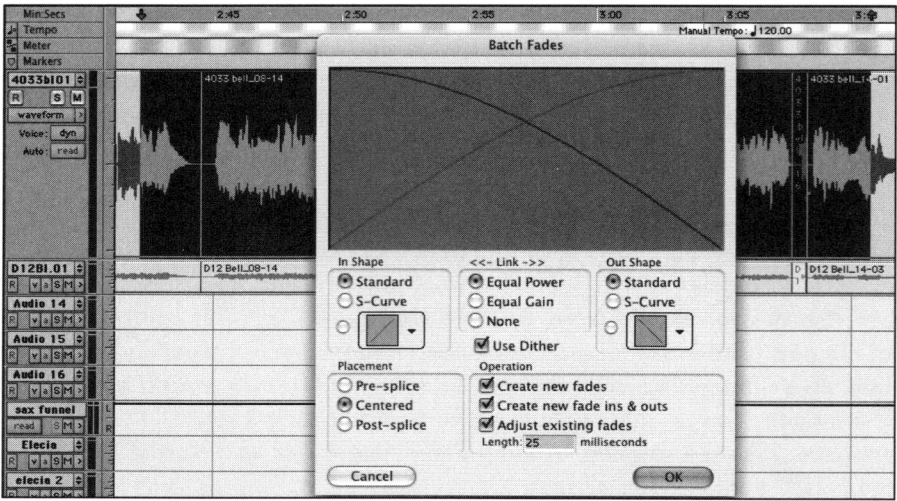

Figure 4.81

The Batch Fades dialog box

After you edit the track to taste, you can save a little time by fading all the parts at once. Select the entire track (CMD+A or triple-click the track) and choose Edit > Batch Fades (CMD+F). When multiple regions are selected, the Fades option naturally becomes the Batch Fades option, as seen in Figure 4.81. With toms, the beginning edit is usually right at the hit, requiring no fade-in (just a fade-out). In these situations, choose the No Fade In option (in the In Shape area), which looks like the top-left corner of a square, shown in Figure 4.82. (You will need to deselect any Link option.) Choose a fast slope fade-out so the tom will ring naturally but get quiet before the next snare or hi-hat hit that would bleed in. This is fast and sounds great for this situation. For other situations in which two regions are crossfaded, choose a length of time that seems fair. The default is 25 milliseconds, but you might need to adjust this to taste. A range from 25 to 150 is good territory for experimentation.

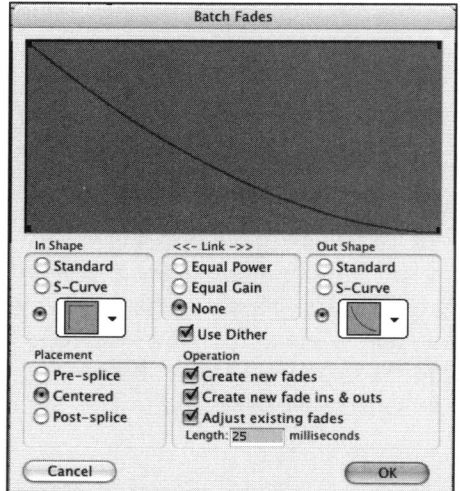

Figure 4.82

The No Fade In and Fade Out Tom batch fades

Faster Fades

When you are editing VOs, awkward room tone can be an unfortunate by-product. VO recorded in even slightly live rooms ends abruptly when simply edited out. Using fade-ins and fade-outs can fix the problem, but they become time suckers if every fade performed needs to be readjusted to a non-default shape.

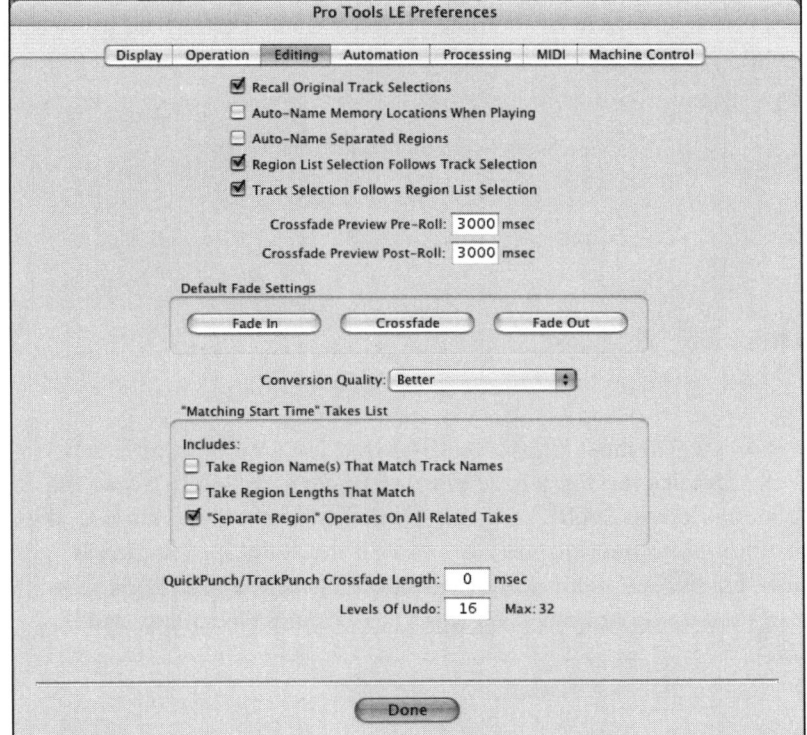

Figure 4.83

The Default Fade Settings in Preferences

For situations like this, in which a fade other than the standard fade is needed for the out-cut, set Pro Tools' default fade to the shape desired by choosing Setups > Preferences > Editing > Default Fade, shown in Figure 4.83, and choosing the fade that works best for the VO.

Repositioning Moved Files

So the bass is just slightly too early, and the producer wants you to play with moving it later to get the feel right. After about 45 microscopic moves, you both agree that it was better off where it was originally. Of course, you've gone way beyond your 32 levels of Undo, so you find that you simply can't get back there from here. Reverting to a saved version won't work because you have been working for hours and you never saved. Recalling a backup won't work because you forgot to read "Don't Lose Your Work" in Chapter 1, and you never acti-vated AutoSave. What do you do now? (Hint: see "Editing Safely" earlier in this chapter).

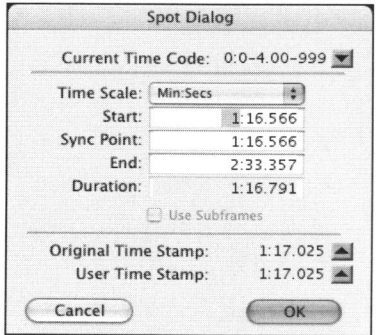

Figure 4.84

The Spot Mode dialog box with original timestamp

Luckily, Pro Tools automatically timestamps every file recorded (including MIDI files) so the part always has its original timing attached to the file. Switch to Spot mode, and click on the file/region with the Grabber tool. Note that this will only work if the Auto-Spot Region is inactive (Display > Auto-Spot Regions). When the Spot Mode dialog box appears, as seen in Figure 4.84, notice the two tabs at the bottom. One is for the original timestamp and the other is for a user timestamp.

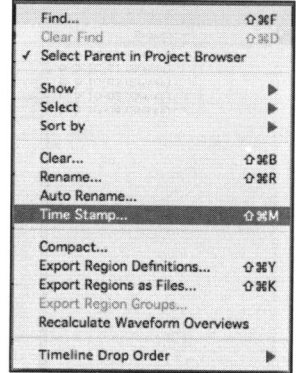

Figure 4.85

The Time Stamp option from the Region List drop-down menu

If you are repositioning to the recorded timing, click the arrow next to the original timestamp, and that timecode (or bars and beats, if selected) will enter into the start of the region. Then, you can click OK, and the region will be spotted to that location. To use the user timestamp, you must first timestamp the region. Do this by clicking on the file and choosing Time Stamp from the Region List drop-down menu, as seen in Figure 4.85. Now you can reposition the file to this location any time using the same process.

Aligning Tracks

There are a few ways to align tracks so they have the same start or end location. If you want to do this by hand (which is slow), you should zoom in and simply line them up manually. However, expect a lot of trial and error and potential phase problems. Here are a few other faster and more exact methods:

❋ Zoom in to each region and trim the beginning to a recognizable zero-crossing point. After you have trimmed each region to the desired start point, zoom out. Using the Grabber tool, click on the first region, setting the cursor to the desired start point (the beginning of the first region). Then, Control-click on the second region (while you are in Slip mode) and watch it snap to the exact location of the first region!

❋ Zoom in to each region and trim the beginning to a recognizable zero-crossing point. After you have trimmed each region to the desired start point, zoom out. Using Spot mode, click on the region with the Grabber tool, and copy the start time from the Spot dialog box, as seen in Figure 4.86. (You could simply copy the numbers from the Main Time Indicator as well.) Because you can't highlight all the start time numbers using the standard Copy and Paste commands, simply write the information down and then type it into the second file's start time in its Spot dialog box. Then, click on the second region and paste the timing into the start time of the second region. Click OK.

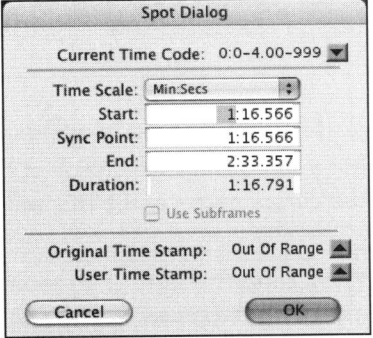

Figure 4.86

Spot dialog box with start time highlighted

❋ Zoom in to each region and trim the beginning to a recognizable zero-crossing point. Create a Sync Point at the start location of each file. Then, you can transfer the Sync Point time information from the Spot dialog box (see Figure 4.87) of the first file to the second.

❋ Zoom in to each region and trim the beginning to a recognizable zero-crossing point. Create a Sync Point at the start location of each file, as seen in Figure 4.88. Position the cursor at the Sync Point of the first region, and then align the Sync Points by SHIFT+CTRL-clicking on the second file.

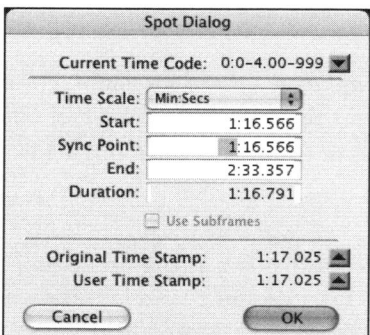

Figure 4.87

Spot dialog box with Sync Point highlighted

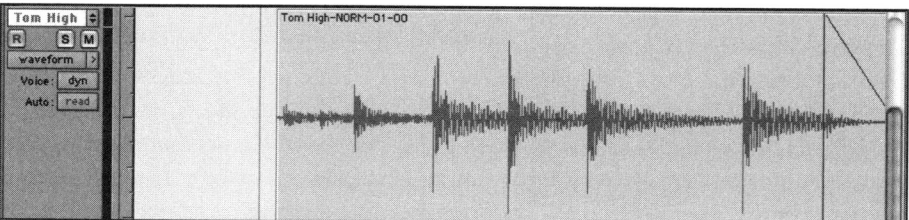

Figure 4.88

Sync Point in a region

* Align the ends of the regions by trimming the *ends* of the files, not the beginnings. Then, CMD+CTRL-click the second file. (Do this after you position the cursor at the first region's end point. You can tab to the end to set the cursor at the end.) This will align the ends of the regions.

* **Y.** With Command Focus active, hitting the letter Y will snap the start of a selected region to the current timecode of playback. While playing the piece, wait for the desired start time to approach and select the region in question. Press Y when the moment comes, and the region will snap its start time to the play position's timecode.

* **U**. Same thing as above, except the selected region's sync point will snap to the play position's timecode.

* **I**. Again, same thing as before with Y except the region's end will snap to the play position's timecode.

* **H.** With Center Playhead scrolling active (Options > Scrolling > Center Playhead) H will snap the selected region to the current position of the playhead. The only difference between Y and H is whether or not Center Playhead scrolling is active.

* **J.** Same thing as U, except that Center Playhead scrolling is active.

* **K.** Again, same thing as the letter I, except that Center Playhead scrolling is active.

Dragging Regions to Locations

When you are trying to drag (or OPTION-drag for a copy) regions to a particular location, exactness can be difficult to achieve. One helpful tip is to look at the cursor location indicator when you are dragging, as shown in Figure 4.89. This will tell you the location of your cursor before you let go, committing the file to that location.

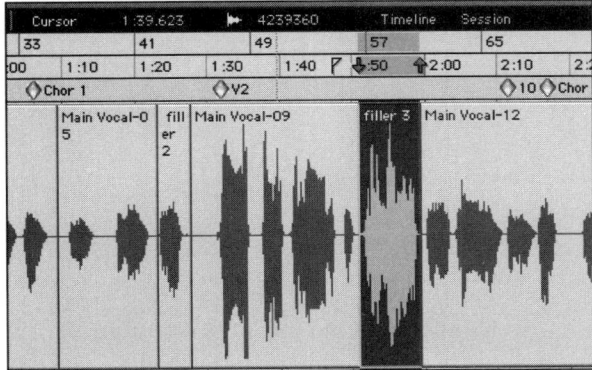

Figure 4.89

The cursor indicator section of the Edit window

If you are dragging the file from the Region List, first position the cursor at the desired location, and then hold the Control key while you are dragging the file to the track. This will position the file to the cursor location, and *only* that location. A third method is to switch to Spot mode and drag the file to any location on the track. You will be presented the Spot dialog box; simply type in the start time, and the file will snap to that location.

Using the Scrubber to Select and Trim

Most of us are comfortable with making selections by eye rather than by ear. This might produce misleading and poor results because the eye might not line up with what the ear wants to hear. To make selections (and move the cursor) by ear, use the Scrubber tool, shown in Figure 4.90.

First, make sure you set your preferences correctly. Choose Setups > Preferences > Operation, and activate the Timeline Insertion Follows Scrub/Shuttle option. This will allow you to scrub (or shuttle) the cursor to any location, and the cursor will "park" at the end of your scrubbing. For example, to find the start of a kick drum, switch to the Scrubber tool and activate the preference, then scrub the cursor back and forth across the visual start of the drum. When your ear is satisfied, let go of the mouse, and the cursor will be positioned at the beginning of the kick.

Figure 4.90

The Scrubber tool

The Trim tool can be changed to the Scrub Trimmer (see Figure 4.91), which accomplishes two jobs at once. It allows you to scrub the audio to audition it at slower speeds *and* trim the region to the position where the mouse was let go. This is a quick way to find the beginning of a file/region and trim it at the same time, while using your ear to make the determination.

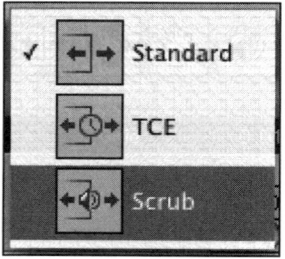

Figure 4.91

Scrub Trimmer

Stutter Edits

If you listen to much IDM or other dance music, you'll recognize the use of stutter edits as creative sound design tools. A stutter edit is a small piece of audio that is repeated to give the impression that the artist or instrument was st-st-st-st-st-st-stuttering. This is easy to accomplish with Pro Tools (or any DAW, for that matter).

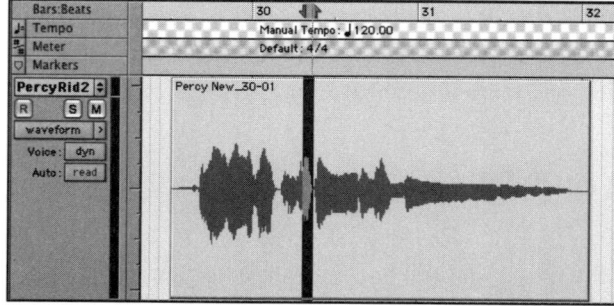

Figure 4.92

A small selection of audio to be used as a stutter

In a musical situation, stutters can be quarter notes, 8th notes, or 16th notes, but they are most often 32nd notes or 64th notes. Switch to Grid mode, and set the grid resolution to the desired stutter length. Start with 16th notes to see whether you need shorter or longer sections, because the 16th note is in the middle.

Using the Selector tool, highlight a single 16th note of audio, as seen in Figure 4.92. You should change the grid resolution to 16th notes to ensure that you capture exactly a 16th note in Grid mode, shown in Figure 4.93. You can choose to capture, separate, or simply copy the region to perform the stutter. Then, paste, duplicate, or repeat the part as many times as desired. (Try filling a half note with the 16th note repeated eight times to see whether that works, as seen in Figure 4.94.)

Figure 4.93

The grid resolution set to 16th notes

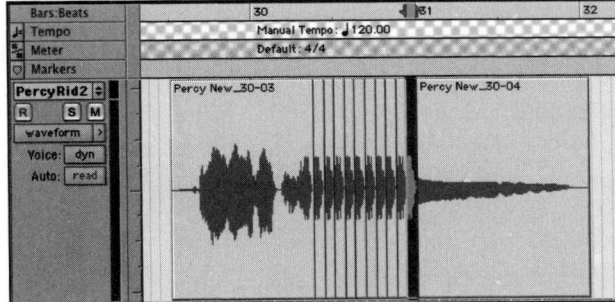

Figure 4.94

The 16th note repeated to create a stutter effect

You can repeat this procedure selecting 32nd notes or 64th notes by changing the grid resolution and selecting smaller sections to stutter. You can also switch to Shuffle mode to paste the part in and shuffle the rest of the track later, but you might alter the timing of other regions on that track accidentally. I recommend you work in Grid or Slip mode for this action.

TCE Smear Edits

The TCE Trim tool (see Figure 4.95) allows you to time compress/expand (TCE) any region to any length by trimming the start or end of any region to any new location. Instead of trimming the extra audio to play, this resizes the region, stretching the audio to fit the new length. This is useful for elastic-sounding audio, but it can produce some nasty artifacts. A before and after TCE Trim view is shown in Figure 4.96.

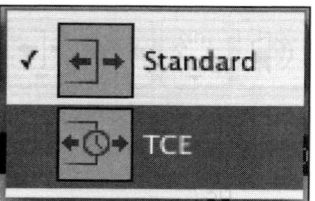

Figure 4.95

The TCE Trim tool

To create a smear effect, use the opposite approach to the stutter edit. Select a small section of audio (a syllable or a note, for example), and then separate the region. This will create the small audio as its own region, allowing you to use the TCE Trim tool. In Slip mode, switch to the TCE Trim tool and click and drag the region to the desired length. (You can use Shuffle or Grid mode, too, but you will be constrained by the functions of each mode.) Pro Tools will create a new audio file with the file extension .tce. Listen and hear how this process stretched the selection over a longer duration, making it sound elastic.

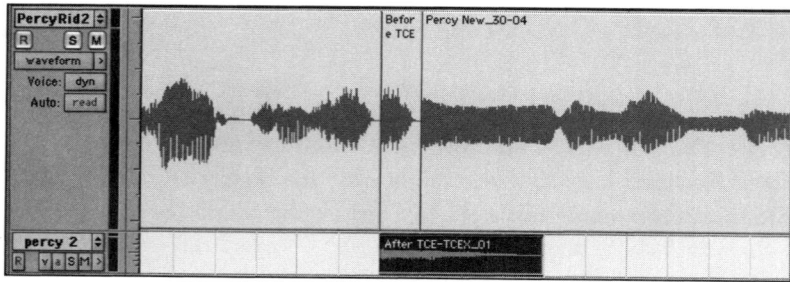

Figure 4.96

A region before (left) and after TCE (right)

For more dramatic effects, use the TCE Trim tool on the entire word (or phrase) to make it twice (or longer) than its normal length. This will make the word play as if the vocalist were on eeeeeeettttttthhhhhhhhhheeeeeeerrrrrrrrrr (ether). You should recognize this effect from the first *Matrix* movie, when Neo takes the red pill, and the quicksilver liquid falls down his throat. Listen for an old modem sound, stretched for liquid (elastic) effect!

Exact Beat Slicing Using the Beat Detective

For loops and performances that don't quite fit the click or grid, TCE stretching may not adjust the loop properly and might yield audible and unacceptable audio artifacts. With version 7, LE users now have access to the same power that TDM users have had for years—Beat Detective. The biggest limitation is that LE users can only use Beat Detective on one track at a time. If multiple tracks are selected, then Beat Detective will only work on the top-most track.

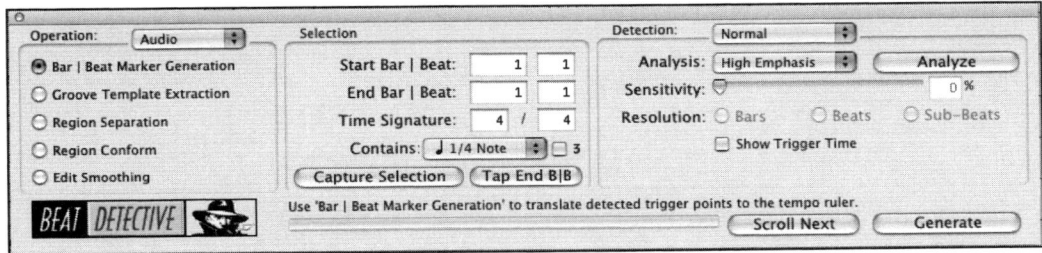

Figure 4.97

The Beat Detective window

Beat Detective has five different functions: Bar|Beat Marker Generation, Groove Template Extraction, Region Separation, Region Conform, and Edit Smoothing. I'll take them one at a time.

✳ **Bar|Beat Marker Generation.** In this mode (see Figure 4.97), Beat Detective will analyze a selection of audio (generally a 2-, 4-, or 8-bar loop) and determine the tempo of the region based on the user-defined resolution. Similar to Identify Beat (see "Using Loops to Create a Tempo Map" in Chapter 5), this mode will extract the tempo and assign it to the Tempo Ruler as tempo markers.

1. Type the desired beginning and ending loop locations in the Selection area, and tell Beat Detective the meter and note resolution (8th, 16th, and so on). I usually stay with quarter notes for 4|4 time and let Beat Detective figure out everything else on its own.

2. Choose your emphasis, which will tell Pro Tools whether the material is focused around high- or low-frequency material.

3. Click the Analyze button, creating vertical lines on the selection matching the resolution chosen. When you are doing this for drums, it works best when *all* the drum tracks are selected. That way, Pro Tools can make an average determination of the timing of the drums to give the best overall feel analysis. If the kick is chosen exclusively, any timing problems on the kick will translate to every other track!

4. Adjust the Sensitivity bar until the lines on the screen match the basic beat of the song at your desired resolution (8th, 16th, and so on), as shown in Figure 4.98.

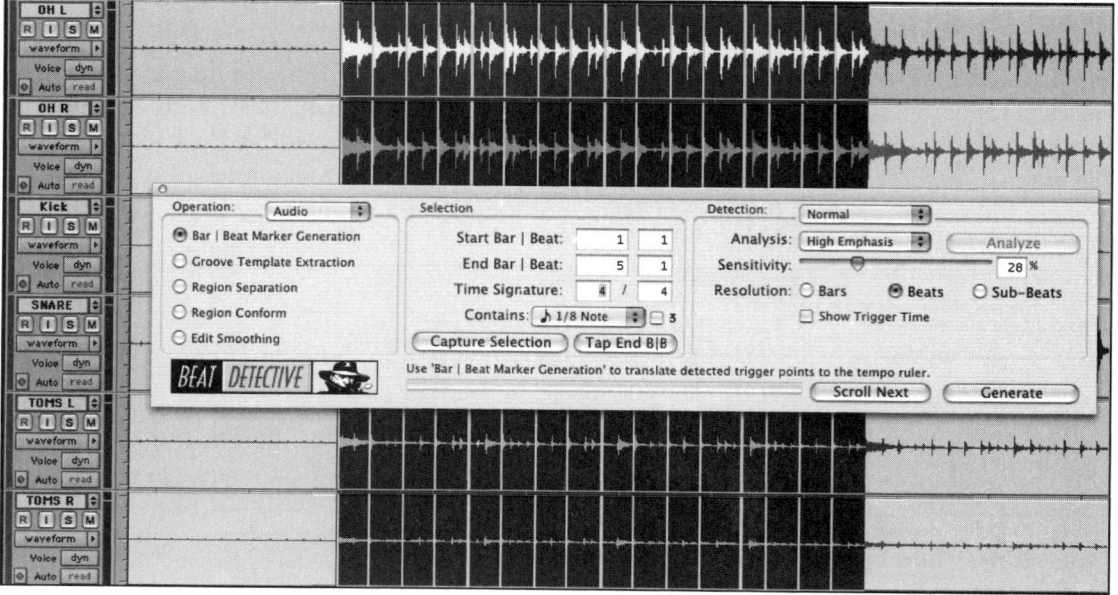

Figure 4.98

Selection of drums—analyzed, emphasized, and sensitized

5. When you are satisfied, click the Generate button, and the tempo will be extracted from the selected loop (at quarter-note resolution or eighth-note resolution, and so on) and tempo markers will be placed across the Tempo Ruler for the length of the selection, as seen in Figure 4.99.

6. At this point, it would be a good idea to create a click track and audition it against the tempo you've extracted from the selection. It should be perfect, reflecting slight feel adjustments from the performance in the click.

NOTE

If the desired effect is to make the recorded drums match a pre-existing tempo map, DO NOT go through the Bar|Bear Marker Generation as you will only destroy the existing tempo map and replace it with the one extracted from the recorded drums! Skip to Region Separation and Region Conform.

❋ **Groove Template Extraction.** After you have analyzed and mapped the tempo to the Tempo Ruler, you can take things a step further by creating a groove from the newly developed click. If a loop has swing, the Groove Extraction feature (see Figure 4.100) will allow you to create a user groove, which can be saved and made available to any song you create in Pro Tools!

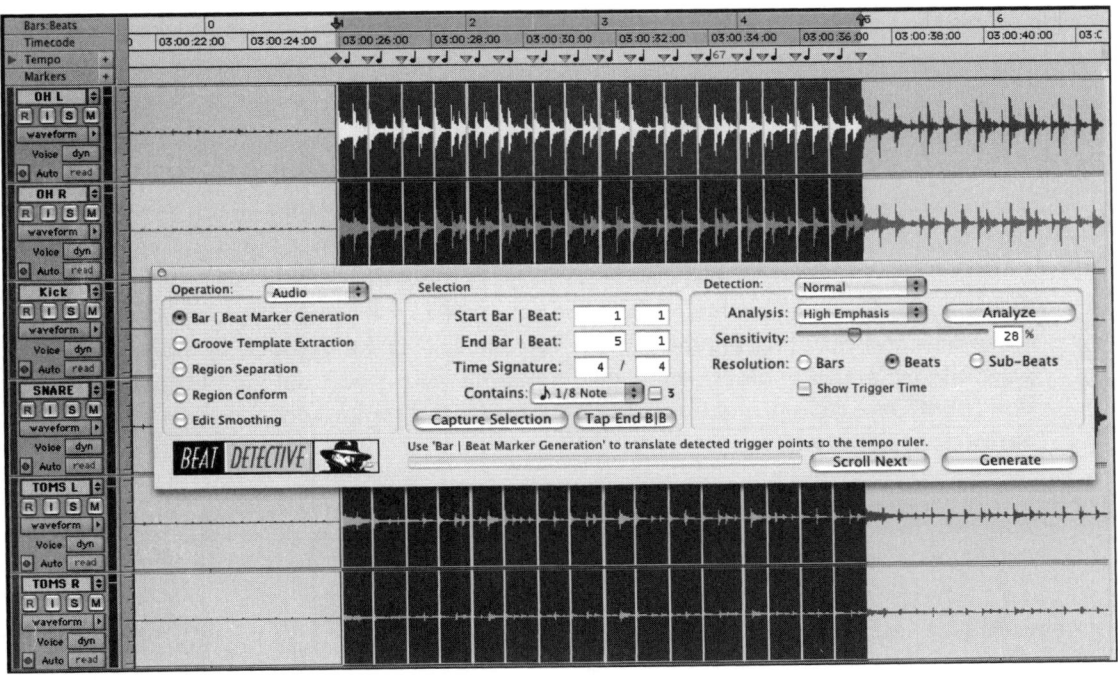

Figure 4.99

Tempo map generated across the Tempo Ruler

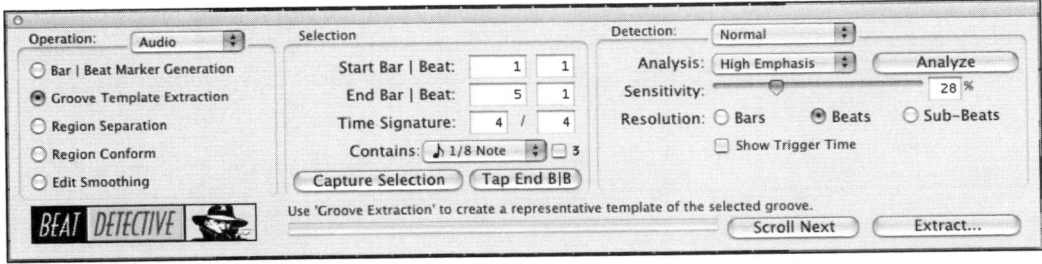

Figure 4.100

The Groove Extraction window

❊ **Region Separation.** This is the part that works like Recycle. (See "Sending Your Loop to the Dr. Rex Player in Reason" in Chapter 5.) Pro Tools and Beat Detective can analyze the beat and separate the selection hit by hit, allowing you to "gridify" the sections to perfect quantization with the rest of the performance (see Figure 4.101). Make the bass player hit exactly as the drummer and vice versa!

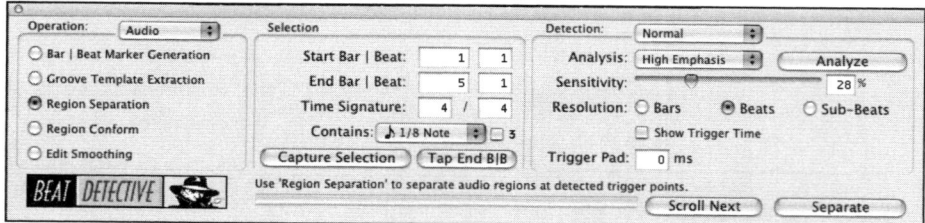

Figure 4.101

The Region Separation window

※ **Region Conform.** After the regions are separated, you should conform them to the tempo and click (see Figure 4.102). Remember that if the goal is to make the performance match another, you should generate the tempo from the best performance (Bar|Beat Generation) and then region-separate *and* region-conform the weaker performance to match.

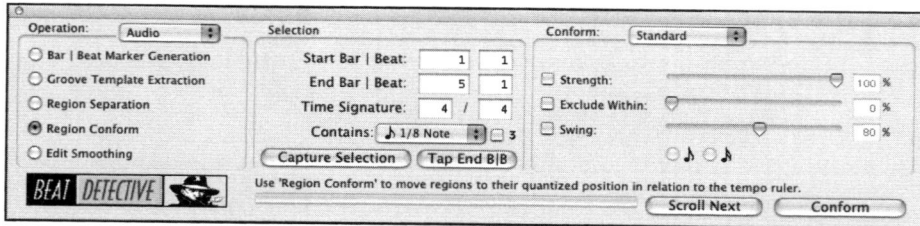

Figure 4.102

The Region Conform window

※ **Edit Smoothing.** When regions are conformed to the better performance's timing, there will usually be gaps left over from shifting the parts around slightly. You can quickly tame and clean this up by clicking Fill Gaps (see Figure 4.103). As the name implies, gaps are filled by crossfades, which removes any clicks or unwanted silences.

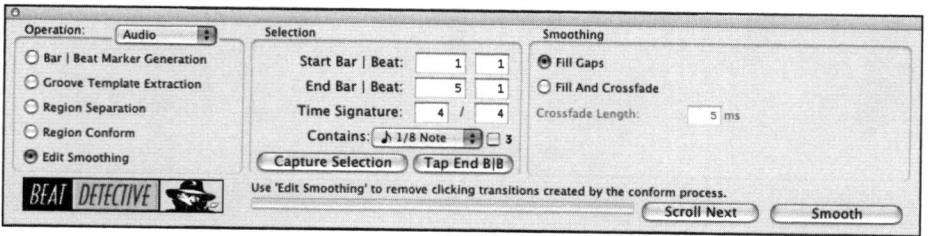

Figure 4.103

The Edit Smoothing window

Troubled Trimming

There will be occasion when trimming a region back to its original form is impossible, even though you know that there is more audio beyond where Pro Tools stopped trimming. No matter how you stretch the audio back, the cursor simply stops short.

In this case, you're not crazy and there's nothing wrong; it's simply bad editing. In the process of cutting and pasting, there are often orphans that are simply not visible. If you have difficulty stretching audio, try zooming in to the fullest view possible.

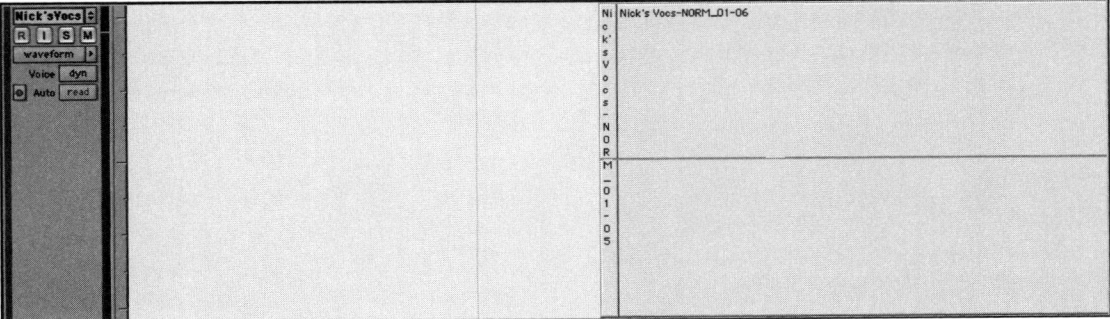

Figure 4.104
Zoomed in all the way with a sliver of audio left over

You may recognize a small sliver of audio, like the one in Figure 4.104, stuck at either the head or the tail of your region. This sliver is stopping you from trimming the region back to full size. Delete the sliver and try again.

5 } Composing with MIDI and ReWire

Pro Tools has always been an engineer's tool. During the late 1980s and '90s, Pro Tools dominated the digital-audio world while other applications competed for dominance in the MIDI world. Today, MIDI applications are equally powerful in the digital-audio world and Pro Tools has matured in the MIDI world. There are still a few distinctions between Pro Tools and MIDI-centric applications, but the line between them has blurred significantly—and with version 7, the line has almost been erased!

Pro Tools now ships with a few different programs to allow the new owner to compose using MIDI and software synthesizers that are all in the package. The most popular of these is Reason, from Propellerhead Software. Reason is so pervasive that this chapter covers almost as much territory in Reason as it does in Pro Tools and general MIDI concepts. The tips listed here cover simple and complex structures with MIDI and composing in general. A background in MIDI is helpful here, as is a background in music theory. Although not entirely necessary, some of the power behind Pro Tools' new MIDI engine will be lost on you without this knowledge.

Do yourself a favor—take piano lessons!

The AMS and Setting Up the MIDI Environment

The AMS (*Audio MIDI Setup*) is Apple's MIDI and audio utility that organizes how software recognizes the MIDI interfaces and the audio interface through the OS itself. This *must* be configured properly for Pro Tools to see any incoming MIDI, including MIDI timecode.

From Pro Tools, choose Setup >MIDI> MIDI Studio, as seen in Figure 5.1, and Pro Tools will launch AMS (shown in Figure 5.2). AMS lives on the hard drive at the following hierarchy (in case you need to find it outside of Pro Tools): Applications > Utilities > Audio MIDI Setup, as seen in Figure 5.3. It is a good idea to drag this utility to the Dock so you can quickly navigate to it. (See "Keeping the Dock Out of the Way" in Chapter 1.)

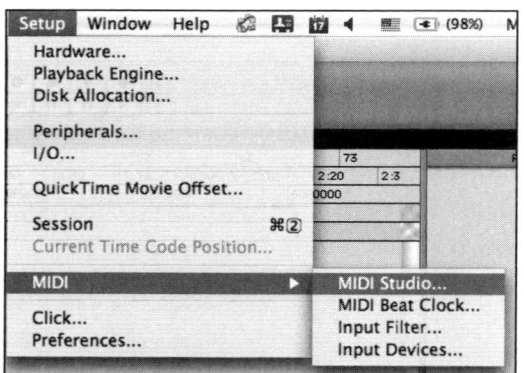

Figure 5.1

Getting to the AMS from Pro Tools

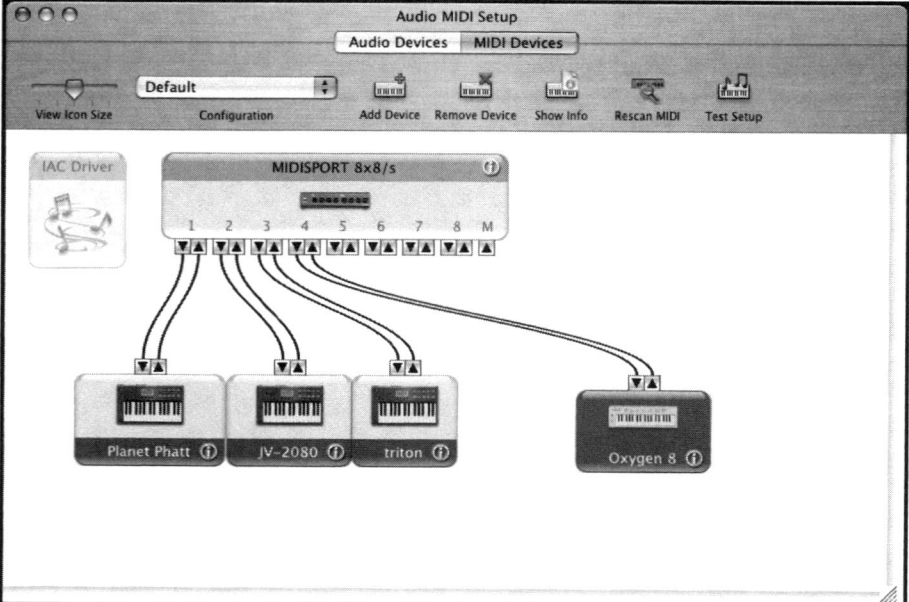

Figure 5.2

The AMS MIDI window

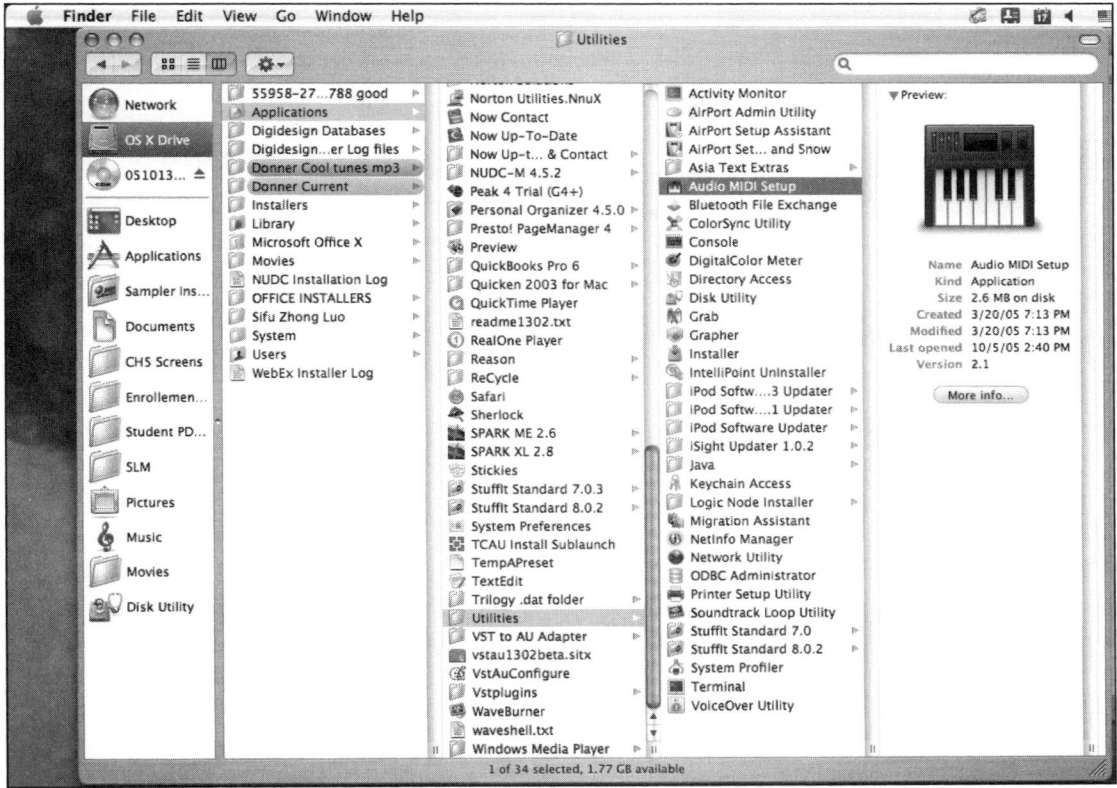

Figure 5.3

AMS from the Utilities window

Click the MIDI tab at the top to see the MIDI configuration. This should be familiar to anyone who has experience with OMS or FreeMIDI. If not, you should see some familiar faces already, such as your MIDI interface shown in Figure 5.4. (If you don't see your MIDI interface, you might need to reinstall the driver for it.) You should create a new configuration for your current MIDI setup. Then, add devices to reflect any MIDI device found in your hardware rack. If there is only a keyboard (or a combination keyboard/interface, such as Oxygen from M-Audio), then it should show up as the interface.

When you create new devices, you can choose from a list of preset instruments that might match what's in your rack. This is very important because you will only be able to get your patch names into Pro Tools if there is an exact match to the .MIDNAM file. (See the next section, "Patch Names in Pro Tools.") After you configure your AMS properly, you can return to Pro Tools, and any MIDI track will show the input and output devices from your AMS configuration shown in Figure 5.5.

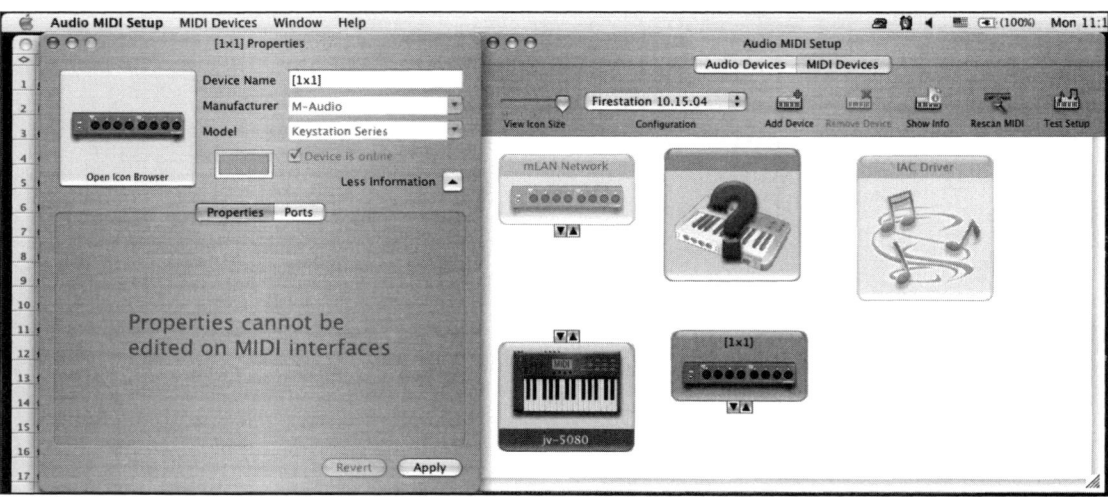

Figure 5.4

The AMS with an auto-recognized 1x1 interface

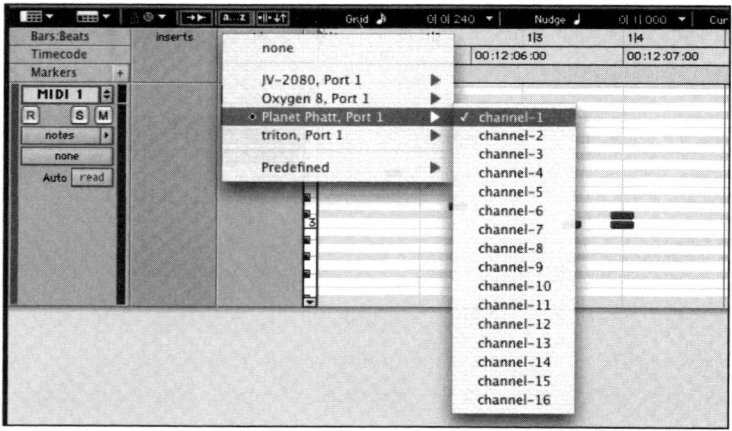

Figure 5.5

Pro Tools MIDI track with outputs set to AMS devices

Note

For the audio side of AMS, you can specify the default output device to be the Pro Tools hardware, and other applications (such as iTunes) will play out of the Digi device. You should also look to the Digi CoreAudio Driver (which can be downloaded from Digidesign's site) to be installed first for AMS to see it at all.

The CoreAudio driver is key (version 6.4 or higher) because it can allow multiple clients (applications) to use the driver at the same time. Launch the Digi CoreAudio driver, and it will tell you how many clients are attached to the driver at once, which tells you how busy the driver is. You can globally set the memory buffer setting, the clock source, and the sampling rate.

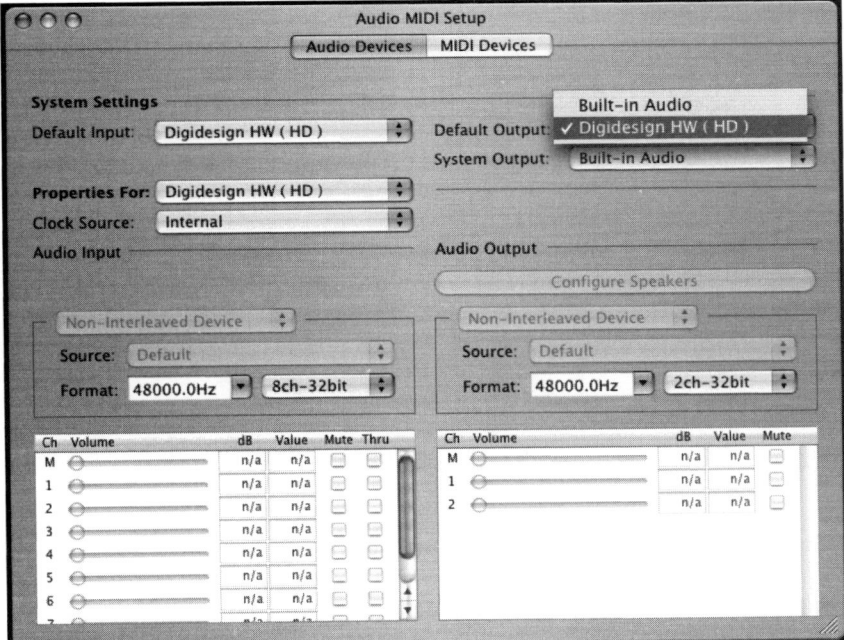

Figure 5.6

The Digi CoreAudio driver seen in the Audio side of AMS

Patch Names in Pro Tools

Unfortunately, when Pro Tools and Mac switched to OS X, so did the technology behind the patch names. Now, patch name files are in XML format, which makes them no fun to edit or create. Pro Tools will recognize the patch name of any synth in your AMS, but it must have exactly the same name in the .MIDNAM file as in the AMS document. The location of these files is shown in Figure 5.7.

Finding the .MIDNAM files can be traumatic, but they are out there on the Web. I found a facility in New Jersey that charges $13 per synth (a small price to pay for the hard work behind the file), and they came across quite well. Download the file, place it in the correct folder, and then verify the title of the file to the AMS document. Did I mention that the file needs to match exactly the name in the AMS?

Create a MIDI track and set the output to the desired synth. Click the Patch Name Settings box under the track information, and the Conform Names dialog box will appear. In the lower-left corner, click the Change box and direct Pro Tools to the matching .MIDNAM file. The patch numbers that were there should become the patch names on the synth, as seen in Figure 5.8. A quick spot check will verify the quality of the .MIDNAM file.

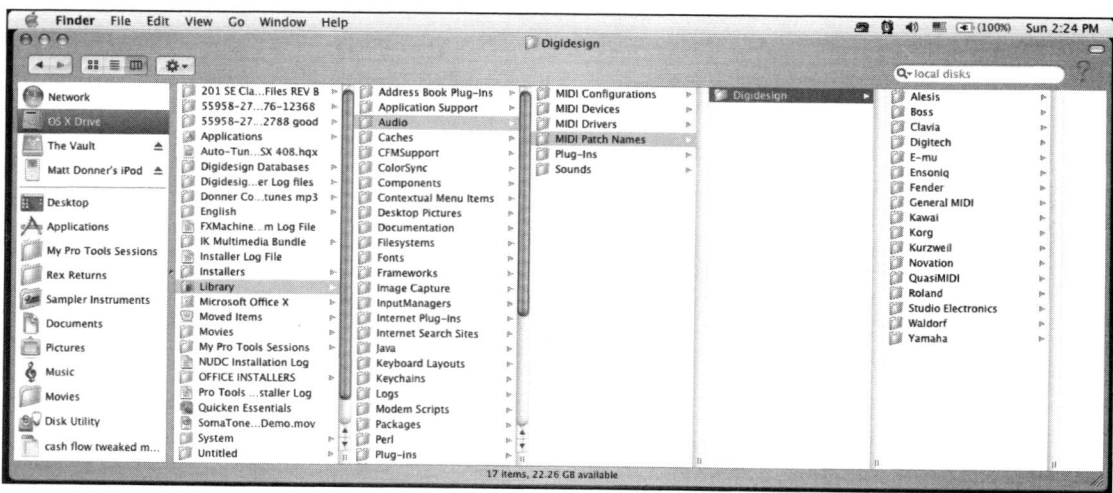

Figure 5.7

The hierarchy to the .MIDNAM files

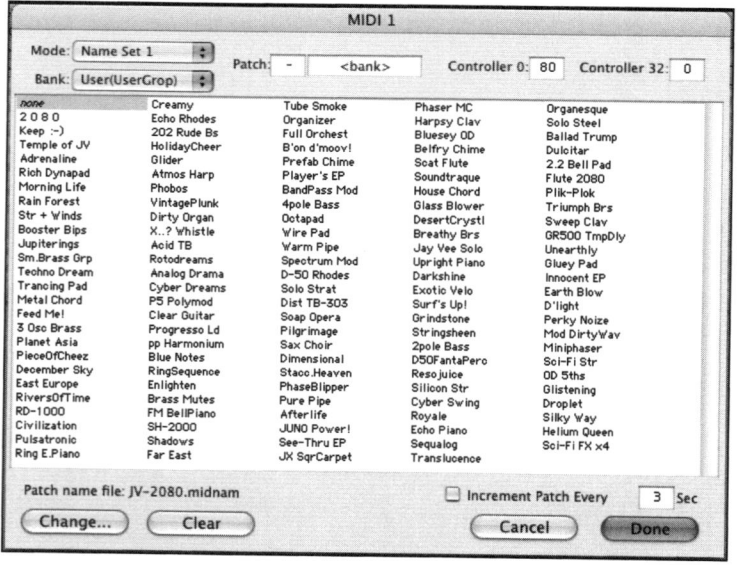

Figure 5.8

Conforming the synth to the .MIDNAM file

Expect to be frustrated with this process. If the names are not perfect, you can try editing the file itself with a program such as TextEdit or sue the creator of the file for your $13 back. I'm not sure which is worse.

Using Program Changes to Save Voices

As a Pro Tools composer working with a single synth, you will quickly realize the limitation of 16 MIDI channels. It is very common to write a piece involving more than 16 sounds, which forces the composer to either record certain parts or buy more gear.

Pro Tools supports the use of program changes on MIDI tracks, allowing the composer to switch sounds on a single MIDI track and a single MIDI channel during the song. This allows certain channels to double up and stretch the effectiveness of the synth. For example, if the verse calls for a piano but the chorus calls for an organ, create a program change to switch from one to the other on the same MIDI track using the same MIDI channel.

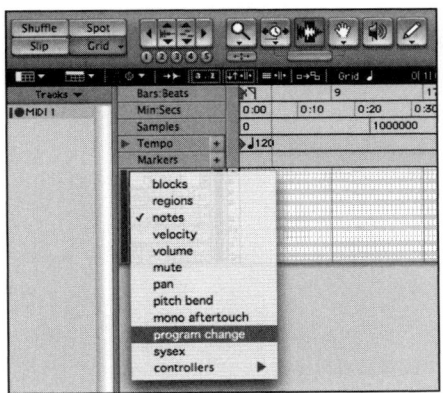

Figure 5.9

The Program Change Selection in the Automation Playlist menu

Once you have created your patch names in Pro Tools, simply switch the MIDI track to view program changes under the Automation Playlist menu, as seen in Figure 5.9. Switch to the Pencil tool and click on any location on the track; the Program Change dialog box will open. Choose the patch of choice, and it will appear on the Program Change playlist at the desired location, as shown in Figure 5.10. Play the song through this section, and listen to the sound change at the chorus!

You can access program changes below the Automation Playlist menu on any MIDI track. This is a fast way to audition the sound before sitting down to compose. Click the Program Change button, and the Patch Name list will appear. Play your MIDI keyboard and audition the first sound on the list. Use the arrow keys to navigate between the sounds to find the one that works best for this track.

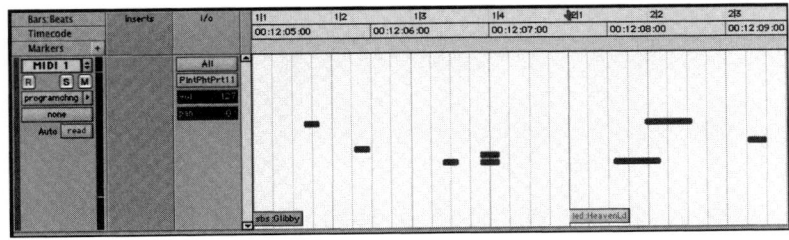

Figure 5.10

Program change data on the MIDI track

Instrument Tracks

One of the biggest complaints among MIDI composers is the clutter involved in the track setup. As you'll see in "Monitoring and Recording Virtual Synthesizers," later in this chapter, Pro Tools would require two tracks to perform the function—one for the MIDI part and one for the virtual synthesizer audio. Now, you only need one—an Instrument track. Instrument tracks are effectively the result of merging a MIDI track with an Aux return. This is a BIG space saver on the Edit and Mix windows and is great for organization.

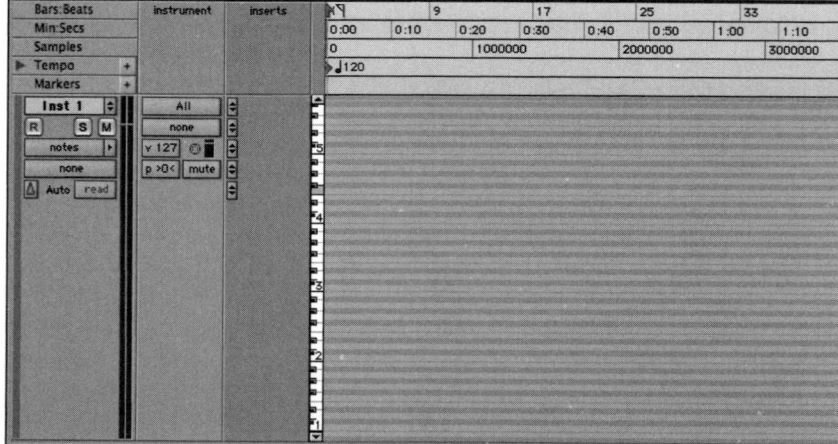

Figure 5.11

An Instrument track with the Instrument column shown

A major point of confusion when first setting up an Instrument track is that the MIDI assignments are not performed at the I/O options. There is a new column of data in Pro Tools 7 that determins where the MIDI data goes called the Instrument column, shown in Figure 5.11. When working with virtual synths, simply insert the synth on the Instrument track, and the Instrument column will instantly assign the MIDI to be sent to the first channel available on the synth.

If your synth is Reason, instant it as a plug-in, choose the ReWire audio channel to receive from, then assign the MIDI to go to the device of choice within Reason, as shown in Figure 5.12. If your synth is hardware, you'll need to set the I/O tab to the input or set of inputs that the synth is connected to. The track data contains the MIDI notes, but the playlist options contain both MIDI data and Aux data, as shown in Figure 5.13.

Figure 5.12

An Instrument track with Reason as the virtual synth

Figure 5.13

The list of Automation parameters on an Instrument track

Monitoring Your Hardware Synths (v6.x and Earlier)

After you've configured AMS and sorted out your patch names, you'll want to start writing music. You'll always need two tracks to work with MIDI in Pro Tools—one for the MIDI information (MIDI track) and one for the synth (hardware or software).

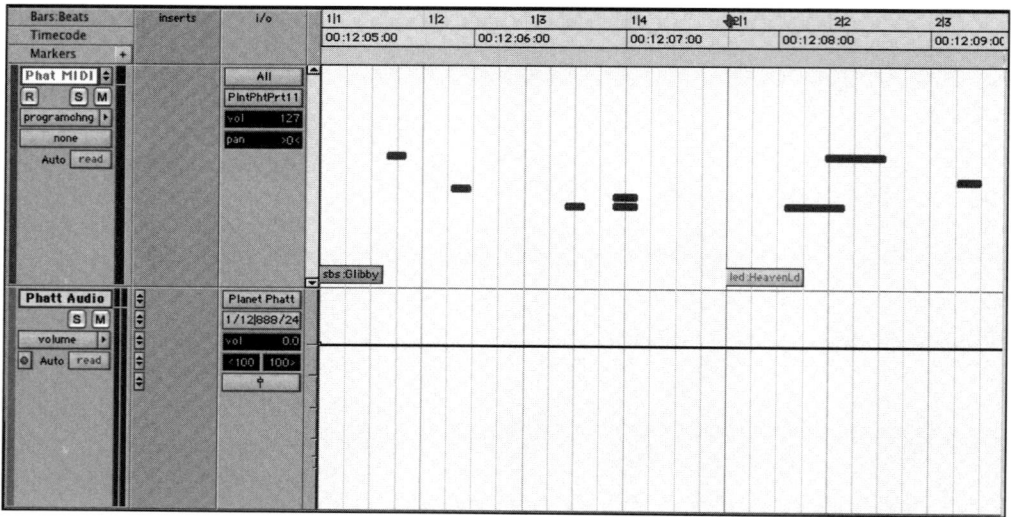

Figure 5.14

A basic two-track MIDI setup

I suggest you get used to creating a MIDI track and an Aux track when you are working with MIDI, like the setup in Figure 5.14. Luckily, PT v6.7 gives you the ability to make several kinds of tracks at once, as seen in Figure 5.15. (See "New Track Shortcuts" in Chapter 2.) You should use the Aux input for your synth monitoring because the Aux inputs allow you to hear the synth without using a voice, as Audio tracks do.

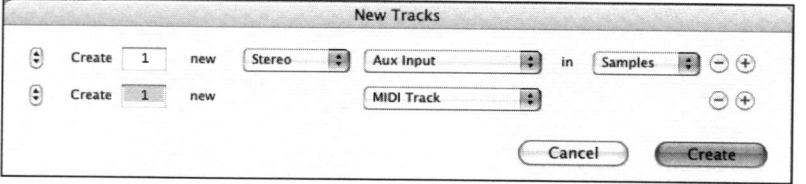

Figure 5.15

Creating a MIDI and an Aux track in v6.7

If the MIDI track has its output routed to the synth, put the track into Record Ready and play your keyboard input device. You should see the meter spike with each MIDI note played if MIDI Thru is activated. (Choose MIDI > MIDI Thru.) Set the output of the MIDI track to your synth and the MIDI channel desired, and MIDI will route through to the synth. Verify that the synth is receiving MIDI on both the MIDI interface and the synth's MIDI input indicator.

Route the audio output of the synth to two inputs on the Pro Tools interface (a patch bay might be useful in your studio if you do a lot of this), and set the inputs of the Aux track to the same inputs used for the synth outputs. (It is wise to label your I/O setup inputs so you recognize the synth output as the title of the I/O interface inputs. In other words, inputs 1-2 become Roland JV-5080, and so on.)

Monitoring and Recording Virtual Synthesizers (v6.x and Earlier)

Working with software (virtual) synths is much like working with hardware synths in that two tracks are needed—one MIDI for the notes (the control track) and one for the synth itself (again, Aux tracks work best here because they require no voice allocation). However, the common question is, Why don't my software synths appear in my MIDI output assignment box (demonstrated in Figure 5.16)?

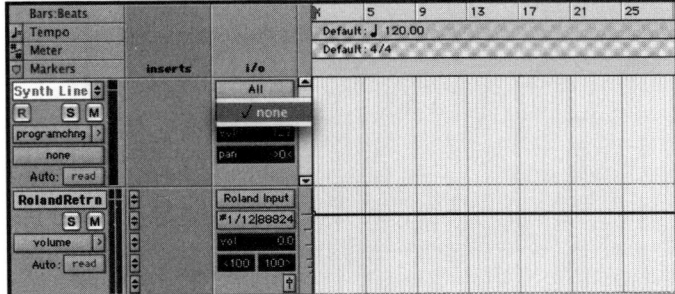

Figure 5.16

MIDI track with no synth available

Software synths are inserted like any other plug-in, and they are always available via the Insert tab. They do not appear in the AMS, ever. They are not seen by the OS because they are plug-ins specific to Pro Tools. Depending on the type of synth, they might also be available to other DAWs as well. To see them in the MIDI track's Output Assign tab, you must first insert them on the Aux (monitor) track. Only then will they be available as output on the MIDI track, shown in Figure 5.17. Prior to version 6.7, any RTAS synths could *only* be inserted on Audio tracks, so you would have needed to create a MIDI and Audio track—not an Aux.

If you intend to print this synth, you might think it is simpler to create an Audio track and simply plug in the synth there, then place the track in Record Ready and click Record to print it. This doesn't work.

Plug-ins are pre-fader on Audio and Aux tracks, but they are post-input, which means that the second you place the track in Record Ready, the synth is killed in deference to the analog input signal (or lack thereof) at the hardware I/O. So hitting Record will record silence and not play the synth. To print the synth, you will need a third track (an Audio track) to which to record.

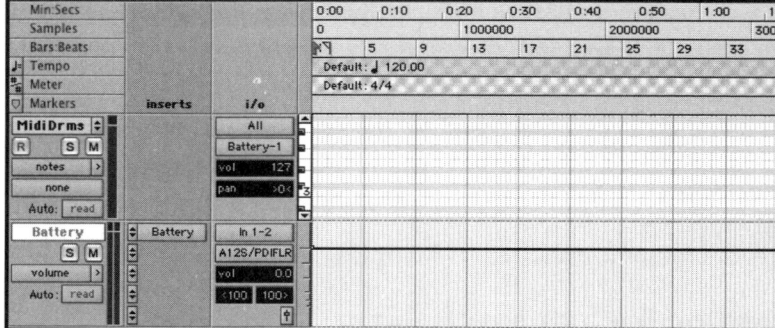

Figure 5.17

MIDI track with synth output assign next to Aux with synth

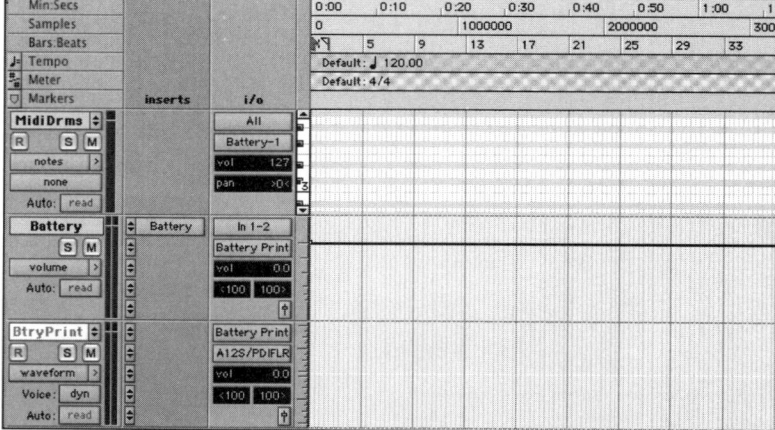

Figure 5.18

Three-track software synth print chain

After your MIDI and Aux tracks are created and music has been composed, create an Audio track to which to record the part. Mono synths should be printed to mono tracks to save voices and keep phase issues to a minimum. Route the output of the Aux to a bus (or a pair, for stereo), and set the Audio track's input to the same bus. This will create the proper signal chain to print the synth: MIDI to Aux and synth, and then out the bus to the Audio track for recording, as shown in Figure 5.18.

Setting Default Thru

Sometimes inspiration comes before the time needed to create tracks and set up the sound to perform. The artist simply wants to hear a C before she sings. Should you tell her to hold on while you create some tracks for that, and then create a MIDI track and an Aux track and instantiate a plug-in, and then load the sound—all while she waits?

If you don't have any hardware synths, then the answer is yes, because there is no other way to get MIDI to play a note. If you have hardware synths, you can activate Default Thru and set it to your favorite piano sound, as seen in Figure 5.19. Provided your synth is patched through to the monitors (it should be normalled if you do this often), simply playing the keyboard will route MIDI to the synth and immediately give you a C on the piano. Instant gratification!

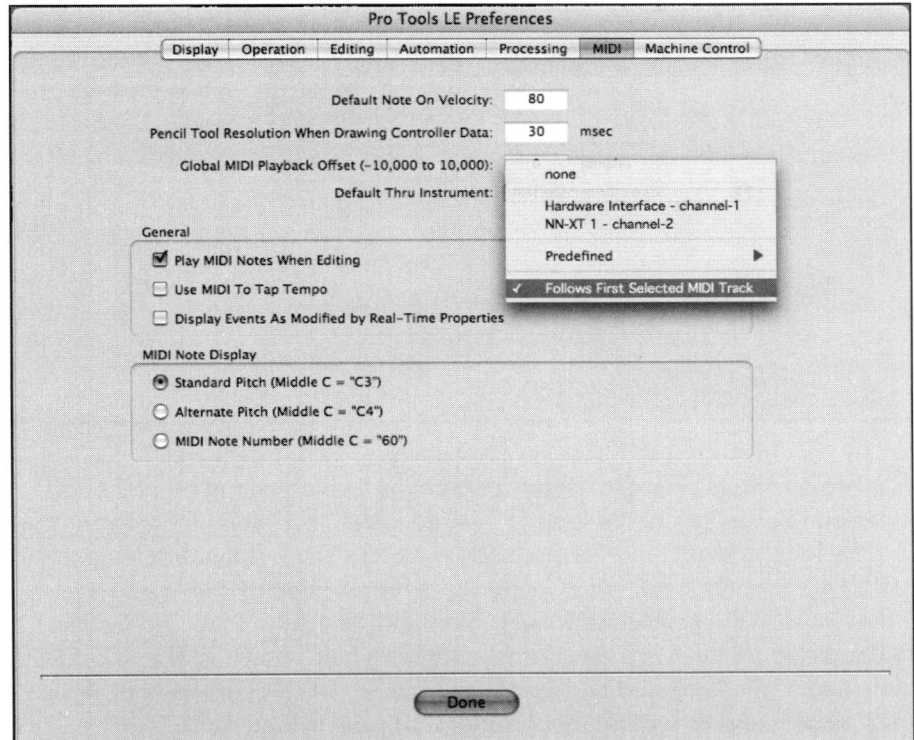

Figure 5.19

Setting Default Thru

Choose Setup > Preferences > MIDI, and set the synth and channel to play as default. If you don't have hardware synths, then you will need to create an Aux with a synth plug-in first to set the Default Thru to play a sound. New to Pro Tools v7 is the ability to set the Default Thru to Follows First Selected MIDI Track. This preference allows the user to change what synth is played as the Default Thru by simply choosing another MIDI track.

In the previous situation, where the singer simply wants to hear C, the producer has the capacity to choose what sound he plays for her by choosing a different MIDI track. If the original Default Thru had a sound with a slight chorus or pitch adjustment, this could throw the artist off. Instead of wasting time switching the Default Thru synth, simply choose a different track until you find the sound you both like!

Using Loops to Create a Tempo Map

How many hours have you spent trying to massage the tempo up and down to a hundredth of a BPM just to get it to line up perfectly with the loop you've chosen to build the song around? It never quite lines up, and you have to deal with it being either slightly shorter or slightly longer than the grid. In either case, it's no fun to have to deal with this for 156 bars.

Figure 5.20

A loop needing a tempo

Figure 5.20 shows a two-bar drum loop that doesn't match the session tempo of 120 bpm. If you know the meter and bar length of the loop (as we do here), Pro Tools can tell you what the exact BPM is for the loop and set your Tempo track to match. You will need to have the Conductor activated to use Identify Beat. (The Conductor is represented by the icon in the Transport window that looks like a conductor waving a baton.) Select the loop and choose Event > Identify Beat to bring up the Bar | Beat Markers dialog box, shown in Figure 5.21. Enter the appropriate meter and start and end times, and Pro Tools will conform your Tempo track to the exact tempo of the loop for that loop's length, as seen in Figure 5.22.

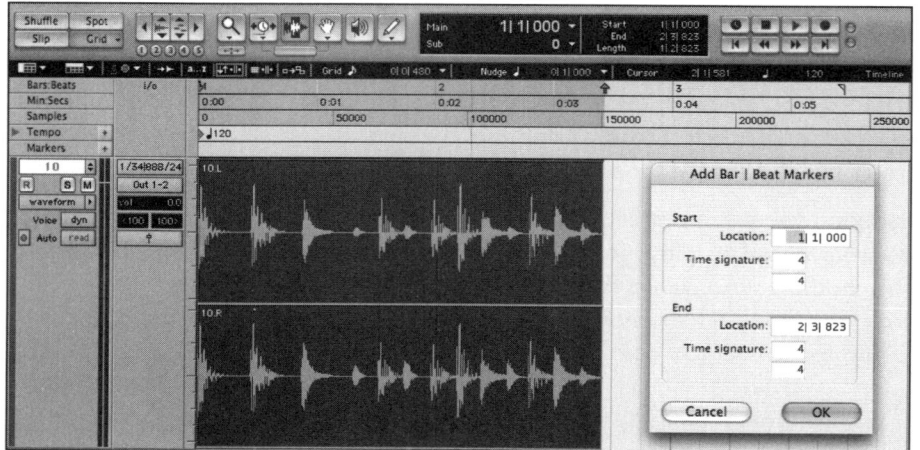

Figure 5.21

The Bar | Beat Markers dialog box as it stands at 120

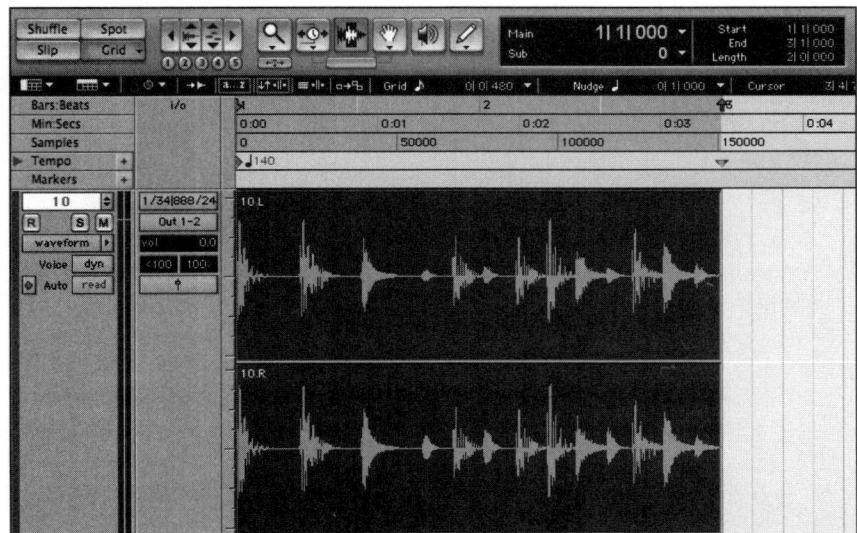

Figure 5.22

The Bar | Beat Markers
dialog box after entering
the proper info

The trick is to type in the desired start and end length. For example, your loop might start at
1|4|325 and end at 4|1|021, making it longer than the two bars you know it to be according
to Pro Tools, which is currently operating at the default tempo of 120. In the Bar | Beat Markers
dialog box, you must tell the program that the desired start and end times are 2|1|000 and
4|1|000. Pro Tools will measure the length of the loop (in samples), and then determine
what tempo fills that amount of samples over the course of two bars. Now your tempo and
your click tracks will play with your loop!

Loops that start and end well with the newly identified beat but drift within the loop require
more work. For these situations, see "Sending Your Loop to the Dr. Rex Player in Reason"
later in this chapter, as well as "Exact Beat Slicing Using the Beat Detective" in Chapter 4.

ReWiring into Pro Tools with Reason

Pro Tools often ships with Reason Adapted, a light version of Reason, giving all Pro Tools
users some software synths to play with right after purchase. One of the best features of
Reason is its ability to link MIDI, timing, and audio information to Pro Tools. Pro Tools can
drive Reason, and Reason can drive Pro Tools. MIDI in Pro Tools can drive the synths in
Reason, making it a dummy synth rack, if desired. There are 64 channels of ReWire audio
available in Reason, but most people only use (or find, for that matter) the first two.

Within the Pro Tools session, create an Instrument track (or Aux track for old-school users) to
plug into Reason. TDM users prior to version 6.x should use Audio tracks because RTAS plug-ins
don't work on Aux tracks. The plug-in, shown in Figure 5.23, will open the Reason application
and the default document set within the Reason preferences. On the plug-in, choose the
ReWire channels desired and you've officially ReWired!

Stereo tracks should instantiate the multi-channel version of Reason. Formerly, Pro Tools' multi-channel Reason plug-in would only see ReWire audio channels, Mix L and Mix R, making the multi-mono version necessary to go beyond these first channels. Now, simply choose the next stereo pair for the next stereo ReWire channels, as seen in Figure 5.24.

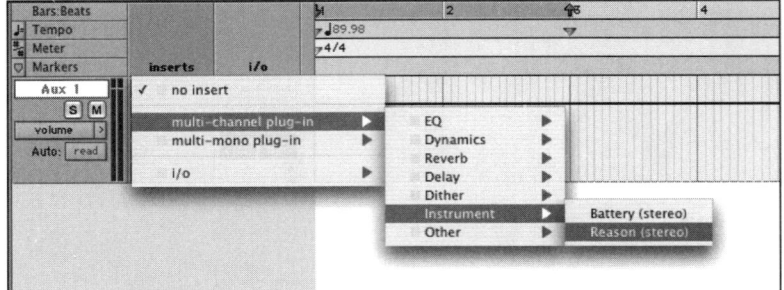

Figure 5.23

Using the multi-channel Reason plug-in

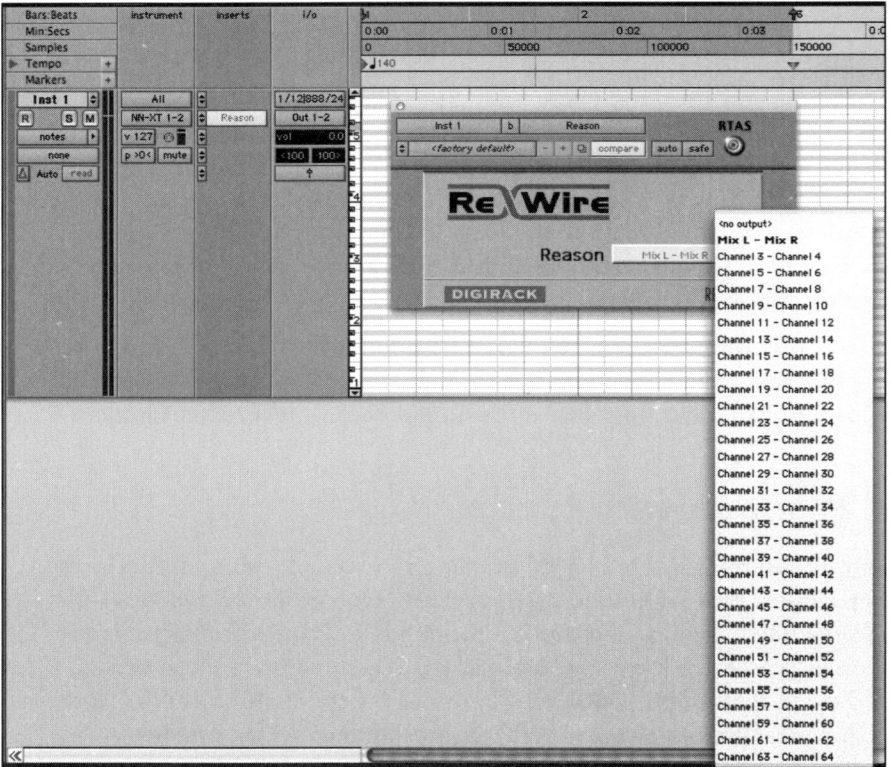

Figure 5.24

Multiple stereo channels available in multi-channel inserts

Printing the Reason Parts

One drawback to running Reason and Pro Tools together lies in the strength (or lack of it) of your system. Reason can be a CPU hog, especially with high track counts and high effect counts. To free up CPU space, it is sometimes necessary to print the Reason parts to audio and trade the available voices in Pro Tools for the CPU power on the computer.

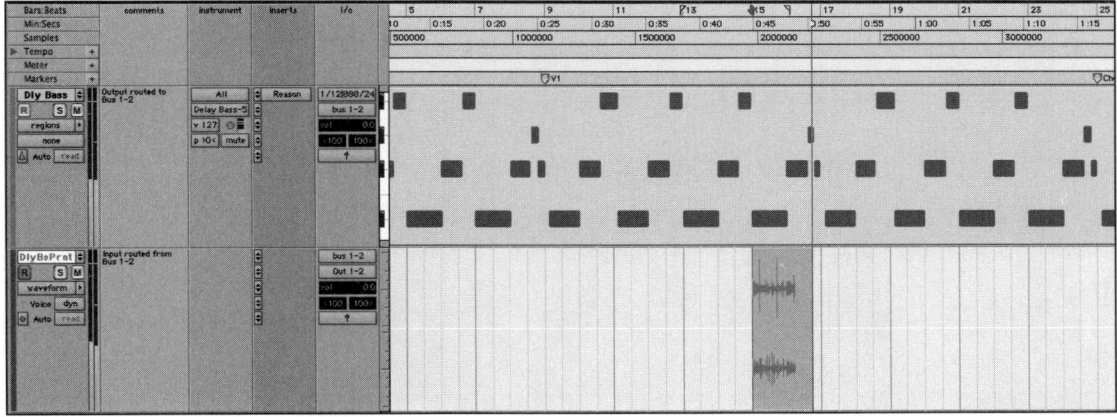

Figure 5.25

The signal chain to print Reason parts

Much like printing virtual synths (see "Monitoring and Recording Virtual Synthesizers" earlier in this chapter), this process requires two tracks if one is an Instrument track (or one track if the MIDI is sequenced in Reason because you won't need an Instrument track in Pro Tools). Assuming the MIDI is in Pro Tools and triggering the sounds from Reason, there are two tracks—one Instrument track for the MIDI data and one Audio track for recording. Route the output of the Instrument track to a bus that matches the input of the Audio track. Record-enable the new Audio track and record the part, as shown in Figure 5.25.

You can then make the Reason return inactive to free up CPU usage in Pro Tools, then delete or remove the part in Reason along with any synths that make that sound. The disadvantage here is that now you won't be able to make changes, and you've committed to the part as it stands. This is unfortunate, but sometimes a fact of life. You should consider upgrading your RAM or CPU if this is common.

Exporting Loops to Pro Tools from Reason

When ReWiring, if you constantly hit the processing wall and run out of RAM or CPU power, you might need to change how you work with these two tools. Try to sequence your parts in Reason (like Figure 5.26) to completion (or at least the completion of the part). Stop thinking about ReWiring and simply export the loop to Pro Tools right out of Reason from the menu, shown in Figure 5.27.

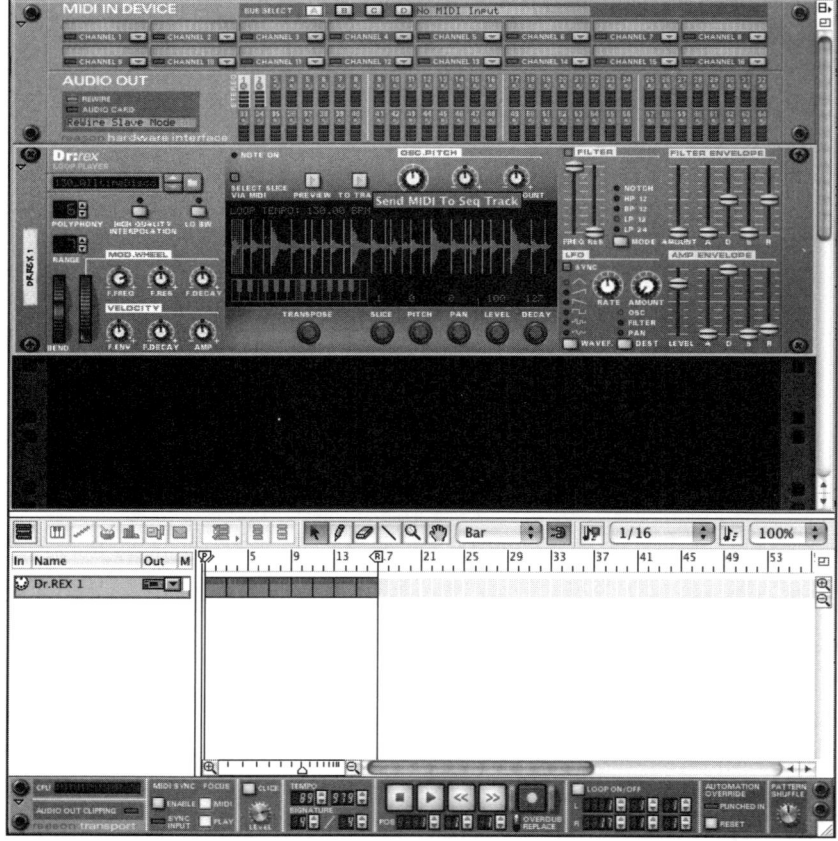

Figure 5.26

A simple loop in Reason

Because ReWire takes up more RAM and CPU, this method is simpler and more efficient than trying to run the two together. Keep in mind that Reason does not give you the Export Loop as Audio function when ReWired. You will need to save your song and quit both Reason and Pro Tools to export your loop from Reason. When you export each loop from Reason, you end up creating the arrangement in Pro Tools with chunks of audio (which take up little room), but you might notice a problem with tempo and sync. Pro Tools has a MIDI clock that can handle tempos to a resolution of a hundredth of a BPM, whereas Reason can go up to a thousandth of a BPM. This means Reason, when not ReWired to Pro Tools, will have a slight variation of tempo

Figure 5.27

The File > Export Loop as Audio File option in Reason

interpretation from Pro Tools. Unfortunately, sometimes loops come across slightly longer or shorter than a perfect one- or two-bar grid region like the one shown in Figure 5.28. Be sure to inspect every loop from Reason for perfection to the tempo in Pro Tools.

You could avoid this by ReWiring the two together and only creating a single stereo ReWire input to monitor (and print) Reason. This will keep the two tempos locked more tightly and should eliminate this anomaly. It does not, however, fix the CPU issue that started it all in the first place.

Another dilemma with exporting loops from Reason into Pro Tools is the non-zero-crossing click. Reason doesn't necessarily create loops cut on the zero-crossing point, depending on the timing of the MIDI track. If a note comes slightly early, the audio loop might come across as if the part played but was cut off at the grid point. You can avoid this by ensuring that your MIDI data in Reason has been quantized.

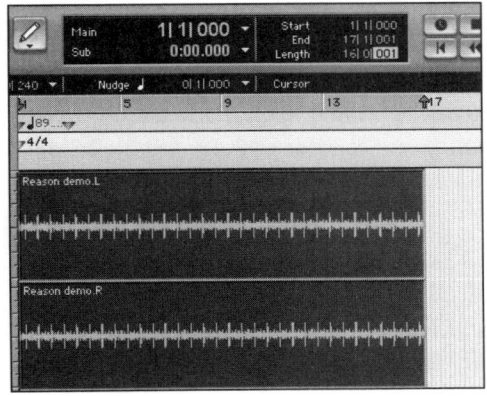

Figure 5.28

Imported loop from Reason off the grid

Sending Your Loop to the Dr. Rex Player in Reason (v6.x Only)

Because Pro Tools LE users didn't have access to Beat Detective prior to v6.7, the next best things were Reason and ReCycle. Pro Tools LE comes with Reason Adapted (a very light version of the popular software sequencer), but ReCycle is sold separately. Buy it. If you work with loops and Reason and you're still hanging on to that old software version, you should buy ReCycle. If you want audio parts you can quantize, buy it. Otherwise, upgrade to v7 and start to use Beat Detective (see "Exact Beat Slicing Using the Beat Detective" in Chapter 4).

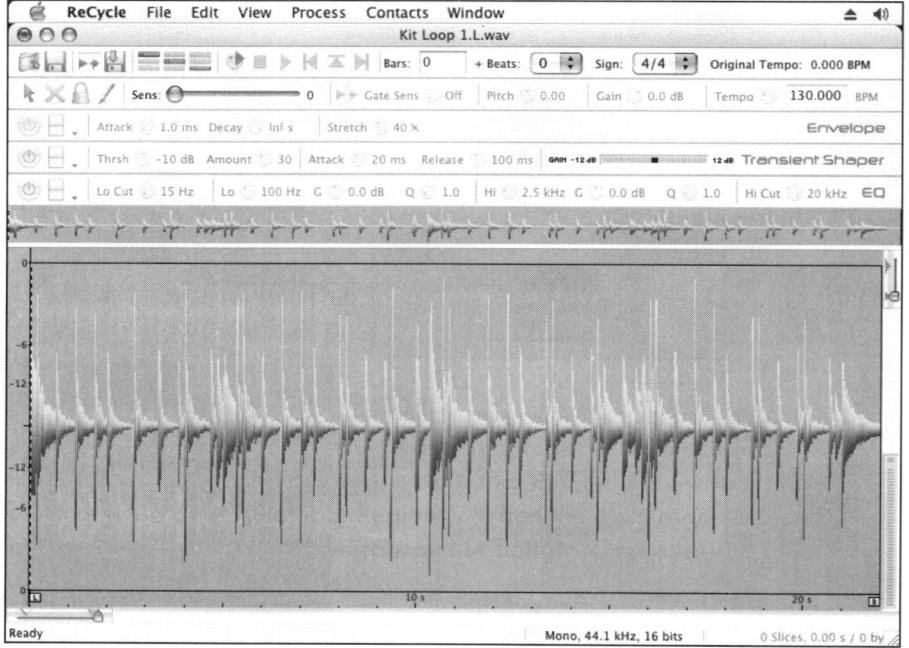

Figure 5.29

The ReCycle window

ReCycle, shown in Figure 5.29, allows you to import audio files, extract the tempo, and create a MIDI file to play the file hit by hit. First, it creates slice points at every transient, and then it measures the distance between the transients, creating a MIDI note timed at the same distance. The MIDI notes are created chromatically, so the first note is C, then C#, and so on, until the file is notated. Each note is assigned a unique slice, allowing the loop to be recreated in perfect time. This is great for replaying any loop at different tempos without having to get into TCE or Beat Detective and mangling the sound. The file is then saved in the .REX format for use in the Dr. Rex Player within Reason.

The Dr. Rex Player, shown in Figure 5.30, plays these .REX files at whatever tempo is set in Reason (or the ReWire host). As the tempo is increased, it plays the chromatic MIDI score faster, making it seem as if the file has been time-compressed. The sound is distinctly better than that by TCE because there are no artifacts involved—only the same audio slices played faster.

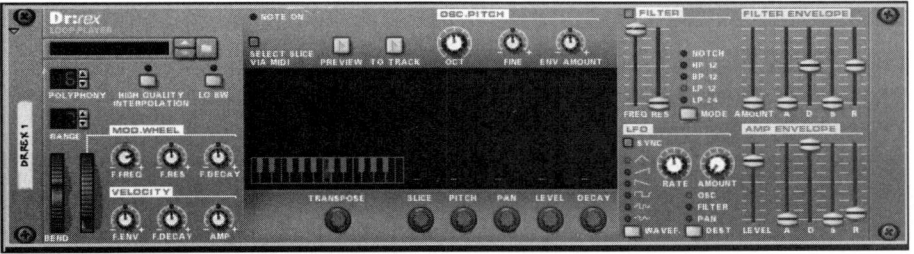

Figure 5.30

The Dr. Rex
Player

For loops that set the tempo in Pro Tools and don't quite fit the click, this is a great workaround. Even if you've identified the beat, the loop itself might have a swing that will never match the straight click in Pro Tools. "REXing" the loop is a great way to keep the audio quality, get it straighter (quantized) to use with the click, and keep the door open to speeding up or slowing down the song without having to resort to the damaging TCE Trim tool later.

Select the loop and export it to ReCycle by choosing Export Regions as Files from the Region List drop-down menu, shown in Figure 5.31. (See "Exporting as Files" in Chapter 3.) I suggest you create a separate folder next to the Audio Files folder called Recycle Exports because you might do this again within the song. Switch to ReCycle by hitting Apple+Tab if ReCycle is already open. If not, find it on the Dock and open it. (See "Customizing the Dock" in Chapter 1.)

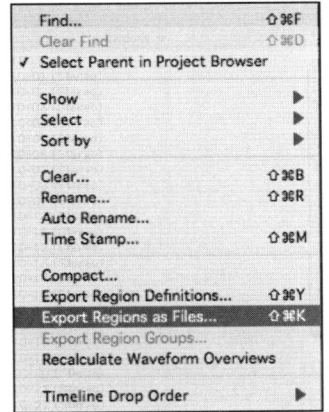

Figure 5.31

Export loop as a separate file to ReCycle

ReCycle won't use the Digi hardware, so you should be prepared to either listen to the computer speaker itself or wire the back of the Mac to your monitor system. Open the file in ReCycle and hit Yes when the software asks you to position the left locator to the first slice point, as shown in Figure 5.32. This sets the first slice at the first transient.

The most important button in ReCycle is the Preview toggle button, shown in Figure 5.33. It allows ReCycle to determine the natural tempo of the loop after you've told it the bar length. If you don't click this button, this process will not work correctly!

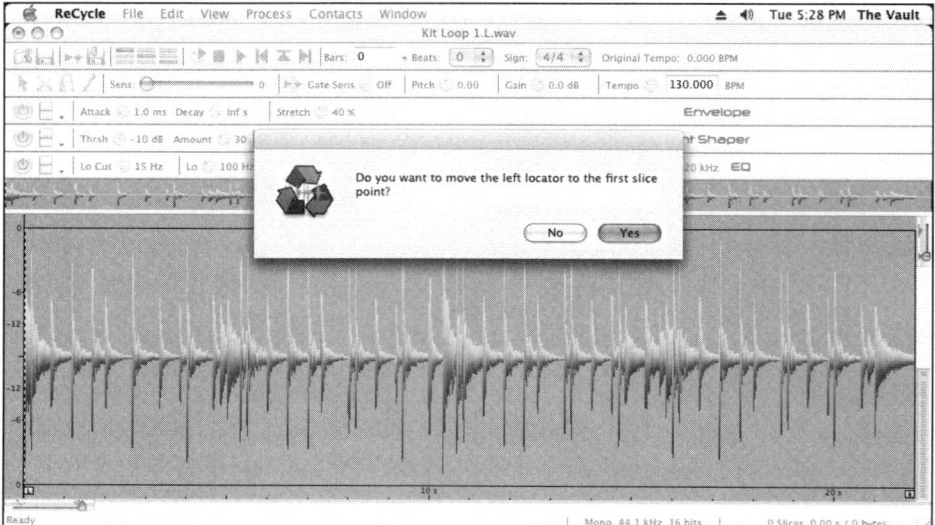

Figure 5.32

The Left Slice dialog box in ReCycle

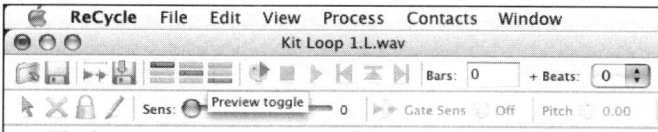

Figure 5.33

The Preview toggle button

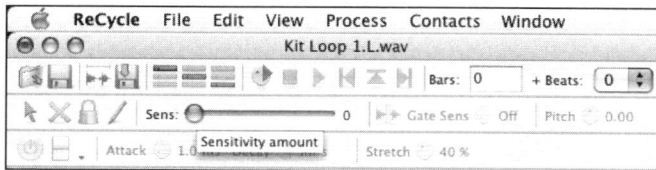

Figure 5.34

The Sensitivity slider

Slide the Sensitivity bar upward (shown in Figure 5.34) until a slice is drawn at every significant transient, as seen in Figure 5.35. You can create missing slices with the Pencil tool, move them with the mouse, delete extras, and audition each slice to ensure good slicing. At this point, picture each slice with a MIDI note attached, with each slice getting a chromatically higher note as the loop goes forward. Save the file in a separate folder called REXs, next to the ReCycle Exports folder you created.

Now, simply open the .REX file in the Dr. Rex Player (shown in Figure 5.36 with the Browse Loop button) and hit the Preview button, shown in Figure 5.37. If you've successfully ReWired into Pro Tools, you should hear your loop at the Pro Tools tempo, which should be the natural tempo of the loop derived from Identify Beat. You can quantize the beat in Reason to some resolution that works and have the loop you want match your click in Pro Tools!

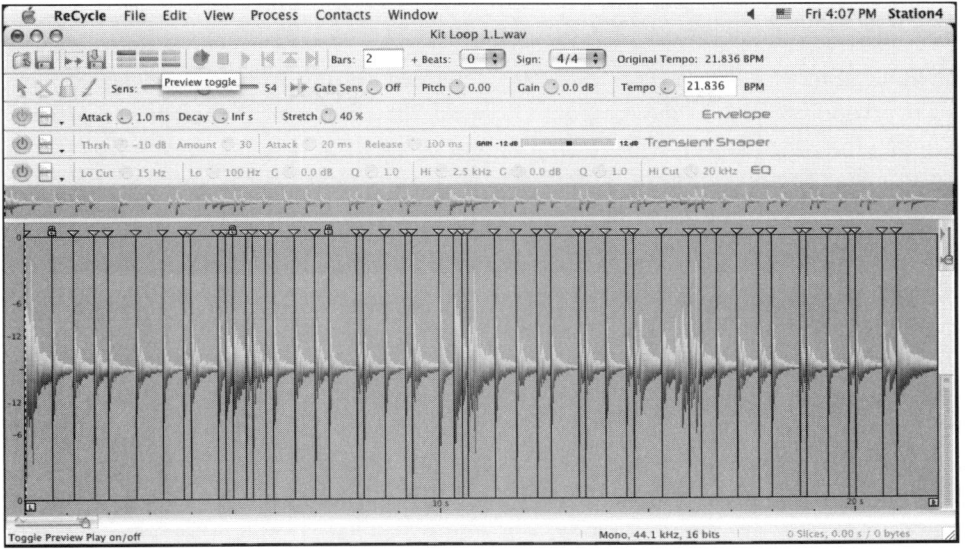

Figure 5.35

The slices drawn at transient points

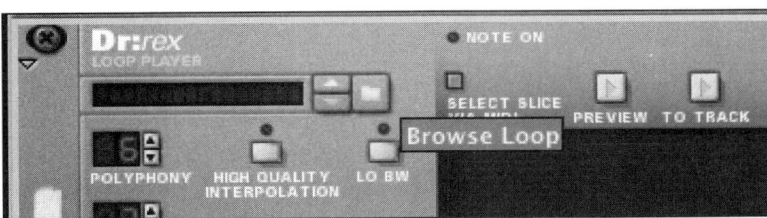

Figure 5.36

Browse loop

Figure 5.37

The Preview Loop button on the Dr. Rex Player

Creating Your Own REX Files

The biggest advantage to REX files is their ability to reconform to any tempo of any song. Since the file is sliced into separate hits, as the tempo is changed, the slices simply realign to the same proportion to match the new tempo. With version 7, one of the secrets is in knowing that tracks can be aligned to either samples or ticks. With tracks aligned to ticks, any tempo change will reconform the regions on the track to the new tempo. With version 7, any loop can be "REXed" by employing one of two methods—Beat Detective (slicing) or Identify Beat (no slicing)

❋ **Beat Detective.** (Use this option when you need to conform the loop to the song tempo and cannot change the song tempo, as it would adversely affect the rest of the tracks.) Since the loop doesn't conform to the session tempo, use Beat Detective's Separate Region function to slice the loop at each transient. Once separated, use the Region Conform operations within Beat Detective to quantize the slices to the grid of the song. Once the slices are in place, select them all and group them into a Region Group by choosing Region > Group (CMD+OPT+G). A good idea would be to export the Region Group to a place on your system where you keep Region Groups. This will make it easy to use this loop at any tempo in any song! For more on how this works, see "Exact Beat Slicing Using the Beat Detective" in Chapter 4.

❋ **Identify Beat.** (Use this option when you have a loop in a fairly fresh song and don't have to worry about changing the tempo.) When you bring the loop into a new song and want to play with the tempo before proceeding with production, first import the loop to its own track. Once there, drag the beginning of the first downbeat of the loop to the beginning of a bar in Grid mode. Select the entire loop and choose Event > Identify Beat. Select the desired start and end bar markers and hit OK. This will conform the session tempo to the length of the loop. Now that the loop matches a tempo, choose Edit > Separate Region > At Transients. A completed version of this process is shown in Figure 5.38. Now that the loop is sliced, I suggest you create a Region Group from it and export it to a place on your system where you keep Region Groups. This will make it easy to use this loop at any tempo in any song!

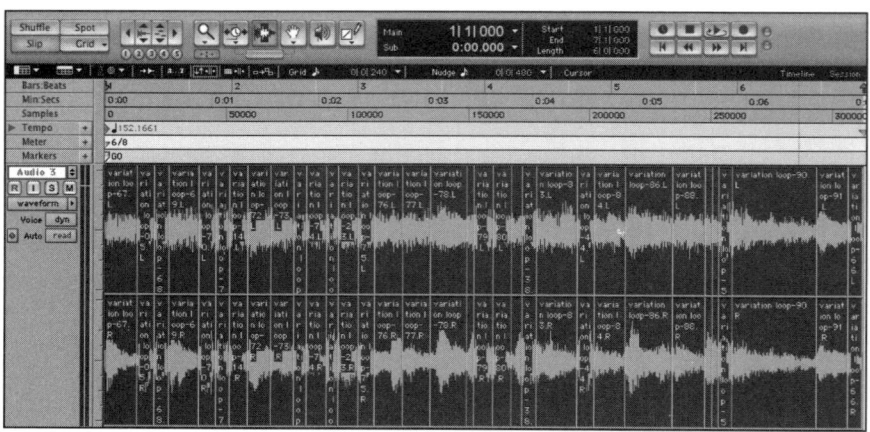

Figure 5.38

A loop now conforming to a tempo, ready for Region Grouping

Exporting MIDI Files to Pro Tools

Some people complain about the lack of quantizing options within Reason. They feel that Pro Tools gives them more options and more control over the MIDI data. If you're one of these people, you'll be happier bringing your MIDI from Reason back into Pro Tools.

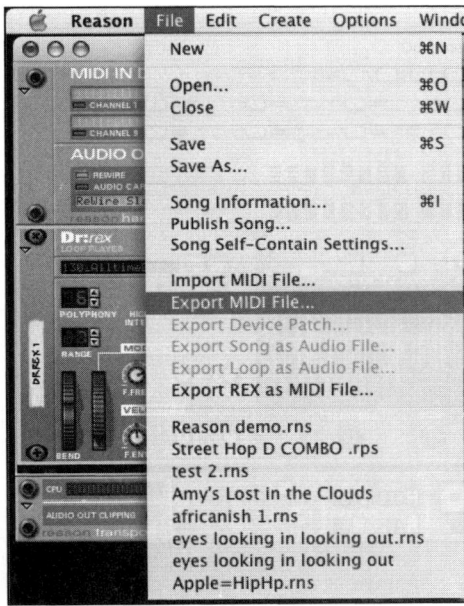

Figure 5.39

Exporting MIDI loops from Reason

First, you exported the loop from Pro Tools to ReCycle, and then to the Dr. Rex Player (as a .REX file). Now you send the MIDI file derived from ReCycle to Pro Tools again. Select the length of time of the loop (two bars in the original example) and choose File > Export MIDI File, as shown in Figure 5.39. Create a separate folder called MIDI Files next to the Audio Files folder because you might do this a lot. In Pro Tools, choose File > Import > MIDI to Region List (shown in Figure 5.40) and grab the Reason file.

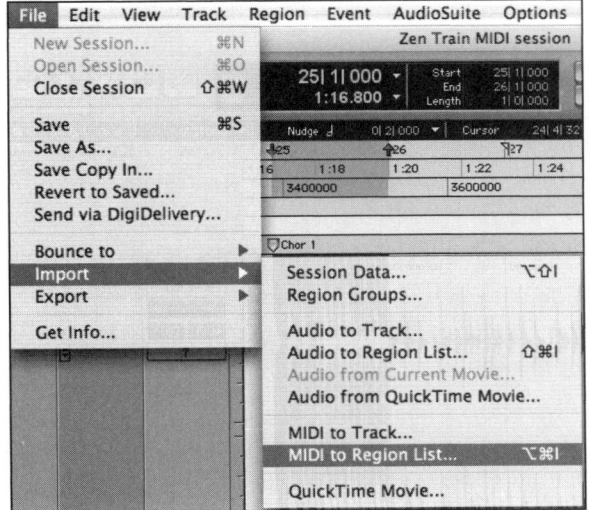

Figure 5.40

Importing MIDI to the Region List

If your Region List fills with a lot of tracks, you will need to either find the one labeled properly or individually drag them onto MIDI tracks to inspect them. The .REX file will look like a diagonal line from the lower-left to the upper-right, as shown in Figure 5.41, because it is chromatic and forward in time. Set the MIDI track's output to the Dr. Rex Player in the Reason document and hit Play. Your .REX file will still play as before, but now you can manipulate the MIDI data as you like using the increased MIDI manipulation available in Pro Tools. For more on this, check out flattening performances in the section "Some Quantizing Tips" later in this chapter.

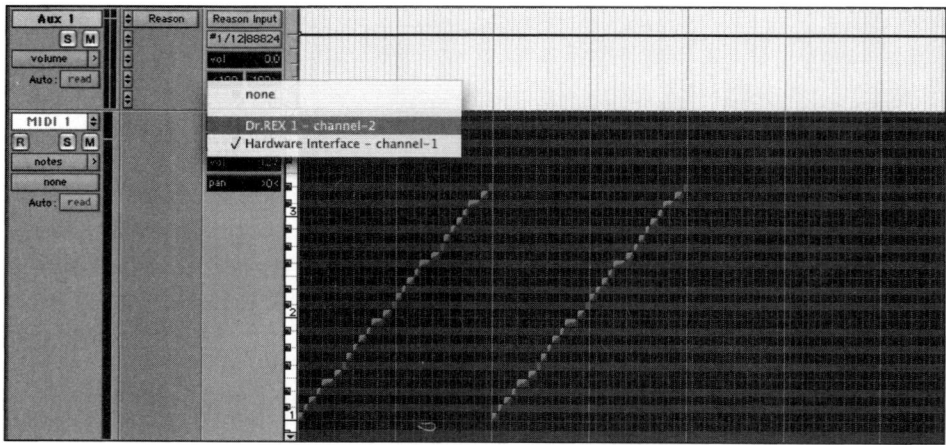

Figure 5.41

A .REX file on the MIDI track in Pro Tools

Thickening the Dr. Rex Parts

A common complaint about Reason in general (as well as the Dr. Rex Player) is the sound quality. It is commonly held that the mixer engine in Reason is thin, and all sound in Reason sounds better when it is ReWired into another DAW host. However, the Dr. Rex Player (at least the presets within Reason) doesn't improve this very much because most of the presets available are somewhat older-sounding and might not be useful by themselves.

A great way to thicken the Dr. Rex loop and maintain the feel involves time-intensive copying of the MIDI data. You'll basically recreate the performance and use the recreation to trigger *other* sounds, keeping the groove but improving the sound.

First, create another Aux track and plug in your favorite drum module or sampler. Open your favorite drum patch (or at least a patch with drums that match the song). Copy the MIDI data from the Dr. Rex track to another MIDI track. Instead of feeding the second MIDI track to the new drums, assign it to the Dr. Rex as well (a duplicated playlist could work, too) to determine the notation of the original drum part. This duplicated MIDI track setup is demonstrated in Figure 5.42.

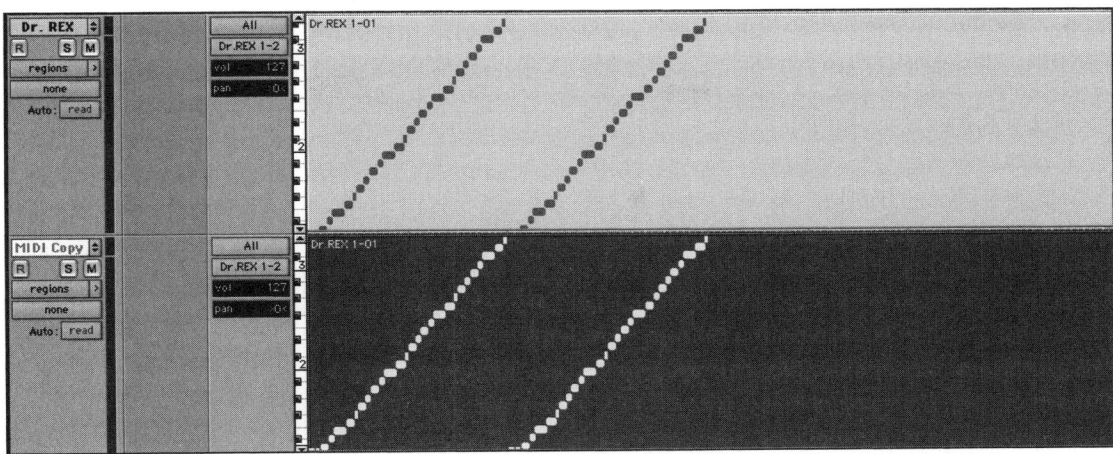

Figure 5.42

Two MIDI tracks with the same MIDI data going to the Dr. Rex

On the duplicate track or playlist, identify each MIDI note as kick, snare, hat, tom, or cymbal. Clicking on the note will audition the Dr. Rex sound associated with it. Control-drag each duplicated note to the same note as the first note that plays that part. For example, if the first note (C) is the kick and the fifth note is also a kick (E), Control-drag the E to the C. Control-drag locks the note in place and allows vertical transposition, keeping the timing and the feel of the part. Continue this until all the kicks are on one note (in this example, C). Continue this process for all sounds on the track until you are presented with one MIDI note for every instance of every sound, as shown in Figure 5.43. For simple loops, you'll end up with three notes: kick (C), snare (C#), and hat (D).

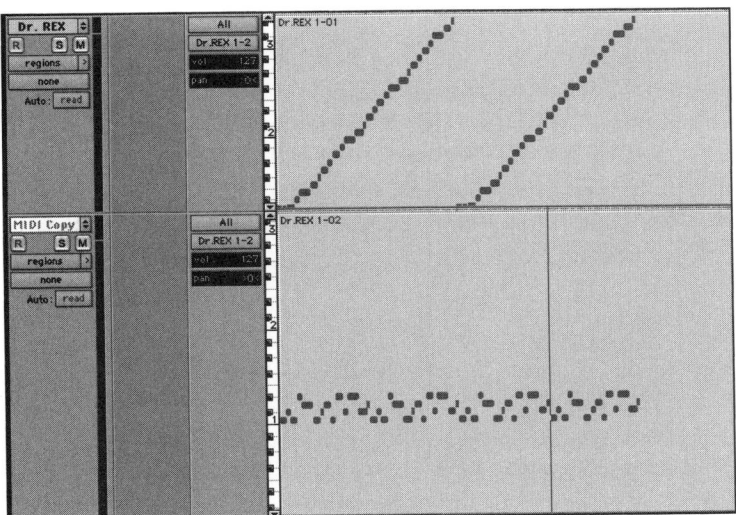

Figure 5.43

A consolidated Dr. Rex track

Now, take this consolidated MIDI track and assign it to the new drum sounds, as shown in Figure 5.44. You'll find that the feel and timing of the Dr. Rex part is perfectly assigned to the new sounds. Mix the two to keep the original tone of the Dr. Rex and the clarity and punch of the new drums.

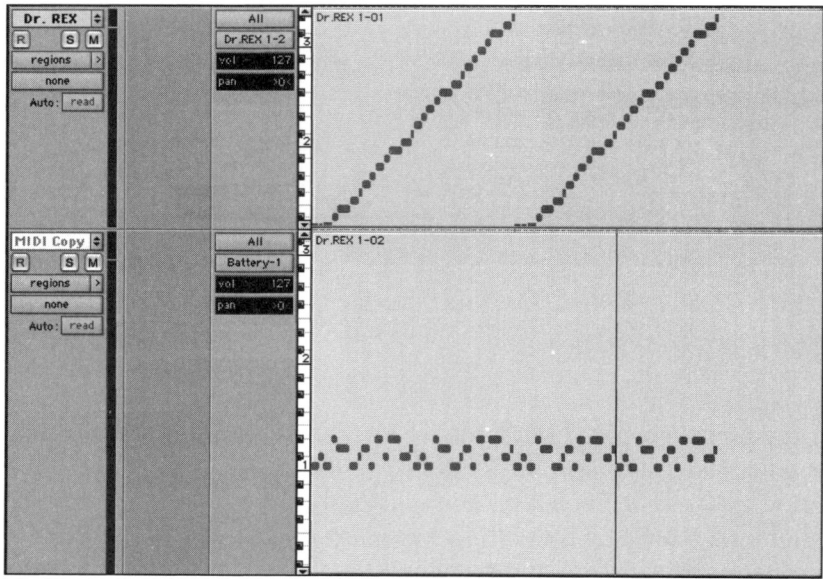

Figure 5.44

Two MIDI tracks to two drum machines

Thickening Other MIDI Parts

If the sound quality of Reason's synth sounds is still suspect after ReWiring into Pro Tools, consider doubling or thickening the parts with multiple synths.

One of the issues with the sound might be color. If you only use Reason as your sound module, you are only working with one color—Reason. If you have another virtual (or hardware) synth, use a similar sound for color variation. After the MIDI is sequenced, be sure to export it to Pro Tools for importing into a fresh MIDI track. Assign the copied MIDI track to the second synth, choose a sound that is similar to the first, and blend the two with the faders, as shown in Figure 5.45. You will maintain the flavor of the part and the feel while borrowing another synth for a different color.

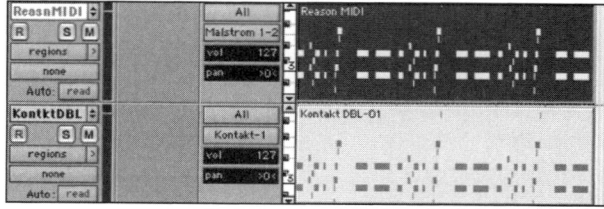

Figure 5.45

A copied MIDI part for thickening

Sampling Pro Tools Regions with Reason

Since the invention of the sampler, audio has been sampled and either triggered repeatedly to create a stutter effect or played up and down the keyboard with interesting pitch and tempo by-products.

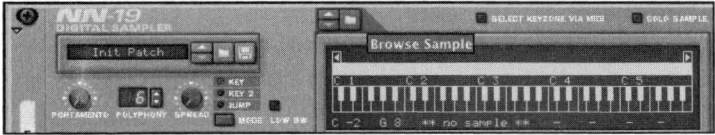

Figure 5.46

Loading samples in the NN-19

To use Reason's samplers to play the region desired, first export the region from Pro Tools by choosing Export Regions as Files from the Region List drop-down menu. Switch to Reason and create a sampler of your choice (NN-10 or NN-XT). Click the Browse Sample button on the sampler (shown in Figure 5.46), and position it to play all over the keyboard (or a certain range of notes). You can now trigger the sample to stutter by playing in repeated notes at the root key (usually C3) or create interesting effects by playing up and down the keyboard. (Consult your Reason manual for details about the sampling functions contained in Reason.)

Effects, ReWire, and DSP

One of the benefits of ReWiring into Pro Tools is the access to the high-quality plug-ins available within the Pro Tools environment. The delays and reverbs in Reason don't always stand up to the ones available in Pro Tools.

Whenever possible, I recommend you use the effects in Pro Tools instead of those in Reason. You will find more automation control and cleaner sound. However, there might be times when you run out of DSP (as seen in Figure 5.47) and those plugs, and you'll need to shave off some DSP.

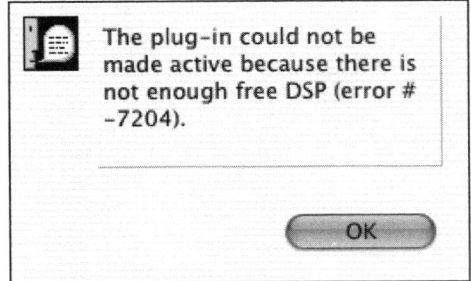

Figure 5.47

DAE 7204: not enough DSP

In this situation, you need to analyze the part that has run out of DSP and what is desired. For example, if the lead vocal needs a delay line set up, you won't be able to get one out of Reason easily. You will need to inspect your ReWire parts to see whether there is an effect being used on them that can be replaced from within Reason. If your drums have a fat reverb on them in Pro Tools, but the sounds come from Reason, you might choose to remove the reverb from Pro Tools and create one in Reason.

Before you make this decision, you'll need to balance the quality of the reverb on the drums against the need to get a delay on the vocal. If you determine that it is worth it to switch the reverb, I suggest you ReWire the reverb on the drums in Reason to its own track in Pro Tools (see Figure 5.48) because you might need some EQ on it to make it come to life. This will take up more DSP, so balance that, too. (Now might be a good time to Save As and try the move to see whether it works.)

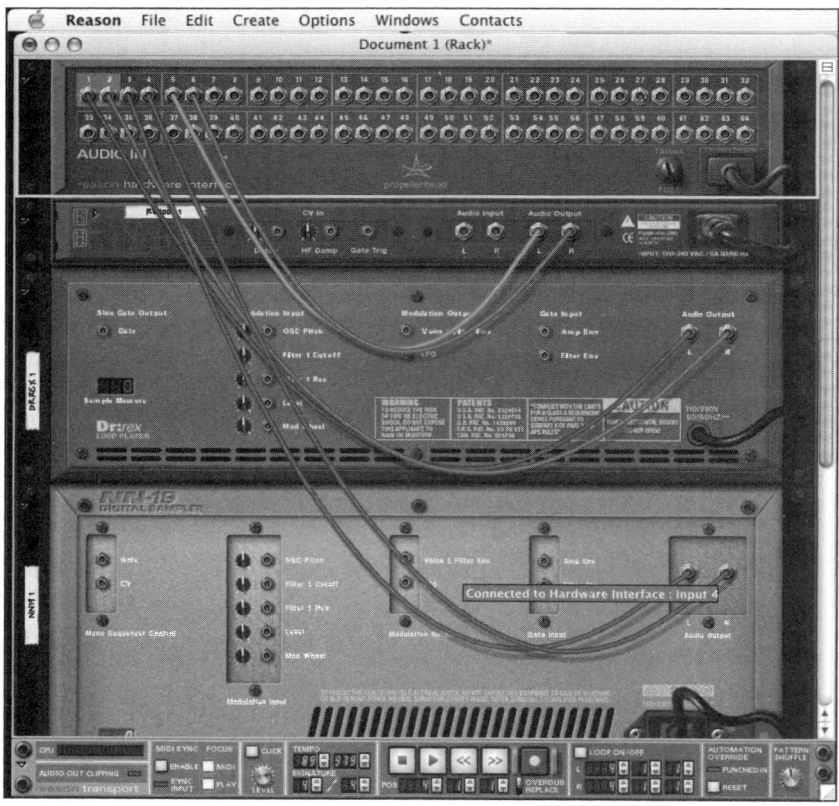

Figure 5.48

ReWiring the drums from Reason into Pro Tools (ReWire 3/4), and ReWiring the reverb from Reason into Pro Tools (ReWire 5/6)

You should make a similar decision with hardware synths. Whenever possible in this case, I suggest the opposite. If your synth has an effect module on it, use it. The effect was built with the synth in mind, so the sound should be good. In addition, you'll get the sound right out of the synth with everything needed, and it should sit in the track better. Only if the synth has a poor-sounding effect module should you use the Pro Tools effects (or if the synth simply doesn't have the desired effect). This will save system resources.

MIDI Beat Clock

When the song speeds up, does your delay speed up too? What about your arpeggio synth line?

MIDI Beat Clock is an old but useful technology that allows multiple MIDI devices to work in time with a common tempo. Beat Clock sends a MIDI message telling the device what the tempo is, as well as tapping out the beat. This allows synths and effects to follow along and keep musical with changing tempos.

Some of the built-in effects naturally default to keeping up with the tempo, such as the delays. Reason allows most effects and LFOs to follow as well by clicking their Sync buttons. For other synths, such as Native Instruments FM7, you will need to activate Beat Clock and send it to that synth in particular, as seen in Figure 5.49. Now any tempo-based sound on the FM7 will tap along with your custom tempo. Unless you are going for that out-of-time effect, you should send Beat Clock everywhere.

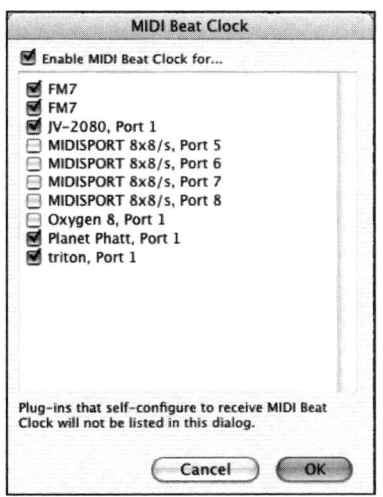

Figure 5.49

The FM7 getting Beat Clock

Using Reason as the Click

Version 6.0 of Pro Tools brought a new tool—the built-in Click insert, seen in Figure 5.50. With this plug-in, an activated click would naturally drive the sounds built into the plug-in. However, the clicks in the preset list (see Figure 5.51) aren't necessarily what your talent wants to hear. Although the sounds are very percussive (they cut through a heavy mix), they can be very sharp and potentially painful.

For those who are using Reason, any module there becomes a potential click sound. Use two slices of the Dr. Rex or two samples in the Redrum as your click module, if you prefer those sounds. You could also use a percussive synth sound if the song calls for it. Assign the click to your module of choice in the Click/Countoff Options dialog box, as seen in Figure 5.52. This should play during countoff as well.

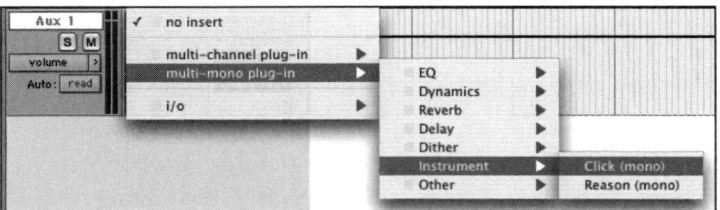

Figure 5.50

The Click Instrument plug-in

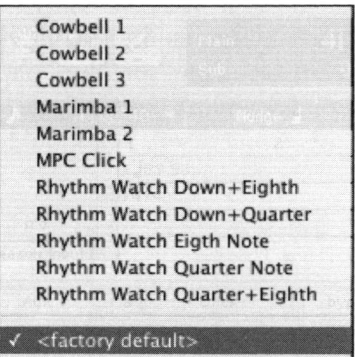

Figure 5.51

The Click plug-in sound options

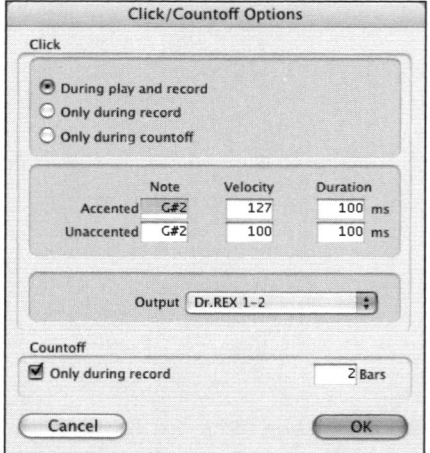

Figure 5.52

Click options with click assigned to Dr. Rex

Keep in mind that you will need to choose the accented and unaccented sounds as C(1) and C#(1) for the first two slices of the drum modules. Both the Dr. Rex and Redrum modules take their first slices at C, an octave below middle C, so try lower Cs if you can't find the right sound at middle C.

Triggering MIDI from Audio

There have been several attempts throughout the last decade to create an analysis program to analyze audio and extract MIDI data, including pitch and velocity. They classically haven't worked very well because it is extremely difficult to analyze this data. This needs to be done by hand...mostly.

Assuming a monophonic audio source (vocal, lead line, sax, and so on), a plug-in such as Antares Auto-Tune can do a pretty good job of performing the pitch analysis. If you don't have a tool like this, you may need to decipher the note data by ear. From there, you can apply the melodic notes to the timing in the audio file. You'll need to separate the file at the transients and create a MIDI note at the right pitch to align with the transient. You can do this by hand with Tab-to-Transient (in Figure 5.53) or faster with the Edit > Separate Region > At Transients option (shown in Figure 5.54).

Activate the Tab-to-Transient feature in the Edit window, and tab through the audio file transient by transient (note by note), slicing the audio at each transient. This performs a similar function to ReCycle. Create a MIDI track directly below the Audio track. Return to the beginning of the audio file and tab into the first transient. Switch to the Pencil tool, and click on the cursor location to create a MIDI note at that location on the MIDI track, as seen in Figure 5.55. You may need to trim the length of the note, since the Pencil will not guarantee a match between the original audio length and the created MIDI note! Because the Pencil tool can also perform quick transpositions, position the cursor over the note to switch it to the Grabber tool, and then drag the note to its appropriate pitch.

With the Separate Region at Transients option, simply select the region and separate it at the transients. This will save a bit of time. You'll still need to manually create MIDI notes to align to the beginning of each region. You can audition the pitch of the MIDI note against the region by looping the region (if it's long enough: a half second or longer) and dragging the note up and down until you find the right note. For pitches between standard notes, you need to transpose the synth itself by cents to fine-tune the MIDI performance to match the audio. Be prepared for this to take some time.

Figure 5.53

The Tab-to-Transient feature activated

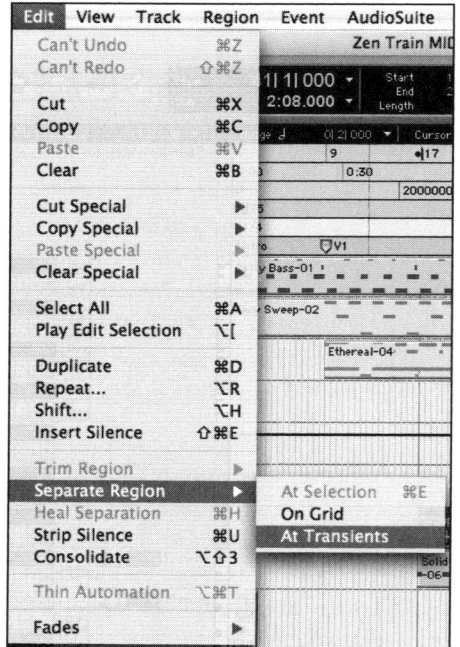

Figure 5.54

The Separate Region > At Transients menu

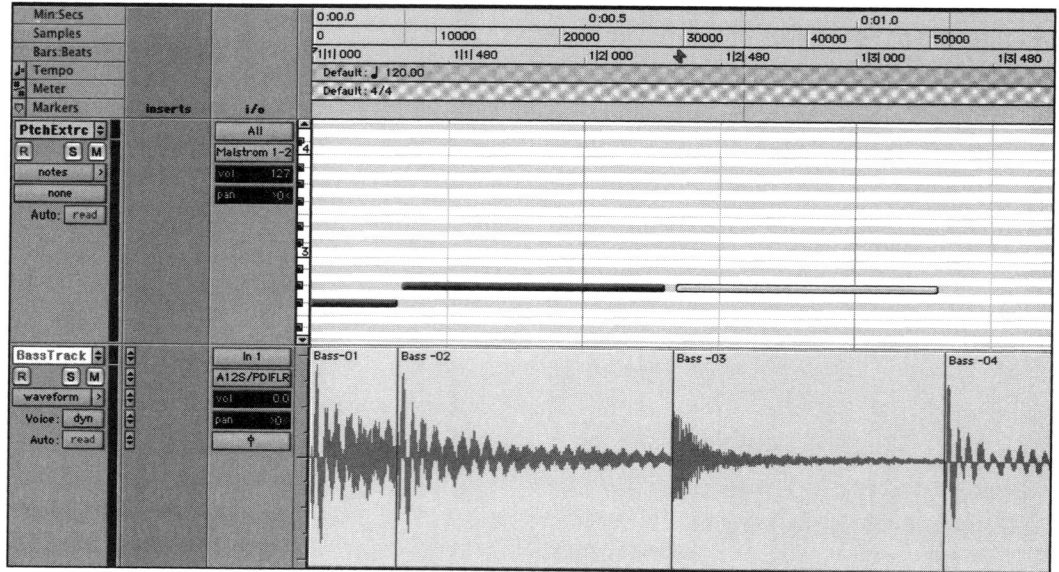

Figure 5.55

MIDI notes drawn in at transients

Quick Chord Creation

Let's face it—not all of us play the piano very well. For some of us, creating chords is simply not an option on the MIDI keyboard. If you know what notes you want to hear, but you can't figure them out on the keyboard, try OPTION-dragging a single note upward (which copies the notes) to make a chord.

If it's a small section, set Pro Tools into Loop Playback (choose Options > Loop Playback or SHIFT+CMD+L) and OPTION-drag the note up or down to audition different chords until you get what you want. You should be in Slip mode (or Relative Grid mode) because the note from which you want to build the chord might not necessarily be on the grid. If it is (verify this by selecting the note and inspecting the Start/End/Length Indicator), you should use Grid mode. If you OPTION-drag the note once and make a copy of it, you can CTRL-drag it up and down in place, ensuring the consistency of the timing of the note. Of course, you can be slick and CTRL+OPTION+drag to both copy the note *and* lock its position at once! If this hunt-and-peck method of chord creation is what you use, take some piano lessons.

Quick Chord Changes

Suppose somewhere in the middle of composing the song the artist notices that the big note in the chorus no longer sounds right. Some investigation determines that the big chord under the big note is major but should be minor. You are now presented with the joy of finding the major third in the chord (in every instance) and dragging it to the minor third.

CTRL+CMD-clicking the MIDI keyboard on the left of the track will select all the MIDI notes at that pitch and allow you to globally transpose the note down a half step to accomplish the task; but surely the notes are right in some other chord, making this procedure somewhat useless to you. A quick collection of steps can potentially save you some time over doing it by hand, especially if the problem occurs in some places but not in others.

Switch the view of your MIDI track to Regions, and separate all the chords that need adjusting. Choose the Object Grabber (TDM) and only select those chords. (Use the SHIFT key to select multiple chords). If you work with LE, you might need to separate the regions in question and drag them to a unique track for this maneuver, as shown in Figure 5.56.

Copy the chords and paste them onto a new MIDI playlist. Switch back to Notes view and CMD+SHIFT-click the bad note on the MIDI keyboard to select all the notes that need transposing. With them all selected, drag the notes down a half step (or whatever is appropriate) as seen in Figure 5.57. Switch back to the Regions view, and copy the regions again using the Object Grabber (TDM—with LE systems, you should have the regions on a unique track or playlist, so simply copy and paste them back to the original track or playlist). Switch back to the original playlist, and paste them back into position. Your big chord under the big note is now minor, and you've quickly made the artist smile...again!

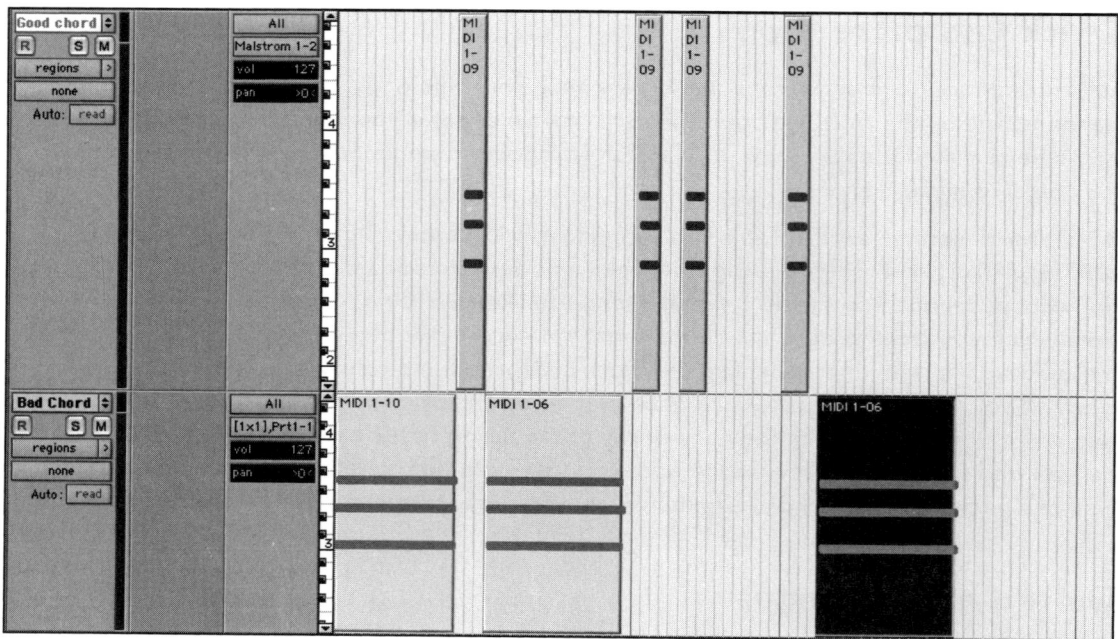

Figure 5.56

Multiple regions selected on a unique MIDI track

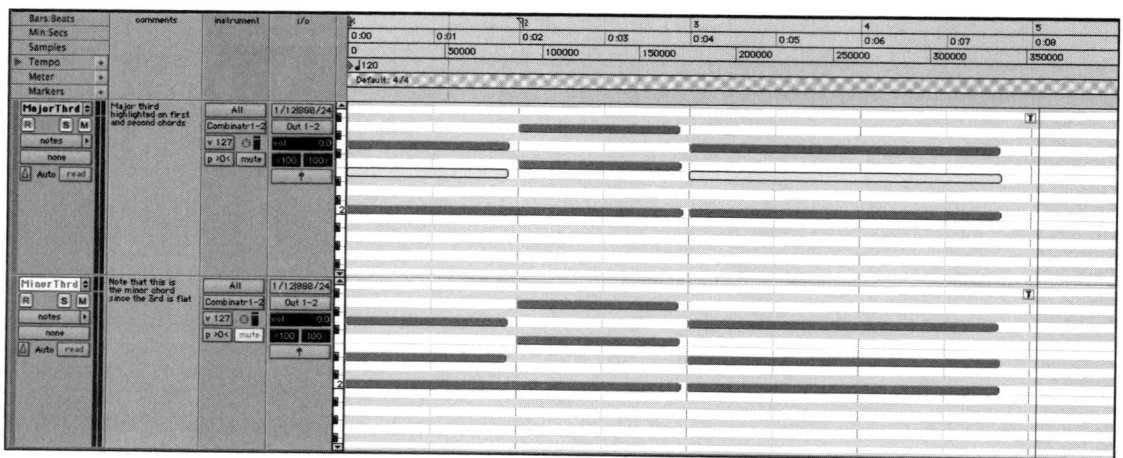

Figure 5.57

Two versions, one major and one minor

Splitting Hands

So you happened to be recording your MIDI track on the piano patch, and you love what you improvised. However, now you want to produce the song for real, and you feel that the left-hand part should play an upright bass and the right hand should play a jazz organ.

After you've determined your tempo and sufficiently quantized the performance, a quick way to split hands is not as simple as you'd think. While viewing the notes on the MIDI track, if you try to select the notes above the left-hand divider and copy and paste them onto another MIDI track, you'll find it doesn't work. Unfortunately, you must perform the move somewhat backwards.

Version 7 has a new function for performing this task within the Select/Split Notes menu, found by choosing Event > MIDI > Select/Split Notes (OPTION+Y). At the bottom of the dialog box, shown in Figure 5.58, you'll find the Action section where you can have Pro Tools split notes based on your criteria. You can copy or cut the data either to the clipboard or to another track— including copying each note to a separate track.

Without version 7, you'd need to copy the MIDI to a second track and delete notes on each. On one track, select all the left-handed notes and delete them, leaving the right-handed notes. On the other, perform the opposite move. Then assign the left-only track to one sound and the right-only track to another.

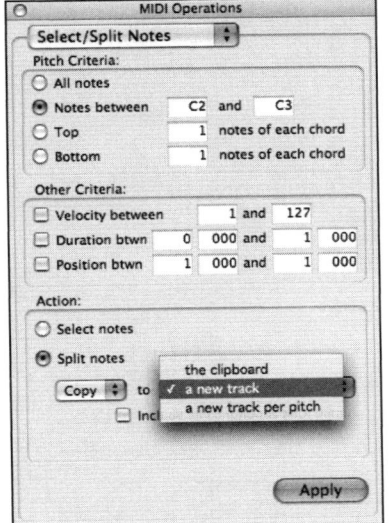

Figure 5.58

The MIDI Operations dialog box with the Select/Split Notes options

When Reason Loses the First Hit

One of the greatest functions of Reason is the ease of loop creation. Through the Dr. Rex and the pattern sequencers (on Redrum and the Matrix), loops are easy to create and play. However, when you are ReWiring into Pro Tools, loops can get funny.

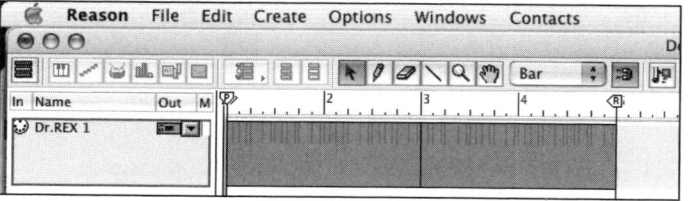

Figure 5.59

Four-bar loop in Reason with a Dr. Rex part

Unfortunately, when you set up a loop in Reason and then play the loop, like the one in Figure 5.59, sometimes the first hit of the Dr. Rex loop is cut off on each successive loop play. One fix (which is only useful during loop playback because that's where the problem manifests) is to massage the start time of the first hit to slightly later so it doesn't hit exactly on the one in Reason, as seen in Figure 5.60. This is a *major* problem for proper start-finish playing, but for temporary fixes (and insanity management), it works okay.

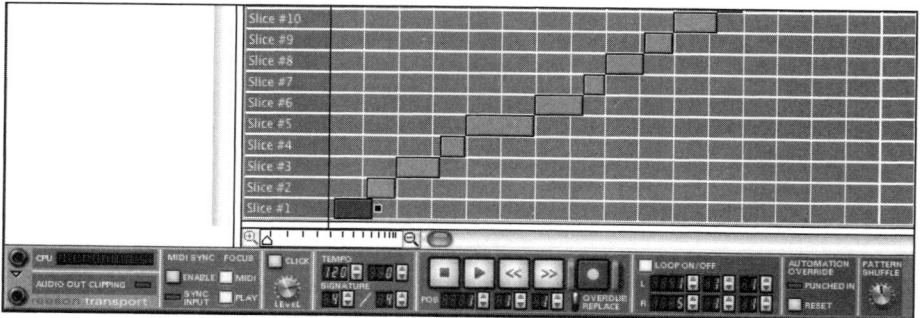

Figure 5.60

Reason sequence with first hit off the grid

A better fix is to know this ahead of time and deal with the problem once and for all. For some reason (ha!), a Pro Tools loop of the same MIDI information plays just fine. Set up your loop in Reason and simply export the MIDI file for the track. Import the MIDI file into Pro Tools, and set the Track view to Regions. Trim the region to match the desired length and position it to the Bar|Beat desired, then loop. You will find that the same Rex part plays (and loops) just fine with the first beat quantized to perfection, as shown in Figure 5.61. You will need to arrange the part throughout the song in Pro Tools now.

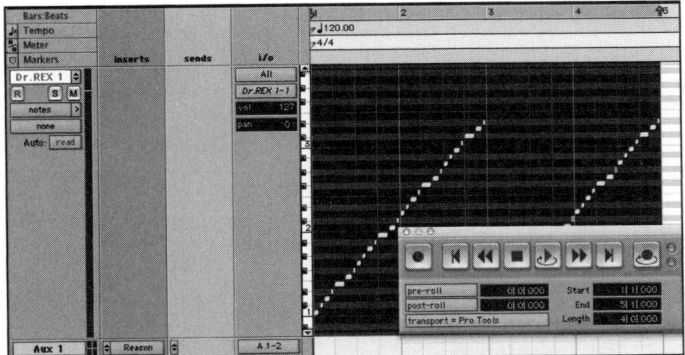

Figure 5.61

Same Rex sequence in
Pro Tools looped just fine

Some Quantizing Tips

For electronic music, the quantization of notes can produce the timing that gives the song its
feel (or kills it). *Quantizing* is simply the mechanizing of the performance timing, velocity,
pitch, and duration that can even out the notes and lock them to a tempo grid. Although the
process is easy, there are several factors that can help give you the flavor and tightness
desired. I suggest you experiment to find which settings work best for you and your song.
I propose the following as a list of good ideas.

❋ Real-Time Properties, which is new to version 7, is the ability to apply real-time properties
to any and all MIDI tracks. Real-time properties are simply MIDI properties (like quantize, duration, velocity, and so on) that are applied in real time and are bypass-able at
any time by simply disengaging the button! The Real-Time Properties column is shown
in Figure 5.62. These properties can be applied to the entire track by using the column
data, or they can be applied to any region by selecting the region and choosing Event >
MIDI Real-Time Properties. This brings up the dialog box shown in Figure 5.63.

Figure 5.62

The Real-Time Properties
column

Figure 5.63

The Real-Time Properties dialog box

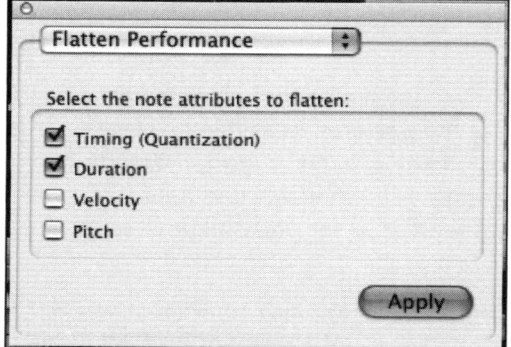

Figure 5.64

The Flatten Performance option

❋ Flatten the performance (shown in Figure 5.64) before you do any quantizing. Because the process of quantizing takes you through several steps and settings, it's easy to get lost, and it can be difficult to regain the original performance. Flattening the performance will store the original timing of the part to the actual MIDI region, making it simple to restore the performance. Select the region and choose MIDI > Flatten Performance to lock in the original take.

❋ The Grid/Groove Quantize menu is the standard way to quantize your parts. You'll need to select the region first, then choose Event > MIDI > Grid/Groove Quantize to open the dialog box. The Preserve Note Duration option (see Figure 5.65) should be active when you are quantizing if you want to adjust the timing of the notes but not the lengths. Deactivate this option and choose the Releases function if you want all the notes to play exactly the same length. This is useful when you are creating fast arpeggios or "tech-y" sounds for which you don't want a human feel. It is mostly useless if you are quantizing drums because most drum samples only play as long as the sample anyway.

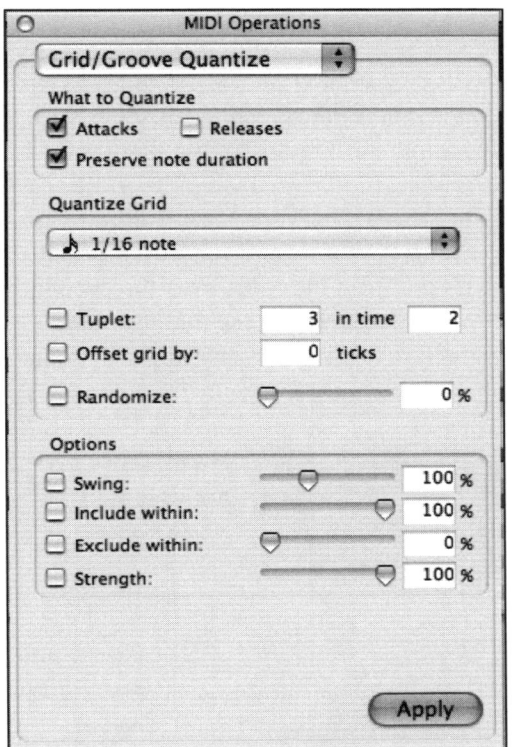

Figure 5.65

Choose the Preserve Note Duration and Attacks options

❉ Truncated drum sounds are easily achievable when you quantize without the Preserve Note Duration option selected. Even though it is mostly useless (drum sounds tend to have a short attack and release anyway, so shortening the MIDI note usually doesn't affect the sound), if you select several MIDI notes that trigger snares—for example, quantizing them to the same length makes them all even and highlighted. You can then use the Standard Trim tool to resize the end length (in Slip mode) to shorten them all simultaneously, creating truncated snare hits that are either unreal or tighter. This can create an interesting drum effect or help the long snare sample get out of the way to allow other sounds to play through.

❉ Offset the grid by about 20 ticks to create a laziness in the timing. This can add back-beat feel to a part that is too stiff and mechanized.

❉ Adjust the Options settings at the bottom to get a mixture of quantized and human performances. If you quantize the notes, excluding notes within, say, 20 percent, then notes that fall within 20 percent of the nearest grid will not be quantized, keeping the feel of the close notes and only quantizing the notes farther away from the grid. You should also set the strength to 80 percent to match. That way, notes further away than 20 percent will be quantized to within 20 percent of the grid, matching your original feel.

Loop Recording with MIDI

A common error when trying to loop record MIDI is to activate the Loop Record function by choosing Operations > Loop Record. This works great for audio but is unnecessary for MIDI. There are some potential advantages (see "Loop Recording" in Chapter 2), but there is another potentially cooler way to do it with MIDI. For layered MIDI recording (for example, the first pass records the kick and the second records the snare), activate MIDI Merge mode, as shown in Figure 5.66. Now you need only activate Loop Playback and record on the MIDI track. MIDI Merge will keep the MIDI from the first pass and add the MIDI from the second pass. This is a fast and fun way to layer the MIDI notes and loop record them at the same time. Figures 5.67 through 5.69 demonstrate a MIDI track recorded one instrument at a time while looping in MIDI Merge.

Figure 5.66

Activating MIDI Merge mode

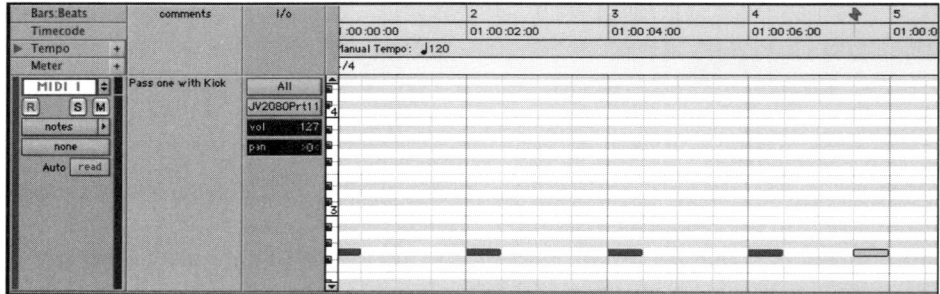

Figure 5.67

Pass one with the kick recorded

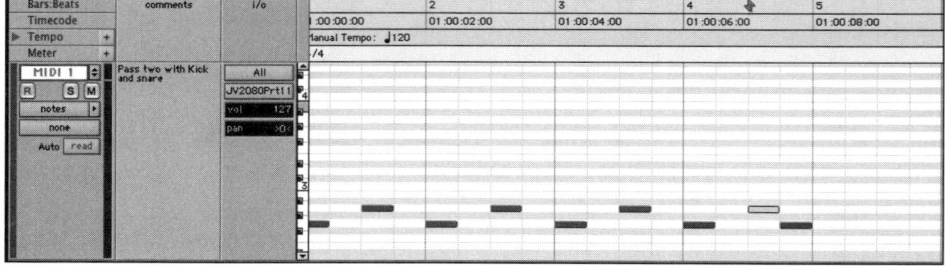

Figure 5.68

Pass two with the snare recorded

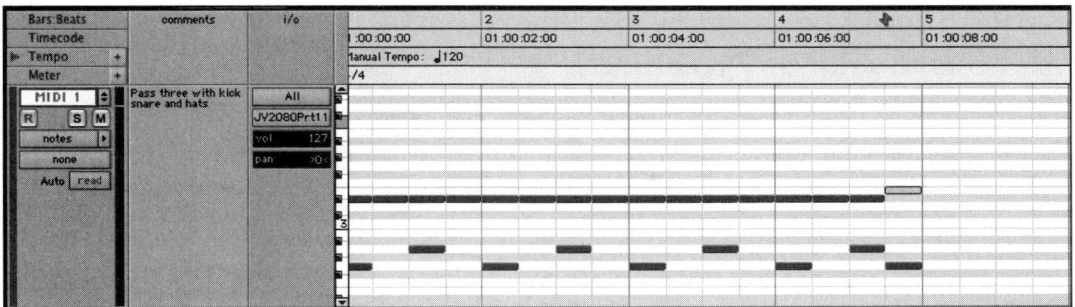

Figure 5.69

Pass three with the hi-hat recorded

MIDI Offsets and Bad Timing

There is a little-known side window in Pro Tools that can seriously affect your timing of notes. No matter how well you play them in or quantize them, they can still play late (or early) if you don't know where to look.

Click the Event > MIDI Offset menu, and you'll be presented with the MIDI Track Offsets window, seen in Figure 5.70. This window allows you to program, either globally or track by track, the amount of latency (or latency compensation) for each MIDI track. For example, if your version of your favorite soft synth comes with 1,024 samples of latency (you can some-times see this in the synth's Control Panel or Preferences page), then you can program the MIDI track feeding it to play 1,024 samples early. You can also measure by ear or eye and adjust the latency by milliseconds.

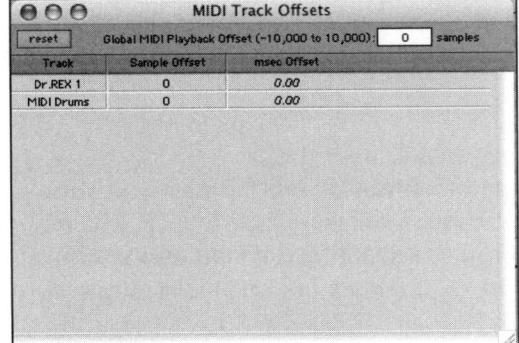

Figure 5.70

The MIDI Track Offsets window

Be careful with this window because the standard key commands don't work with the window open. For example, the spacebar (normally reserved for Play and Stop) erases the Global MIDI Playback Offset value and does not actually play.

Automating Reason from Pro Tools
(Hideki Yamashita, Pyramind)

Hideki Yamashita—or Dex, as he's known to most—is one of the most industrious hackers I know. He can figure out almost anything related to music technology software, which is why I hired him! Hideki serves as Pyramind's assistant technical director, and he is responsible for the proper upkeep of our multi-station lab and our two production studios. I set him to task on figuring out this section and, as usual, he came up shining.

Because Pro Tools will be the main application when ReWired with Reason, it is reasonable (ha!) to want to do everything from Pro Tools and relegate Reason to a sound bank library only. However, one last frontier of control lies in real-time automation of everything in Reason from Pro Tools.

The first step is to obtain the CC (controller change) numbers of the individual modules so they can be mapped and controlled from PT. This information is contained in a document that you can find within the Reason application folder. The reason for this (ha ha!) is that Pro Tools unfortunately does not enable the user to use the Learn from MIDI function in Reason.

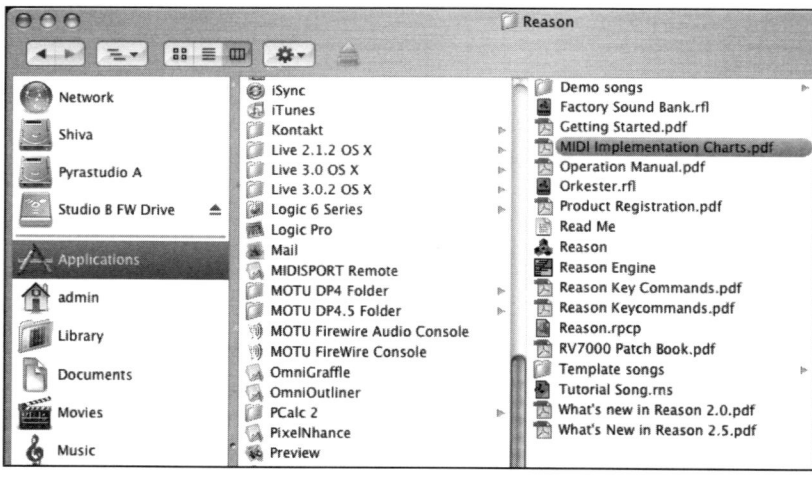

Figure 5.71

Finding the Reason implementation chart

Suppose, for example, that you want to automate the Maelstrom's Filter Frequency. If you refer to the MIDI implementation chart, found in the location shown in Figure 5.71, you will see that controller #79 is assigned to that parameter of that synth. You should also ensure that no MIDI receive function is active in Reason, both on the track (no MIDI icon to the left of the track name) and in the Preferences, as seen in Figures 5.72 and 5.73.

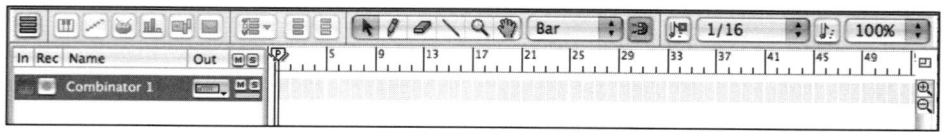

Figure 5.72

MIDI deactivated in Reason 1

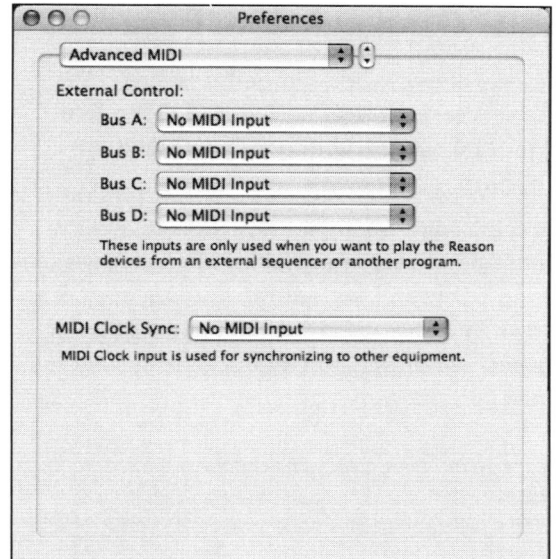

Figure 5.73

MIDI deactivated in Reason Preferences

On the MIDI track assigned to play that Maelstrom, switch your view to the Controller Data view and add controller #79 to the list of controllers to be shown and automated. You can automate the parameter using either the Grabber or the Pencil tool if you want, drawing curves that now apply to the Filter Frequency, as seen in Figure 5.74.

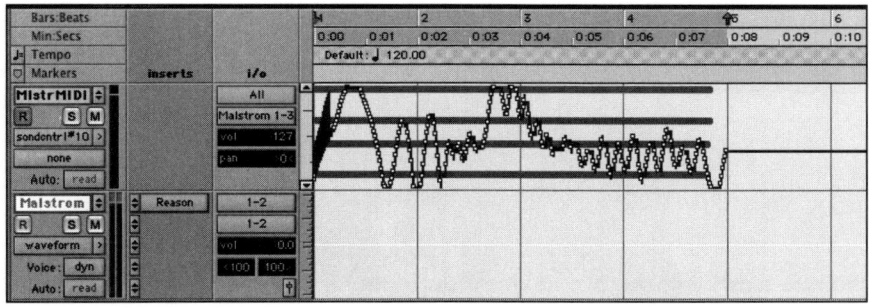

Figure 5.74

Controller automation in the Maelstrom MIDI

If you want to twist knobs on a certain controller, you might need to refer to the manual for that controller to assign a knob to a controller data value. For example, with most USB keyboards you can easily assign a knob to be controller #79, allowing simple automation of the Reason synth by twisting the knob, which will then be recorded into Pro Tools.

Tempo Shifts from Live to Pro Tools (Greg Gordon, Pyramind)

Greg Gordon founded Pyramind in 1987, and he and I have worked together since 1996. He has proven himself to be a cutting-edge producer who is always well-versed in the latest electronic and electronica tools. I asked him to figure out what's wrong with Live and Pro Tools (if anything) and tell me how he would fix it. Here is a doozy.

Another application that allows the connection of audio and MIDI into Pro Tools is Live by Abelton. Live is a very powerful loop-based tool that allows for many forms of interactive performance and is generally used, well, live. ReWiring between Live and Pro Tools is easy and very similar to the same process with Reason (shown in Figure 5.75), with the exception of the number of channels—only 16 stereo default buses, although you can hack the system to deliver up to 64! (See www.abelton.com for details.)

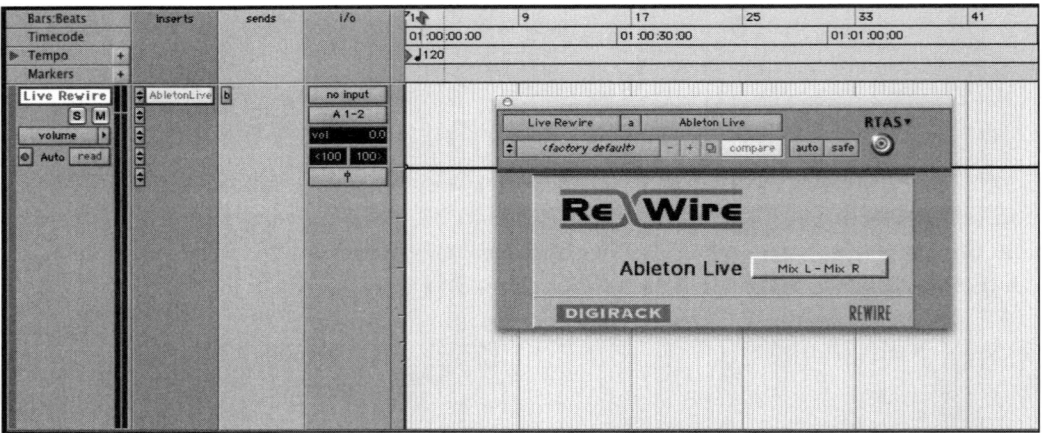

Figure 5.75

Live inserted into Pro Tools

A problem between the two exists with regard to workflow in that if you create a song entirely in Reason, you can export the audio, the MIDI, or both, and recreate your move in Pro Tools. This is not so with Live. With the ability to create a custom master tempo track in Live, digital audio files can gradually change tempo over time without needing to be rendered to disc. However, with Live in ReWire mode, Pro Tools will ignore the tempo track in Live. While Live 5 allows you to export MIDI, you are unable to export the tempo changes with it. If you have drawn in gradual tempo changes in Live, you have two choices to recreate these tempo changes in Pro Tools—both involve rendering some of your Live set to audio for importing into Pro Tools.

Render and Beat Detective

1. Select the length of time in Live that represents the tempo change (slow down or speed up) and choose File > Render to Disk, as shown in Figure 5.76. This creates a stereo (or mono) audio file that has the tempo changes embedded in it. If you are currently ReWired, you'll need to reassign the outputs to Master to create an audio file that isn't silence. If you render without reassigning, nothing goes to the Master bus and nothing gets rendered. It's a good idea to ensure that the section you highlight has a solid transient every quarter note (like a kick or a click) so that Pro Tools will read it well when you render it.

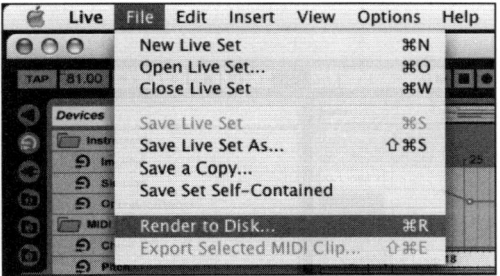

Figure 5.76

Render to Disk option in Live

2. Import the rendered file to a track (Track > Import to Track) in a brand-new Pro Tools document. You now have two ways to recreate the tempo adjustment—Identify Beat or Beat Detective.

   - **Identify Beat.** Separate the audio at every point at which the tempo changes, leaving regions that are individually set to a single tempo. Then, region by region, use Identify Beat (Event > Identify Beat) so the Tempo Ruler in Pro Tools has tempo changes made at every region separation (Figure 5.77). This is time consuming and doesn't account for tempo curves where the tempo changes unevenly.

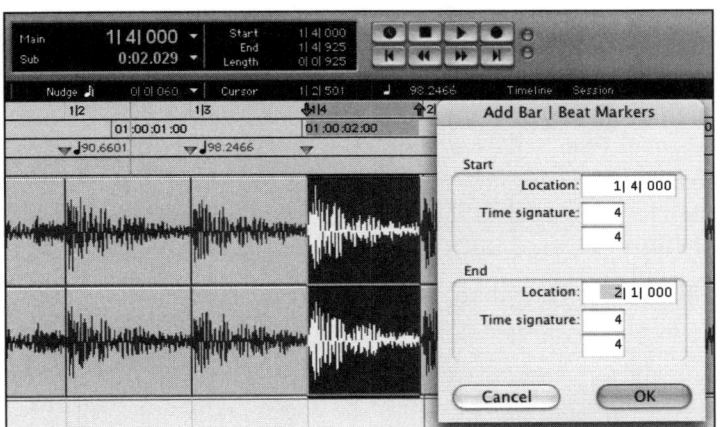

Figure 5.77

Identify Beat performed on the exported Live file

• **Beat Detective.** Using Beat Detective in Pro Tools, analyze the reference file and set the threshold to quarter notes (or 8th notes, as necessary). Upon analysis, make sure that all the gridlines align themselves with transients placed on all your down-beats (Figure 5.78). When you are satisfied with the alignment, output the new tempo track with the Bar|Beat Marker Generation. (See "Exact Beat Slicing Using the Beat Detective" in Chapter 4.) The new tempo track should now drive the Live session, just as the original one did.

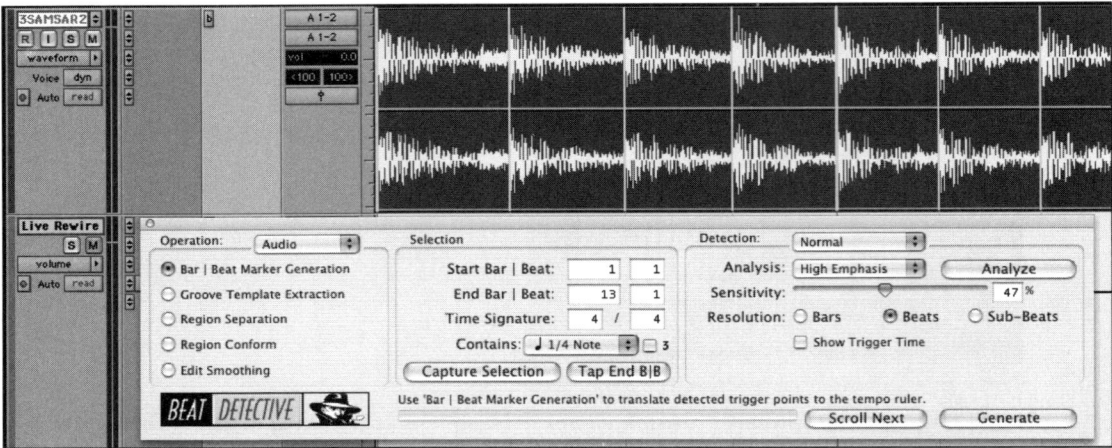

Figure 5.78

Beat Detective on the exported file

Cut-Time MIDI Parts (Version 7)

For MIDI parts in a slow tempo song that need to be played cut-time (twice as fast), version 7 allows an easy solution. Prior to this version, audio tracks had the ability to align to either sample-based rulers or tick-based rulers. Now, MIDI tracks can do the same!

If you're happy with the timing of all of your other MIDI parts and you're NEVER going to change the tempo again, set all of your MIDI tracks to sample-based. Then, simply copy your cut-time MIDI region and paste it to a new MIDI track assigned to the same synth/drum machine. Set the track to align to ticks, as shown in Figure 5.79. Then, you can double the tempo of your song and *only* the tick-based MIDI part will be cut-time!

If you're *not* comfortable with locking your song's tempo to accommodate the cut-time part, you'll need to do it the old-school way, shown in the next section.

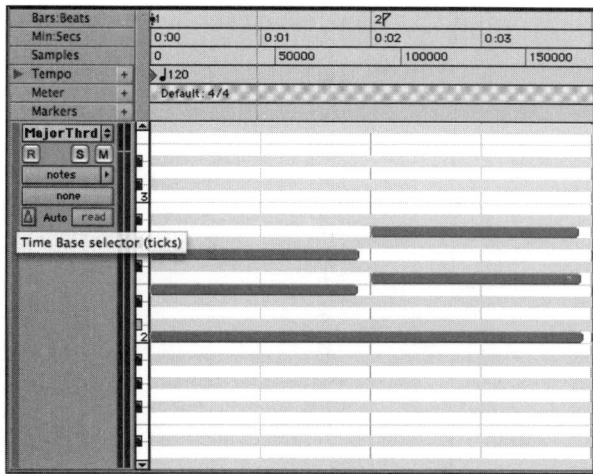

Figure 5.79

A MIDI track set to ticks

Cut-Time MIDI Parts (Version 6.x)

Prior to version 6.7, creating a cut-time MIDI involved changing the master tempo to half of its original BPM. This made all the MIDI parts play cut-time, which might not have been the desired effect. If you only want one MIDI part to play cut-time (such as the drums), you can simply use the TCE Trim tool.

1. Slice the MIDI region into the loop that needs to play cut-time by switching to the Regions view and separating the region.

2. It's a good idea to quantize the parts to perfection because the TCE trimming will not change the relative position of the notes. If the performance is slightly off, it will stay off after TCE. This is particularly true if you are extending the region, not shortening it.

3. After the MIDI regions are separated, switch to the TCE Trim tool.

4. Switch to Grid mode, and set the grid resolution to Bars.

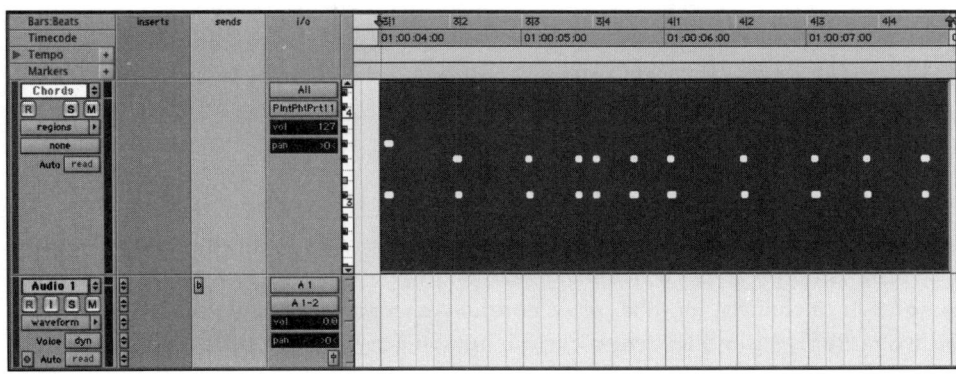

Figure 5.80

MIDI region before TCE

5. Click and drag the end of the region to the left to a position halfway between the start and the previous end, making the region half as long as it was. It will regenerate itself at half-time, and all MIDI notes will adjust relative to their current positions, keeping their performance feeling. Figures 5.80 and 5.81 show a MIDI region before and after, respectively, TCE trimming to cut-time.

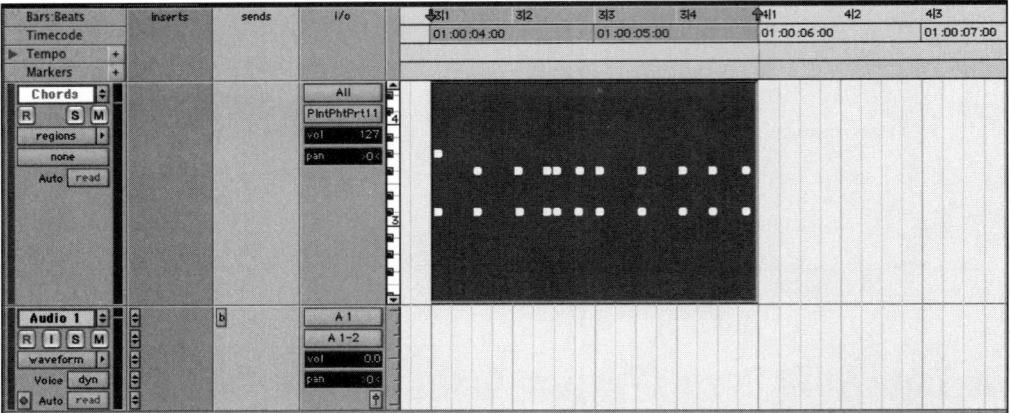

Figure 5.81
MIDI region after TCE

Difficult MIDI Parts

Let's face it—you're not a classically trained and practiced piano player. There is simply no way you can play that 32nd-note run in C# diminished at 155 bpm, right? Wrong. Here are three different ways to pull it off: half-time recording, step recording, and the Pencil tool.

* **Half-time recording.** If you can't play it at 155 bpm but you can play it at 77.5, then record the part in using the Half-Speed option.

    1. Press SHIFT+CMD+spacebar to set Pro Tools to record at half speed and play the part at the slower tempo. When you play back at normal speed, the part will also play at normal speed, making it seem like you played it at twice the speed.

    2. Quantize the part either before or after returning to normal speed. Just because you can play it at half speed doesn't mean you played it well!

* **Step recording.** By choosing Event > MIDI > Step Input, you'll be presented with the Step Input options, shown in Figure 5.82. Here, you'll be able to literally play the part in note by note (step by step) at whatever resolution you choose. You can choose to step the notes in at random lengths (or at carefully chosen lengths, if you know how long you want them to play) to give a certain human flavor to the part. Otherwise, all the notes will be of even length, and they might sound mechanical.

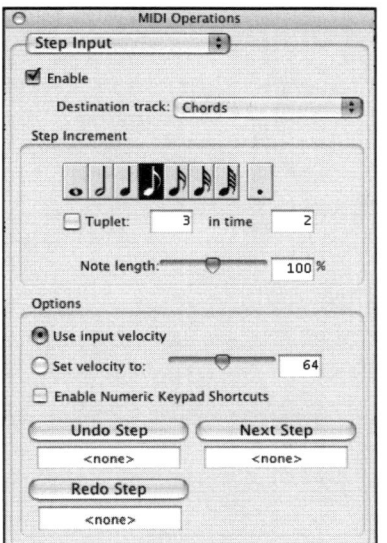

Figure 5.82

The MIDI Operations Step Input options

❋ **Pencil tool.** By choosing the Pencil tool, you can draw in the notes at any resolution you desire.

1. Set your note resolution by setting the grid resolution to the desired note length, as seen in Figure 5.83.

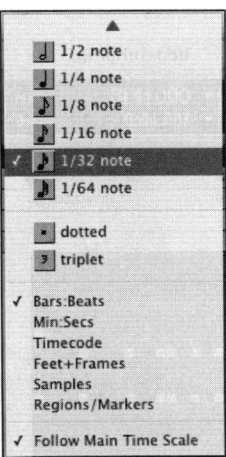

Figure 5.83

Grid resolution set to 32nd notes

2. Every time you click on the MIDI track, a note of the grid resolution length will appear at the pitch clicked, shown in Figure 5.84.

3. Repeat this process until all the notes are in place.

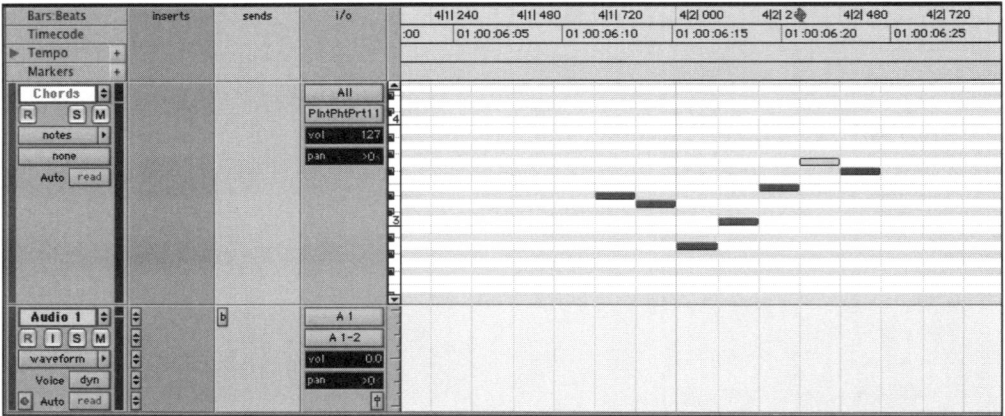

Figure 5.84

The Pencil tool creating MIDI notes

4. Select all the notes in this section, and move the cursor (still the Pencil tool) to the end of the note. The tool will switch to the Standard Trim tool and allow you to adjust all the notes to the desired length. Select some of the notes to adjust only those notes' lengths.

Meter and Tempo Changes

Some programming is required for songs that require alternate meters, multiple meters, or multiple tempos. Pro Tools documents default to a meter of 4|4 and a tempo of 120 bpm. This is visible in the Tempo and Meter Rulers (choose View > Ruler > Tempo and Meter). They are both displayed in Figure 5.85.

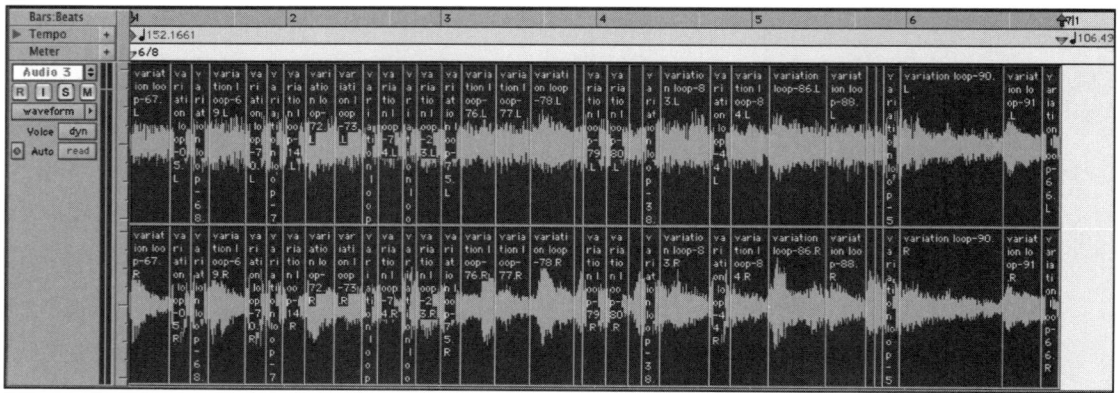

Figure 5.85

The Meter and Tempo Rulers

Suppose the song needs all of the above—alternate meters, multiple meters, and multiple tempos. It starts in 7|8 time at a BPM of 95, switches to 6|4 time at 92 bpm for the chorus, and then back to 95 7|8 for the verses. You will need to do the following:

1. Set the start to 7|8 time and the BPM to 95.

   a. Position the cursor at the beginning of the song and choose Event > Tempo > Tempo Operations to bring up the Tempo Operations dialog box, as shown in Figure 5.86. As a shortcut, go directly to Constant under the same menu, if you know your tempo change occurs at a specific location.

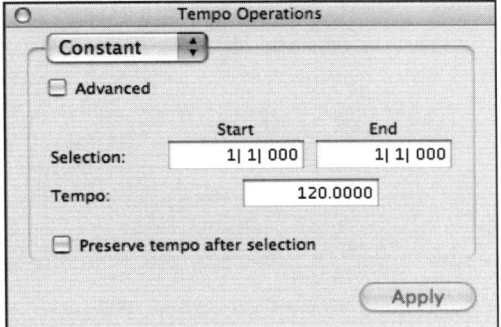

Figure 5.86

The Tempo Operations dialog box

   b. Re-enter (if necessary) the position 1|1|000, and select the end measure after the length of the verse. For a song with 8 bars of intro and a 16-bar verse, the end locator will be measure 25|1|00.

   c. Choose Event > Time > Time Operations. As a shortcut, go directly to Change Meter under the same menu, as shown in Figure 5.87. Choose the same starting and ending bar|beat marker and choose the starting tempo—in this case, 95 bpm.

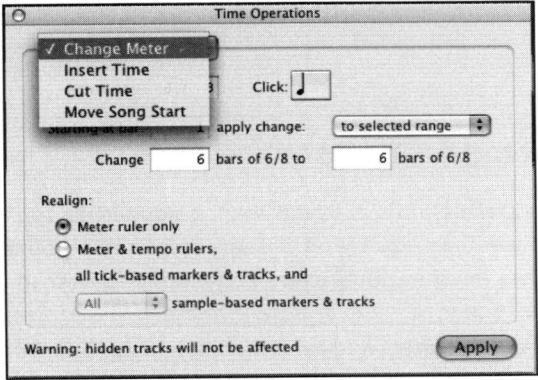

Figure 5.87

The Time Operations dialog box

2. Mark the chorus for the next change.

    a. You have to know the song to do this ahead of time. If you already know that between the intro and verse 1 you have 24 bars, great. If not, you will need to play the song against a click at 7 | 8 and count the measures.

    b. Choose Event > Tempo Operations > Constant, and enter the bar | beat position of the beginning and end of the chorus. Change the meter to reflect 6 | 4, and then hit Apply.

    c. Choose Event > Time > Time Operations, and set the position of the chorus. Type in the new tempo of 92, and hit Apply. Figure 5.88 shows the result of these maneuvers.

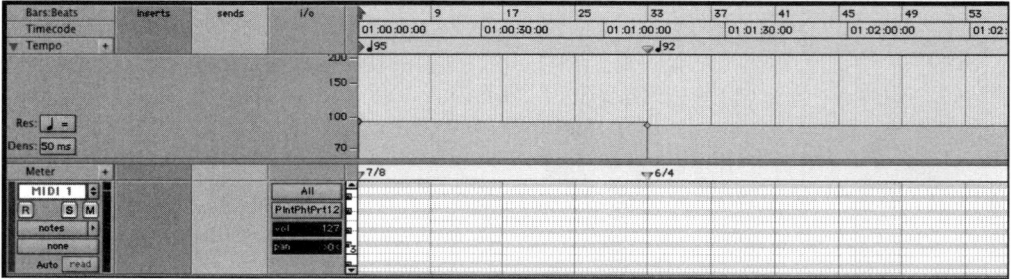

Figure 5.88

Results of Chorus Meter and Tempo changes

For an idea of what this might sound like, check out "Carry Me Home" on my CD, *Donner, Party of One*, available at www.cdbaby.com and www.itunes.com. Enough shameless self-promotion; now go compose!

Note

For changing tempos in version 6.7 and information regarding tempo changes over time, see "Tempo Shifts in Pro Tools" in Chapter 8.

Dealing with Audio and Tempo Changes

So the song is tracked, all the parts are perfect, and it's time for the vocalist to show up and do her thing. Everybody's excited because they can't wait to hear what she's gonna do for the song. Finally, she shows up and hears the tune, and everybody waits for her to get up, get in the booth, and get down! Instead, she looks you squarely in the eye and says, "It's great, but it's too fast. Slow it down about 15 bpm, and let me do my thing." At this point, all the tension in the room now focuses on you, and you realize that you now have the dubious honor of figuring out how on earth to slow down this all-audio song. Deep breath now—there's just a little pressure on you, but you can do it! It might just take a few hours....

If you have a TDM rig with a sync I/O, you can change the settings in the session to vary the sample rate, slowing the song down—this also *pitches* the song down, so it may not work if the vocalist feels funny about the new pitch.

Remember that audio's timing is referenced to the Min:Sec count, not the tempo. This means if you simply slow the tempo down 15 bpm, you do *not* slow down the audio, just the click and the MIDI. If you did, you'd need to respot every region of audio *and* slice and respot all the consolidated audio!

Many producers create music by finding the sounds they want to use and grid-pasting them to every quarter note (or 8th note, and so on). An example of this is shown in Figure 5.89. This means that for one tempo they play in perfect sync, but if the tempo shifts, they stay in their Min:Sec timing and do not adjust to the new tempo. For tracks like this, requantizing the audio to a new tempo is easy. Switch the track to lock its timescale to ticks instead of samples (as shown in Figure 5.90), and it will conform to the grid and not the Min:Sec. This means when your vocalist asks you to switch the tempo, you need only switch tracks like this to ticks and readjust your tempo at will. All regions will instantly reposition themselves to the new tempo, and you're finished! An example of what happens when you change tempos with some tracks set to ticks and others set to samples is shown in Figure 5.91.

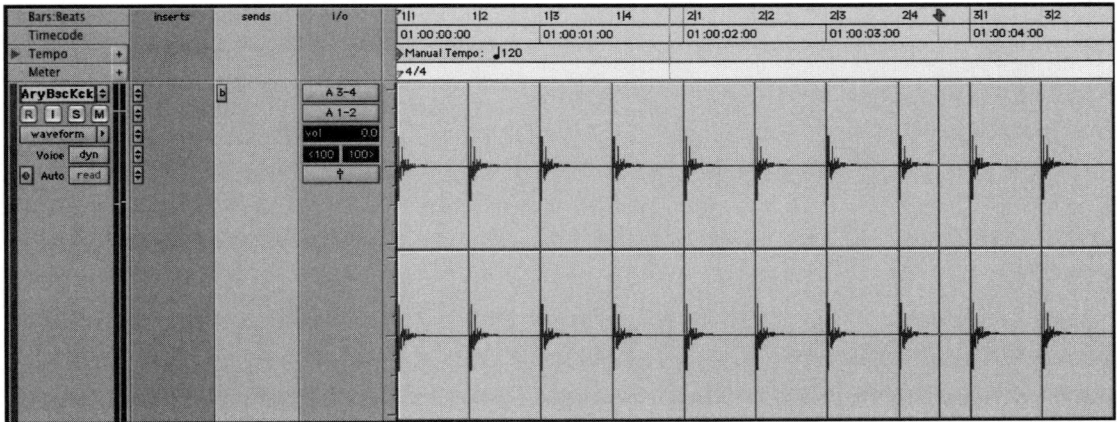

Figure 5.89

A track with grid-repeated audio every quarter note

For tracks that are composed of other performances, such as guitars or live (or printed) drums, you will need to use Beat Detective to separate the regions based on their performances. To use Beat Detective, see "Exact Beat Slicing Using the Beat Detective" in Chapter 4. After the tracks are separated, switch each of the tracks to ticks, and your hits should readjust to the new tempo. You could also requantize within Beat Detective. However, you'd need to requantize every time you adjust the tempo. This is why ticks are much handier!

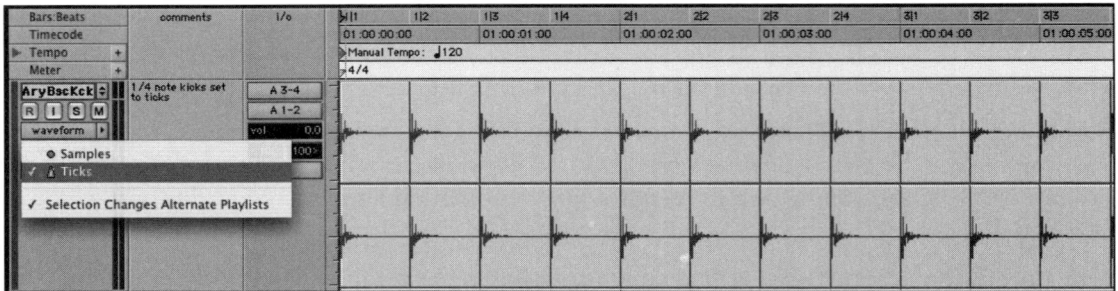

Figure 5.90

Timescale set to Ticks on kick track at 120 bpm

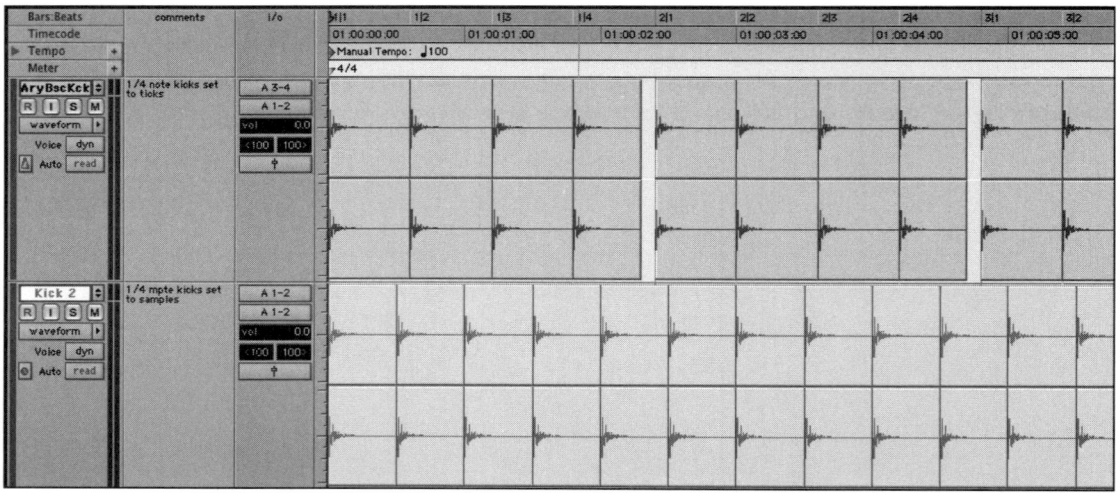

Figure 5.91

Tracks before and after tempo shift with one at Ticks and one at Samples

6 Inserts, Sends, and Effects

When it comes to fun with Pro Tools, this is where it counts. Adding effects and making the sound great is always the fun part, but most often it is done improperly. In this chapter, I'll cover the right way to work with inserts and sends to create some standard (and creative) sounds before and during the mix stage. Keep in mind that the ideas presented here are meant to be a good start but not all-inclusive. Use these techniques where they fit your work and style, and then develop your own from there.

Hitting the Wall and Getting Stuck (TDM)

It never fails. I always get the important frantic tech call at the worst possible time. A good friend of mine called me in a panic from New York while I was home babysitting my seven-month-old. Diapers were flying, the crying had just started, and I knew I was in trouble. I got back to him an hour or so later, and he told me his saga, to which we all can relate.

In the middle of the session, he went to insert one last plug-in, but his system was already at capacity. While trying to add the last plug-in, DAE began to deassign and then reassign the plug-ins for efficiency (shown in Figure 6.1), and it eventually got to a breaking point and froze repeatedly. My friend had hit the wall.

Figure 6.1

The DAE Reallocation taskbar

His best workaround in the heat of battle was to fire up the session in OS 9 (after about 45 minutes of head-meets-wall self-teching), and when the session came up without his newly-added troublesome plug-in, he resaved it as a new version and then went back into OS X to press onward.

Normally, DAE will reallocate plug-ins according to efficiency. Mix Plus systems (such as his system) offer three types of DSP chips—A, B, and C, in decreasing-power order. When C plugs are first inserted, they go to the A chips, only to get kicked out later when an A-only plug is inserted—much like the guy who stole your seats on the floor because he didn't want to sit in his nosebleed seats. When DAE tries to reshuffle things, it often does a fine job. If there is no room left, you should receive a DAE Error - 7204 (shown in Figure 6.2) indicating that the wall has been hit. In my friend's case, DAE was out of chips and couldn't give my friend the last plug-in. Instead of just providing an error, it simply crashed. Subsequent attempts to reopen the session kept giving him crashes, and there was simply no other way in.

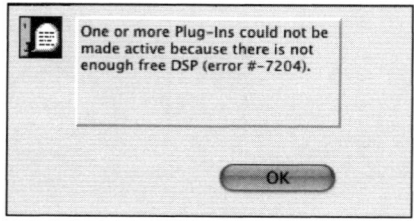

Figure 6.2

DAE Error - 7204

Had my friend read "Don't Lose Your Work" in Chapter 1, none of this would have happened. *Always* activate the AutoSave function by choosing Setups > Preferences > Enable Session File Auto Backup, and have Pro Tools save every two minutes, keeping the last 10 to 20 sessions. In my friend's case, he could have reopened the AutoSave from four minutes before and kept working. He would have saved an hour and a half, as well as a lot of skin on his forehead.

What Do You Do When You Run Out of Plug-In Power? (Hitting the Wall—TDM and LE)

You can guarantee that no matter how much plug-in power you have, you will eventually use it all. The plug-in power you have won't be enough (even though you are probably using twice what you need) of course, but at least you'll know where the wall is!

Similarly to "Printing the Reason Parts" in Chapter 5, you can (and should) print your effects tracks to save DSP and allow yourself to go over the wall. Choose an expensive plug-in or track with lots of plug-ins on it to print. It should be a track for which you've settled on the sound and are comfortable moving beyond. You can tell which plug-ins are more expensive by measuring how much DSP they use; do so by choosing Window > System Usage and seeing which plugs use the entire chip (TDM only; LE users can't really tell which ones use up the most, but you can start with reverbs and soft synths, as they tend to be the biggest CPU hogs).

When you've found a good candidate, create an Audio track of matching channels (mono or stereo) right below it, and set the new track's input to an unused bus (or pair). Set the output of the source track to the same bus, and record-enable the receiving track. Before you record, you should name the track something like Kick with Effects or Kick FX Print so you'll know what it is later. Record the track in its entirety, as seen in Figure 6.3.

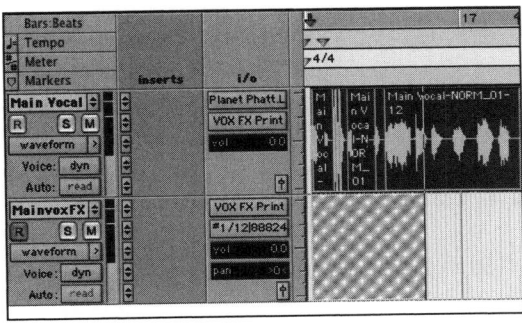

Figure 6.3

Signal flow for printing the effects

Some people make a *big* mistake here. They delete the track after printing the effect to free up DSP. This is fine if you are *sure* you're *never* going back to those plug-ins and settings! This is probably a delusion you're having temporarily—it's late, and you're not thinking clearly.

After you delete the track, you can *never* go back. Although you do get the DSP back, there is a better way. Select the original track, and choose Track > Make Inactive (see Figure 6.4). Now you've reclaimed the voice, freed up DSP for more plug-in fun, *and* left yourself the option to go back and tweak the settings!

Figure 6.4

The Track > Make Inactive menu option

Multi-Mono versus Multi-Channel Inserts

An often overlooked facet to stereo plug-ins is the ability to create separate settings for left and right plug-ins on a single plug-in. For example, if I record two guitar parts and choose to merge them onto a single stereo track for screen ergonomics (see "Stereo or Dual Mono?" in Chapter 2), I might then process the two parts with two different EQs to give a unique stereo image. One might think it wise to separate the two back into two mono tracks (or simply keep them mono to begin with) and plug in two different EQs to achieve the effect. However, this is wasteful because you will double the amount of DSP needed.

In this example, use a Multi-Mono plug-in, as shown in Figure 6.5. This gives you the ability to set different settings for the left and right channels on a single plug-in. In the upper-right corner, you'll notice a small stereo indicator with two small black dots. This represents the stereo selector. When it is set to L, the settings affect the left channel only. When it is set to R, the settings affect the right channel only. When the Link button is engaged, one side or the other will be the master, affecting both sides equally.

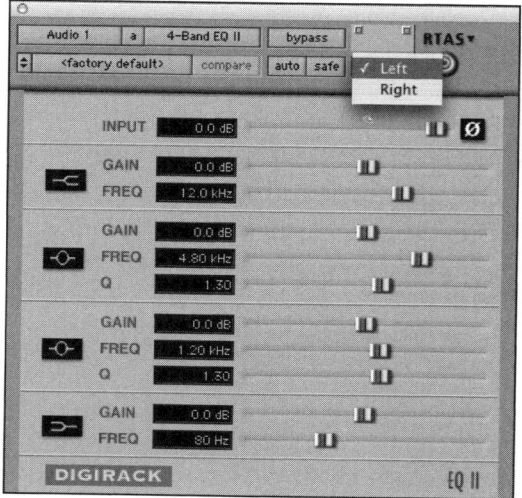

Figure 6.5

A Multi-Mono plug-in

If there are unique settings to both sides (after delinking), then the Link button is re-engaged; Pro Tools will ask you which side should be the new master and inform you that the other settings will be lost, as seen in Figure 6.6.

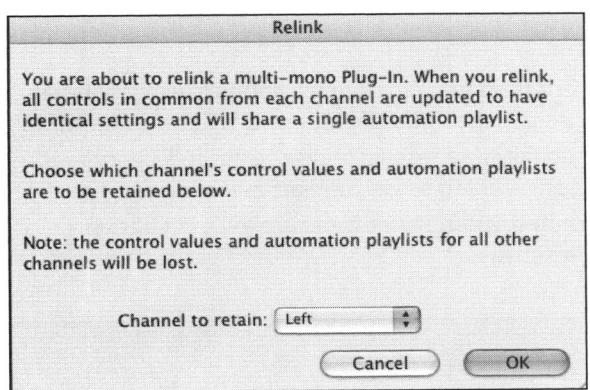

Figure 6.6

The Relink dialog box

The AM Radio Effect

The AM Radio effect is a very common request in post-production as well as in music. This effectively makes the audio sound really bad, as if it were on AM radio. (This is sometimes called the Telephone effect.) The AM Radio effect has an extremely limited frequency bandwidth and dynamic range, so a cheap way to get this effect is to plug in an EQ (make sure it has at least filters and a parametric EQ) and either a compressor-, limiter-, or distortion-style plug-in (such as something like Sans-Amp, Amp Farm, Chrome-Tone, Guitar-Rig, and so on). You can use the stock Digidesign plug-ins if those are all you have, as shown in Figure 6.7.

Start with the EQ and roll off all bass below 400 Hz. Roll off the treble above 2k. This is already pretty close, but not unique enough. I like to boost about 4 dB (at narrow bandwidth) of 440 Hz, but you can sweep the frequency to find the band that works best for you. When the tone is sufficiently horrid, add the compressor and set it heavy. Start with the threshold at –20 and the ratio at 4:1, and adjust from there to taste. For that last bit of crunch, add the distortion and set the crunch to medium-light. Different amps have different crunches, so play around a little until you find your friend. I use Amp Farm and set it to my favorite amp—the 1959 Bassman, which has a particular "honkiness" that I like for this effect.

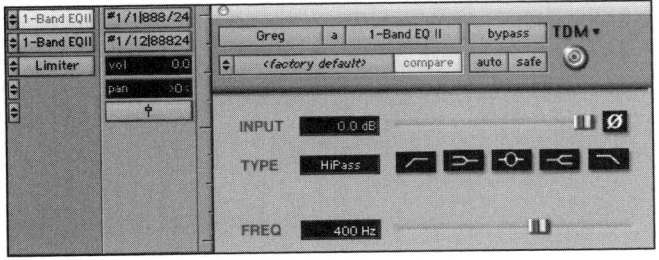

Figure 6.7

The plug-in chain of an AM Radio effect

Offsets as Chorus

Although chorus effects are great for creating width in tracks, you can achieve similar effects through editing alone if you don't have a chorus effect or you are out of DSP. For example, a track I worked on recently had a single lead and a single background (harmony) vocal (see Figure 6.8). I found this to be boring because both wanted to be panned in center, but I *really* wanted the background to be in stereo and panned wide. Instead of applying a chorus effect, which can be unnatural, I used editing instead!

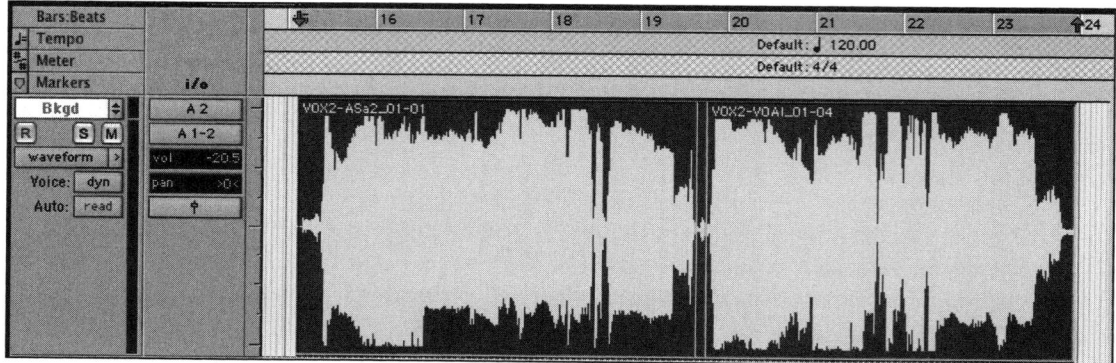

Figure 6.8

A single background voice

If the song is set to a click or conforms to Grid mode, set your Nudge resolution to 64th notes. Create a new track (for voice, choose mono) and OPTION-drag the single voice onto the new track. This will exactly double the part, but panning wide will achieve no great effect. (In fact, it will still sum to mono.) Highlight the copied track, and nudge the track later by one 64th note. (You can nudge it earlier if you want, but it can be weird to hear it before the beat. Experiment and see which you like better.) Press the + (plus) key on the number pad to nudge it later, as shown in Figure 6.9. (Laptop users press Fn+SHIFT+?) Use the – (minus) key to move the track earlier. (Laptop users press Fn+SHIFT+;) Now, if the two tracks are panned wide, you'll have a natural chorus without any digital artifacts from your chorus plug-in!

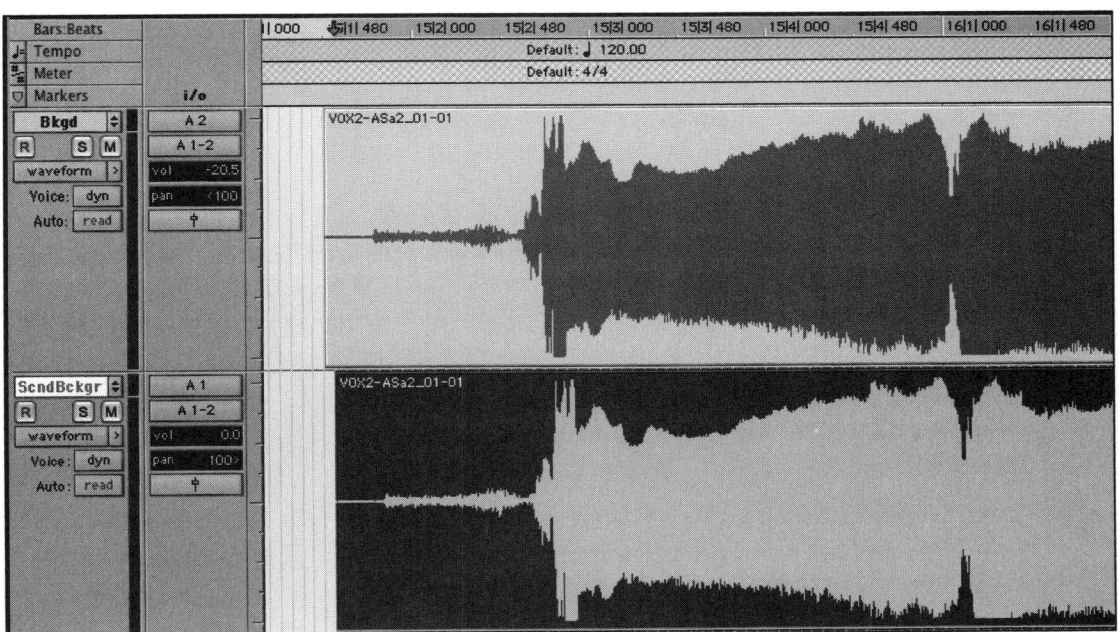

Figure 6.9

Copied, shifted, and panned wide

Offsets as Delay

Instead of using a Delay effect, try creating a similar effect with editing. OPTION-drag your track to an empty track next to it, and nudge it later by your desired delay resolution (quarter, 8th, and so on). This will be a cleaner delay, but it will only repeat once. This effect is best used for a particular word or phrase and will be tedious if applied across the whole song, as seen in Figure 6.10. Use this on key phrases that demand a single tap (...single tap...) only (...only...).

If your song is not laid out to the grid, you can create one through Beat Detective (see "Exact Beat Slicing Using the Beat Detective" in Chapter 4), or you can guess and adjust it by ear. If you use this technique, it is advisable to set your Nudge resolution to 10 milliseconds (set the Main Time Scale to Min:Sec) and nudge it into place [+ and – on the numeric keypad will shift the region earlier (–) or later (+)].

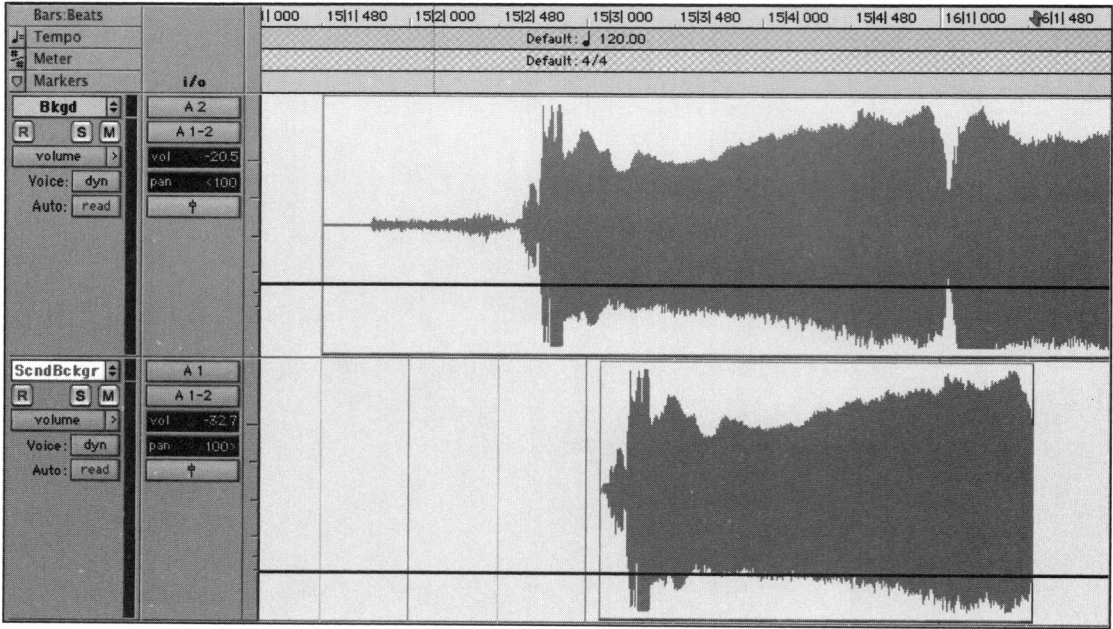

Figure 6.10

A copied and delayed track

Side-Chaining

An old trick in analog mixing is to side-chain certain effects together in such a way that the sound of one track directly affects the effect of another. For example, you might want the kick drum to control the compression on the bass, making the bass "tuck in" every time the kick hits. This is useful in situations in which both the bass and kick share similar frequency content. Not every plug has a side-chain input, but those that do get their chain signal through the buses.

In the kick/bass example, start by compressing the bass to taste and trying to adjust the kick volume so they start to elbow each other for space. Create an Aux send on the kick, and send it to a mono bus. (Remember to label your I/O and buses; see the next section, "I/O Labeling.") Then, set the side-chain input to the same bus; it's the button that looks like a key, as shown in Figure 6.11.

Now whenever the kick hits, it sends a signal to the side-chain input of the bass, telling the compressor to get its threshold level from the kick (when it hits) and *not* from the bass. When there is no kick send, the bass is compressed normally.

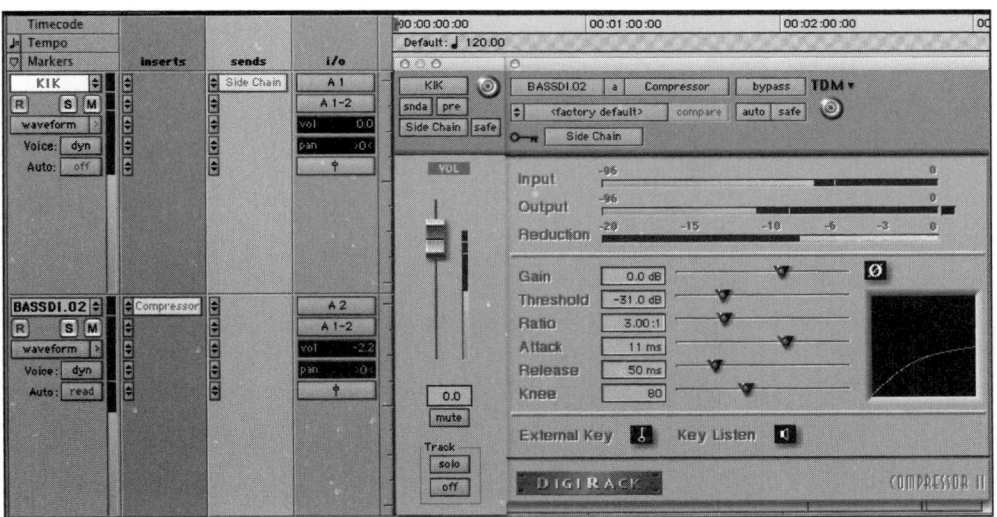

Figure 6.11

The side-chain set up with kick and bass

I/O Labeling

If you read "Labeling the I/O and Template Settings" in Chapter 1, then you already know some of the benefits of labeling your I/O. Choose Setups > I/O Labels, and you will be presented with the I/O Setup dialog box shown in Figure 6.12.

When you are mixing or sound designing, it is a very good idea to label your I/O. That way, as you use more and more buses for effects, you can easily see which bus goes to which effect. This will save you lots of time. In addition, if you are not the final mixer or producer on this session, it will make the next engineer very happy to know that he or she doesn't have to reinterpret your routings; he or she can simply pick up right where you left off. You'll get professionalism points for that one!

However, you will lose professionalism points if you name your buses Funky Delay or Tapper City, as opposed to Snare 1/4 Delay. Assume the next person working on your song knows nothing about you or your setup, and remember, Keep It Simple, Stupid! A good idea is to use the lower-numbered buses for effects, such as reverb and delay, and the higher-numbered buses for subgrouping sounds for group processing. (See the next section, "Subgrouping Sounds.")

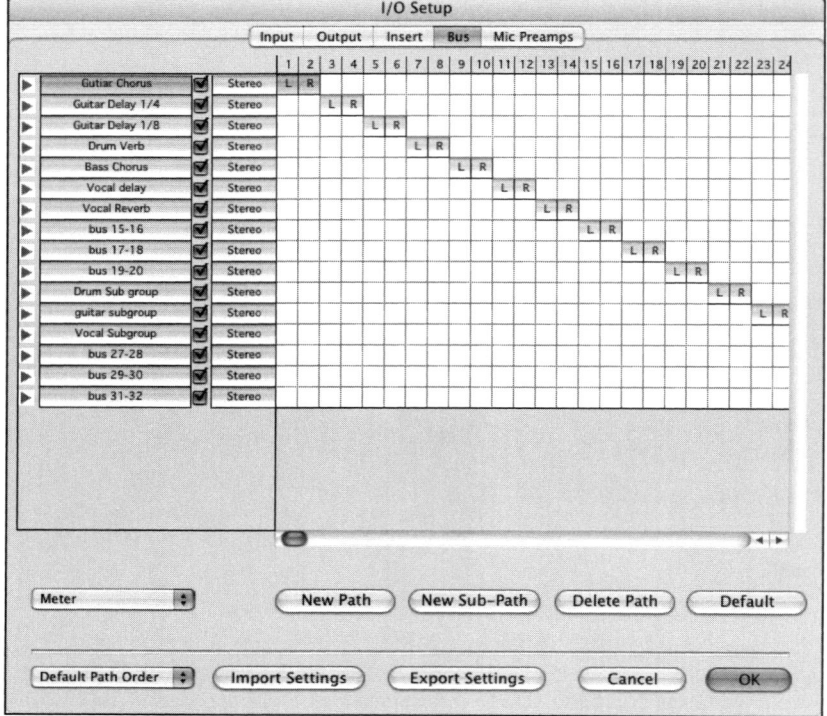

Figure 6.12

The I/O Setup dialog box

Subgrouping Sounds

So the producer wants you to put the newfangled compressor on the entire drum set; but you only have enough DSP for one compressor, and you need seven more. Should you put the compressor on a track, print it, make it inactive, and put one more on the next track?

To save time and DSP, the best move here is to sub-group the tracks together, and then add your compressor. To do so, route the output of all the drum tracks to a stereo bus labeled Drum Subgroup or something similar. Create a stereo Aux input and name it Drum Subgroup (creative, I know). Set its input to the bus Drum Subgroup (hey, they all have the same name!), and you've just routed all your drum tracks to the one Aux input, as seen in the Mixer window shown in Figure 6.13. You can now safely put that newfangled compressor on the Aux track, compressing all the drums at once!

Note

When you do this, remember that the entire set will be compressed based on the mix of the drums. This means if the kick is too hot, it might affect your mix strangely, so be prepared to readjust your drum mix to suit the single compressor. Remember that the group drum compression will sound different than compressing each part individually because the compression is now triggered by all the drums, not each one individually.

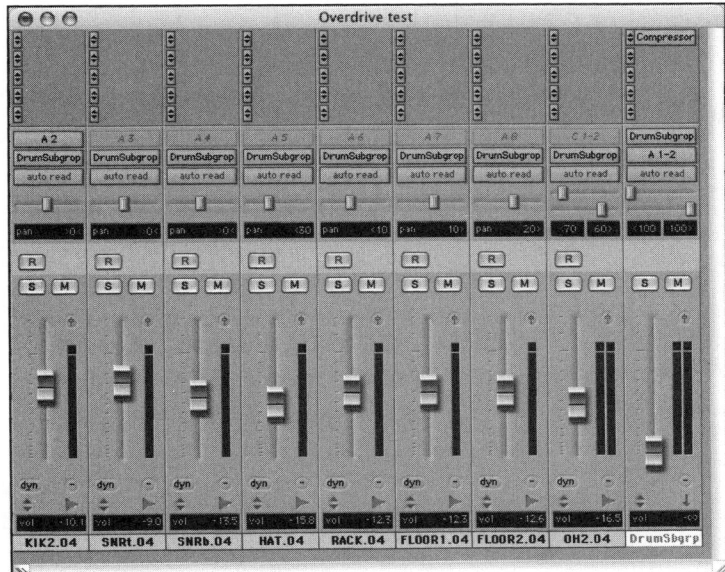

Figure 6.13

Ten drum tracks subgrouped with compressor

Faster Plug-In (and Send) Creation

For situations in which you will need to create several plug-ins or sends at once, following are a few shortcuts to save time.

❋ When you are creating inserts on all channels, hold the OPTION key before creation. When you hold the OPTION key during most maneuvers (mute, record ready, solo, assign, and so on), Pro Tools knows to do that maneuver to all tracks at once. This is certainly true for plug-ins and sends (see Figure 6.14). Use this technique when you create headphone mixes. (See "Headphone Mixes for a Single Artist" and "Headphone Mixes for Multiple Artists" in Chapter 2.)

❋ When you create inserts or sends on selected channels, hold the SHIFT+OPTION keys before creating the insert. Like OPTION, this will create the insert or send on all tracks, but the SHIFT key also tells Pro Tools to limit the creation to the selected channels. Select multiple channels by SHIFT-clicking the Channel Select buttons.

❋ If two mono tracks share a sound and require similar (but not the same) treatments, OPTION-drag the plug-in from one track to the next while Pro Tools is parked. This will copy the plug-in from the one track to the next, keeping the same sound but allowing different settings. This is useful for two mono guitar tracks in which the left one is EQed bass heavy and the right one is EQed mid-range heavy. In this case, having the two guitar parts on one stereo track could also work using a Multi-Mono plug-in, but changes made to the EQ during automation can become unmanageable.

❋ New to version 7 is the ability to drag-copy your sends as well as your inserts. Simply OPTION-drag the send to another channel, and you've copied the send.

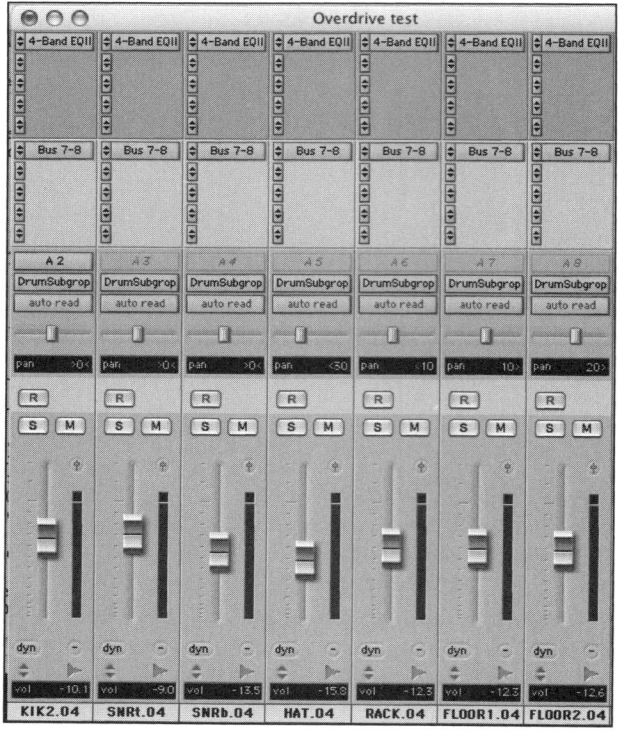

Figure 6.14

The Mix window after OPTION-insert and OPTION-send

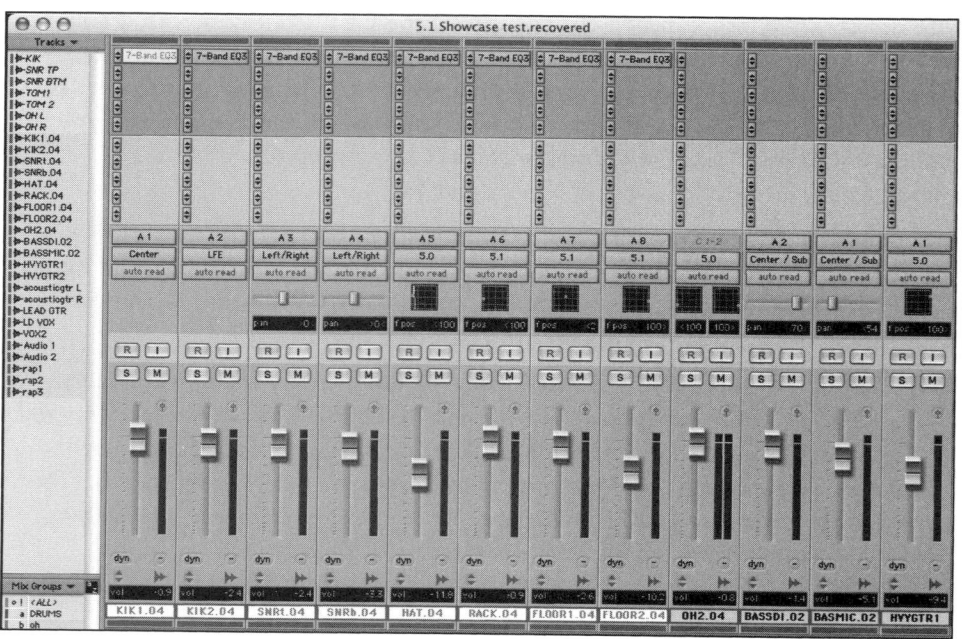

Figure 6.15

Multiple channels selected with inserts created on only those selected

Storing and Recalling Your Favorite Insert Chains

Over time, you'll develop an arsenal of plug-ins and an array of favorite signal-processing chains. Every rock drum set will get your favorite rock EQ/compression chain, and every hip-hop loop will get its treatment, too. You'll also develop Carpal Tunnel Syndrome from mousing every track and repeating this process setup for every song you work on.

When you are sold on your favorite signal chains, you should store a copy of the session in some remote location on your hard drive for later recall. You can create a folder next to the Pro Tools application called Signal Chain Sessions.

Suppose you're working with drummer X, and you love the drum set configuration like the one in Figure 6.16. Choose File > Save As, and direct it to your Signal Chain Sessions folder. After it's there, you can always refer to it to import your settings into another song. For example, if a week later you find yourself working with drummer Y and you want the signal processing from drummer X, simply choose File > Import Session Data and direct Pro Tools to the session with drummer X in your Signal Chain Sessions folder. You can select to import the tracks corresponding to the drums only (you remembered to name your tracks, right?) and choose only the Plug-In Assignments and Plug-In Settings options from the Playlist Import drop-down menu, as shown in Figure 6.17.

Figure 6.16

Drum set with collections of inserts

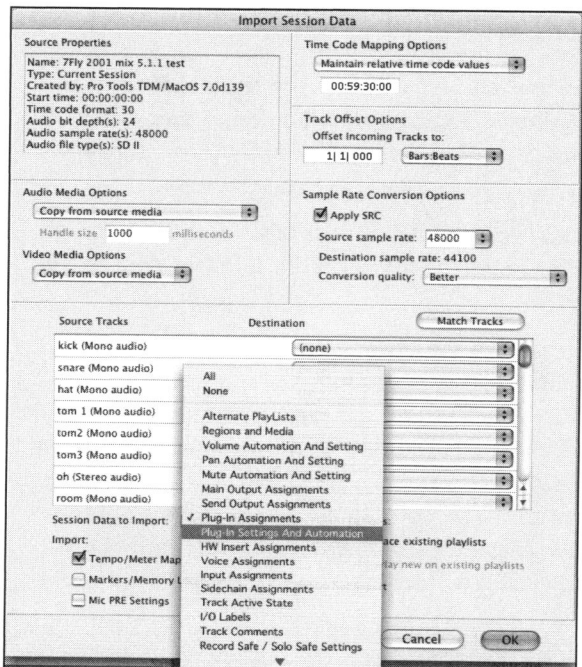

Figure 6.17

The Import Session Data feature importing inserts and settings only

You can choose to direct these tracks to import on top of your existing tracks (kick to kick, snare to snare, and so on) so your new session is still intact with the addition of only the pre-existing signal chains and settings. You can tweak from there.

Old-School 808s

Nothing busts a Jeep like a good ol' 808 kick drum. If you don't know this sound, listen for the bass coming from the hip-hop track playing out of the Escalade next to you at a red light. The rumble that makes you want to use the bathroom is probably the 808 kick, made famous by the Roland drum machine of the same name. If you can't find the sample (get out from under that rock, my friend!), then try to create your own, like we used to in the old days!

The signal chain is simple: A 60-cycle tone is generated by an Oscillator and is then gated closed. A kick drum performance triggers the gate to open when the kick plays and the gate shuts after a certain (user-defined) amount of time. The following steps detail how it's done.

1. Create an Aux input next to the kick performance. You can create a discrete track with a single kick hit (say every eight bars) that does the triggering. Otherwise, you will need to determine when you want the 808 to play and create a track with audio hits that plays that way. Insert Signal Generator (Figure 6.18) on the Aux track and set it to 60 Hz at 0 dB. Later you can adjust the frequency to match the pitch of your song.

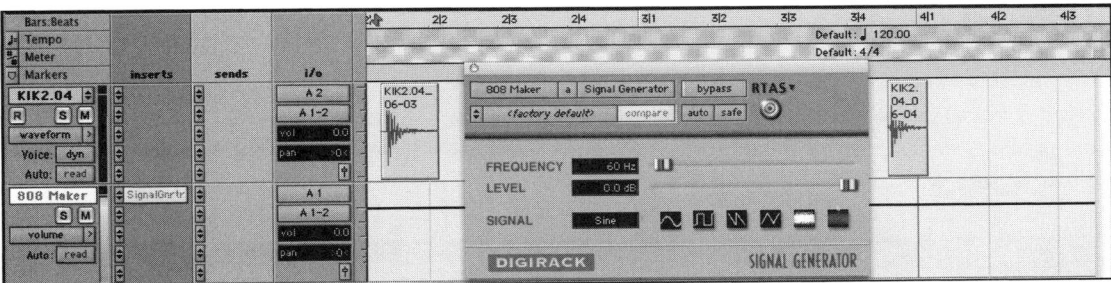

Figure 6.18

Kick on the Audio track with Signal Generator set to 60 Hz on the Aux track

2. Insert a gate on the Signal Generator track. You will tweak the settings later, but for now simply adjust the gate open to a high enough threshold to cut off the signal completely.

3. Route a Send's output of the trigger track to a bus labeled Side Chain (see "I/O Labeling" earlier in this chapter) and set the fader to 0 dB.

4. Set the key input on the gate to Gate (Figure 6.19). Now whenever the trigger part plays, the gate is triggered to open, generating a rumbling 60-Hz tone in sympathy with the trigger part...semi-instant 808!

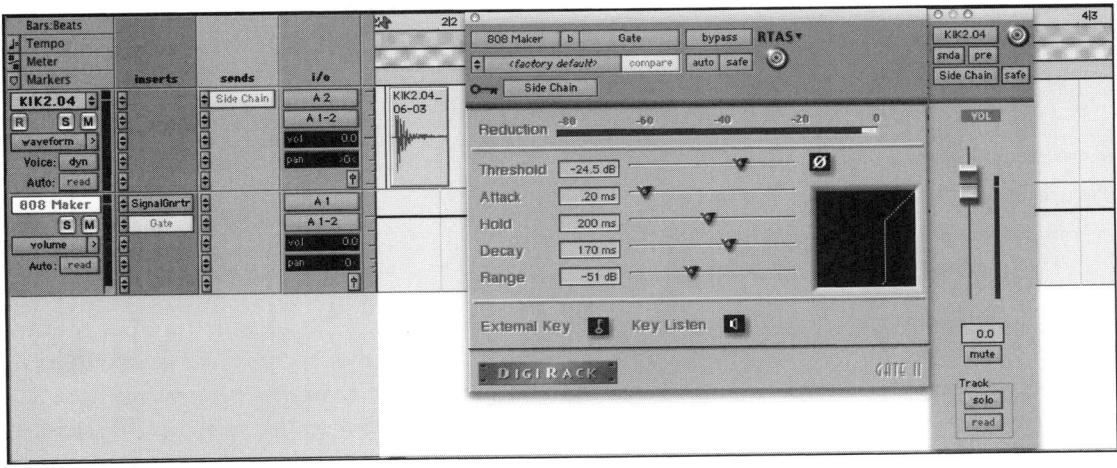

Figure 6.19

A Gate trigger on the Signal Generator with key input from the Side Chain bus

Helicopter Vocals

This move is very popular in drum and bass music, but it's not limited to that genre. The idea is that a vocal track plays while very small, repetitive sections of the vocal are cut out so it seems like a helicopter blade sliced out sections very quickly. As with the 808, the secret is to use a gate with a side-chain signal.

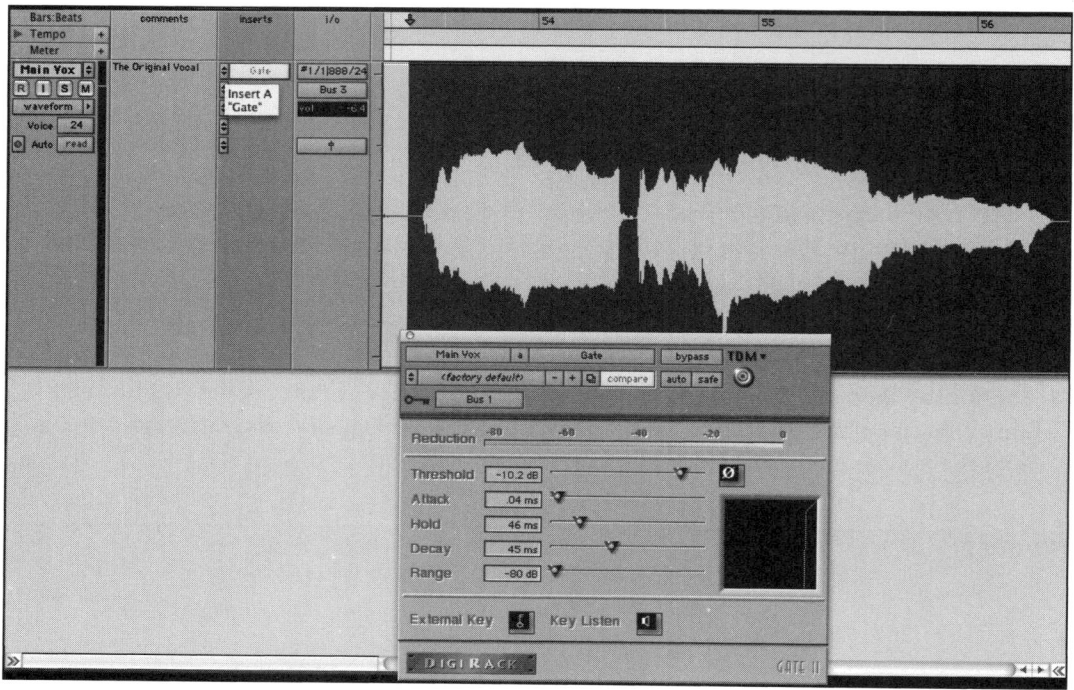

Figure 6.20

A vocal track with a gate inserted on it.

Insert a gate on the vocal track in question, as shown in Figure 6.20. As with the 808, route a send output of a trigger track to the side-chain input on the gate. You can use anything as a trigger like a hi-hat pattern or a drum loop. If you don't want to hear the trigger track too, don't route the send to the side-chain, route the output of the track to the side-chain instead. If you route the output of the trigger track so you don't hear it, too, the part will play silently to the gate triggering it to open and allow the vocal through. Figure 6.21 shows the vocal track recorded after the gate is triggered by a drum pattern.

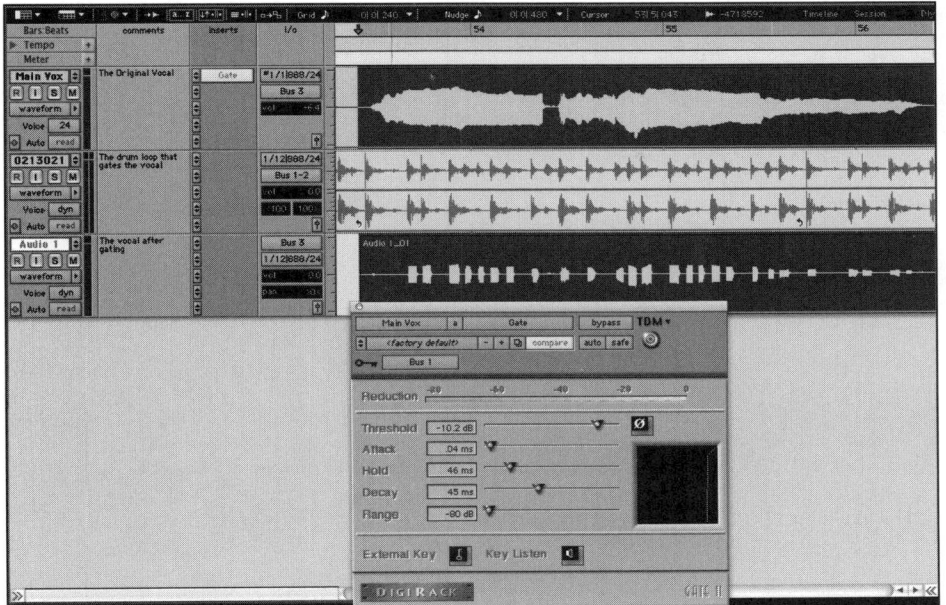

Figure 6.21

A vocal triggered by a drum pattern.

Replacing Drum Sounds During the Mix

More and more these days, I find myself mixing projects that were recorded by the bands themselves in their not-so-perfect rehearsal space with a lot of cheap mics. Invariably, I'm asked to perform miracles and make the drums sound huge when they sound very small. Here are two ways to deal with drum sounds that don't work—both of which involve replacing the sounds with better-sounding samples of other drums.

❋ **Sound Replacer**. This very handy AudioSuite plug-in (Sound Replacer and batteries sold separately) allows the user to analyze any drum track and replace the sound with up to three different samples based on volume. First, select the regions that need replacing, then open Sound Replacer. On the left of the screen, you'll see three vertical sliders that can be linked to three different samples. Click the folder icon at the bottom of each slider to load a sample to replace with. As you bring the slider down, you are setting the volume at which the track will be replaced with the sample linked to the slider. In the main window, you'll see the volume range shrink around the track and the transients that poke out above the volume threshold you set with the slider. Figure 6.22 shows a track with a single replacement sample loaded, where the volume threshold has been lowered to allow transients to poke through. You have the choice to process this setting to an existing track or to a new track. In addition, you can simply replace the original with the replacement snare or you can blend them together into a new track with the mix setting at the bottom of the window.

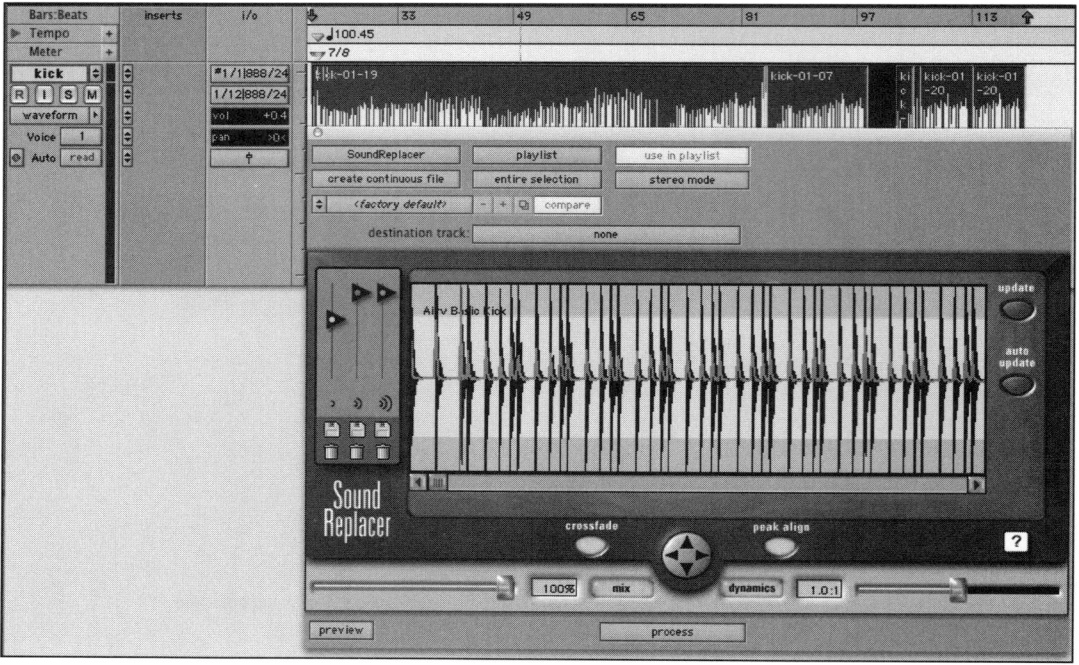

Figure 6.22

Sound Replacer with a track and a replacement sample loaded

❉ **By hand**. Long and slow, the only advantage to this method is that you are guaranteed accuracy. (Sound Replacer can make timing mistakes at times.) First, import the sample you'd like to use as the replacement to the Region List. Select the region in question, and choose Edit > Separate Region > At Transients. Once the region is separated, create a new track underneath it. On the original track, tab to each transient, move to the track below, and drag the replacement region to that location—feel free to copy the replacement sample region and simply paste it into place after moving the cursor to the replacement track!. A handy shortcut is to hold the CTRL key while dragging the region to the new track. You could also CTRL+OPT-click on an instance of the replacement region. This will copy the replacement region and paste it to begin at the cursor location (which should be the point of the transient on the original track). This will import the sample to the exact location of the cursor (which should be the location of the transient). Continue this process until you have a replacement sample at the location of every transient. You can then choose to use both tracks and blend them with the faders or mute the original and just use the replacement. Figure 6.23 shows the track before and after the replacement.

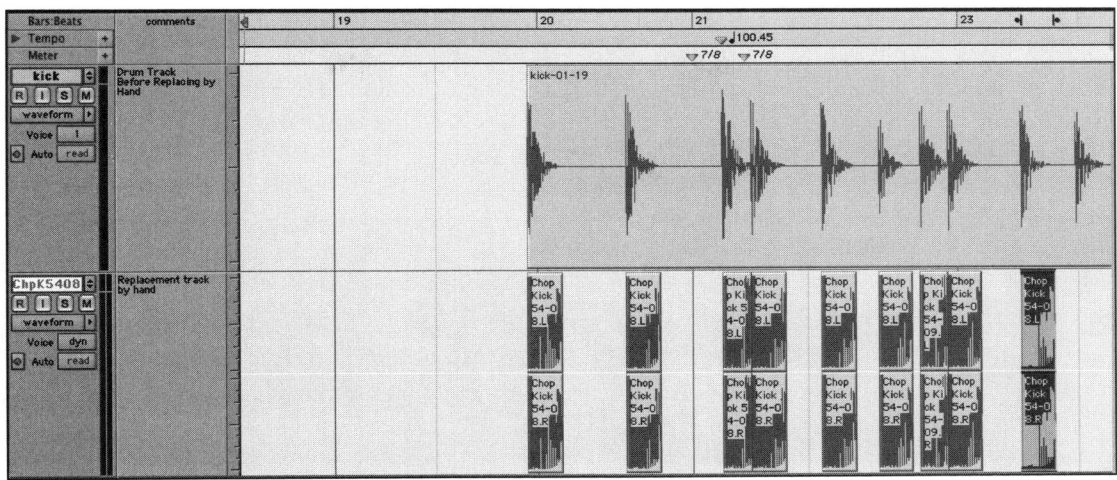

Figure 6.23

A track with transients replaced by hand

Mono Effects on Stereo Sounds

I like distortion. Maybe it's because I play guitar or maybe it's because I grew up in the 1970s with classic rock, but I like distortion. I REALLY LIKE distortion. I'll put it on drums, bass, vocals, pianos—it doesn't matter. The problem is that my favorite distortion plug-in, Amp Farm, only supports mono sounds. What is a poor rocker to do?

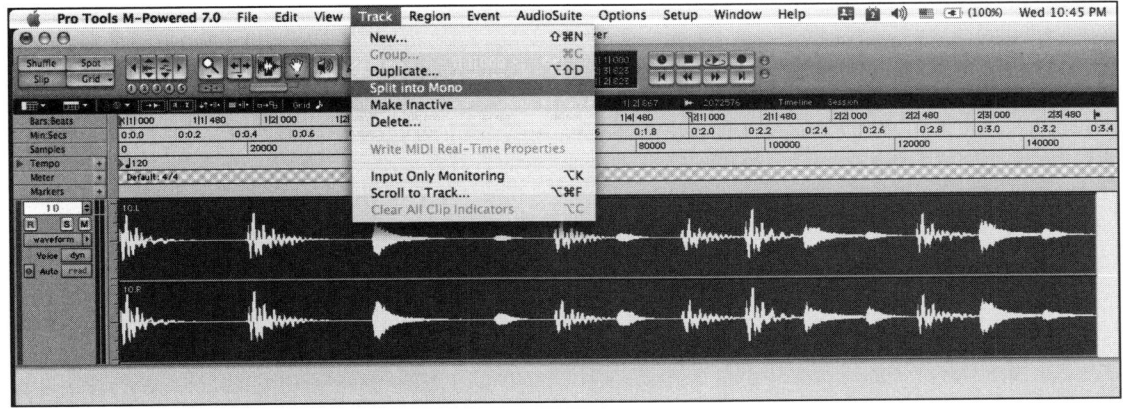

Figure 6.24

The Track > Split into Mono option

When I need to run a stereo loop through Amp Farm, I select the track in question and choose Track > Split into Mono (Figure 6.24). This creates two new mono tracks and copies each of the loop sides (left side to new track 1 and the right side to the new track 2) to the new tracks. From there, I'll often remove one track and run the other through the plug-in. Figure 6.25 shows the result of a loop split into stereo.

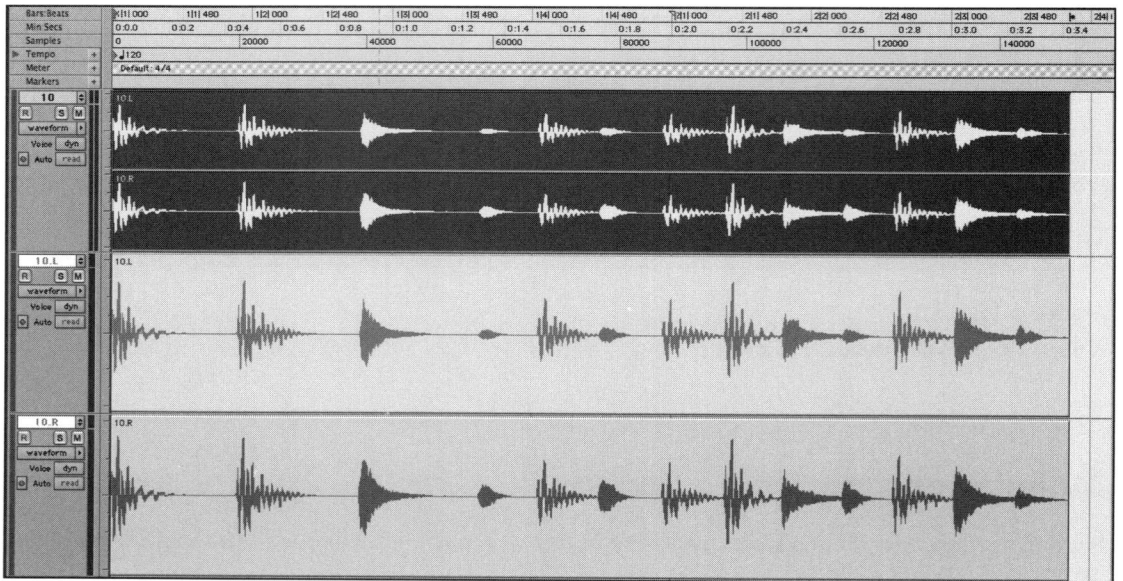

Figure 6.25

The result of the Split into Mono function

Simple Send and Return Configurations

I see a lot of producers who insert reverbs and other time-based effects directly on a track. I believe this is often a mistake. With the reverb inserted on the track, the only way to create a blend with the reverb and the dry sound is to adjust the mix parameter. The problem is that when the blend is even, you lose the presence and punch of the original sound. With a send and return configuration, you get the wet sound and the dry sound with all its punch on two faders. You can then blend them with the faders and get the best of both worlds!

Figure 6.26 shows a simple send and return configuration. First, create an Aux channel (stereo for stereo time-based effects and mono for mono time-based effects). Then, create a send on the dry signal to a bus. Set the input of the new Aux track to the same bus (a good idea is to label the bus at this time to avoid confusion). Lastly, insert the reverb on the Aux track. If you want more reverb, increase the send from the dry track or simply turn up the fader of the Aux. This way, you can keep the punch of the dry sound and have reverb too!

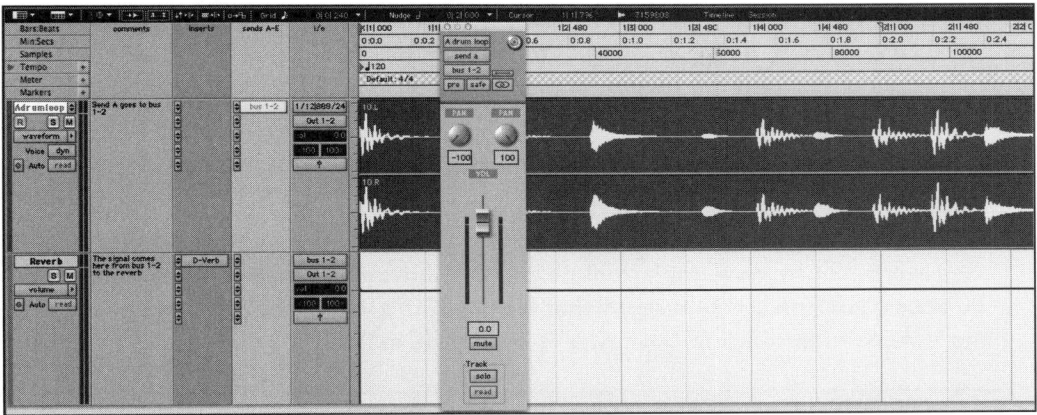

Figure 6.26

A simple send and return configuration

Reverb-Only Setups (Instant Distant)

Ever want to hear the sound as if it's so far away that it's been swallowed in the reverb? When this is the desired effect, there are two ways to accomplish it, one better than the other.

❄ Insert the reverb on the track in question, as in Figure 6.27. Pick your favorite reverb and set its mix to 100% wet. This will give you instant distant signal. However, you will run out of control and options if you want the sound to change from all wet to all dry because the only control you have is the Wet/Dry mix. Unfortunately, finding a balance between wet and dry may land at 20% wet and will be distinctly quieter than if you set it up the right way.

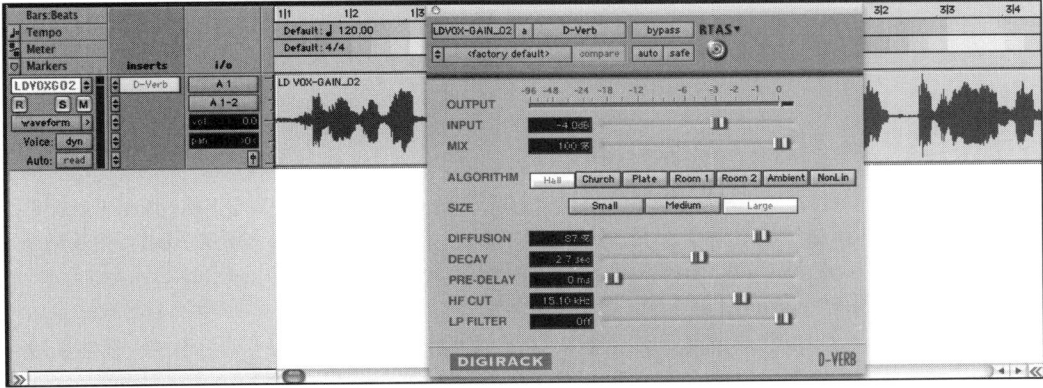

Figure 6.27

Reverb directly inserted on the track

✻ Create a send and return signal chain. This is the fundamental setup for any time-based effect, such as reverb, delay, or chorus. You'll need two tracks—the dry track and an Aux input (return). Insert the reverb on the Aux track, and set its input to a bus labeled Reverb, as in Figure 6.28.

1. On the dry track, create an Aux send to the bus labeled Reverb and turn it up to 0 dB.

2. Click the Pre-Fader Send option. This separates the Send volume from the Fader volume, allowing you to turn the fader down to minus infinity and still send signal to the reverb. You've now got instant distant! The advantage here is that if you change balances, you can create a signal that is both 100% wet and 100% dry by bringing the Volume fader back to 0 dB. This is impossible in the first setup.

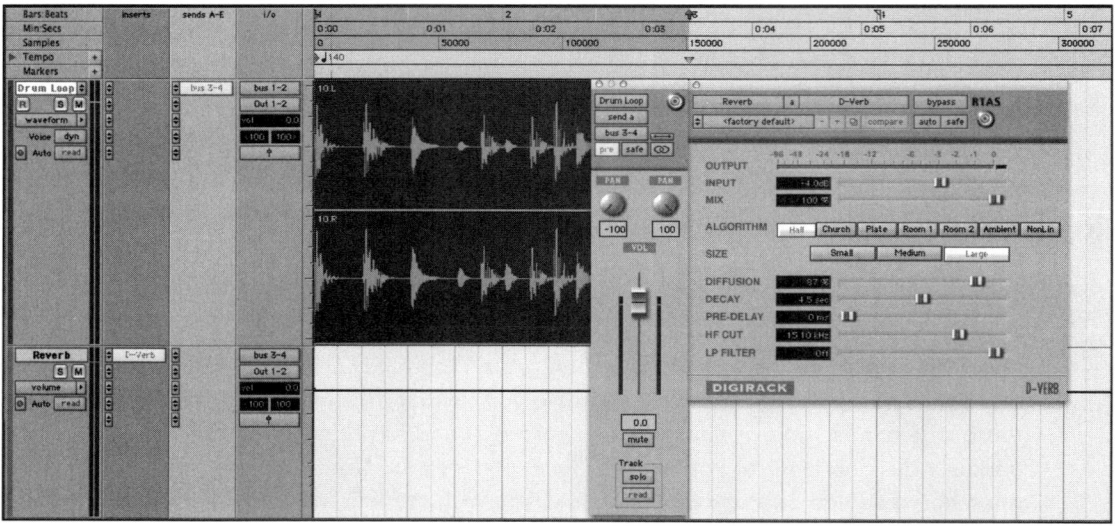

Figure 6.28

A pre-fader send and return signal chain

Shaving DSP in TDM Systems

When you use TDM systems, the first thing you'll notice is the quality of DSP available and the dedicated chips for DSP (TDM Farms or Accel Farms). Having these dedicated chips to do the heavy lifting is great, but it is not infinite—eventually you hit the DSP wall and run out of processing power. (See "Hitting the Wall and Getting Stuck (TDM)" and "What Do You Do When You Run Out of Plug-In Power?" in the beginning of this chapter.) Instead of having to print your effects and burn voices, you can shave DSP by switching some plugs around.

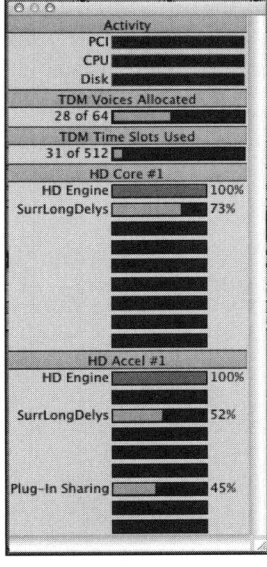

Figure 6.29

The System Usage window

You'll know you've hit the wall when you receive the DAE - 7204 error telling you you've just hit the wall. It's nice that Pro Tools tells you this because I know it can be hard to tell when you've hit the wall—the bruises on your nose aren't always enough. Once you shake off the sting from the impact, open the System Usage window by choosing Window > System Usage, and you'll be presented with the list of plug-ins that are currently inserted, as shown in Figure 6.29. Look for the hogs (100% for one plug-in) and start shuffling from there.

If you run out of TDM DSP, try switching one or more plug-ins to RTAS (see Figure 6.30), lightening the load on the DSP chips and sending some of it to the Mac CPU. This will work *only* if the TDM plug you switch is the first plug in the chain because RTAS plug-ins can't follow TDM plug-ins. Keep in mind that if you often use virtual synths (most are RTAS style and already tax the CPU), there might not be much room on the CPU left to switch to. It might be worth printing to audio to free up CPU, and then switching TDM plug-ins to RTAS.

Figure 6.30

Switching to RTAS

You might find yourself with a slower computer when you switch, but at least you can get around the wall. You can keep doing this until you run out of CPU, in which case your back will be truly, well, against the wall.

You should look to print and deactivate some DSP tracks at this point, or you can buy a beefier computer if one exists! If not, then learn to get comfortable printing your tracks with DSP—or learn to mix with fewer effects (yeah, right).

Chaining Effects

If you don't already know, the five insert points on any track are preconfigured to be in a series. This means that insert point 1 flows into insert point 2, to 3, to 4, and then to 5. When you create your chained plugs in this way, it is sometimes a good idea to set your first one to insert point 2, leaving point 1 open for the option of switching around.

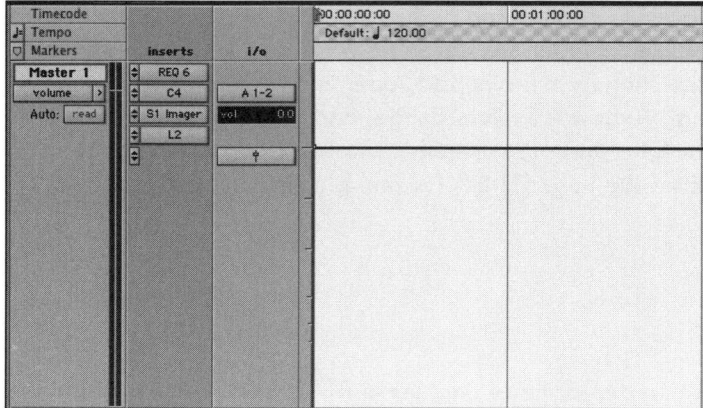

Figure 6.31

Four chained inserts on a track

Insert overload like this can happen often on the Master Fader when the mix is almost over. Many producers pre-master on the Master Fader, and often several effects are inserted there, as seen in Figure 6.31. When you pre-master, it can do more harm than good in the long run, and it can be frustrating when you want to change only the first plug. You'll need to move each plug down individually, and then create the new plug at the top. If you start at insert point 2, you can sneak in that different first plug with little problem, as seen in Figure 6.32.

Figure 6.32

Shuffled plugs one at a time

The flip side to this argument says that if you start at insert point 2 and you need a fifth insert after the other four, you still need to shuffle the plugs around to make room. It's true. You just can't win sometimes. However, if you are chaining plugs on a track other than the Master Fader, you can route to another channel and get five more plugs, as shown in Figure 6.33!

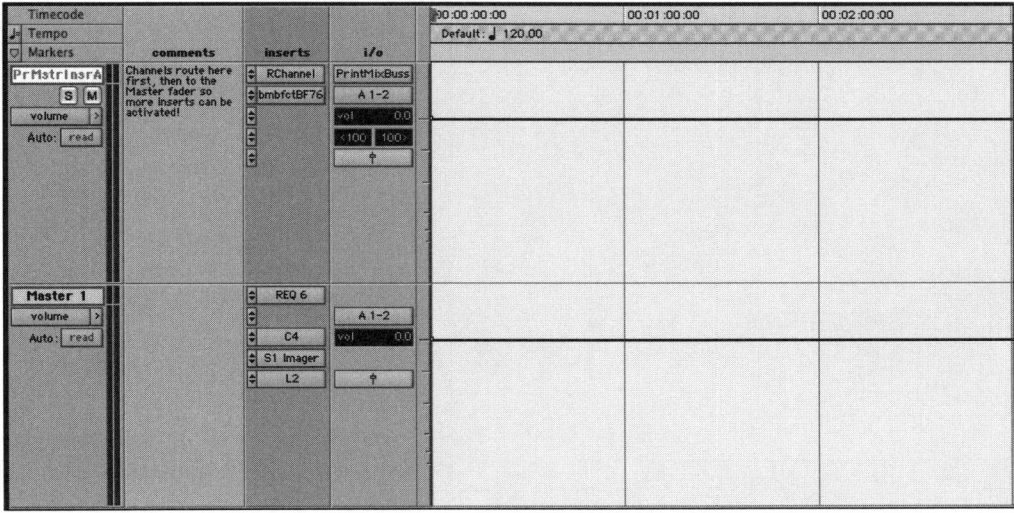

Figure 6.33
Setup with more than five plugs

If you route the output of a filled-up track to a bus labeled Five More Effects and create another track named Five More, whose input is set to Five More Effects, you now have five more insert effects available. Some might say you've over-processed the signal, but what do they know? You love it!

Of course, you have just hit the wall again...ouch.

Clipping the Plug

Ever wondered why you keep seeing red Clip indicators on your track no matter how low you drop the fader? Check under Options > Pre-Fader Metering to see whether this option is active, as shown in Figure 6.34. If so, your Clip indicator is telling you that the clip is already written on the file and you need to pencil it out. (See "Erasing with the Pencil Tool" in Chapter 4.) However, if there is no obvious clip on the file, then check your plug-ins—you might be clipping the plug itself, as shown in Figure 6.35.

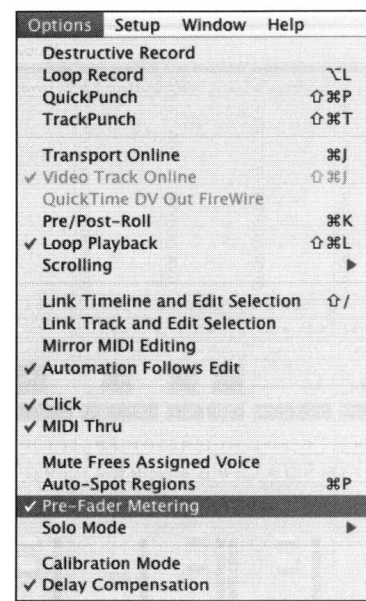

Figure 6.34

The Options > Pre-Fader Metering option

Figure 6.35

A clipped plug-in

When this happens, your channel will tell you you've clipped, but you can't get the red Clip indicator to go away, even after dropping the fader and turning off pre-fader metering. This is a surefire indication that you've clipped the plug-in. This can add undesirable digital distortion to your sound. In this case, adjust the input to the plug until there is no clip, and turn up the gain afterward if necessary.

Storing Presets

If you work with the same talent repeatedly, it's probably because they feel comfortable with you, your studio, and your sound. This might be due to the room, the mics, or your particular plug-ins and settings. As a measure of customer service, if your talent needs to go elsewhere to do a job, make sure they travel with their plug-in settings, too.

When you determine that the settings you have on this plug-in work for this talent, be sure to save the preset. When you click the Save Settings button, Pro Tools defaults to saving the setting in the Root Settings folder on your hard drive; but it is also wise to put it in the Session folder so that it lives right next to the session itself, as seen in Figure 6.36. Once there, it is easy to burn the file to CD as well as save it to the talent's hard drive.

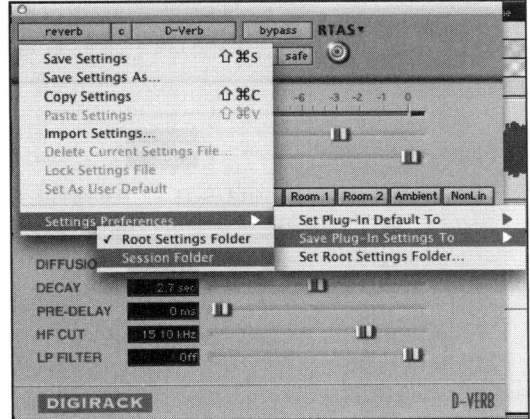

Figure 6.36

Changing the Save Plug-In Settings default folder

After you've saved the session to the Session folder, it is available to anyone with that plug-in and that session's drive attached. Although the current session saves the setting within the Pro Tools document, it does not make it immediately available to another session.

Dealing with Plug-In Delay

Users of Pro Tools TDM prior to version 6.7 (or HD users at 6.4 or higher) need to manage the latency created by inserting plug-ins. Latency is a natural function of inserts, and it can be measured by CMD-clicking twice on the Volume indicator on the track itself, as seen in Figure 6.37. Continuing to click there will cycle through volume readout, peak readout, and sample delay readout. Following are three ways to deal with sample delay.

Comments and Nudging

1. First, you should determine which plug-ins you will be using on the track and plug them in. When you are satisfied, measure the sample delay and mark it in the Comments field, as shown in Figure 6.38. Your comment should read something like, "Oxford EQ, BF 1176, Waves L1- 75 samples."

2. Then, select all the regions on the track by either triple-clicking or choosing Edit > Select All (CMD+A). Set your Nudge value to samples, and nudge the tracks earlier by the sample delay amount. The theory is that the plugs make the track late, so measure the delay and move the region earlier by the same amount, keeping the track phase and sample accurate with the rest of the tracks.

Figure 6.37

CMD-click the Volume indicator twice to determine the delay caused by inserts

Figure 6.38

The Comments field showing the plug-in chain and sample delay

Timeadjuster

1. Digidesign has a built-in plug-in that deals with plug-in delay—it's called Timeadjuster. This works counter-intuitively by adding delay to the other tracks. It adds sample delay itself, slightly defeating the purpose. First, measure the track's sample delay.

2. Insert Timeadjuster on all the other tracks by OPTION-inserting it in the fifth insert position, and then removing it from the track in question. Timeadjuster has an inherent minimum sample delay of four samples, so simply adding it adds four more samples of delay! You can already see this is going to be fun.

3. Adjust Timeadjuster on the other tracks to delay them to the same level of delay as the original track, basically making every one late to match. If your largest delay is 74 samples, then adjust all other tracks by 70 samples because adding Timeadjuster already shifts the track by 4 samples, as seen in Figure 6.39.

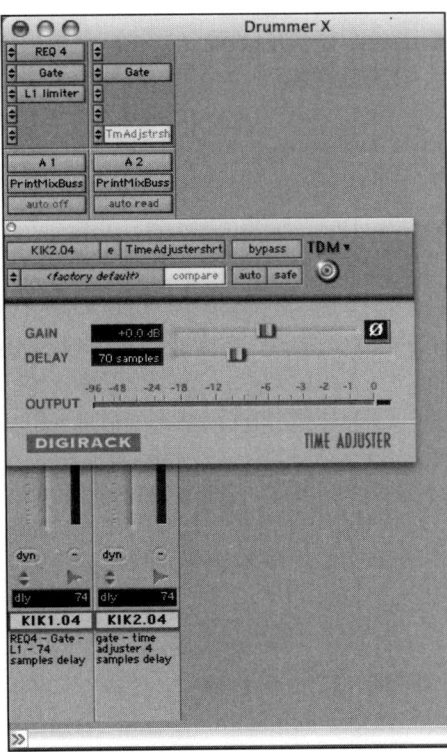

Figure 6.39

Timeadjuster set up for managing sample delay

Print and Shift

1. Route the track with sample delay to a bus labeled Delay Print.

2. Create a new Audio track with the input set to Delay Print.

3. Record the entire track from the beginning of the first region to the end of the last region.

4. Because the delay of the insert chain doesn't show up on the new track, you can zoom in to the beginning of the original track and compare the beginning of it to the beginning of the printed track, as shown in Figure 6.40.

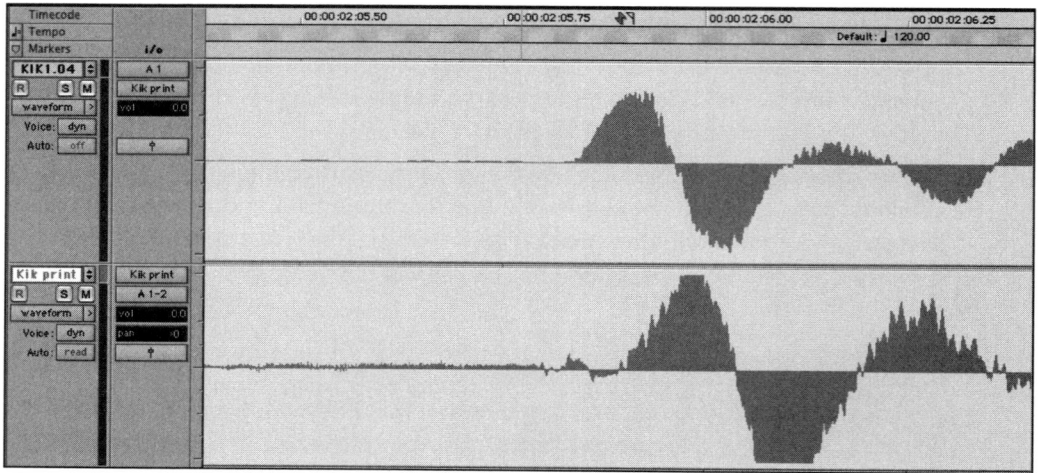

Figure 6.40

Printed track after plug-in delay versus the original track

5. Position the cursor at the beginning of the original track, and switch to the Grabber tool.

6. Control-click the printed track to align it to the same sample point as the original track.

7. Deactivate the original track to free up DSP and keep the sound sample accurate.

A-B Tests with Plug-Ins

The Compare button on the plug-in will allow you to audition between the current preset and a tweaked version of the plug-in. Once you change from default, the Compare button illuminates, telling you that you've left the preset and are now working with custom settings, as seen in Figure 6.41. There will always be a decision process between the settings you have currently (after tweaking the preset) and the settings you think will sound better with more tweaking. To perform this A-B test, you need to do a bit of setup first.

Generally, you'll insert a plug-in and adjust the settings from the factory default settings to taste. If you like these but you want to experiment with another setting, you really have no way of getting back to these settings unless you save them as a preset. After you save the default settings, you can tweak again until you think you've got it better. Then, you can click the Compare button to go back and forth between the current settings and the saved ones.

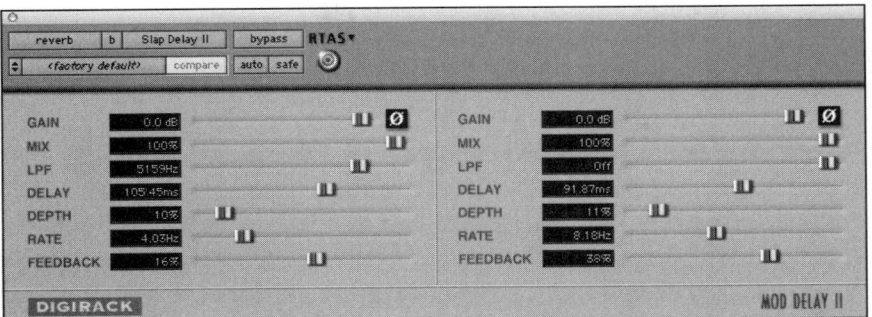

Figure 6.41

EQ with custom settings tweaked from the factory default

Solo Safe with Reverbs

An organized Pro Tools session might be arranged with all the MIDI and Audio tracks at the top and all the Aux inputs at the bottom. The Aux inputs probably hold a synth or two and a few reverbs and delays, like the one in Figure 6.42. This is great for organization, but really annoying when you try to solo an Audio track with the reverb. You'll need to solo the track, and then navigate to the end to solo the reverb, and back and forth. The same goes for MIDI tracks and synths. So how can you keep the synths playing while only soloing the MIDI track and keeping your tracks organized?

Normally, when one track is soloed, all other tracks are muted. This is shown by the yellow solo light on the soloed track and the grayed mute on all others, as shown in Figure 6.43.

Figure 6.42

The Mix window organized by track type

Figure 6.43

Solo light and grayed mutes

You can activate Solo Safe by Apple-clicking on the Solo button, either in the Edit or Mix window. By putting a track in Solo Safe, you can solo any *other* track, and the Solo Safe track will *not* mute, as seen in Figure 6.44. This is handy when you are auditioning parts with their reverbs against other parts and their effects too. If you Solo safe the vocal reverb, you can solo *just* the vocal track and the vocal reverb will also play.

Figure 6.44

A Reverb Aux input in Solo Safe mode

Delay Compensation

New to version 6.7 is Delay Compensation (introduced with 6.4 for HD users), which removes any induced delay by inserting a plug-in. Remember from the "Dealing with Plug-In Delay" section earlier in this chapter that every plug-in induces a certain amount of sample delay on that track. You also remember how annoying it is (was) to deal with that delay.

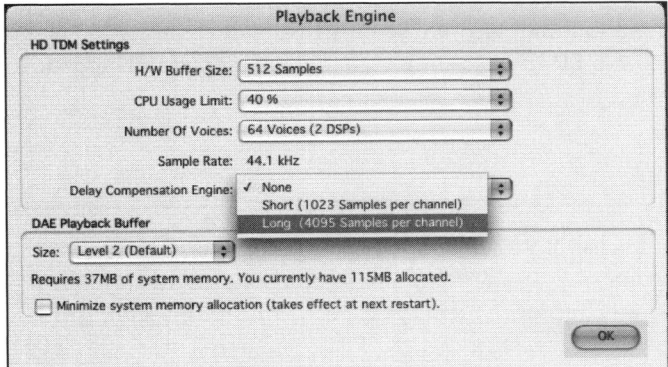

Figure 6.45

Playback engine with Delay Compensation

Now, you simply tell Pro Tools which level of compensation you require (Setups > Playback Engine > Delay Compensation), and it will automatically absorb the delay until you go over the limit, as seen in Figure 6.45. Because adding Delay Compensation steals DSP, start with the smaller setting first. You can activate the compensation by choosing Operations > Use Delay Compensation (see Figure 6.46).

Figure 6.46

The Operations > Use Delay Compensation option

Remember that sample delay only becomes audible on two tracks that normally play in sample-accurate phase together (stereo overheads, kick mic against the snare mic with bleed through, and so on). By inserting a delay on one track, you smear the phase of the two tracks played together. It is a harsh, digital noise that starts to sound like a tunnel. Once you hear it, you'll know it forever.

If you're not sure whether there's delay affecting your sound, save your settings, de-insert the plug-ins, and listen. Unfortunately, bypassing the plug-in doesn't remove the delay. A neat trick here is to CMD+Control-click the plug-in to deactivate it. This removes the DSP usage as well as the insert delay *and* keeps your settings. In the case of a kick drum from a live drum set, it will most likely show up when soloed against the overhead mics. Because the kick always bleeds into the overheads, any smearing of phase would be readily apparent when the two play together.

Solo the kick and overheads and listen without plugs. Then, re-insert (or reactivate) your plugs and listen. If the sound gets funny, revisit the "Dealing with Plug-In Delay" section or upgrade your software to use Delay Compensation!

Tempo Shifts and Delays

When you compose music in Pro Tools, it's likely you'll use more than one tempo and meter—not for all music, but for some. In particular, if you extracted the tempo using Beat Detective (see "Exact Slicing with Beat Detective" in Chapter 4), then your tempo probably changes every quarter note!

Usually this is no problem, but if you are using tempo-specific effects or tempo-specific LFOs on your synths, then every time the tempo changes the effect or LFO won't keep up! This can sound like a train wreck if the tempos shift drastically and the effect doesn't keep up.

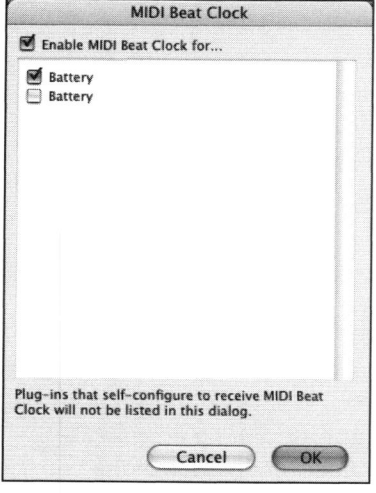

Figure 6.47

MIDI Beat Clock

As you saw in the "MIDI Beat Clock" section in Chapter 5, activating the Beat Clock and assigning it to your synth (see Figure 6.47) is vital to keeping everything together. However, some effects don't require the Beat Clock to be turned on. If you are using Reason parts, Reason effects, and LFOs, you only need to assign the effect or LFO in Reason to the note resolution (quarter, 8th, and so on). Because Reason gets its tempo from Pro Tools, it will naturally follow any tempo changes you program.

Synths created in Pro Tools, however, require the MIDI Beat Clock to be activated so they stay in time. Keep in mind that any delay created that emulates analog delay will get funky whenever you change tempos. Delay signals naturally pitch shift (radically) when the delay time changes in the middle of audio running through it, and emulated delays are no different. If this happens to you, you should consider using a different effect, printing the effect prior to the tempo change, or killing the send to the delay as the tempo changes. Every situation is different, so trust your ears.

7 Mixing and Automation

More an art than a science, the process of mixing is one of the most fun and most challenging in all of audio. The sounds created and recorded have to balance to create an emotional response that works with the nature of the piece and keeps the listener engaged from the first note to the last.

The mixer has to take the elements as they are, on "tape," and blend them like a master chef creating the perfect meal. Beyond the obvious list of plug-ins, the mixer's greatest tools are imagination and a good ear. This chapter will cover a few ideas and techniques to make your mixes (and voice productions) stand out.

A Word on Automation

When you talk about mixing, one thing truly makes mixes stand up and get noticed—automation. It's the process by which vocals can stay loudest in the mix, make parts instantly disappear and then reappear one word later, or change the entire song into an AM radio sound. More than EQ or compression, automation can make a mix sparkle, and it can smooth out any inconsistencies.

If you own a control surface, such as the Command 8, Control 24, Pro Control or ICON, automation through the Automation modes (see Figure 7.1) is the most fun you can have during mixing because you can touch the faders as well as control the movement of more than just the faders—and best of all, you can move more than one fader at a time! If you don't own a control surface, you'll need to use the mouse and the Automation Playlist curves to draw in automation (see Figure 7.2).

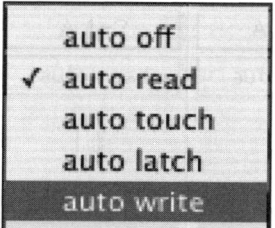

Figure 7.1

The Automation modes

It should go without saying that everything in Pro Tools can be automated. Some of what you'll see in this chapter involves automating functions you might not be used to, such as EQs, sends, and reverbs, as well as shortcuts to making your mixes unique and exciting.

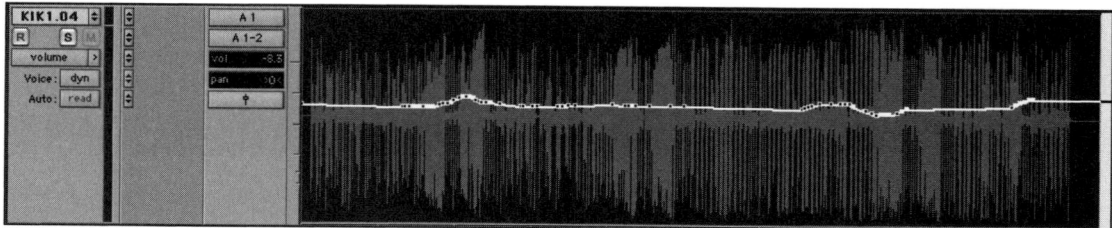

Figure 7.2

Automation Playlist for volume

Levels, Bandwidth, and the Master Fader

Depending on your level of hardware, you might be disappointed when you hear your mix on CD as opposed to hearing it right out of the mix. There are several functions at play during the mix process, including your hardware, DA converters, your levels, and your Master Fader processing. Although most of the discussion in this tip is true for all DAWs, you should experiment with the methods listed here to determine which work best for you.

A common theme in record production is *loudness*—how loud can you make it without distortion? This is not necessarily the best approach, but it might be appropriate for the style of music with which you are working. No matter what you choose to do on the Master Fader, you should pay attention to all your faders and meters.

Master Fader Meters in 24–Bit Sessions

You never want to see a clip because it means you are over-processing or you've over-recorded. This can lead to distortion and just plain poor sound. Pay extra attention to the Master Fader to make sure your levels are under clip. A good target is to make sure that the Master Fader reads between –6 and 0 dB. (Figure 7.3 shows a Master Fader with good level. Notice that the yellow break lines at the top indicate that the mix hit between 0 dB and –6 dB for a moment, also indicating a dynamic mix.) This way, you can be sure you're using all 24 bits of your mix and getting the most dynamic range (or the loudest signal, whichever is desired) without distortion or introducing extra quantization errors.

It's a good idea to have the Master Fader's volume indicator measure the peak value for the track (see Figure 7.4), telling you what the highest signal was to ensure that you hit the 6-dB range (or that you don't peak).

Figure 7.3

Master Fader
with full level

Figure 7.4

Peak measurement
on the Master
Fader

Level of the Master Fader

When there are clips on the Master Fader, most people drop the Fader until the peak goes away. This is not the best maneuver, however, because you might be curing the symptom but not the problem. The problem when you peak the Master Fader is generally that you have too much signal in your mix. Put simply, the mix is overly hot and is filling the Master Bus to overflowing. When you lower the Master Fader, you lower the capacity on the Master Bus, not the amount of signal going to it. Eventually, you might go beyond the 6-dB range (you lose one bit every time your volume falls below –6 dB), shrinking your bit count and reducing the image width, clarity, and dynamic range of the mix.

Unfortunately, a better method is not so easy. You need to lower the faders for all the channels *before* the Master Fader. If you have automation, this is even more painful. If you are submixing channels, then there is even more to do.

Activate All Group, and switch any track to the volume curve. Because the vertical size of the track determines the accuracy of volume automation trimming, switch any track to Large view. Using the Grabber tool, create breakpoint automation at the beginning and end of the song. These two automation breakpoints will indicate the bookends of the volume automation. Select the entire song, including these two new points, and switch to the Trim tool. (Note that the Trim tool only performs one task when the track shows automation—trimming the automation curve up or down—so don't bother distinguishing between the various trimmer tools.) Lower the Volume Automation Playlist for any track, which will lower the volume curve on all tracks proportionally, as shown in Figure 7.5. Use small amounts at first to see if it alleviates your problem.

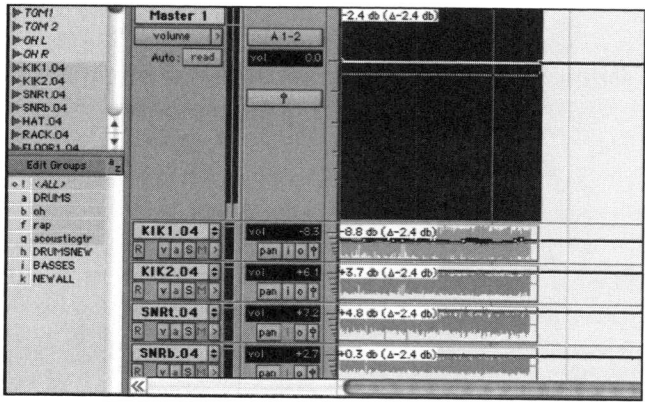

Figure 7.5

All Group lowering the volume curves

You will notice a quieter mix because you also lowered the Master Fader. Deactivate the All Group setting, and adjust the volume curve on the Master Fader to be at 0 dB again, as shown in Figure 7.6. Your mix should get louder again, but you might also notice that the levels have changed among your tracks. Any tracks that are subgrouped together should have the Aux track's volume curve readjusted as well. You will need to go through this process repeatedly until your mix sounds right; your Master Fader is at 0 dB; and the meter doesn't hit 0, doesn't peak, and sits within the 6-dB range. Expect this to take a little while. It is a good idea to save your mix before attempting to adjust the levels to make sure you know what you liked before you recognized the problem.

Figure 7.6

The Master Fader readjusted to 0 dB

Plug-Ins on the Master Fader

Most people put lots of stuff on the Master Fader before they put the song on CD and call it done. Most mastering engineers will not thank you for this because it is their job, and they have better tools to do it. It might sound better now in your less-than-perfect listening environment, but when you go to master, you will hear the third degree from the mastering engineer (unless you are very light-handed about it...and most people aren't)!

However, if you have a good Dither plug-in, you should use it if you intend to bounce to disk at 16 bits for CD. If you are not aware of dither, it is a process that helps you convert your 24-bit song to 16 bits with better clarity. If you don't own a good third-party Dither plug-in, use POW-r (which comes with Pro Tools). The three different dither settings are used for different material—sparser material should be run through Type 1 and denser material should be run through Type 3, as shown in Figure 7.7.

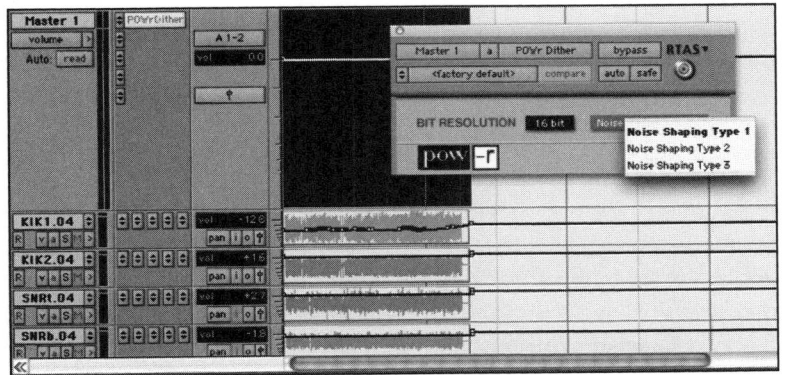

Figure 7.7

Dithering with POW-r

Printing versus Bouncing

One of the biggest questions and debates in digital audio, and especially with in-the-box production systems such as Pro Tools, is about *summing*. Some feel that when you try to sum (add) all the tracks together in digital systems, you simply run out of room at the Master bus, with the audible result being a lack of clarity, dynamics, and image. The previous section, "Level of the Master Fader," is one workaround to this solution, but for some that's simply not enough. If you are one of those people, I suggest you look at performing your mix through analog summing as opposed to bouncing or printing. Following are three methods of finishing your mix with differences in quality and operation; try them and see for yourself which works best for you.

Bounce to Disk

By far the simplest method, bouncing the mix is the process of playing the mix as a whole and concurrently creating a stereo (or dual mono) file for CD burning or file transferring. The biggest advantage of this move is speed. Although this occurs in real time, so it takes as long as your song, in the Bounce dialog box (see Figure 7.8) you can choose the Convert During Bounce option, which takes a 24-bit mix and converts it to 16 live. The same goes for sample rate conversion. However, one problem is that if you bounce the file to 16 bit for CD, you have to rebounce it to 24 bit for mastering, doubling your workload. The biggest downside to this method is that the conversion, while occurring real time, might introduce audible artifacts and give you a smaller-sounding mix. Choose this method for convenience and speed only.

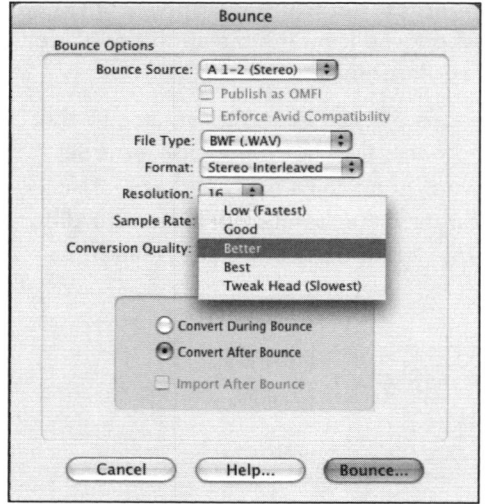

Figure 7.8

The Bounce dialog box

Record to Tracks

By busing all the tracks to a single stereo Audio track and recording the mix (shown in Figure 7.9), you avoid any unwanted conversion noise during bouncing, and you simultaneously create your 24-bit file for mastering. Keep in mind that the file is 24 bits but two tracks—left and right. You will need to drag both out of your Audio Files folder to bring them to mastering. You can export the file (SHIFT+CMD+K) to 16-bit for a reference CD, preserving the quality of the 24-bit for the mastering engineer. This is preferable to bouncing to disk for quality, but it can be a real hassle to set up, and it doesn't avoid the summing issue. There simply might be too much information for the stereo bus, and the mix might sound crunched in the end anyway.

Figure 7.9

Multiple tracks routed to a single stereo track

Analog Summing

In this situation, you'll need an analog line mixer with a clean signal path. Several companies make them, and some of them are specifically designed for this purpose. Instead of relying on Pro Tools and your hardware and software limitations, route all your tracks out separate outputs to the line mixer instead of the Master Bus. This removes the Master Bus logjam and can keep your sound quality at its highest. If you can't afford 24 to 48 tracks of console, a simple 8-channel mixer might suffice. In this case, subgroup your tracks into clusters (rhythm sections, guitars and pianos, lead vox and effects, and so on). Reroute the output of the mixer back into Pro Tools, and record the mix to a Stereo track. You will then have a clean, analog-summed mix printed at 24 bits for mastering. You will need to export the reference for CD, but you maintain the quality and avoid artifacts generated by bouncing. However, you are performing two extra conversions between the digital and analog domains, and this can also affect your sound. You might notice a change (or lack) of color in your mix that may prove to be unacceptable—or exceptional. The quality here depends on both your Pro Tools interface (DA and AD conversion) and your line mixer.

As you can see, there are just as many decisions to make at the final stage of your mix as there are during it. The best thing to do is experiment with the various options at the Master Fader to determine which is best. Personally, I always keep my Master Fader meter between –6 and 0 dB, and I constantly adjust the channel faders to keep it there. I don't usually put much on the Master Fader—I leave that for the mastering engineer. I also don't generally analog sum my mixes, but occasionally I get requests to run the whole mix through a colorful compressor in the analog world. More often than not, though, I print the mix and then export to CD. Again, experiment to see which method works best for you.

When to Use the Various Automation Modes

There are five Automation modes (review Figure 7.1) that allow you to interact with the parameters you want to automate and that give you different options for how you interact.

❋ **Auto Off.** When you turn the Automation mode off, you temporarily bypass all automation written to the track. This is by far the smartest way to audition the channel at a different setting than is currently automated. For example, when the producer wants to listen to the song without the lead vocal, but the lead is automated to always play, temporarily set the lead vox to Auto Off. Then when you mute the track, it will stay muted.

❋ **Auto Read.** This is the default mode for all tracks. It basically means that any automation written to the track will play back. In fact, it will always play back the automation until you choose a different mode.

❋ **Auto Write.** This mode is dangerous because it creates new automation on everything that can be automated on the track from the moment you hit Play to the moment you hit Stop. *Don't use this mode if you only want to adjust one parameter!* Use this mode when you want to write a blank pass across the track from start to finish, or you want to erase automation parameters for sections of a song (or the whole thing).

❋ **Auto Touch.** Auto Touch mode writes new automation from the moment the parameter is touched (clicked on) until it is released. This is the best mode to use for quick updates, such as increasing the volume for one word that got swallowed by the guitars.

❋ **Auto Latch.** Auto Latch mode starts when you touch the parameter but keeps writing automation until you hit Stop. This is great for adjusting the parameter for a section while keeping your hands free to do another move. It is also good to let go of the parameter and keep automating, removing the probability of writing a jittery curve (because you'd have to hold the mouse button to keep the automation writing with Auto Touch). Of course, it could just be the second cup of coffee kicking in.

Keeping Organized by Colors

New to version 6.7 is a color palette, as shown in Figure 7.10. You can now color-coordinate tracks and groups (my wife likes that!) to visually help you tell what's occurring. During the mix stage, it is a good idea to determine which colors best represent which instruments, and then label all related tracks and groups that color.

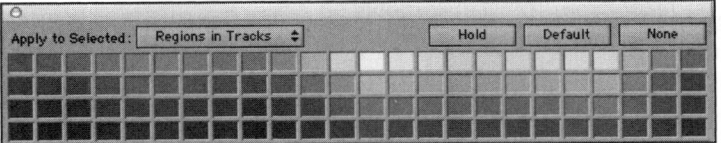

Figure 7.10

Color palette

For example, you might start your mix with drums, a drum sub-mix, a drum reverb, and a drum group. Within these, you might have groups, such as toms, kick, snare, hat, and OH and room. If your color is orange, then the drum tracks all get orange, the sub-mix gets dark orange, the reverb gets light orange, and the groups all get dark orange. That way, if they're orange, you can tell that they're drums.

Keeping the Edit and Mix Windows Linked

If you're like me, you do most of your mixing in the Edit window with automation, but most of your processing in the Mix window with inserts and sends. Constantly jumping back and forth is fine (especially if you have two monitors), but with high track counts you might find it annoying to be at the top of your Edit window on one screen and the bottom of the Mix window on the other.

By Control-clicking the Channel Select in either the Mix or Edit window, you will link the two together for that track (see Figure 7.11). That way, when you switch from the Edit window to the Mix window, you will always have the linked track in your view.

Figure 7.11

The Mix and Edit windows linked

Creating Drum Punctuations

Often it's the kick, but it could be the snare. Maybe it's the toms or maybe it's the hi-hat, but one thing is for sure: Somewhere in the song, one of your drum tracks will get buried at the big hit moment, and you'll want to punctuate the moment with a temporary increase in level.

If you're going to use the mouse, simply select the kick hit (or snare, and so on) and switch to the Volume Automation Playlist. Figure 7.12 shows a kick drum Volume Playlist that is flat throughout. Switch to the Trim tool and trim the volume slightly higher. The Trim tool increases or decreases the volume curve across the entire track, between automation breakpoints or across the selected section only. Keep in mind that the Trim tool will change automation values in different increments based on the vertical size of the track—the larger the track, the more accurate the volume change. Figure 7.13 shows the first kick hit punctuated after trimming the volume upward. Repeat this process wherever the sound requires a moment of punctuation.

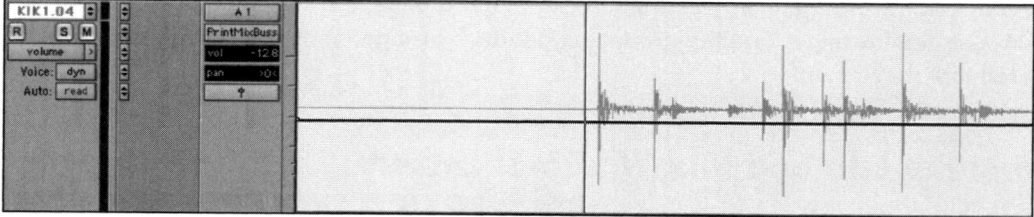

Figure 7.12
Kick drum volume curve flat at the big hit

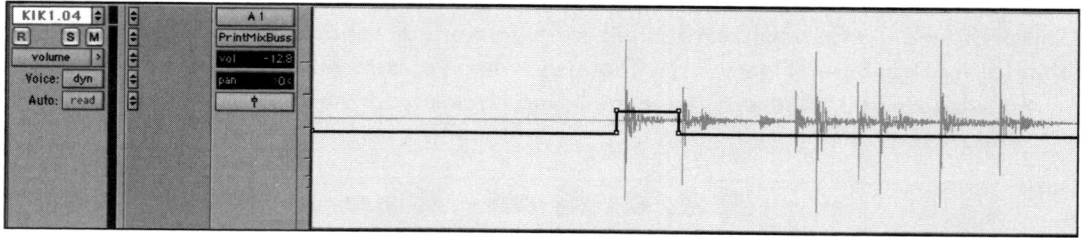

Figure 7.13
Kick drum curve trimmed for the big hit using the Trim tool

Note

Holding CMD while trimming will allow you to change the curve by finer amounts.

Keeping Automation Curves Clean

An unfortunate by-product of trimming volume curves (or any curves) in sections is that the volume curve is actually a square wave, as shown in Figure 7.13. There are vertical lines representing the change in volume at the corners of the curve, but sound doesn't work that way; it needs time to "ramp up." In synthesis terms, this is called the *attack* of the sound.

The audible by-product of this square wave is usually an unacceptable click. The click will only occur if the square wave occurs over actual audio, not between the audio. If the square wave occurs over audio and you notice a click, you can remove the clicking by adjusting the corners slightly inward, creating a slight angle to the square wave, as seen in Figure 7.14. Even a sample's indentation will remove the click; as long as there is *some* angle to the square wave, there will be no clicking.

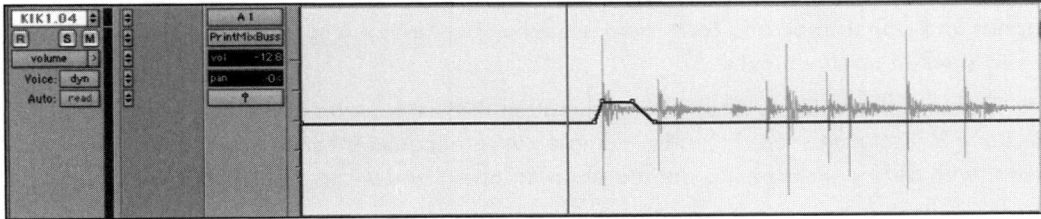

Figure 7.14
The square wave after adjusting the corners

De-Breathing Naturally

As you saw in the "Stripping Vocals" section in Chapter 4, you can edit vocals to provide a cleaner vocal audio. But voice can be unnatural when *all* the breaths are removed this way. A better way to de-breath vocals is to leave some of the breaths intact, but much quieter than the rest.

For breaths between sentences, editing is fine because no one wants to hear the talent take a deep breath before the next big sentence. However, no one believes that *anyone* can read 20 pages of copy without a single breath!

For the breaths in the middle of a sentence, try dropping the volume automation curve by about –20 dB instead of editing. Using the Selector tool in Slip mode, select a breath, and switch to the volume curve. Switch to the Trim tool and drop the volume until the volume curve reads –20 dB. You could accomplish the same thing with the Grabber tool by clicking the two edges of the selection, and then dragging from between the two breakpoints down –20. If you use the Trim tool, be sure to adjust the corners to create a slight angle to the curve to remove the click potential, as shown in Figure 7.15.

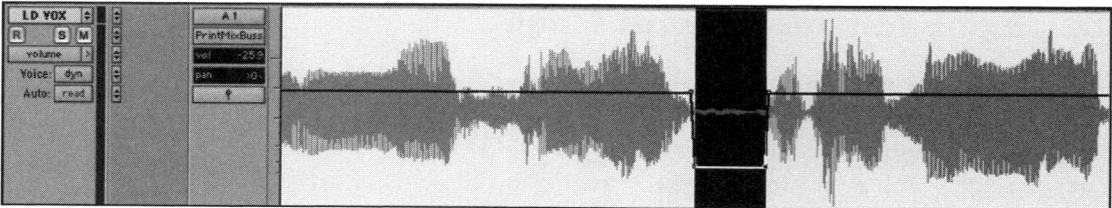

Figure 7.15

The Vocal track with the breaths dropped –20 dB

Auto-Pan (the Reincarnation of the Pan Scan)

Back in the old days, there was a box called the Pan Scan whose job it was to take a single mono signal and pan it back and forth across stereo speakers at a set rate. It was kind of like a *Pong* bar stuck in up-down cycle.

With Pro Tools, you can simply draw the Automation Playlist for pan in the shape you want, and you have instant pan scan. I like the triangle curve because it keeps the cycling even. Experiment with different shapes to get the panning effect you want.

For music set to the grid, switch to Grid mode and set your grid resolution to the desired pan rate. Choose the pencil shape desired (see Figure 7.16 for the list of pencil shapes) and click-drag to the right over the length of time that you desire panning. Dragging to the right will extend the length of time, and dragging up and down will extend the width of the pan after using the triangle pencil (see Figure 7.17).

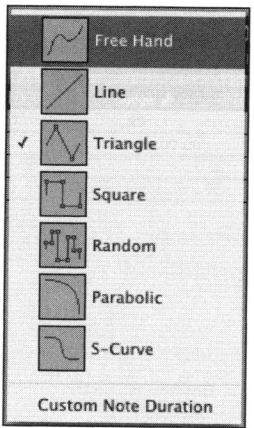

Figure 7.16

The various pencil shapes

Note

You can use the Pencil tool in this manner for all kinds of different effects. Try using it on volume with guitars to emulate a vibrato sound for blues!

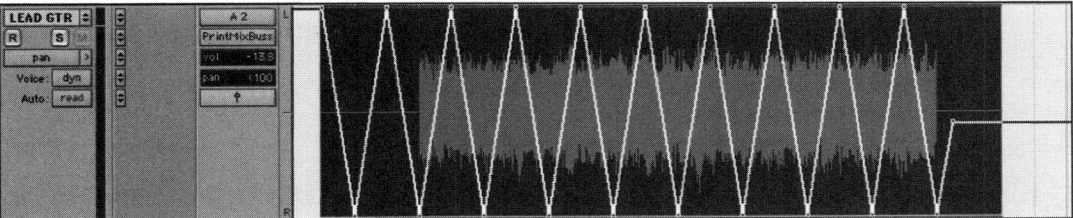

Figure 7.17

The pan automated at quarter-note resolution with the triangle pencil

DJ Filtering without a DJ Mixer

Almost every DJ on the planet knows how to crank the EQ knob or filter knob on the mixer and make the track sound super thin (removing all the bass) or super dark (removing all the treble). The trick isn't necessarily that simple in Pro Tools; however, it just requires a little automation and the right plug-in.

Frequency Only

Although it's not pretty, Digidesign's one-band EQ works, and it's in every Pro Tools system. If you simply need to make an idea for someone else to recreate with a better EQ, this will do just fine. First, decide whether you are filtering out the treble or the bass and choose the most appropriate filter. Both the HiPass and LoPass filters are shown in Figures 7.18 and 7.19, respectively.

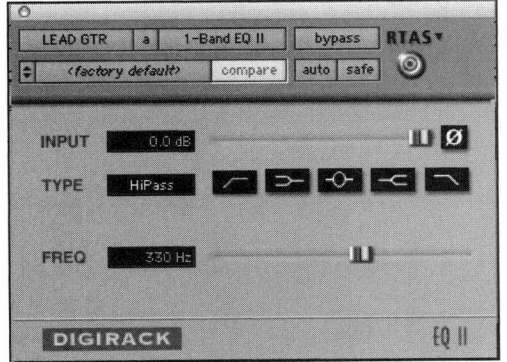

Figure 7.18

HiPass filter

Set the frequency to be automated by choosing Auto from the plug-in itself. This presents a list of parameters you can automate, as seen in Figure 7.20; you should add the filter frequency. After you are finished, you will notice that you have an Automation Playlist available for the frequency of this plug-in.

Figure 7.19

LoPass filter

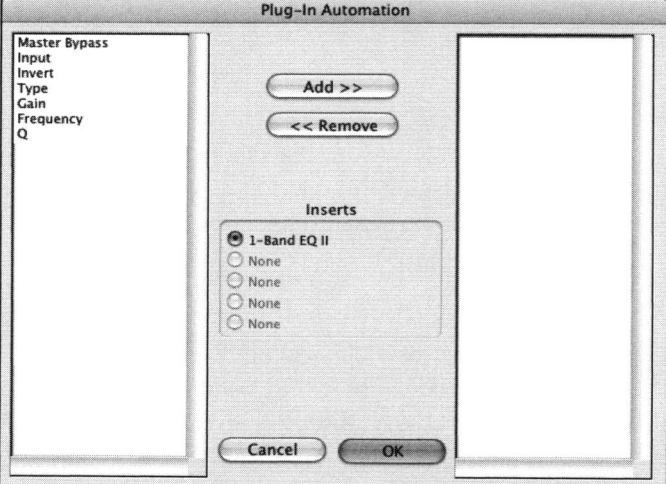

Figure 7.20

The Plug-In Automation parameter list

You can automate the filter move with the mouse using one of the Automation modes (see "When to Use the Various Automation Modes" in this chapter), or you can draw the desired curve using the Pencil tool, as shown in Figure 7.21. Keep in mind that you can make very accurate automation lines (or curves) by choosing different-shaped lines with the Pencil tool, depending on the move desired.

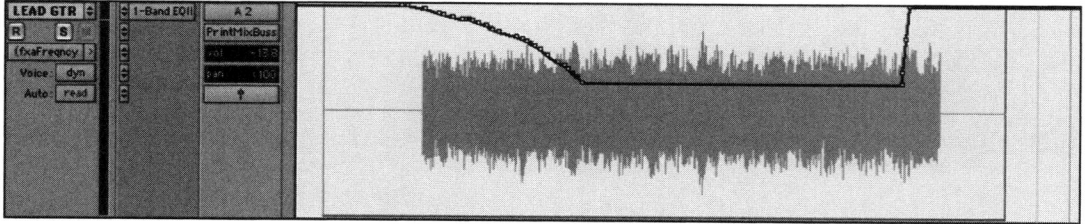

Figure 7.21

The Automation Playlist for filter frequency with a curve drawn with the free pencil

Peak Adjustment

The peak is similar to the resonance parameter found on almost every synth. Automate the filter frequency as you did previously, but in addition, adjust the peak upward to give more bite to the filter. The idea here is that the frequency determines the point of filtration, called the *cutoff frequency* (all sounds above this point are removed), and the peak adds more of the cutoff frequency. This really emphasizes the effect of the filter sweep and "points" the sweep frequency for more distinct sounds.

Note

Any EQ or filter will work for this move as long as it has the filter frequency (cutoff) *and* the peak adjustment.

Fast Synth Automation (or Any Plug-In)

I use the synth as the example here because, classically, synths have more parameters to automate than almost any other plug-in out there. Because there are so many to automate, it's nice to find a quick way to get to just the desired parameter for automation.

Normally, you would have to click the Auto button on the synth to bring up the Plug-In Automation list and sort through the various parameters (see Figure 7.22) until you find what you are looking for. This is a tedious and error-prone process. (You might accidentally add the wrong parameter, have to remove it, and then search again for the right one.)

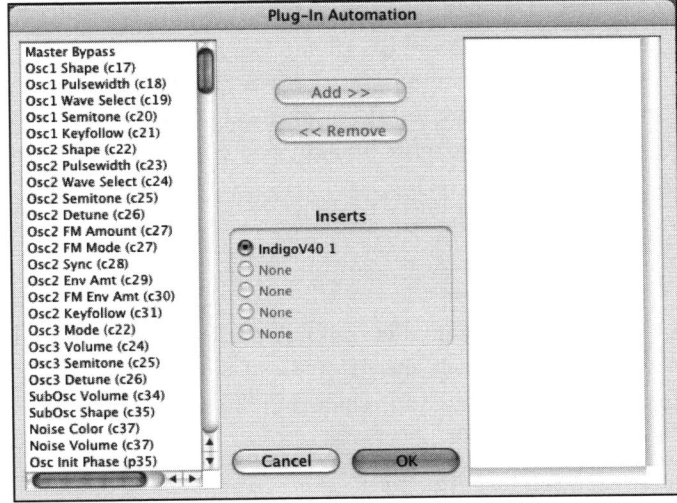

Figure 7.22

Access Virus Indigo's Plug-In Automation list (partial)

Position the cursor over the desired parameter and CMD+OPTION+Control-click the parameter. You will see a short pop-up list allowing the user to enable automation for this parameter, as seen in Figure 7.23. After you choose to enable automation, the same methods still apply—either write in the move with the mouse using an Automation mode, or draw in the curve using the Pencil tool.

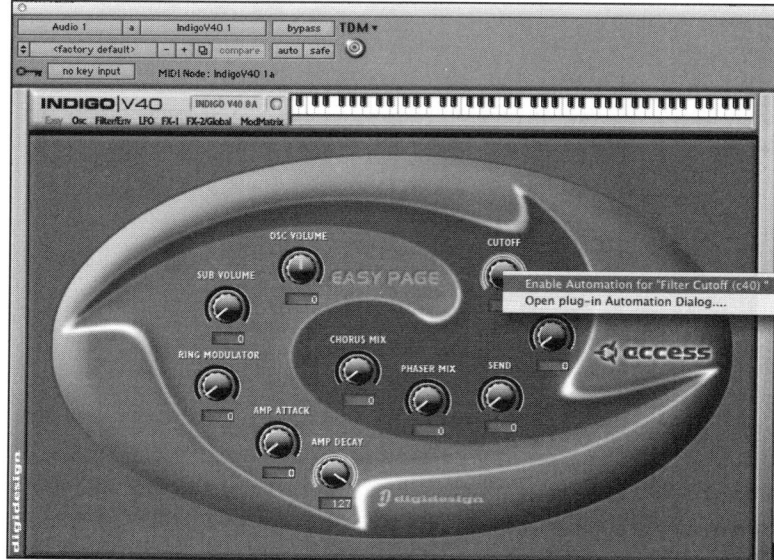

Figure 7.23

Virus Indigo shortcut to enable automation for a parameter

Yet another shortcut is available if you know you want to enable all the parameters at once. Hold the CMD+CTRL+OPTION modifiers, and click the Auto button on the plug-in. Nothing will happen visually, but you will notice that every parameter of the plug-in is now available to automate and has it's own automation playlist available for editing. You can also choose to go to the full Plug-In Automation list, but why bother?

The John Bonham Special

The list of possible effects I could cover here is probably infinite, but this particular example of automation is very ear-catching and extremely cool (in one man's opinion, of course). I call it "Phasers on Stun" or "The John Bonham Effect"—it's what happens when the drums run through a phaser like the end of Led Zeppelin's "Kashmir."

Insert your favorite phaser plug-in on the drum sub-mix Aux input (see "Subgrouping Sounds" in Chapter 6), and set the parameters to your favorite '70s flavor. I strongly suggest you subgroup multiple drum tracks to a single Aux track to pull this off. If you don't, you run the risk of developing Carpal Tunnel Syndrome or a mental breakdown by trying to insert and copy the automation move across multiple tracks!

After the plug is inserted, set the mix to 100% dry and adjust for any sample delay that exists. Enable automation on the Mix parameter (CMD+OPT+CTRL-click the Mix parameter knob.) When it's time for the Bonham séance, automate the mix to increase to 100% wet over the desired length of time, as shown in Figure 7.24.

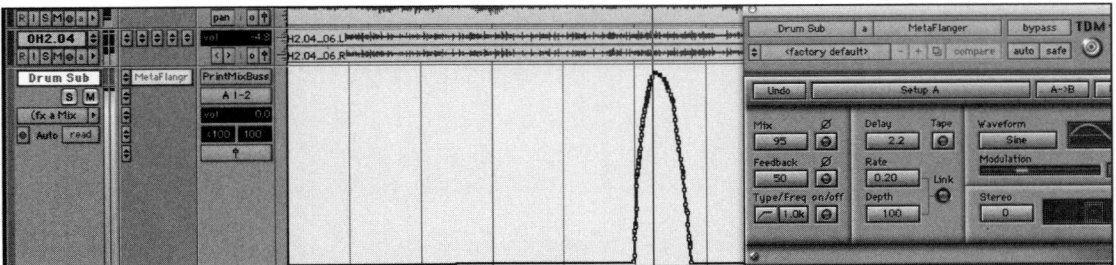

Figure 7.24

Automation of mix of drum sub-mix on the Phaser effect

If you've set all your other parameters to the desired effect, then as you increase the mix, you'll get phased drums for the length of time at which the mix is 100% wet. You'll also get the sneaking suspicion that your lava lamps need dusting, and you'll develop a desire to wear orange and brown together with red sunglasses. Don't do it! Unless it's Halloween or a '70s night with your significant other....

Reggae Reverb Explosions

A favorite among reggae and dub producers is the occasional explosion of reverb on the snare or timbale track. Delay works here, too, so just replace reverb with delay as you choose. (Use both for more dramatic effects.)

As you saw in the "Reverb Only Setups" section in Chapter 6, the best way to create a reverb configuration is with the dry audio track and an Aux input that holds the reverb plug-in, as shown in Figure 7.25. Create an Aux input and insert your favorite reverb. Set the input to a bus called Reverb Explosions. Create a send on the snare track that is assigned to Reverb Explosions.

As the moments arise demanding the snare reverb explosion, automate the send to increase to the desired level by either adjusting the Send fader with the Automation modes or drawing the move in with the Pencil tool, as shown in Figure 7.26. It's a good idea to ensure that there are no vertical automation curves or that they occur slightly before the snare sound so there is no clicking. Also, ensure that the send curve is drawn down to nothing before the next snare hit to avoid accidentally getting too many snare explosions.

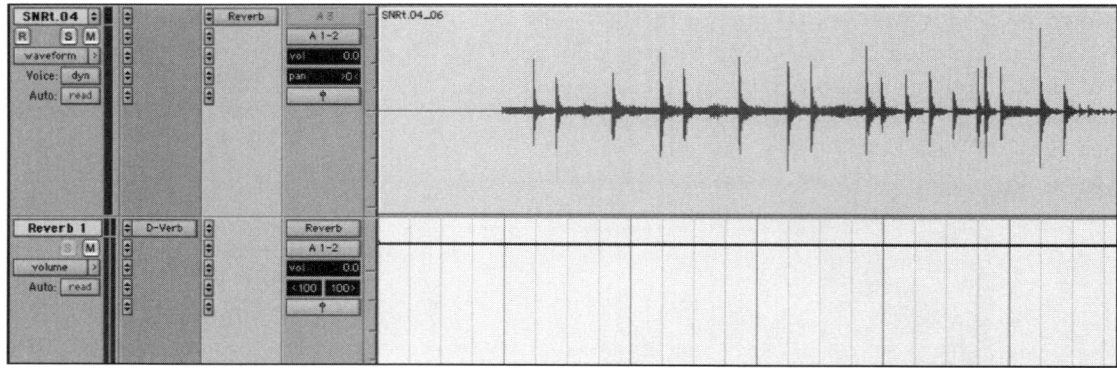

Figure 7.25

Standard send and return configuration with snare and reverb

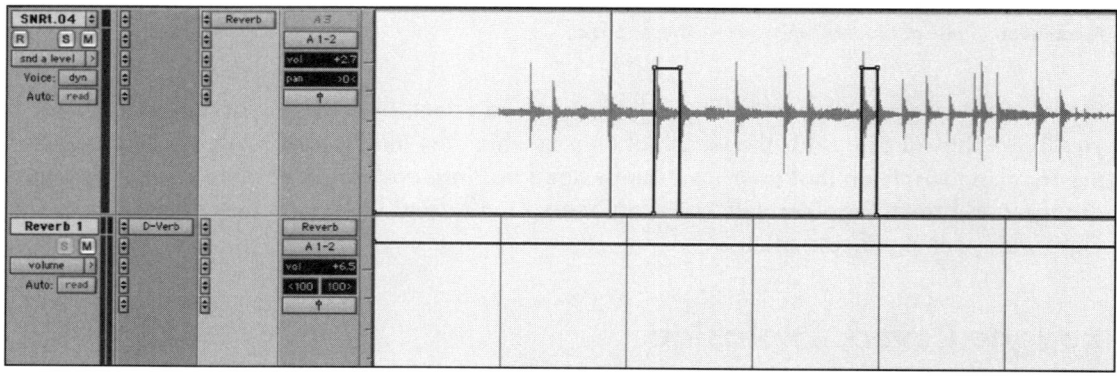

Figure 7.26

Automation of the send to Reverb Explosions Aux input

Automating the Whole Mix

I get a lot of requests to make the entire song flow through an AM radio effect, as if the song decided to find its way onto the other end of a phone call. It might not be obvious, but you can bet that I'm not going to insert an EQ on every track and automate each one! You can also bet that I'm not going to insert the EQ on every track and copy the move from track 1 to track 2, and so on! What am I going to do, you ask? Simple—automate the Master Fader!

If you read "DJ Filtering without a DJ Mixer" earlier in this chapter and "The AM Radio Effect" in Chapter 6, then you already have a sense of what to do. Insert your favorite EQ or filter on the Master Fader. For a true AM radio effect, you might need a combination of filters (Hi and LoPass) and a parametric EQ. After you've set the AM radio effect to your liking, you have two ways to create the automation: bypass or parameter automation.

❋ Bypass automation

1. Set the AM effect to your liking, and enable automation for the bypass.

2. Automate the effect to be bypassed for the majority of the song, until the effect is called for.

3. Display the Automation Playlist for the bypass, select the length of time desired, and switch to the Trim tool.

4. Use the Trim tool to change the curve to reflect the deactivation of the bypass for the selection (so the effect is now active; see Figure 7.27), and then listen. You should find the whole song switching to the AM radio sound for the desired length of time. You might also find some audible clicks as the bypass activates and deactivates. This is due to the vertical lines drawn when automating the bypass, which are unavoidable. If clicks occur, either adjust the timing of the automation or try the parameter automation method that follows.

Figure 7.27
The Master Fader with EQ inserted and bypass automation for filters

❋ Parameter automation

1. Because you might experience clicking using the bypass method, enable automation for the parameters required for the effect—probably filter frequency (Hi and LoPass) and the gain for the parametric EQ, as shown in Figure 7.28—you'll notice small blue boxes around the three parameters being automated.

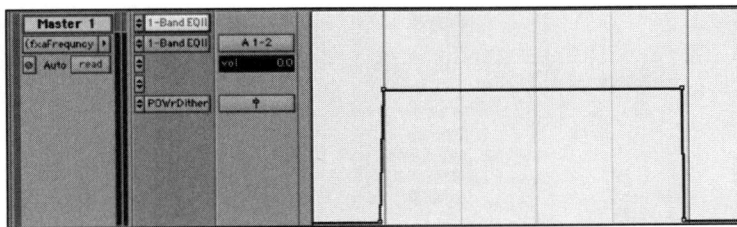

Figure 7.28
Three parameters able to be automated

2. When it's time for the AM radio effect, draw in curves that reflect the parameters shifting to the AM radio settings. Be sure to draw the curves steeply if you want the effect to seem instantaneous. It might be wise to write down the settings, and then draw in curves to those settings.

If you mix without a Master Fader, you can still automate the entire mix. Instead of creating a Master Fader, create a stereo Aux input and route the outs of each channel to it. Keep in mind that you only want to route channels that would normally play directly to outputs 1-2 to the new Aux input. Don't mess with subgroups!

Exit Stage Left

A fun way to end a song involves the piano drifting off into the ether, slowly getting farther back and wetter as she goes. The move makes it sound as if the piano is being wheeled off with the player still attached—I call it "Exit Stage Left." It doesn't have to be piano, though— you could pull this move on any sound that you want to fade into the distance before the song fades down.

The secret is to set up a similar chain to the one found in the "Reverb Only Setups" section in Chapter 6.

1. Create an Aux input and insert the reverb on it. Set the input to a bus called Reverb Send.

2. On the piano track, create a send set to Pre-Fader and assign it to the bus called Reverb Send.

3. Near the end of the song, as the song fades out leaving only the piano, slowly automate the piano fader down, as shown in Figure 7.29. This will drop the signal of the dry piano but leave the pre-fader send going to the reverb channel, making it seem as if the piano fades into the distance.

4. Lastly, just as the sound gets to be reverb-only, automate the pan to slide to the left.

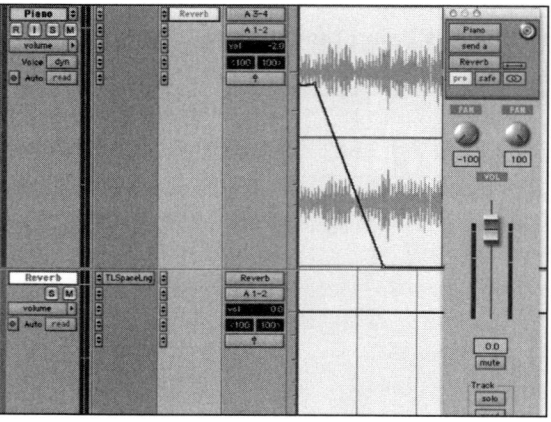

Figure 7.29

Pre-fader reverb configuration and automation during Exit Stage Left

Fast Session Merging

You may have to explore many different mix ideas to satisfy the client. This can make life hard if you keep working in one session, constantly saving and having to backtrack to follow a different mix idea. If you turned on the AutoSave function, you might be in luck, but you might also find that you only have the last 20 minutes of work, not the last two hours.

You might want to save a few versions of the mix as you go. Instead of calling these versions simply "#11" or "Thursday Afternoon," keep the title in line with the quality of the mix, as shown in Figure 7.30. For example, your first one should be called "Raw Track." This should tell you that you've done nothing to the song. If the producer ever wants to go back to the dead beginning, this is it.

Figure 7.30

A list of Pro Tools mix titles denoting the mix characteristics

Another good idea is to save one called "Rough Levels" for the state with no inserts but with good relative fader levels—a starting point. That way, instead of having to go all the way back to the beginning, you can simply start from the point of first inspiration. If you take a path that stops working, save the session as "Guitar Edit 1-DNU" (Do Not Use) so you know what the idea was and that it didn't work. That will keep the producer from going in circles.

As you go, you might like two different mix directions at once—beefier drum ideas mixed with crisper vocal ideas. If they live on two different sessions, such as "Beefy Drums" and "Hot Vox," then you'll want to merge them into one master session. Remember your Import Session Data window? (See "Switching Songs" in Chapter 2 and "Importing Session Data" from Chapter 3.) Create a new session called "Merged Drum and Vox Mix," and import the session data—drums from "Beefy Drums" and everybody else from "Hot Vox." You now have a blend of two great mix ideas in one master session!

In this situation, while it is cleaner to import the tracks from one session on top of the tracks currently in the session, you can import the tracks to new playlists and simply mute the old tracks to quickly A/B the two mixes to see which you really like better. It might be wise to group the tracks (both original and newly imported), then mute them as a group when you audition mix idea 1 (original tracks active) versus mix idea 2 (newly imported tracks active).

Looped Regions and Automation

It may seem silly, but unfortunately, its not—automation does NOT follow a looped region! When a region is duplicated (CMD+D) or repeated (OPT+R), the automation across all parameters copies with the region. That way, all instances of the region will behave exactly the same. However, with looped regions, this is not so—the automation only covers the territory of the original region! You will need to copy this automation by hand.

A simple way to do this is to copy the automation across the first region then duplicate it (CMD+D). Be sure you've selected the entire region—no more and no less. Otherwise, as you duplicate, you'll eventually fall off the grid, and your automation will not match the looped regions. Figures 7.31 and 7.32 show a looped region before the automation copy and after the automation has been pasted and duplicated a few times, respectively. Of course, this is all much faster if you repeat the automation copy instead of duplicating it.

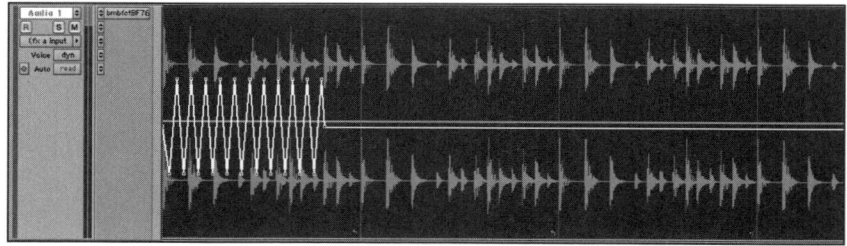

Figure 7.31

A looped region with automation only shown on the first instance of the region

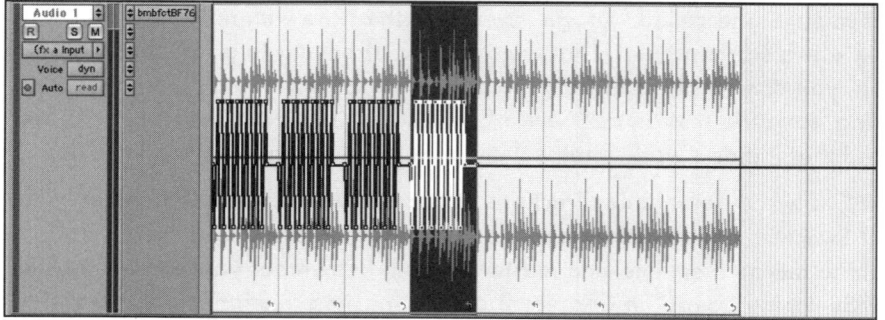

Figure 7.32

Automation duplicated to cover the looped regions

8 } Working with Picture and Surround

As the price of digital production tools decreases, more and more people have access to equipment that enables more productions. However, access to the tools and knowing the best way to use them are not always the same! Two high-end subjects are approached here with the desire to give you some legs up when working in these two fields—post-production (working with picture) and 5.1 surround sound.

While both fields are generally best served with TDM rigs, post-production can be approached with LE systems. 5.1 surround sound, however, is reserved for TDM rigs, as the LE systems simply don't support it without other hardware like 5.1 consoles. This chapter will cover how to work faster and smarter in these two fields with Pro Tools with the hopes that you can avoid some potentially damaging mistakes as well as provide your clients with better work faster!

Setting Up the Picture Session

One of the most important steps in working with picture is the setup. Most professional video and film post-production studios have a dedicated hardware device to play the video, but for most project studios, the picture will be digitized into the QuickTime format.

You can import any QuickTime video file into Pro Tools by choosing File > Import > QuickTime Movie, as seen in Figure 8.1. After it is in, you can do a few things to make sure you've set up the session correctly.

Figure 8.1

The Import > QuickTime Movie menu

Set the Start Time

When you work with picture, it's a good practice to set the session start to before one hour in timecode. Most synchronization sessions like this hate to cross midnight (00:00:00.000, where the numbers mean hours:minutes:seconds:frames), so it has become standard practice to set up to start the session at one hour. If you own an LE system, which doesn't support timecode, consider purchasing Digidesign's DV Toolkit to get that support. Pro Tools M-Powered will not support DV Toolkit, so if you need to work with picture, don't get the M-Powered version!

Set the session to start somewhere before one hour, preferably a full minute (or more) before. Choose Setup > Session (CMD+2 on the numeric keypad; laptop users press FN+CMD+K), and click in the Start Time window, as seen in Figure 8.2. Type in the numbers for the desired start time, and hit Enter. If you don't know when to start the session, ask the supervising sound editor. If there is no supervising sound editor, go with something safe, such as 00:59:00.000 (59 minutes).

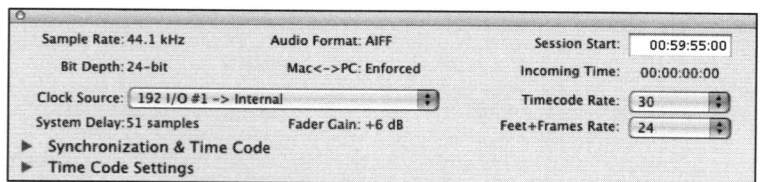

Figure 8.2

The Session Start Time window

What Happens When You Change the Start Time?

If you are importing a movie against a pre-existing session (such as an OMF delivered from Final Cut Pro), then it is entirely likely that when you change your starting time, Pro Tools will want to know what your intention is, as seen in Figure 8.3. You want to keep everything where it is—only change the timecode of the session start (Maintain Relative Position) or move everything to the new start time (Maintain Time Code). Generally, you will choose to maintain the timecode, leaving everything where it is and simply changing the start of your session—especially if you are working to a pre-existing Final Cut Pro session. In this case, the audio needs to stay in place, as it is locked to the position of the picture. If you are starting a session from scratch, then it is okay to maintain relative position.

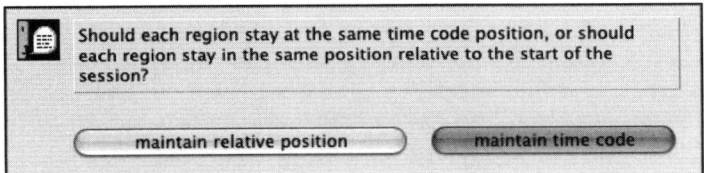

Figure 8.3

The Maintain Time Code window

Create and Line Up the 2 Pop

When working with picture, everything starts at the 2 pop—the moment two seconds before the show starts (generally 01:00:00.000). There generally will be a beeping sound in the session to line up to. If there is, it should be spotted to 00:59:58.000, as seen in Figure 8.4. If it isn't, you'll need to move the entire session so it lines up. Activate the All Group option, and select the entire the session (CMD+A). Switch to the Grabber tool, and drag the 2 pop until it lines up to 00:59:58.000. The entire session will move with it, and your files will be lined up to the proper timecode.

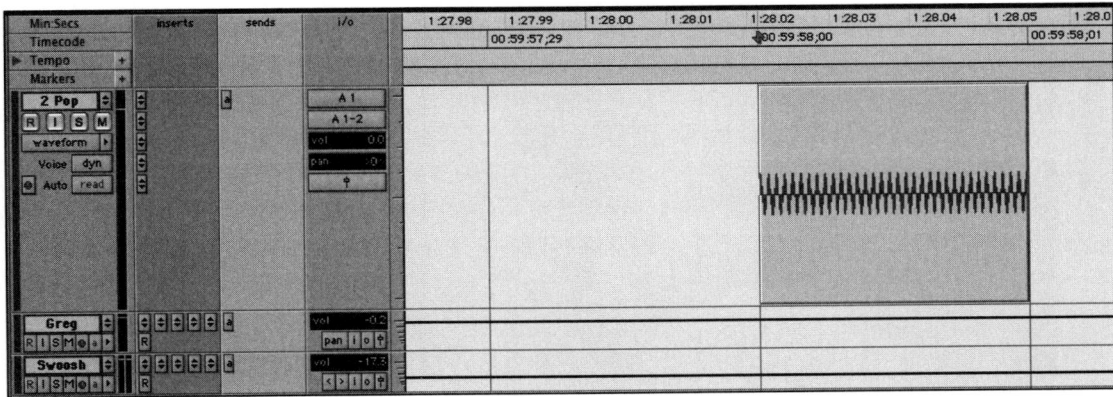

Figure 8.4

2-pop audio at 59:58:00.000

Spot the Picture

On importing the movie, Pro Tools will create both a new movie track to house the picture and frame clips, visible in the Edit window. However, Pro Tools will want to spot the picture to the beginning of the session. This may or may not be the proper location. Often, the session will be preconfigured to start at one hour, while the picture might be set up to start 10 seconds or more beforehand.

If you don't know when the picture is supposed to start, but there is a 2-pop frame, you'll need to mark the 2 pop on the picture track and spot it to 00:59:58.000. Set your Nudge value to the timecode (one frame resolution, shown in Figure 8.5) and position the cursor at the beginning of the movie file. Hold down the + key until the picture flashes with the 2 pop. It is generally seen as a black frame with a white hole in the middle (or the number 2 as seen in old movies). Go back and forth by nudging, using the + and – keys, until your cursor is parked on the 2-pop frame. Create a Sync Point by choosing Region > Identify Sync Point (CMD+,). Then switch to the Grabber tool and Spot mode, as seen in Figure 8.6. Click on the movie file, bringing up the Spot dialog box. Type 00:59:58.000 in the Sync Point window. Back up a few seconds and hit play to verify the spotting of the picture. You should see the 2-pop frame as you hear the 2 pop.

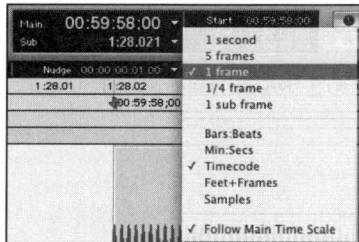

Figure 8.5

The Nudge value set to 1 frame

Figure 8.6

The Spot mode dialog box with 2-pop frame

Working with Sound Effects Libraries and Catalogs

Within the Workspace is a folder called Catalogs (see Figure 8.7; note that catalogs are HD only!) in which you can store aliases to all your favorite and much-used audio. Creating a catalog is easy and generally dependent on your searching (and labeling) skills with audio. If you always search for gunshots, create a catalog of gunshots so you'll never have to search again!

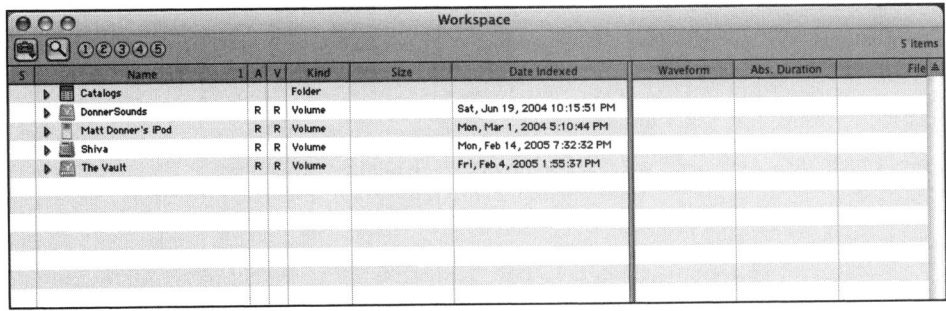

Figure 8.7

The Workspace Catalogs folder

First, conduct a search for "gunshots," like the one in Figure 8.8. You can widen your search by typing "**g*n**." In this case, any file with the letters "g" and "n" separated by one letter will show up (gun, guns, gunshots, gin, began, and so on), as seen in Figure 8.9. This might yield a result list that is too wide, so use trial and error to hone your searching skills. After your search list is complete, you can select all the files found, and choose Workspace > Create Catalog from Selected. Then whenever you need gunshot sounds, simply locate the catalog subfolder called Gunshots (see Figure 8.10), and you'll find all your favorites!

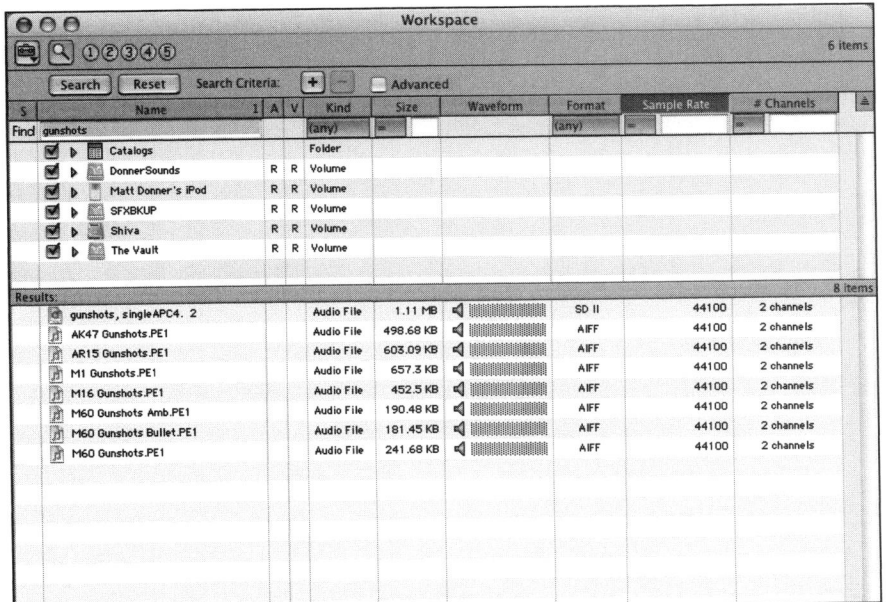

Figure 8.8

Search results for "gunshots"

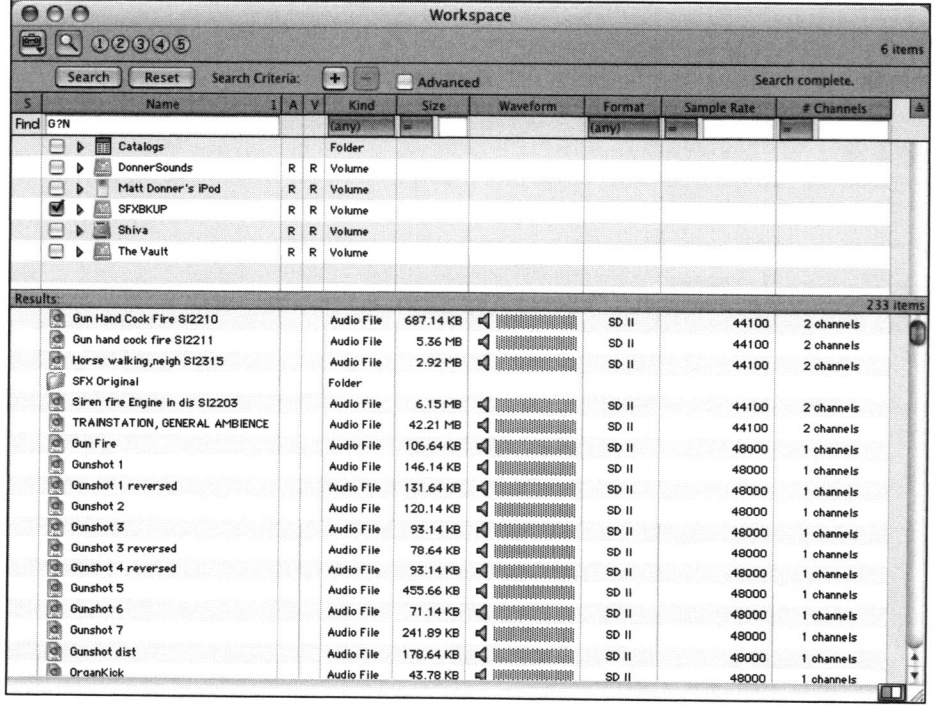

Figure 8.9

Search results for "g*n"

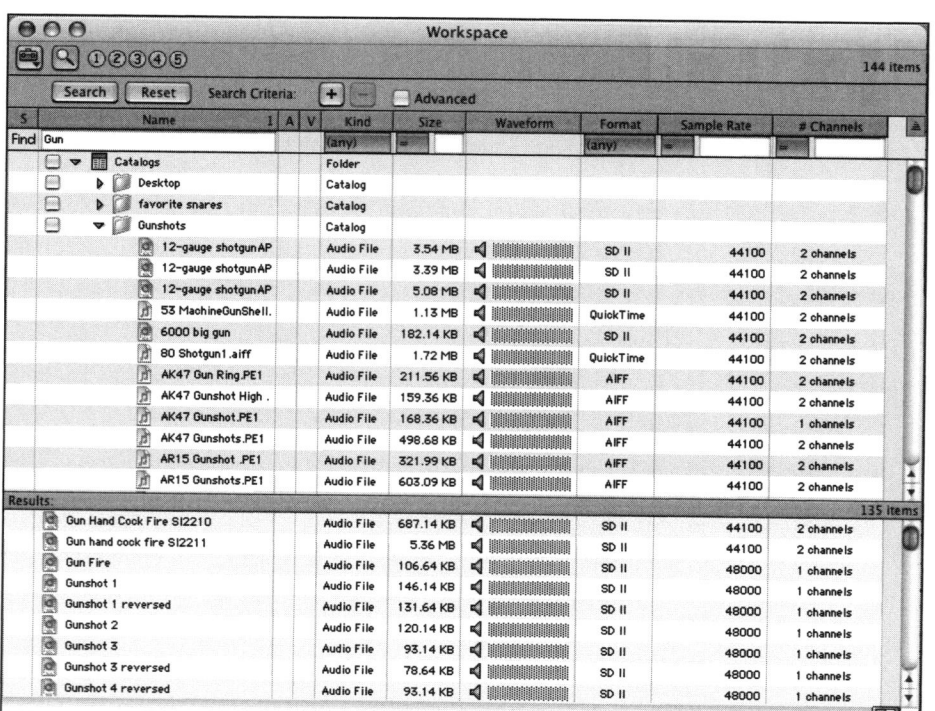

Figure 8.10

Catalog of gunshots

Movies Playing Out to TVs (Mac Only)

When digital movies are created in the .DV (digital video) format, they can play as digital information directly out of the computer's FireWire port (IEEE 1394). With proper hardware, you can convert this FireWire signal to NTSC video and connect directly to a TV. This is tremendously valuable because the video can take up serious RAM and screen space when played directly on the computer monitor.

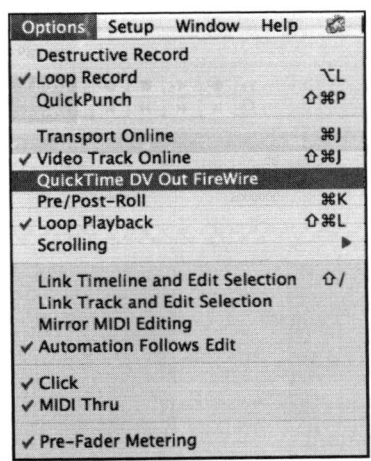

Figure 8.11

The Options > QuickTime DV Out FireWire menu

Pro Tools began supporting playing QuickTime movies in the .DV format through the FireWire port with version 6.0. Prior to this version, third-party software was required to play the movie out to a regular television. Now, simply choose Options > QuickTime DV Out FireWire (see Figure 8.11), and Pro Tools will look for FireWire hardware, routing the movie out the FireWire port to your converter and your TV. This process does not happen in real time, however. There is a small delay involved, but you can compensate for it by choosing Setup > QuickTime Movie Offset. Generally, this offset will be around 22 quarter frames, but you should check in the converter box manual to determine exactly how many frames are necessary.

Working with Music and VO

It is common in video post-production for the VO to be the most important performance, with intelligibility and clarity of the dialogue as the focus of the piece. However, music and sound effects often come along to boost the energy and feel of the piece. So where do you balance the energy of the music and sound effects against the volume of the VO?

A common trick in these situations is to work with volume automation to create a "ducking" of the music and effects under dialogue when the VO starts. Generally, the music (probably a stereo file) will duck by 20 dB under the VO, but if it ducks too quickly or too early, it will feel empty for a moment (which is unacceptable). If it ducks too late, intelligibility of the first word might get lost (which is really unacceptable).

Line up the VO track against the music track, and set the music track to the Volume Automation Playlist. Zoom in, if necessary, but look at the curve of the music volume, and draw (or automate with the mouse and modes) the curve to start just as the VO starts, as shown in Figure 8.12. It should sound like the VO forces the music downward, emphasizing the crispness of the first word and making the music dip natural.

Figure 8.12

Automation curve on a music track

Helpful Hints for Final Cut Pro Users (Scott Hirsch, Pyramind)

Scott Hirsch is one of the other certified Pro Tools instructors in San Francisco, and he teaches the Pro Tools Operator Certification series for Pyramind. He is a film post-production audio engineer and a member of The Court and Spark group. Following are his tips for Pro Tools users working with Final Cut Pro.

❋ OMF has an internal limit of 2 GB. This translates into roughly six tracks of mono 16-bit audio, each an hour long. (A 16-bit mono audio clip is roughly 5 MB per minute.) If your total audio is bigger than that, use ins and outs to break your sequence into sections and export each section as its own OMF file.

1. Create your sequence. Place a 2 pop (one frame of tone matched with a frame of color bars) two seconds before and after your sequence. You will use this later to make sure everything came into Pro Tools and maintained sync.

2. Levels and transitions do *not* get copied into the OMF from FCP, so don't spend too much time on them unless it is necessary to have a version of a complicated mix to reference. If this is the case, then a useful tip is to export the bounced FCP audio

clip onto the video reference movie. Then the Pro Tools editor can bring the stereo reference mix from FCP onto a track into Pro Tools by choosing File > Import > Audio from Current Movie, as seen in Figure 8.13. Keep in mind that you may need the audio from another movie, but you'll need to conform it to the current movie. In this case, import the audio from another QuickTime movie under the same menu options.

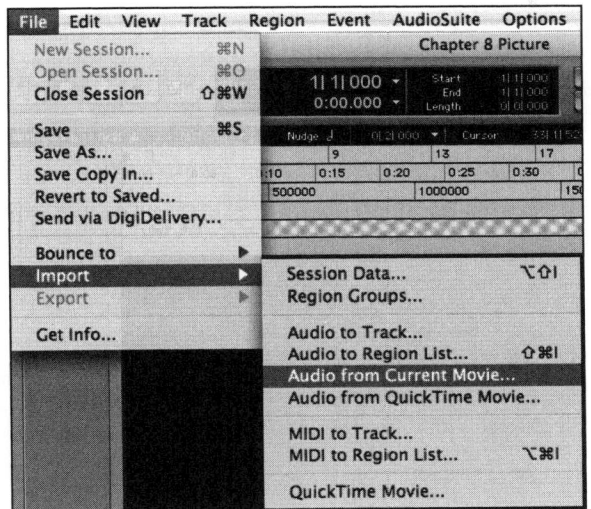

Figure 8.13

The File > Import > Audio from Current Movie menu

❋ In Final Cut, choose File > Export > Audio to OMF.

1. Because Final Cut supports bit depths of 12 and 8, be careful what you choose for your settings. Ask your supervising sound editor what the preferred audio specs are; if there aren't any, ask the Pro Tools editor what is preferred.

2. Choose a handle length of five seconds (or more) so the Pro Tools editor has some crossfade room.

3. Choosing to include crossfade transitions from the FCP OMF Export window can throw your files out of sync by leaving gaps in your sequence that get shuffled together, like a ripple edit. Although this is supposedly fixed in version 3, it is safest to leave this option unchecked.

Pro Tools and Film Mixing (Dave Nelson, Outpost/Pyramind)

Dave Nelson is dedicated to independent films. He has worked on hundreds of such films, including *Lost in Translation* with Sofia Coppola. He also teaches film sound at the University of California at Monterey, San Francisco State University, and Pyramind. The following is Dave's advice for both Final Cut Pro users and the Pro Tools mixers who work with them.

Final Cut Pro Users

❋ Because FCP doesn't export volume automation, keep all FCP volume moves to a minimum, or at least very rough. Because you'll be exporting the OMF to Pro Tools for audio mixing, anything you do will need to be recreated in Pro Tools, so don't waste your time. If you like what you've done, you can export a reference mix with the OMF, but you might never use it—so again, you might be wasting your time.

❋ When exporting the OMF, choose an OMF with embedded audio. When the Pro Tools mixer unpacks the OMF, he will most likely choose to copy the audio to new files, anyway. Then, you can toss the OMF (unless you're paranoid and worry about losing the Pro Tools drive and the original OMF).

❋ Deselect the Pan Even/Odd Tracks Left/Right option when you unpack the OMF (see Figure 8.14). Because most tracks coming from FCP are dialogue, having them panned left and right makes more work later when you re-pan the dialogue to the center.

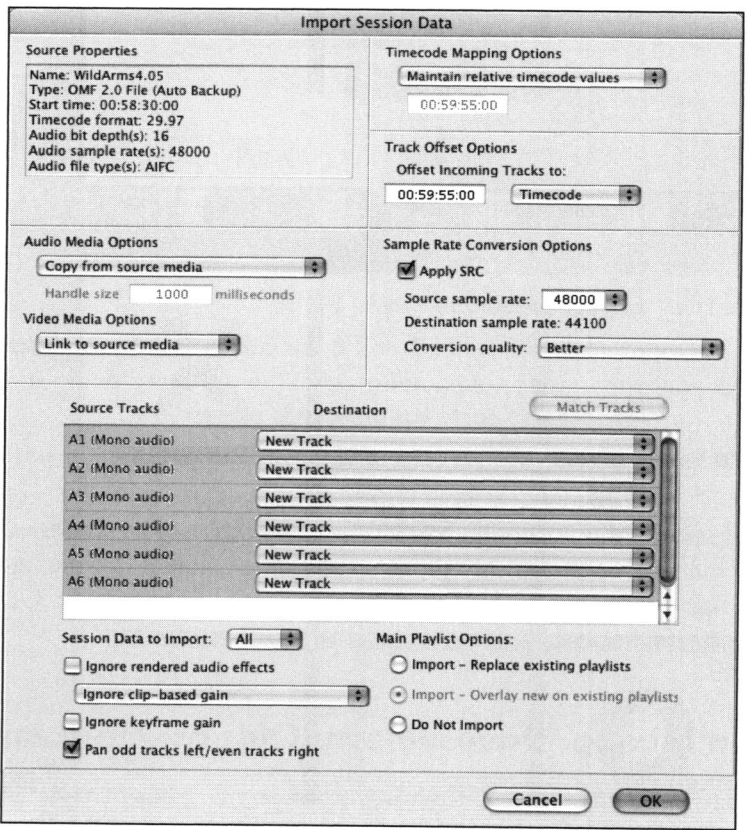

Figure 8.14

Deselect the Pan Tracks option in the Import Session Data dialog box

✳ If you don't know how to create a 2-pop frame in your picture, at least set your show to start at 01:00:00.000. If you can't do that either, then create a reference mix with your QuickTime picture export. When the Pro Tools mixer imports the OMF, he will most likely reconform the session to start at 01:00:00.000. If there's no visual 2 pop and no audio 2 pop, then the Pro Tools mixer can compare the exported reference mix to line up the OMF tracks and the picture.

✳ If the Pro Tools session was reconformed to 01:00:00.000 and that timecode doesn't line up to the Final Cut session, bounce the mix starting from 00:59:58.000. When you deliver it to the Final Cut Pro editor, he need only line up the mix to two seconds before the show start to ensure sync between FCP and PT.

Organizing Pro Tools

✳ Once you unpack the OMF into Pro Tools, reorganize the tracks to your liking, but be sure to rename the tracks intelligently. If a track is related to dialogue, call it "Dialogue," not "D." In film, as in music, several Pro Tools mixers and sound designers might work on the session. In large facilities many people work on the session, so the more organized the session, the better.

✳ In film, most audio boils down to three types, known as *stems*—dialogue, music, and effects. Create stereo (or 5.1) Aux inputs as subgroup masters, and position them at the head of the session. Set their inputs chronologically from 1/2 for dialogue, 3/4 for music, and 5/6 for effects.

✳ Contrary to the "Labeling the I/O and Template Settings" section in Chapter 1, Dave never labels the I/O buses. For him, the time spent takes away from valuable mixing time, and if the buses aren't labeled well, the next Pro Tools mixer may not be appreciative. If you do label the buses, keep it very obvious what the bus leads to.

Quick Spotting Techniques

First, a quick review of the "Aligning Tracks" section from Chapter 4:

✳ **Control-drag.** When you drag in audio from the Region List, you can quickly spot the region to the cursor location by Control-dragging the region from the list. If you have marked the SFX location with the cursor, simply hold Control while dragging from the Region List, and the file will lock to that timecode only. Remember to nudge the position of the cursor (along with the movie) by clicking the + and – keys. After you're spot-on (ha!), perform the Control-drag, and move on to the next sound.

✳ **Control+Shift-drag.** This one works just like the Control-drag, except that it lines up the Sync Point to your location upon dragging from the Region List. If your file has no Sync Point, Pro Tools assumes that the Sync Point is the start point. In this case, the process is exactly like the Control-drag.

✳ **CMD+Control-drag.** This will line up the ends of the regions upon dragging from the Region List.

✳ **Aligning regions.** The functionality of the above three dragging methods works exactly the same for audio already on the tracks. To line up the beginnings of two regions, place the cursor at the beginning of the desired location, and Control-click the second region. Use SHIFT+Control-click on the second region to line up the Sync Point to the beginning of the first region. If you want to line up the two Sync Points, first position the cursor at the first region's Sync Point, and then SHIFT+Control-click the second region. To line up the ends, position the cursor at the end of the first region, and CMD+Control-click on the second region.

✳ **Replacing regions.** If you've used a particular SFX throughout the movie and the producer no longer likes it, you will be most upset if you have to find every usage of the region and replace it by hand. This file might be spread across several tracks and several scenes, so finding the usages is no fun, nor is replacing them. There is a little known secret here that might make your work faster if you have to replace re-used regions.

You really only need to find one instance of the region, and Pro Tools will allow you to replace all instances in one move. Highlight the region to be replaced, and Apple-drag the new region on top of the old one. This will bring up the Replace Region dialog box, shown in Figure 8.15. Depending on your situation, you have a few options.

• **Replace Region versus Replace All Regions That Match Original**. Simply put, one replaces the one instance of the original region while the other finds all regions that match and replaces them all. The only caveat is if an instance of the original region is even slightly altered from its original state (remember that it will take on a new name with the edit number like audio-05), then that instance will not be replaced.

• **Match**. Only available when the Replace All Regions That Match Original option is selected, you can choose either Start Position, End Position, or Region Name as the determining factor for replacement.

• **Find Match On**. Once it is determined that a region matches the description for replacement, you can choose to replace all instances throughout the song or just on the one track. For a snare drum, it is likely that you'd choose the former, but in SFX sessions for example, gunshots (or the like) could be spread across many tracks throughout scenes. For this situation, choose All Tracks.

• **Fit To**. This option is slightly more complex. Once Pro Tools has determined a match, the three options here (Original Region Length, Original Selection Length, or Replacement Region Length) will determine exactly how the region is replaced. For timing specific events, like SFX, you will most likely choose to fit to either Original Region Length or Original Selection Length; but for the snare drum situation, you'll most likely choose Replacement Region Length.

In the aforementioned situation, be sure to check the All Tracks box in the Find Match On section. Pro Tools will seek out the many instances of the bad region and replace them with the good one!

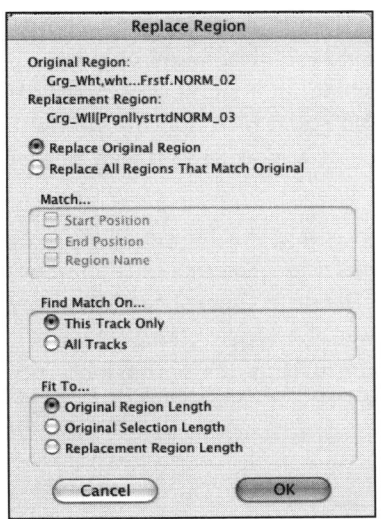

Figure 8.15

The Replace Region dialog box

Tempo Shifts in Pro Tools

Long a point of contention for film-style composers, Pro Tools never quite worked right when trying to create smooth tempo shifts that matched picture. A Pro Tools composer would have to program micro tempo shifts every 8th note to trick the ear into thinking that the tempo was increasing. Even this was challenging because you would sometimes also need to program measures of 1|8 at every tempo shift to keep the bar|beat count accurate, too!

Pro Tools now provides two ways to create variations in tempo—using the Pencil tool on the Tempo Ruler and using Tempo Operations.

* **Pencil tool.** The simplest method to create variations in tempo is to open the Tempo Ruler by clicking on the arrow next to it. Switch to the Pencil tool (click and hold on the Pencil), choose the curve you want to use to shift the tempo, and simply draw in the tempo shift, as shown in Figure 8.16.

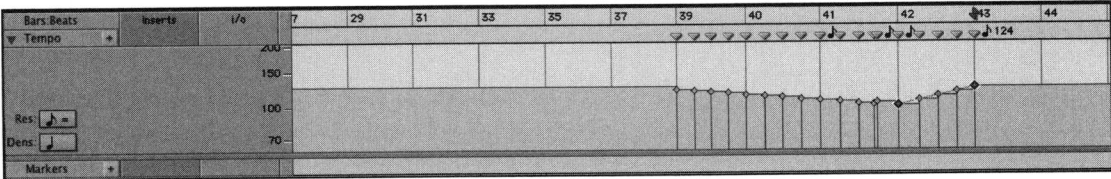

Figure 8.16

The Tempo Ruler exposed with hand-drawn tempo shifts

Keep in mind that when scoring to picture, you should be aware of the location of the first downbeat of the first measure of music. For certain scenes, there might only be enough time for one beat, or even one 8th note. In this situation, it might be simpler to create a single measure of 1|8 meter to fill the space. You could also add an 8th note to the meter before the break, so instead of a measure of 4|4, you end up with one of 9|8 (4|4 with an extra 8th note).

❅ **Tempo Operations.** For very specific tempo maneuvers, using the Tempo Operations feature and entering the data might simply be faster. You will find a tempo shift set of curves and options when you choose Event > Tempo > Operations Window, as shown in Figure 8.17. From this window, you can change the type of tempo operation by selecting from the drop-down menu shown in Figure 8.18; each of these has an advanced mode that allows you to let Pro Tools calculate the shift. Simply choose your curve of choice, enter the data, and your tempo will change as desired.

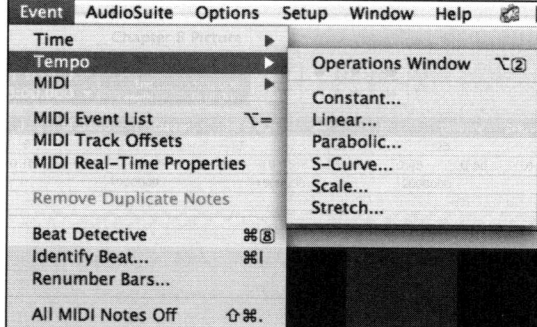

Figure 8.17

Tempo Operation curves menu

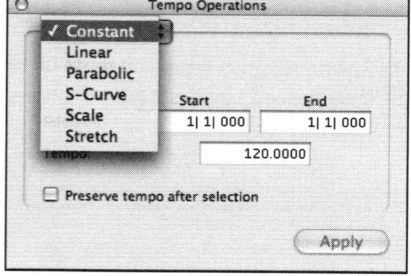

Figure 8.18

The different types of tempo operations

Following are the different types of tempo operations available:

❅ **Constant.** This sets a static tempo for a length of time. If you want the chorus to be at 122 bpm from measures 33 through 41, simply type it in and you're done.

❅ **Linear.** Tempo will increase steadily (linearly) from location 1 to location 2. This is nice if you know the tempo at the beginning and the end of the gap, but not between them.

✳ **Parabolic.** More advanced than the others, this option allows you to tell Pro Tools to either conform to or calculate the tempo, according to a user-defined curve. (The Calculate option is for advanced users.) Drag the Curvature slider to adjust the slope of the curve. Positive numbers will be concave, and negative numbers will be convex.

✳ **S-Curve.** Similar to the parabolic curve, the S-Curve tempo shift allows you to set the midpoint at which the curve switches from convex to concave (and vice versa with positive curvature numbers).

✳ **Scale.** Very simply put, you can enter a percentage and Pro Tools will change the tempo within the selected range to a percentage of the original.

✳ **Stretch.** Very useful for situations where a series of tempo shifts needs to reconform to a new selection. If you have three tempo shifts that cover 16 bars and they need to cover 17 bars (due to say a picture change), then you can stretch the three tempo shifts to cover the new 17-bar length by entering the 17 bars into the window. Choose whether you'd like the start to stretch forward or the end to stretch backward through the Advanced menu.

Note

All the tempo operations have a Preserve Tempo After Selection button which, when clicked, will change the tempo of the piece back to the original tempo before the selection where the tempo was changed. If tempo starts at 120, changes parabolically to 135 at measures 17 through 22, and then this button is selected, the tempo will return to 120 at measure 23.

5.1 Surround in Pro Tools (TDM)

One of the last remaining frontiers in audio production is surround sound. Many experiments have been tried in 3D sound, but the 5.1 surround format seems to have taken hold. There are a few standards in surround sound—which really means there is no globally accepted standard. There are, however, some best practices and lots of ideas on the subject. Pro Tools TDM supports up to 7.1 systems, but I will limit this discussion of surround sound to 5.1 and the three main configurations therein—SMPTE, Film standard, and DTS (also known as ProControl Monitoring).

Choosing Your 5.1 Format

Pro Tools currently supports surround sound setups for three types of 5.1 configurations— SMPTE, Film standard, and ProControl Monitoring. When you create a 5.1 session, it is critical that you choose the correct format because you are almost guaranteed to have problems later (see Figure 8.19). I've heard of stories in which the producer had the format incorrect (and never did a quality-control check, mind you) and pressed 2,000 copies of the DVD, only to find out that the dialogue played out of the right speaker only! For the record, they can throw you out of the producers' club for that kind of mistake.

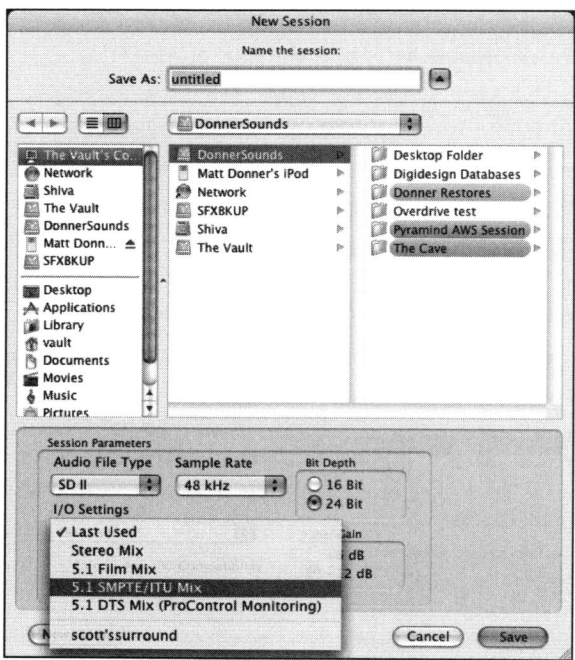

Figure 8.19

The 5.1 options in the New Session dialog box

You should ask your producer (or supervising sound editor) about which format to choose. There is no real standard, but there are several common uses for choosing your format (although that, too, is hotly debated). As you will read, even some of the heavyweights disagree on which standard is the best for Pro Tools, but they all agree that there are tremendous pitfalls to avoid!

* **Film Mix.** The track layout in this format is a direct parallel to what you'd think of 5.1, and the outputs of the interface should respond accordingly. In output order from 1 to 6, the tracks and outputs should line up to Left (1), Center (2), Right (3), Lsurround (4), Rsurround (5), and LFE (6).

* **SMPTE/ITU Mix.** This format is more aligned for compatibility to stereo mixes. Had the aforementioned producer used this standard, he might have saved himself a huge problem (and several thousand dollars). In output order, the tracks should be Left (1), Right (2), Center (3), LFE (4), Ls (5), and Rs (6). This is the hardwired default for the Digidesign Control 24.

* **DTS (ProControl Monitoring).** As its name implies, this format is the hardwired version of 5.1 for ProControl users. Its outputs are Left (1), Right (2), Ls (3), Rs (4), Center (5), and LFE (6).

The good news is that there might be a way around the issue later if you've chosen the wrong format, but I'll touch on that a bit later. In the meantime, check out www.dolby.com for more information on their specifications and speaker placement/calibration ideas.

Setting Up for 5.1 (I/O Configurations)

Just as you'd expect, there are as many pitfalls in setting up Pro Tools for 5.1 as there are in mixing in 5.1. This is a direct result of the choices (and lack of standards) in 5.1 configurations. There will be many little details to square away before you get into the meat of the job; but no matter what the job, you should *always* label your I/O.

After you label your I/O, you should make sure you are compatible with the Default Path Order in the I/O Setup dialog box, as shown in Figure 8.20. This determines what format the next path created will take.

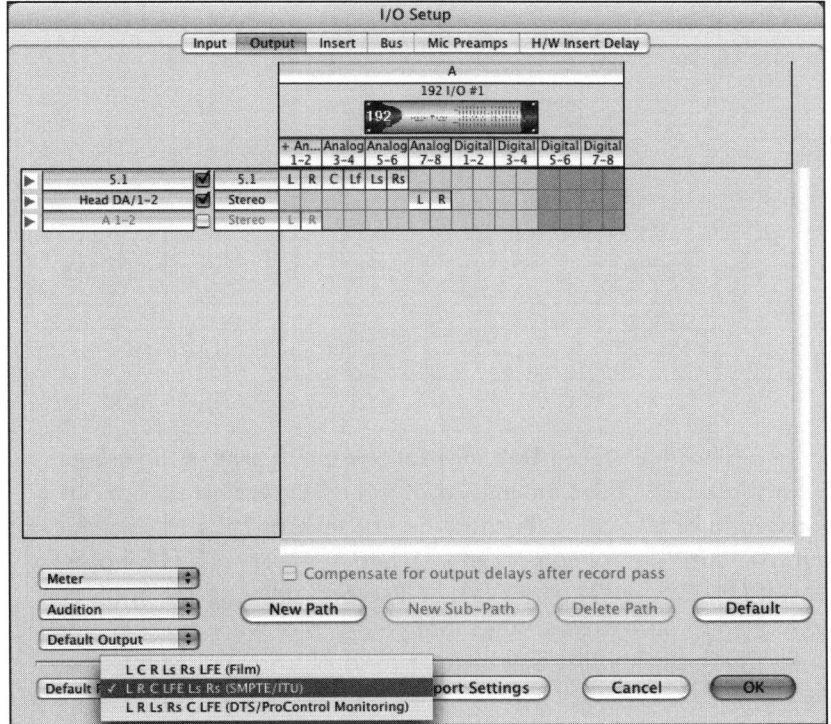

Figure 8.20

The Default Path Order drop-down list

Andre Zweers, Skywalker Sound

Because Andre's job is to man the Pro Tools rig while recording orchestras, he has quite a bit of experience in recording 5.1 sessions. He has several I/O labeling configurations already saved, ready for import as soon as the producer tells him the format. (See "Labeling the I/O and Template Settings" in Chapter 1.) As soon as he knows the format, he'll create a new session and import the I/O settings for that format, like the one seen in Figure 8.21. He works roughly 75 percent of the time in Film standard (L, C, R, Ls, Rs, LFE) and 25 percent of the time in a custom version of the Film standard (L, C, R, LFE, Ls, Rs), but almost never in SMPTE standard.

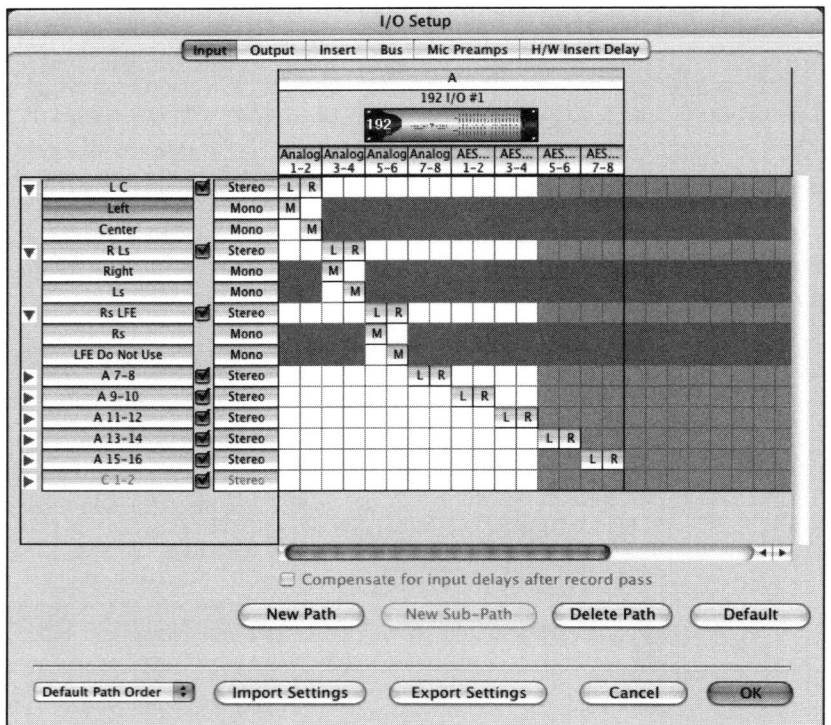

Figure 8.21

Film standard variation (inputs) in the I/O Setup dialog box

Because Andre records quite a bit with a Decca Tree microphone configuration, he creates a dedicated 5.0 input label for those mics. This tree consists of three front-facing mics and two rear-facing mics, each recorded to its own track. Because he has several 192k HD interfaces, each mic gets its own input (standard operating procedure), and he reserves 5/16 inputs for the tree. They are labeled Left (1), Center (2), Right (3), and so on. Although Pro Tools can support tracks of 5.1 (and higher), Andre recommends that you record every track in mono and pan each track accordingly. This minimizes any assignment confusion and keeps everything easy to manage later.

John Loose, Dolby Labs

It's safe to say that the good folks at Dolby know a thing or two about surround formats. John was one of the first to have worked with 5.1, and, as a leader in the field, he has a unique way of doing things that works best for him and his clients. It's not the most common way to work, but in the end it doesn't matter—it does work.

First, John works with SMPTE format as his configuration (a similar I/O setup to John's configuration is shown in Figure 8.22). Although this is not the most common format, it provides him with the most compatibility between stereo sessions and 5.1 sessions. He has lots of gear prewired to his Pro Tools setup, and it would be harder to rewire than to reconfigure Pro Tools for him. Because most of the media that comes to him is not in that configuration, he has to perform several steps to ensure quality, but he also gets the benefit of keeping his studio as is. If media comes to him in a different format (which happens all the time, he says), he'll print it into Pro Tools in his format. This way, his I/O setup never changes.

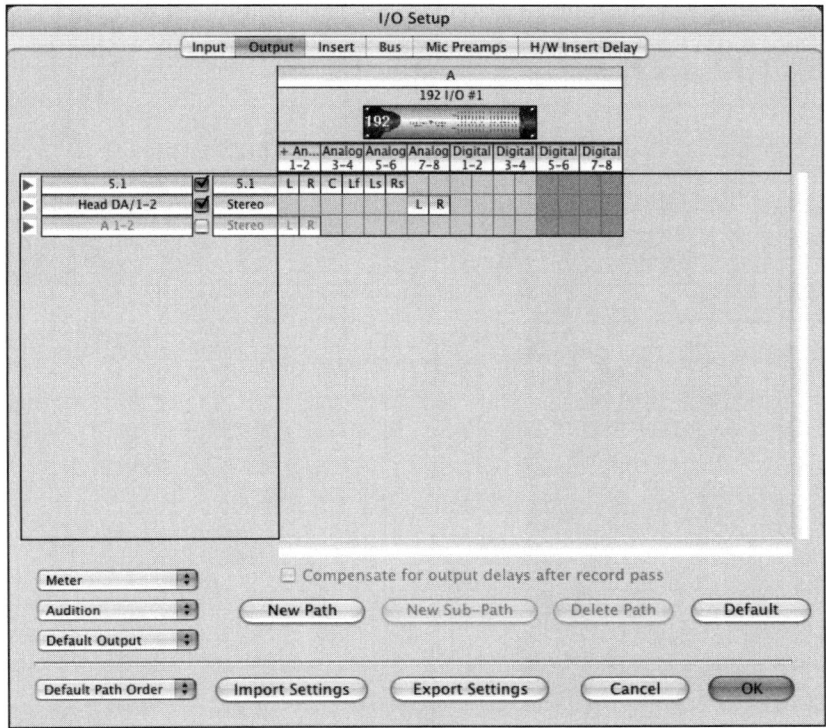

Figure 8.22

An SMPTE I/O setup (outputs)

Of course, he has a template I/O setup that he starts with the labels he likes and every conceivable subpath available. Subpaths are output configurations that live within the master path. In this case, the path would be 5.1 (six outputs), and subpaths would be clusters such as left/right only, surrounds only, LCR, and so on. This way, during the mix he can choose any collection of speakers needed and route the audio to those speakers only to save some DSP. Because he reprints the media into his format, everything plays properly, and he can rely on his configuration.

Gene Radzik, Dolby Labs

Maybe it's a Dolby thing, but Gene also subscribes to the SMPTE format if possible. The added level of compatibility between stereo and 5.1 is the main thing, but he also works with clients who produce in the older Dolby Surround format or LCRS (a potential I/O setup, shown in Figure 8.23, reflects the compatibility with LCRS). With LCRS, the mix is heard in stereo if there is no decoder and in LCRS if there is. Because the SMPTE format is L, R, C, S, Ls, Rs, there are three levels of compatibility: L, R (stereo—the first two no matter what), L, R, C, S (Dolby Surround—the first four no matter what), *then* L, R, C, S, Ls, Rs (SMPTE—the first 6).

For this three-leveled compatibility, Gene also suggests that the 7-8 be used as well as the 5.1 outputs. When the client has mixed the 5.1 session and is happy, they will print the mix to six tracks of Pro Tools (or another medium), and then they'll set to remix the spot for LCRS. Usually, the client will have encoders for the LCRS mix (hardware or software). LCRS goes in, and LR comes out. This matrixed Dolby Surround mix is then reprinted to the last two tracks of Pro Tools. Now, the client has eight tracks of mix in three formats: 5.1 (tracks 1 through 6), LCRS (matrixed on 7-8), and the stereo (matrixed on 7-8).

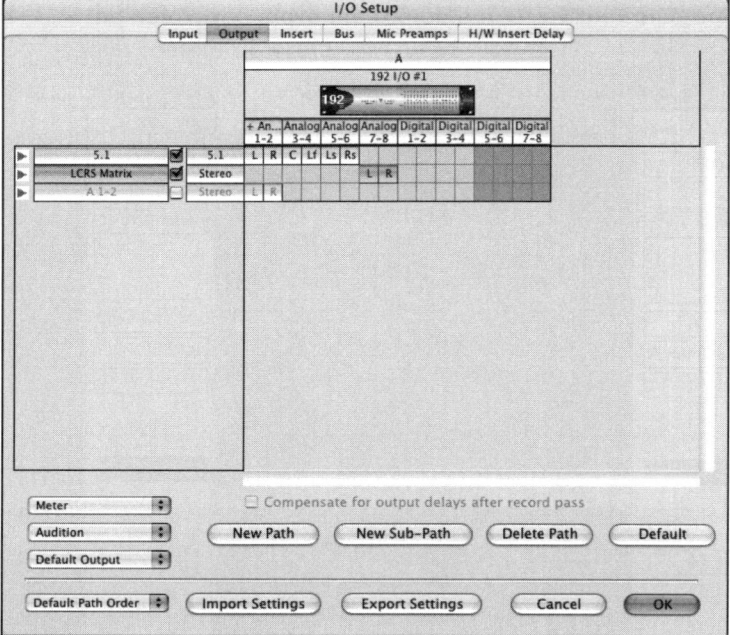

Figure 8.23

5.1 SMPTE format with 7-8 as matrix

5.1-to-Stereo Compatibility

There is always a decision to be made in choosing your 5.1 format. You should check with the producer or supervising sound editor to determine which is the best format for the project. However, if there is no producer, you might have to make the decision yourself.

Andre Zweers, Skywalker Sound

Generally, Andre is not the one mixing in 5.1; the mixes are performed on an automated console and rerouted into Pro Tools for printing. As suggested in the section "Setting Up for 5.1 (I/O Configurations)" earlier in this chapter, Andre records the 5.1 mix to six mono tracks (labeled accordingly—Left5.1mix, Center5.1mix, and so on), and then OPTION-drags them to a 5.1 track of a similar setting (L C R Ls Rs LFE), as shown in Figure 8.24. That way, if another session needs to reference the 5.1 mix, you can import session data for the 5.1 mix and have it available.

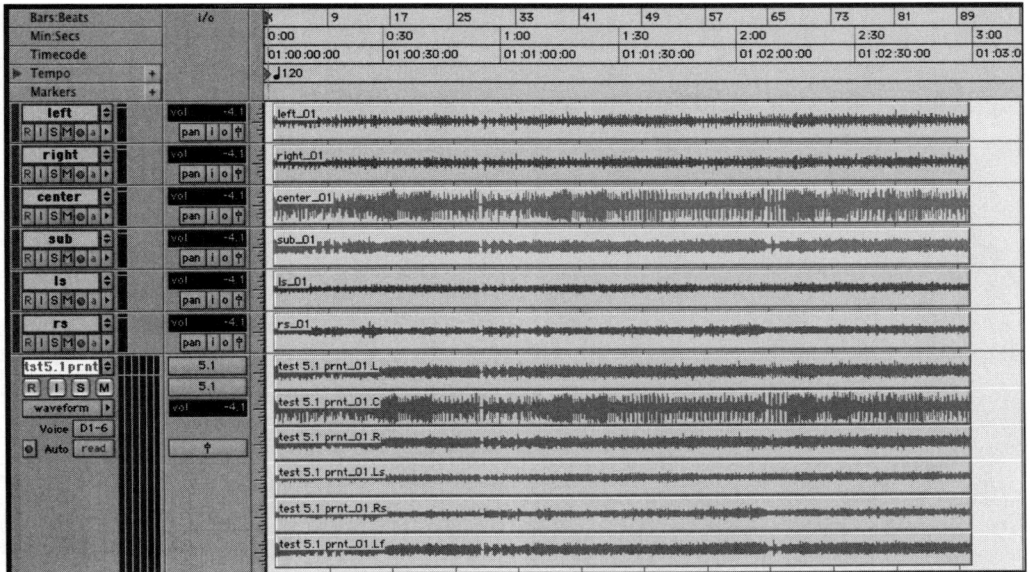

Figure 8.24

Final mix as six mono tracks and a 5.1 track

Because the mixes are all performed at the console and not within Pro Tools, Andre's job is easy when the client needs stereo and 5.1 at the same time—he simply creates a stereo audio track and records the stereo mix, too. However, his suggestion when remixing 5.1 to stereo within Pro Tools is to start by re-panning everybody to the stereo bus. Once there, you'll recognize a difference in the mix, and you'll need to tweak it. This is inevitable, but you can save time by starting with a quick volume dip: –6 dB for the surround channels and –3 dB for the center channel.

Remember from Audio Theory 101 that when stereo parts are panned to mono, they gain 3 dB. Because the surround channels both come to the front speakers, it makes perfect sense to dip them 6 dB (3 dB per channel) and the center by 3 dB. This is only a starting point. You might find other interactions that require adjusting (such as EQ and phase), so trust your ears. When he is finished, Andre simply mutes the 5.1 mix and plays the stereo mix for the producer. He quickly A/Bs for the producer with the Mute buttons only.

John Loose, Dolby Labs

When you work at Dolby, you tend to have more gear than the next guy. Although John isn't crawling around the gear to get to the chair, he does have quite a few toys to work with between stereo and 5.1. For him, either direction is equally easy. If the client needs to go from 5.1 to stereo, he has at least two options—hardware encoding (most likely) and software mixing (occasionally).

Figure 8.25

5.1-to-stereo conversion with Aux sends

※ **Hardware encoding.** There's no mystery here; simply purchase the Dolby boxes (or work at Dolby and get them for free!) and route the signal to the encoder. Six channels go in and two come out. That's it. No adjustments, no nothing—just six to two. Now you are referencing the encoded two-channel mix as you would when you play the movie without a 5.1 decoder. It's a good idea to also reference the 2–6 decoded mix to make sure it goes back and forth properly. Because these encoders are pricey (to say the least), you might want to start with the software-mixing solution first before you rush out and buy the encoder/decoder package.

※ **Software mixing.** If the client needs it done within Pro Tools, John will copy to send (Edit > Copy Special > Copy to Send) the mix so his 5.1 mix shows up on an Aux send going to a stereo output, like the one in Figure 8.25. Similar to Gene Radzik's suggestion, generally outputs 7–8 will be used for this. Now he has his mix going to both 5.1 outputs and stereo outputs at the same time. Both mixes show up at his monitor system, and he can audition between them with the touch of a button.

For stereo-to-5.1 conversion, John relies on outboard gear such as the TC Electronic M6000, which has a function called Stereo Unwrap that takes stereo material and reconfigures it for 5.1. Where outboard like this doesn't exist, simply import the file into a 5.1 session and have fun. Beyond the simple panning options, try creating a 5.1 reverb on the track and adjusting the mix to taste. For more detailed-sounding conversions, create an Aux send and route it to a 5.1 Aux return with a 5.1 reverb inserted on it, as shown in Figure 8.26.

When it's in a good place, be sure to route both tracks to a single 5.1 track for printing so you have it. If John were Andre, he'd print it to six mono tracks, then OPTION-drag it to a 5.1 track so both versions would be available!

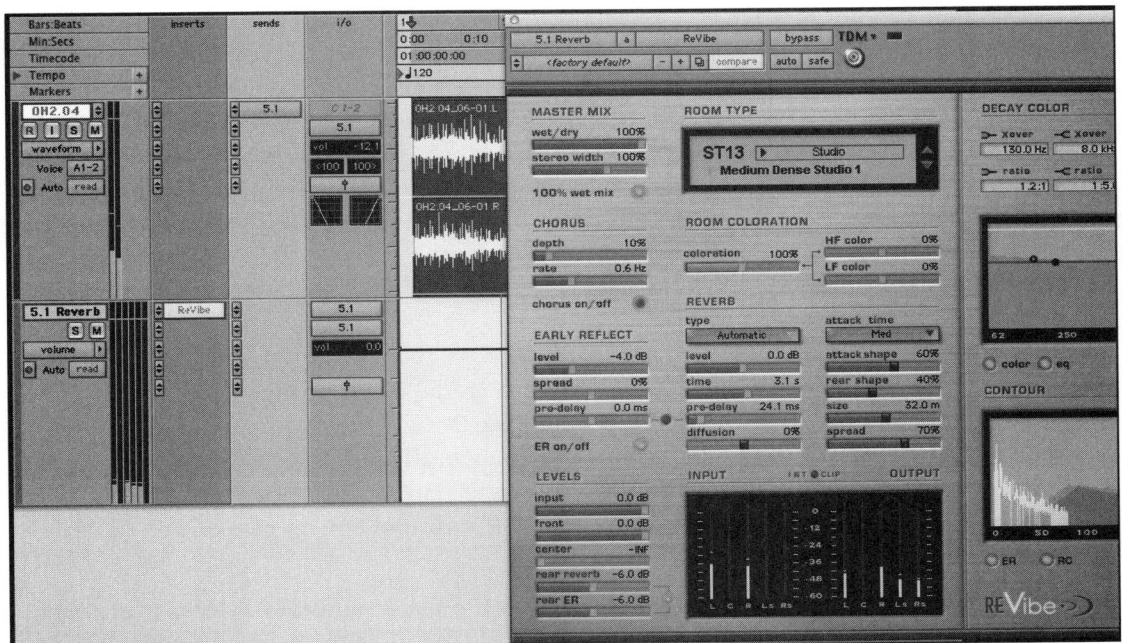

Figure 8.26
Stereo file with Aux send to 5.1 reverb

Rewiring in 5.1 (John Loose, Dolby Labs)

Not to be outdone, John Loose offered a view into the future of 5.1—ReWire in surround. Because John composes equally between Pro Tools, Reaktor, and Live, the necessity of creating in Live and rewiring into 5.1 immediately became apparent. The secret is to pre-mix in Live, and then pan 5.1 in Pro Tools.

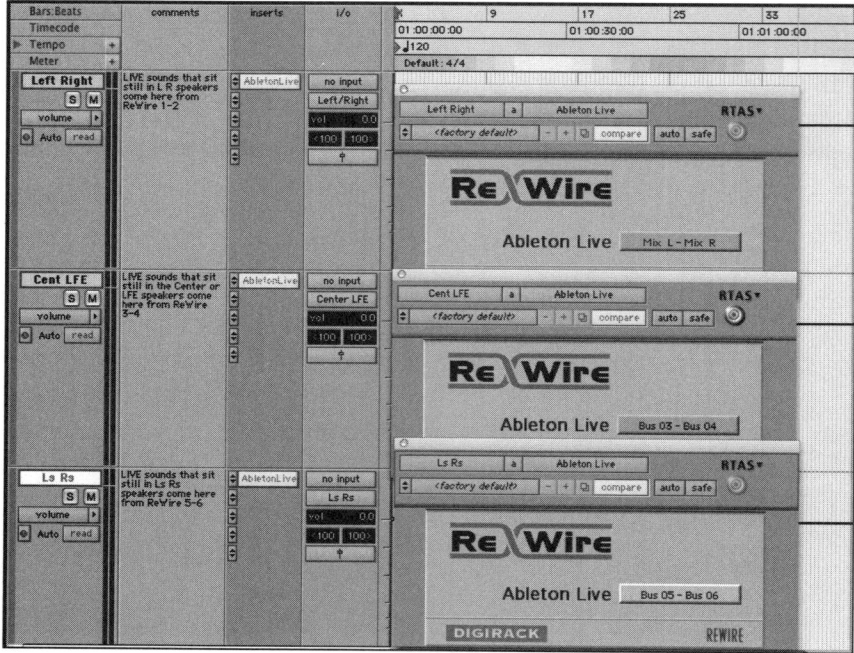

Figure 8.27

Aux inputs with Live inserts and I/O

Because Live doesn't really support 5.1, John had to create a system that works this way. Live supports 16 stereo ReWire paths, but John will only use three of them—one for the L-R channels, one for the C-LFE channels, and one for the Ls-Rs channels (Figure 8.27). When he's satisfied with the composition, he'll decide which parts in Live will go to which speakers and route them to the appropriate buses. Then he can work the Surround Panner in Pro Tools to decide where the sounds go.

The C-LFE pair is note-worthy (Figure 8.28). This ReWire bus is generally reserved for sounds that are mono- or bass-driven, so the mono sounds will end up in the center speaker only and bass sounds end up in the LFE channel. Whatever is low frequency in Live gets routed to the LFE channel. Sounds that shouldn't go to the LFE may have the bass filtered out of them in Live so they don't accidentally go to the sub, but stay in the center speaker.

John could create multiple Live inserts and multiple stereo chains to accommodate more than the standard six-channel routing, but it generally gets unmanageable and can hog the CPU, too. In either case, the idea is to predetermine which sounds should be grouped and ReWire them together, with all the 5.1 panning occurring within Pro Tools.

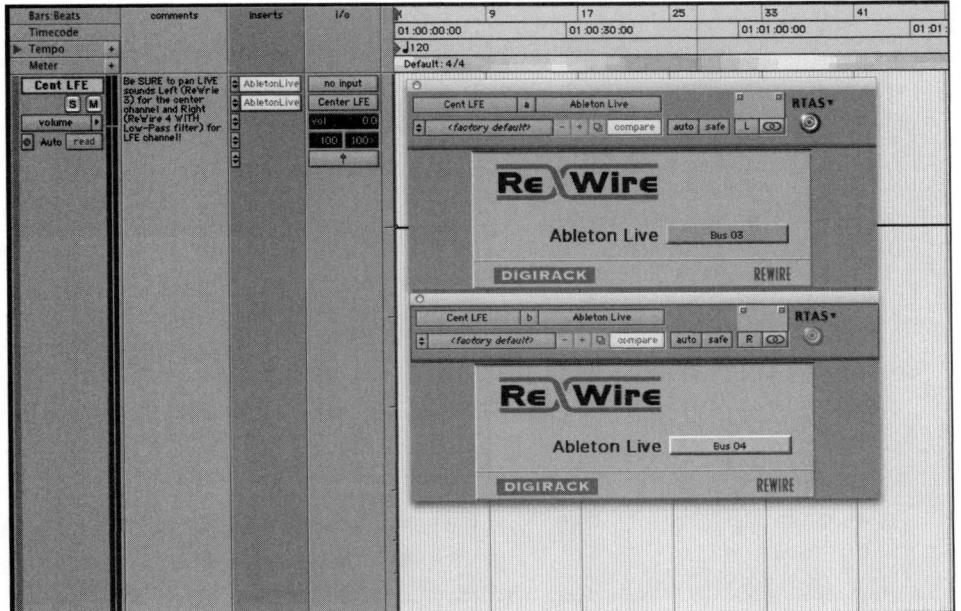

Figure 8.28

Pan output on the C-LFE pair

Mixing Pitfalls in 5.1 (John Loose, Dolby Labs)

Take everything you know about mixing and multiply it by four. Well, 3.1 at least. That's basically what happens when you mix in 5.1. Because Pro Tools doesn't really behave any differently than it does in stereo, everything you already know about Pro Tools mixing is true in 5.1, with two pitfalls thrown in to keep you honest! Check out these potentially job-threatening pitfalls and best practices.

✼ **Multiple pan automation.** One of the biggest complaints about the built-in panner is the separation of parameters when you are spinning sounds around. Although the three knobs for position link (when the three-knob button is activated—the green dot at the bottom of the black field), there is no linking the green dot in the middle of the black field to divergence or center %. For this, John has a secret weapon he shares with us all: Control+CMD-copy. This secret move will allow you to copy unlike information to other parameters. Like the curve of the position and want it to happen on the center %? Control+CMD-copy the curve, and then Control+CMD-paste the move onto the Center % Automation Playlist (Figure 8.30), and off you go! This is solved in version 7 with the addition of the Copy Special command, found under the Edit menu (see Figure 8.31).

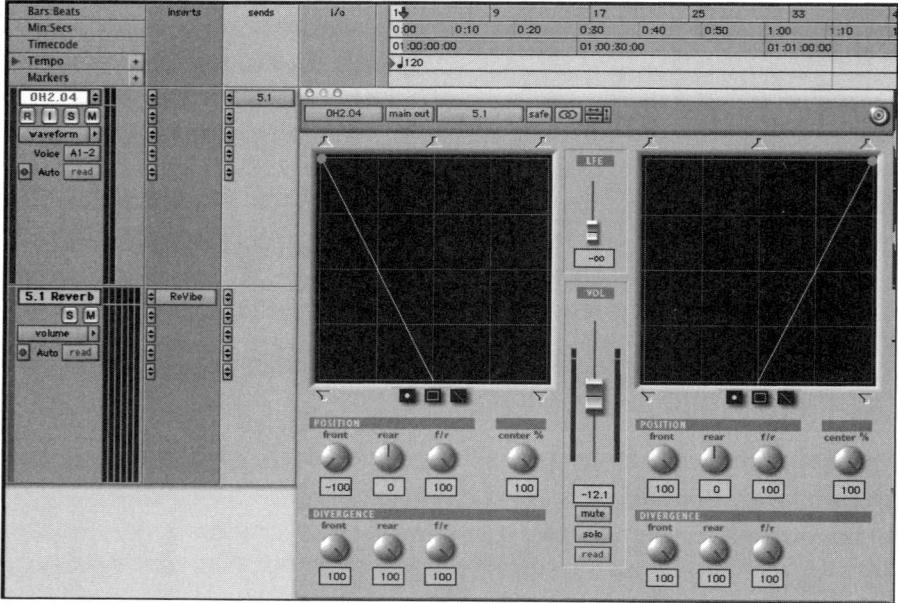

Figure 8.29

The 5.1 panner

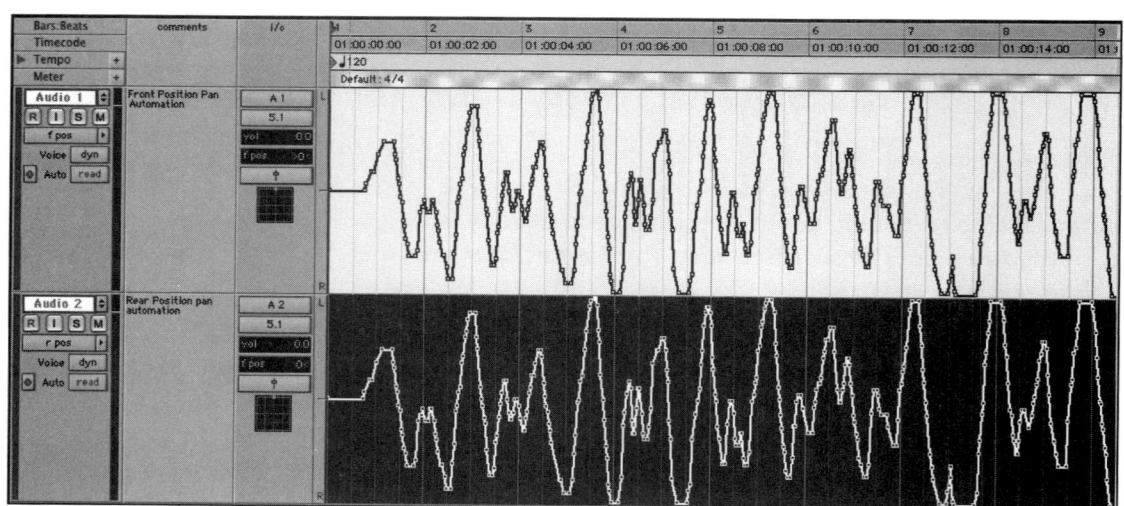

Figure 8.30

Control+CMD-copy and paste curves on unlike parameter Automation Playlists

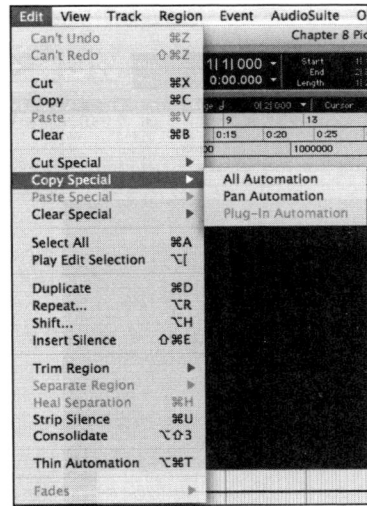

Figure 8.31

The Copy Special command under the Edit menu

❊ **Cross-named files.** The manual makes slight reference to this, but man, is it a problem! Remember the story about the producer who printed 2,000 copies of the DVD with the tracks in the wrong format? Here's how it might have happened. (It wasn't anyone involved with this book, by the way!)

1. After you've chosen your 5.1 format, it will (should) be consistent throughout your session. That means that all your I/O labels, all your track names, and all your files (prints, too) should conform to the same specification. Pro Tools, however, seems to disagree.

2. If you route your mix to a single 5.1 track, Pro Tools will print the file in L, C, R, LFE, Ls, Rs format, anyway, as seen in Figure 8.32!

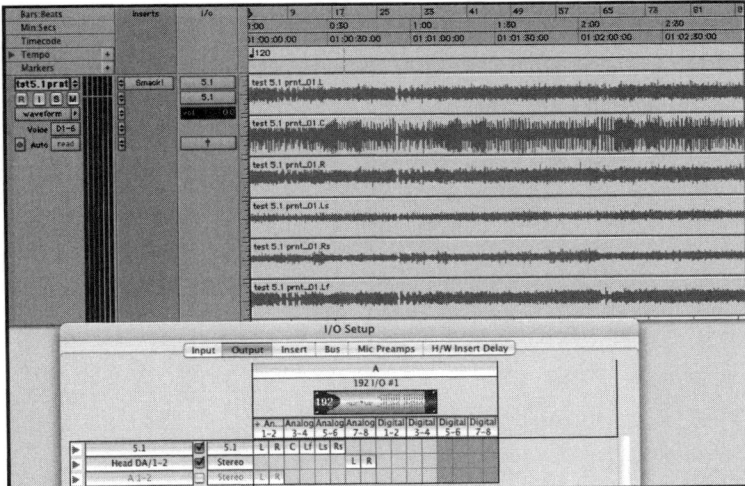

Figure 8.32

Printed mix in the wrong track format

3. If your session conforms to SMPTE format, you would expect that a 5.1 track created in this session would conform as well. Unfortunately, the printed file will retain the naming convention for L, C, R, LFE, Ls, Rs! That means while your session plays fine, prints to the 5.1 track (and still plays fine), the track names will *not* be fine!

4. When you export these tracks as mono tracks for encoding elsewhere, the Left sound will line up to the Left file, but the Right sound will line up to the Center file. As you can see, this potentially leads to serious issues.

5. If you work in SMPTE, you need to be conscious of this fact and should verify by listening to each file after export to ensure that the names match the appropriate channel. If not, then you should rename the file after exporting to ensure that you don't end up with dialogue in the right ear only!

❊ **Surround busing.** Most people use many of the 64 internal buses (128 for HD) during a mix, and in a Film mix you might use all of them. Even in 5.1, the temptation to go nuts with 5.1 busing is generally overkill, and most people go back to using stereo buses mainly, with the occasional 5.1.

1. To keep things simple, start by creating a single 5.1 Aux return with a 5.1 reverb and have it be the only 5.1 bus.

2. Or, if you need to print to six mono tracks, create the single 5.1 bus for printing first, shown in Figure 8.33.

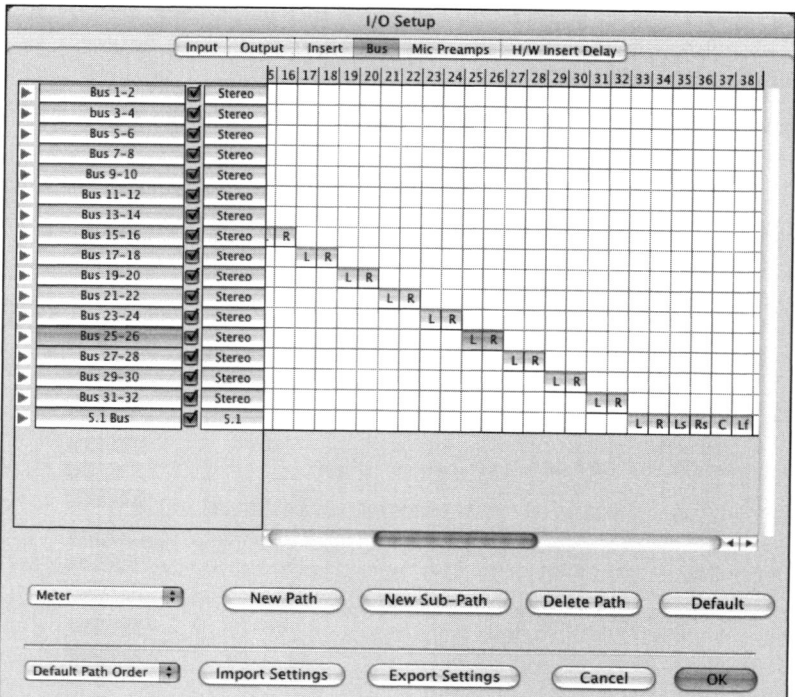

Figure 8.33

I/O setup with single 5.1 bus

3. John's suggestion is to keep the first buses stereo and create the 5.1 bus at the bottom (buses 58 through 64). That way, your temptation to grab a 5.1 bus will be visually less when you see the bus list.

✻ **Printing stems.** In the film world as well as in the world of orchestral recording, there is a need for multiple 5.1 prints. For film, you'll need 5.1 prints of all your D, M, and E tracks (dialogue, music, and effects) for delivery. In this case, you'll need three 5.1 buses to route to three sets of six mono tracks for recording (see Figure 8.34). All told, you end up using 18 buses (and 18 tracks), but that's how it is!

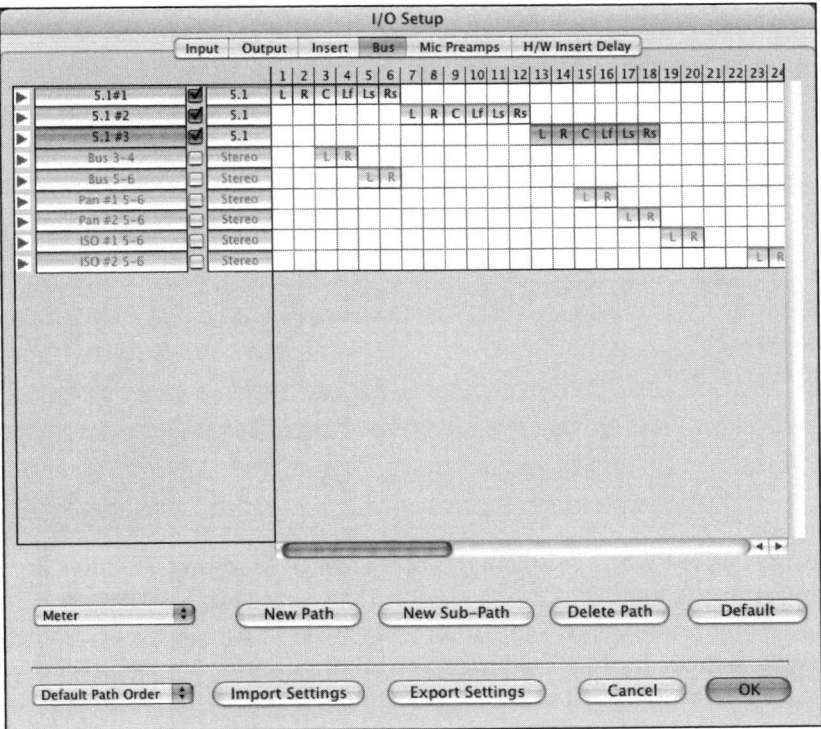

Figure 8.34

I/O setup for three 5.1 buses

Keeping the Music/SFX Still When the Picture Changes

The real title here should be "The Picture WILL Change, So Get Used to It and Deal with It." Deadlines are always present, and a few hours before then you'll get the frantic call from the producer or director saying that the love scene is all wrong and he's gone ahead and trimmed 3 seconds from the first kiss to the cigarette. It's only 3 seconds and 12 frames, right? It's not that big of a deal, right? It's not like your whole document is gone to hell because of it, right? Right?

Sigh . . .

The good news is that there are a few tricks to keep in mind should this happen to you.

Music Sessions

Keep your tracks in tick-based resolution. As you find yourself rescoring the scene, you can simply change the meter or the tempo for those 03:012 (3 seconds, 12 frames) to fit the new shortened scene. This way, all of your MIDI parts will instantly reconform to your new tempo/meter, and the missing time won't be missed at all.

Remove the time from the timeline completely by choosing Event > Time > Cut Time (shown in Figure 8.35). Enter the start of the 03:012 and the end (ensuring that the length is 03:012), and Pro Tools will remove the amount of time and reconform the rest of the song to the new picture with all other markers, meters, and tempos intact. BE SURE to select the Meter Tempo Rulers option to make sure that the rest of the session conforms correctly.

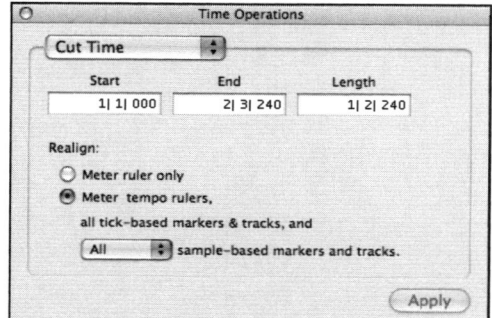

Figure 8.35

The Cut Time option in the Time Operations dialog box

Post Sessions

Keep all your tracks in sample-based resolution. If you use MIDI to trigger SFX, this is especially true. As you remove the 03:012 with the Cut Time operation, you may find some unwanted tempo and meter adjustments. With all of your tracks in sample-based resolution, your SFX will still trigger exactly as they used to. If you need to perform a tempo change for a small music cue, your SFX triggers will remain locked to the timecode of the picture—a HUGE time saver!

} Index

Numbers

A

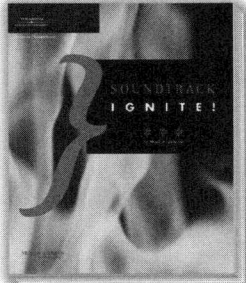